May 24, 1989

Vince,

Best regards and success
in your career.

Dick Sullivan

Software Engineering:
An Industrial Approach
Volume 1

Ronald A. Radice and Richard W. Phillips

Rensselaer Polytechnic Institute
and
International Business Machines Corporation

Prentice Hall, Englewood Cliffs, New Jersey 07632

Radice, Ronald A. (date)
  Software engineering.

  Bibliography: v. 1, p.
  Includes index.
  1. computer software—Development. I. Phillips,
Richard W.   II. Title.
QA76.76.D47R327 1988 005.1   87-30037
ISBN 0-13-823220-2 (v. 1)

Editorial/production supervision: *Gloria L. Jordan*
Cover design: *Photo Plus Art*
Manufacturing buyers: *R. Washburn, C. Grant*

The publisher offers discounts on this book when ordered in bulk quantities.
For more information, write:
Special Sales/College Marketing
Prentice Hall
College Technical and Reference Division
Englewood Cliffs, N.J. 07632

Ada is a registered trademark of the United States Government (Ada Joint
Program Office)
LOTUS is a registered trademark of Lotus Development Corporation
PSL/PSA is a registered trademark of ISDOS, Inc.
SADT is a registered trademark of SofTech, Inc.
SREM is a registered trademark of TRW Corporation
VisiCalc is a registered trademark of VisiCorp

Reproduced by Prentice-Hall from camera-ready copy prepared by the authors
using the IBM Publishing Systems BookMaster ™.

Printed in the United States of America

10 9 8 7 6 5 4 3 2 1

ISBN 0-13-823220-2

Prentice-Hall International (UK) Limited, *London*
Prentice-Hall of Australia Pty. Limited, *Sydney*
Prentice-Hall Canada Inc., *Toronto*
Prentice-Hall Hispanoamericana, S.A., *Mexico*
Prentice-Hall of India Private Limited, *New Delhi*
Prentice-Hall of Japan, Inc., *Tokyo*
Simon & Schuster Asia Pte. Ltd., *Singapore*
Editora Prentice-Hall do Brasil, Ltda., *Rio de Janeiro*

Dedicated to Claire and Lee

Contents

Part 2. The Software Product   55

Chapter 3. Planning the Product   56

Chapter 4. Requirements Engineering   69

Part 3. Software Engineering Methods   171

Chapter 6. Planning the Project   172

Chapter 7. Design of Software   205

Foreword

Software Engineering is only a human generation old. At that age, civil engineering had yet to discover the right triangle. While more people are working on software engineering now than worked on civil engineering then, fundamental ideas and principles still take time to emerge. For example, it took the genius of Edsger Dijkstra several years to articulate the idea of structured programming after the advent of ALGOL 60.

Even before the discovery of structured programming, IBM undertook the largest, most complex software development project of its time, OS/360, under the leadership of Frederick Brooks. Although software systems have seldom had lifetimes of more than ten years (with changing hardware generations), OS/360 has been evolved and extended over twenty years, and no horizon is yet in sight. With requirements of hundreds of thousands of installations accepting ever new generations of hardware and operational conditions of distributed real time data processing, the methods and tools used in this evolution have been subjected to an uncompromising, relentless proving ground without precedent.

The demands of all this massive and continuing software development have led to a new understanding and crucial perspective that embeds methods and tools into a framework of intellectual and management control. This framework is called the IBM Programming Process Architecture, and it is the central and unifying theme in this book. As the authors state:

> The Programming Process Architecture is the highest representation of the software process. While it includes the concept of a software engineering environment, it contains much more in a broader framework.

In short, it is an industrial strength process that has been developed and used in large scale practice with consistent results and control.

Two principles learned from large scale software development are brought forward in this book: (1) rigorous definition and management of the process beyond the levels exerted by individual tools and techniques are essential, and (2) the evolving process, as architected and practiced, must be allowed to govern the requirements for new tools.

In accordance with the scope of software development supported by the IBM Programming Process Architecture, this book provides a broad coverage of software methodologies, from formal procedures to creative heuristics, with many references to original work in the field. Classroom-tested in university courses, this book represents a first in bringing the lessons of megascale software development from the industrial crucible to the university classroom.

Harlan D. Mills

Preface

Why Another Book on Software Engineering?

There are many excellent books already available, and we have used a number of them over the years in the course we have taught at Rensselaer Polytechnic Institute (RPI). While we were developing our two-semester graduate-level course sequence in Software Engineering, we realized that none of the existing books fully met our needs for the sequence we were teaching, as none specifically represented an industrial view. The industrial view we wanted to focus upon required a book that was: (1) based on industrial experience and examples and (2) emphasized the engineering of software. We therefore found ourselves developing volumes of course notes and handouts to document our lectures for our students. The course notes for the first semester have now completed their migration into this book. This volume represents the first in a proposed series which will address the complete life cycle of programming development. The first two volumes will cover the life cycle of software development, and it is intended that succeeding volumes will cover in more detail each of the stages of development. Emphasis in this volume is placed on the methodologies within each development stage, and for each stage we note our recommended approach. This volume directly maps to the first semester as we teach it at RPI.

Enough has been written over the last twenty years about the software crisis to cause one to wonder if it will ever be solved. Clearly, since it was first uttered in 1968 at the North American Treaty Organization (NATO) conference in Garmisch, Germany, the problem has changed somewhat. Indeed much has gotten better and much will continue to further improve in the coming years. The combined and increasing focus of industry and academia on this problem will bring the evolution of Software Engineering to its required maturity in the industry and engineering disciplines. We will explore some of the historical aspects of this crisis in Chapter One. However, we do not intend to belabor this crisis in this book, but will, by example, speak more optimistically about how it can best be addressed today and what the near future holds as opportunity.

Any technical book can soon become out of date, especially in a field that is evolving as quickly as Software Engineering. Nonetheless, we believe the basic underlying principles that we highlight are necessary to both short-term and long-term Software Engineering solutions. In fact, these basic principles are evident in many of the successful project solutions we have seen. Some of the specifics we discuss in the book are undoubtedly evolving even as we go to print, but we believe the basics will persist.

It is essential that computer science and software engineering students get an industrial view in their education. It is important to reiterate here that the academic world must do more to introduce and address the realities and the problems of industry in the Computer Science/Software Engineering curricula. It is important at this time, given the maturity level of software engineering, that the industry and academia be more widely integrated. This can be accomplished by having academia draw people from industry to teach graduate and undergraduate programs, or by having universities assign members of their teaching staffs to industrial sabbaticals.

The alternatives within Software Engineering that we have chosen as best or preferred are naturally influenced by our experiences at the International Business Machines Corporation (IBM), but we have, in almost all cases, gone beyond our immediate experiences to confirm the effectiveness of our preferences or recommendations. Inside IBM, our focus is predominantly determined from personal knowledge in System/370 software product development. This history spans a combined 55 years in the industry. Our backgrounds cover a multitude of products from operating systems, to telecommunications, to languages and applications. It includes work across all stages of the programming development life cycle. Since 1972, we have been involved in defining, implementing, and changing Software Engineering within IBM. The views and opinions we hold in this book, although influenced by our work at IBM, are ours alone and not necessarily those of IBM.

Is This Book for You?

This book was written first with our students of Software Engineering at RPI in mind. As we developed the book, we realized that it applied as well to all software workers in the industry, whether they are students, new programmers, experienced programmers, or managers of programmers; and whether their focus is systems, embedded, or application programming. The book is appropriate to both academia and industry, and, therefore, we believe we have met our original objective when we were first asked by RPI to bring an industrial view of Software Engineering into the academic environment.

What Is This Book About?

The primary focus is *software process*: what it is, what is meant by it, why it is important, what its underlying principles are, and how it is managed. The result of a good process, in general, is a good product. There are exceptions on both sides of this relationship, but we believe that a good process is required to achieve good products repeatedly. There are other important aspects in the software environment, such as tools and methodologies, but we believe that the process should determine the tools and the methodologies and not vice versa. Throughout the development life cycle any particular process is only as good as the people who work with it and believe in it. Without good programmers and managers behind it, no process by itself is sufficient to achieve the goals of better quality, higher productivity, and shorter development cycles.

In this volume we describe the project development stages through to the code stage. In each stage we emphasize the process paradigm we recommend in Chapter Two. Again in each of these stages we focus on an industrial approach.

A Quick Outline

Chapter 1 introduces the topic of Software Engineering: its purpose, problems, and evolution.

In Chapter 2 we present the dominant theme of the book, the software process. We discuss

1. Evolution and prevalent views of software process

2. Principles relevant to software process management

3. A recommended approach for a process definition and management

In Chapter 3 we explore how the software product should be planned. This product-planning activity is central to the first portion of the Requirements and Planning stage. It is a precursor to determining the feasibility of continuing the product's actual development.

In Chapter 4 we discuss the need for alternative methods and a recommended approach to Requirements Engineering.

Chapter 5 explores a number of ideas about human factors in software, including the idea that human factors should be treated as any other functional requirement for the product, but that specific process focus must be brought to bear in order to achieve it.

Chapter 6 is focused on the planning of the project, that is, what is the best way to plan, execute, and control the project process to deliver the product.

Chapter 7 introduces the design of software and relevant concepts necessary to engineer the design.

Chapter 8 discusses approaches for validating and verifying the completion of the various work items that are developed during the product cycle. We recommend preferred approaches.

Chapters 9 and 10 discuss relevant concepts, methodologies, and representations for completing software design at three discrete design levels: Product Level Design, Component Level Design, and Module Level Design.

Chapter 11 completes this book and addresses the Code stage of software development.

Subsequent stages of the software development process will be discussed in Volume 2 of this textbook series.

How to Use This Book

Our lectures follow the text, and are coupled with three other activities:

1. Course projects

2. Case studies

3. Additional readings

We follow a 14-week sequence and try to address the chapters in the following sequence:

Chapter 1: The State of Software Engineering — Week One

Chapter 2: The Process of Software Production — Week Two

Chapter 3: Planning the Product — Week Two

Chapter 4: Requirements Engineering — Weeks Three and Four

Chapter 5: Human Factors and Usability — Week Five

Chapter 6: Planning the Project — Weeks Five and Six

Chapter 7: Design of Software — Weeks Six and Seven

Chapter 8: Validation and Verification — Week Seven

Chapter 9: Product Level Design and Component Level Design — Weeks Eight and Nine

Chapter 10: Module Level Design — Weeks Ten and Eleven

Chapter 11: Code — Week Twelve

The course projects are designed to support Software Engineering. Students work on projects that address requirements formalisms, project history repositories, project tracking, design language processing, code restructure engines, reverse engineering, code generation, test coverage, test case generation, and software metrics, among others. Projects are assigned to directly reinforce the software engineering principles we teach in our lectures.

The case studies are intended to simulate specific types of problems that the software engineer might encounter in industry, and to structure a level of project progress during the semester. While we are hesitant to do anything to subvert the software principles we teach, we do have to contend with the artificial environment of a 14-week course. The focus during this semester, therefore, is in creating a learning environment more than in requiring a fully functional project at the end of Semester One. Nonetheless, the project teams are required to demonstrate the capability of their "product" at a level of test completeness by the end of the semester. Usually the teams achieve completion at a Unit Test level, a test effort which immediately follows the completion of the code. In some cases testing has gone well beyond the Unit Test level. Basically we are simulating a product development cycle for the initial release of a product within a 14-week constrained period. During the second semester the projects are rotated, the teams are kept together as much as is practical, and the teams are asked to continue with

1. Completing Release 1

2. Using it throughout the rest of the semester

3. Maintaining their "product"

4. Developing the requirements for Release 2

5. Completing Release 2 through the System Tested level in the life cycle

Finally, additional readings are assigned to either stress major points we want the students to explore or to take advantage of current findings in the software engineering literature.

A student using this book can either do so directly in a course that uses the text or read it as stand-alone text. While it is anticipated that the text be used in a Software Engineering course, we wrote it so that it will also stand by itself.

Acknowledgments

As with all books of this nature, there are more people who deserve recognition than we can adequately acknowledge in our words here. First, we must thank our secretaries, Gloria Murphy and Anne Wendt, who helped us in so many ways with typing, editing, copying, making the graphics, and the numerous last-minute requests for changes. Fortunately, they had a well-defined process and good text processing tools to keep us under control and to help us make this text. We thank Ron Wendt for showing us the powers and intricacies of Publishing Systems BookMaster, the product we used to produce this book in camera-ready form. Next, we have to thank the many past students at RPI who were in our classes and worked with our notes as they evolved towards this book. We also thank Herb Freeman, who initially contacted us for RPI. We want to thank IBM for giving us first the experience and then the support while we worked on this book. Finally we thank all of the reviewers who helped make this a better book than it otherwise would have been.

R. A. Radice and R. W. Phillips
Poughkeepsie, New York

Reviewers

Joan Carl	Almerin C. O'Hara, Jr.
Gerhard Chroust	Leonard Orzech
Robert Goldberg	W. C. Peterson
Jack T. Harding	A. M. Pietrasanta
Gene F. Hoffnagle	Bernie Rachmales
Ev Merritt	Claire L. Radice
Harlan D. Mills	Hans A. Schmid
Robert P. Mueller	Carol A. Schneier

Part 1. The Basis of This Book

Chapter 1. The State of Software Engineering

1.1   Introduction

This book was written 40 years after the ENIAC, short for Electronic Numerical Integrator and Computer, ushered in the computer age. In these 40 years, we have seen a phenomenal and almost unbelievable growth in the use of computers. Who would have guessed that in such a brief time we would see the power of ENIAC surpassed by a chip well over one one-millionth its size, or that processors with stored programs would be used in automobiles, watches, appliances, and countless other day-to-day applications interfacing people and machines? Not even Thomas J. Watson, Sr., who did so much to develop the computer industry, envisioned its present state. In fact, in 1946 Watson proclaimed that "the world could probably not find a use for more than five computers."

It is easy to look back at software industrial development and feel that we have progressed unpredictably far since 1946. Indeed we have, but not yet far enough. We, as an industry, are still only in the beginnings of becoming a science. We call ourselves computer scientists or software engineers, but it is more out of anticipation of what those roles offer than from a fully earned position. We, as an industry, still do not consistently keep, analyze, or make public the necessary data to substantially prove our theories or to enable others to repeat our successes. So, we are barely a science. We still cannot consistently and repeatedly do as good a job on a new project as we did on the last. Although better at managing consistency and repeatability, we do not yet deserve the title "software engineer." This sounds harsh, but the evidence of numerous software projects suggests it.

This situation does not mean that the software business is full of slackards or incompetents who are not trying hard enough. This is hardly the case. We are truly fortunate to be in a discipline that has captured the interests of so many talented and motivated people. We would not be where we are today except for the many people who have contributed to the evolution of programming. Some of their names are noted in our chapter references. We must build on the work of those who came before us if we are to attain the desired engineering control we need for repeatedly making software products with better quality at lower cost, and on schedule. We have chosen to base this book not only on our own experiences, analyses, and readings, but on the work of, and our interactions with, others in industry and academia. We have selected our recommendations from those processes, methodologies, and practices that have been successfully used on many projects and that we believe will lead to a repeatable consistency in developing quality software within cost estimates and on schedule. We believe many of the required changes for the business of software production will come about through a well-defined software process. Therefore, we will focus on process definition and process management throughout the book.

In this chapter, we discuss the relationship of this book to the state of Software Engineering. We will look at some of the background, current practices, key problems, and challenges for software engineers.

1.2 Beginnings of Software Engineering

Before discussing the current issues in software engineering, we would like to set the stage by looking at its history, starting with programming in the 1950s. In the 1950s and 1960s programs were perceived by many as merely procedures to run the hardware. Notions familiar today, such as software modules, interfaces, data abstractions, and state machines were not familiar concepts to most software practitioners of those decades.

The typical program was stand-alone and capable of performing all tasks necessary to complete a job, usually without invoking the services of any other program. The programmer's thought processes were highly proceduralized and sequential: "First I do A, then I do B, then I do C." Coding languages were mostly at the assembler level, and flowcharts, if any were used, were the predominant design notation.

The burgeoning mass of procedurally coded instructions soon fostered the emergence of *subroutines* and *macros*. Significant at this time in the industry was the emergence of *monitor* programs that could invoke other programs and provide services to them, such as handling input/output devices. Toward the end of the 1960s, monitor programs had evolved to a fair degree of sophistication, and some were called *operating systems*. The operating system provided general purpose service and control for user-written programs. *Utility* programs were also provided to assist users in performing commonly repeated manipulations of data, such as copying data from one form to another.

FORTRAN for scientific applications and COBOL for business applications were rapidly becoming the accepted computer languages, but many programs were written in assembler languages, with the interface to input/output devices often called at the machine language level. Many times the debugging of these "procedures to make the hardware run" took on some bizarre characteristics.

The amassing of data engendered a new subsystem, that of data bases. Data base subsystems usually ran under control of an operating system. Thus, the 1960s ushered in some highly significant software advances in the actual uses of computers, and programming was on its way.

When the 1970s arrived, software was still exhibiting some disturbing properties and was characterized as complex, error prone, and labor-intensive. Software was viewed as complex because of the rapid growth in size of applications without corresponding breakthroughs in methods to handle the increasing size of programs. Many systems, now huge, were internally still a series of procedures, taxed to a point of collapse under demands for more permutations and combinations of functions.

Software was error prone because (1) the original developer's limited span of control over his work caused errors to be made, and (2) the maintainer or developer who inherited the code from some unknown original author had to decipher the logic of "spaghetti" code and make changes without regressing the program's function. This was a challenge to the best programmer, and all too often it was impossible to avoid creating new errors.

Finally, software was labor-intensive because software development was usually brought about by people doing and redoing their programs with very few good development tools. The severe lack of skilled programmers to maintain and enhance the software products only added to the problem. Cost overruns became normal when the programmers discovered they had to spend more time than anticipated to write, debug, and put together their complex and error prone pieces.

The situation demanded more focus on *how* software was developed or on the *process* of developing software. Many concepts and practices in use today were originated during the 1970s to manage size and complexity. For example, *life cycle models* of the software development process were defined with discrete stages identified for initial specifications, final specifications, high-level design, low-level design, coding, testing, and maintenance. There was also a focus on more efficient ways to detect defects in the product as early as possible in the development stages. Testing methodologies were improved, and disciplines for rigorous *Inspections* of the design material and code were instituted in some organizations. Additionally, program proofs of correctness were added as a discipline to deliver higher quality programs.

In spite of those improvements, the legacy propagated from the 1970s to the 1980s was that programming is a highly error prone and labor-intensive process with major cost overruns prompting many executives to classify investment in software development as a "bottomless pit."

1.3 Software Engineering Goals

In the early 1980s, as hardware costs decreased, software development and service costs for many products were living up to the predictions of the previous decade by becoming the dominant cost factor. This initiated three shifts in emphasis for the data processing industry:

1. Defect Prevention: to improve the quality and productivity of the software development process

2. Defect Removal: to use the software development process to deliver defect-free software products, primarily through application of engineering disciplines

3. Software Development Tools: to replace labor-intensive development activities with capital-intensive activities and thus give software developers more tools and equipment to do their jobs more effectively in shorter cycles

These shifts emphasized the fact that higher quality and lower costs are needed to improve software in the 1980s. Indeed, they have become the goals of the 1980s and 1990s for software production and can be stated as follows:

1. Increase quality
2. Reduce costs
3. Improve schedules
4. Increase production

Figure 1 on page 6 illustrates how these four software engineering goals currently are being focused and addressed in the industry and suggests some practical and successful techniques for achieving these goals. The interface between the goals and the focus areas is shown as a *bus*, indicating that any or all four of the goals can be affected by efforts defined under the focus areas. The focus areas in turn are affected by the techniques shown, and the interface between the focus areas and techniques is again shown as a bus.

The remainder of this chapter elaborates on these goals, how they are being addressed, and how this book relates them to the software development process. It concludes with a look ahead to the challenges of the 1990s.

1.4 Why Are Software Engineering Goals Important?

The four Software Engineering goals are at the very basis of the software industry, and are a reason for the existence of Software Engineering. When we speak of the software industry we mean to include all those application, embedded, and system software products developed for users who expect the products they use to meet the stated requirements, especially reliability, in all respects. Therefore, in the process of achieving the four noted goals, we will be enabling:

1. Improved user satisfaction with software and hardware products

2. Improved management of software product development

3. Increased delivery of function to the marketplace

1.4.1 User Satisfaction

User satisfaction is influenced by many factors and is hard to define. It is not essential that we focus here on the specifics of the measuring gradients of "satisfaction." What we are concerned with is simply producing products that meet the requirements of the user population such that the product meets their needs and is reliable under use. When users are satisfied with excellence in a product, demand develops. Good products seem to create the opportunity for other products to grow and evolve into an expanding marketplace. Thus, good products expand the marketplace and with that expansion bring the need for more products.

For example, when the personal computers (PCs) first came to the marketplace, they were eagerly sought out by experts in programming. Only later were PCs a necessary item for the larger population of average business people. The advent of satisfying spreadsheet programs such as VisiCalc and Lotus expanded the PC

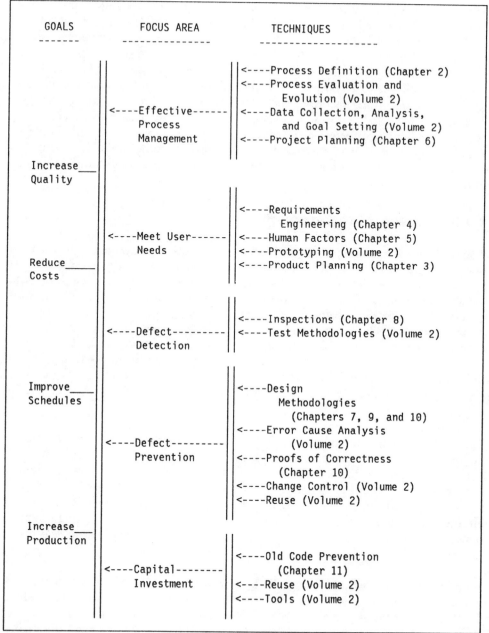

```
    GOALS              FOCUS AREA            TECHNIQUES
    -------           ---------------       --------------------

                                     <----Process Definition (Chapter 2)
                                     <----Process Evaluation and
                                             Evolution (Volume 2)
                     <----Effective------   <----Data Collection, Analysis,
                          Process                  and Goal Setting (Volume 2)
                          Management        <----Project Planning (Chapter 6)
    Increase
    Quality

                                     <----Requirements
                                             Engineering (Chapter 4)
                     <----Meet User------   <----Human Factors (Chapter 5)
                          Needs             <----Prototyping (Volume 2)
    Reduce                                  <----Product Planning (Chapter 3)
    Costs

                                     <----Inspections (Chapter 8)
                     <----Defect--------    <----Test Methodologies (Volume 2)
                          Detection

    Improve                                 <----Design
    Schedules                                   Methodologies
                                                (Chapters 7, 9, and 10)
                                            <----Error Cause Analysis
                     <----Defect--------           (Volume 2)
                          Prevention        <----Proofs of Correctness
                                                (Chapter 10)
                                            <----Change Control (Volume 2)
                                            <----Reuse (Volume 2)
    Increase
    Production
                                            <----Old Code Prevention
                     <----Capital--------          (Chapter 11)
                          Investment        <----Reuse (Volume 2)
                                            <----Tools (Volume 2)
```

Figure 1. Major Areas of Software Engineering Focus for the 1980s and 1990s

marketplace as opportunities to make productive use of the PC by the average business person became apparent and real. The demand of the marketplace for both personal computer hardware and software has been phenomenal and surprising to all who were involved. At this writing, the PC market seems to have been tamed in its outstanding growth. This slowdown in growth is typical of all new, rapidly expanding industries. The slowdown is also driven somewhat by the lack of a satisfactory system solution for the average home user. The combination of a software and hardware system solution is not yet available to help the average person adequately solve his or her problems with home economics, personal communication, security, and entertainment. For the average person, determining what to buy, how to install all the hardware and software parts, and how to avoid collision between the parts, is annoying at best and a clear inhibitor at least. When a satisfactory market solution does become available, and if it is easy to use as a combination of packages, we should see another surge of expansion in the PC market.

1.4.2 Software Management

Today there exists a long history of software product development which should help the product teams to do as good if not a better job than was done the last time a product was developed. However, this history is often not used, forgotten, or not remembered effectively. This problem of not effectively using the lessons of history to develop software products is due to many factors. Primary, however, is that the history or product development memory can only be successfully used in a repeatable manner after a process definition is created to carry the history from one project team to another. Each team in turn can then build upon that memory and add to it from its experiences. Thus, the history of successful product development can be captured and represented for repeated use in a defined process.

Typically today this memory is embodied in the experts or experienced product people who have run the product development gauntlet one or more times and who bring their expertise to bear on the next product under development. This is necessary, but it is not sufficient. The unsolved issue is to transfer this expertise fast enough and effectively enough from one software development project to another. In a rapidly expanding industry there are never enough experts or experience to transfer the memory across the population base, even within one manufacturer.

Additionally, many who have had the benefit of being in product development do not have an easy way to develop or maintain a repository reflecting the product development memory, so a number of the same mistakes are repeated again and again. Indeed, most of the mistakes being made today are not new, they have been occurring over the last 40 years. We, as an industry, need, hope, and expect to eliminate these repetitions in error as soon as possible. Failure to set goals from the knowledge of software project history is a key contributor to the problem of repeated failures. Setting incremental improvement goals based on product development memory brings with it improved focus on software management. If the goals are taken seriously by all involved parties, and are achievable, then incremental and orderly improvements can be made.

1.4.3 Increased Function

There is an ever-increasing demand for more and more software. Yet we do not educate and train enough programmers, who are becoming software engineers, fast enough to fill the ever-increasing demand. This is not a bad problem to have in and of itself, but unless we solve it, it can delay the evolution of hardware-software solutions. If we cannot educate and train enough programmers to meet the demands for new function, then we will need to improve the way we do business such that programmers can more easily develop products at higher quality, faster, and at lower cost. To do this we will need to understand and remember the lessons of past projects. We will have to effectively manage the process of software production.

1.5 Effective Process Management

It is generally thought that improved programming tools, processes, methodologies, education, and training will create an environment conducive to improved defect prevention, defect detection, and process management [BOEH84]. In addition, there is growing recognition that an integrated, well running, and controlled process is essential to derive the true benefit from these tools and methodologies [HUMP85].

Process data collection, analysis, goal setting, and improved estimating methods all play an important role in establishing such a basis, as shown for example in the work of both Boehm and Wolverton [WOLV83]. An example of progress from a pragmatic view may be seen in the productivity measurements of products developed for large systems [FLAH85].

In addition, industries are devoting attention and resources to reviewing, refining, and evaluating the effectiveness of their in-place software development processes. For an example of this, one may look at IBM's integrated effort for

1. defining and documenting the process of their large-systems development process [RADI85A].

2. instituting specific improvement actions based upon evaluations of the actual development process, as practiced at the operating technical level [RADI85B].

3. automating the management of the development process, and automating the actual process tasks through tools [HOFF85].

We believe that if Software Engineering is to advance rapidly as a discipline it requires a set of principles to guide its direction. We believe that these principles include the following [RADI85A][HUMP85]:

1. The process of software production must be formally defined.

2. The process must be actively, continually, and consistently managed to achieve consistently improving quality and increasing productivity.

3. The process must be defined into stages. Each stage must be decomposed into tasks, each of which has an entry criteria, validation mechanism, and exit criteria.

4. Each work item exiting from a task must be validated before proceeding into another task as input.

5. Data capture, analysis (which includes feedback), and goal setting are essential for improving both the product and the process. Periodic process assessments must be planned and executed to monitor effectiveness.

6. Procedures must be established to certify product quality and implement any necessary corrective actions as they may be needed.

7. Problems with the product or process must be recorded and analyzed for cause, effect, and improvement. This is to be done both from a statistical assessment and from a defect extinction perspective [JONE85].

8. Changes to the product or process must be controlled. They must be recorded, tracked, and evaluated for effectiveness.

9. The software production process must be concerned with not only the development viewpoint, but must include the viewpoints of testing, publications and related materials, build and integration, marketing and service, and process management. The overall product is composed of all of these viewpoints.

These principles are the basis of a quality process which we believe is a necessary ingredient to achieve a quality product.

We discuss details of the software development process in Chapter 2 of this book. Data collection, analysis, and goal setting, although discussed in this volume, will be addressed in detail in a subsequent volume, along with process evaluation and evolution.

It is one thing to have a process definition and another to ensure that the process is being managed effectively, efficiently, and consistently. Adhering to the process management principles will assit, but success can be easily mitigated by day to day issues which work against a smother running process engine. Indeed, it is unlikely that a complete process engine will exist in the near future. Rather, the process requires management involvement, risk taking, and decision making, none of which can be fully relegated to a "process engine." The success or failure of a project in many instances is determined by how well the project was planned and then managed from the original plan through changes required to meet the project objectives. These and other aspects of project planning are discussed in Chapter 6.

1.6 Meeting User Needs

In all cases with products, the user prevails. If the product does not satisfy the user community it will probably fail. If the user does not have a need for the product, it will fail unless the product marketing team has cultivated a market for the product. If the product meets the users' needs, but is too costly, it will probably struggle to survive, unless it has carefully assessed its market niche. If the product is price competitive and meets the users' needs, it should reap all the successes it warrants. How then can a new product reduce its chance of risk by meeting a need in the user community? This is the subject for Requirements Engineering.

1.6.1 Requirements Engineering

Requirements Engineering has been viewed by many as the weakest part in the entire software development process. Perhaps because of increasing recognition of this problem, work that was begun in the 1970s for adding rigor to this stage of the process has intensified in the 1980s [ROMA85]. Progress is occurring in many software development enterprises in the areas of:

- Systematic methods for gathering initial user requirements, rigorous problem analysis and matching solution definition, proper design placement of the solutions, and realistic prioritization of requirements

- Exit criteria for requirements specification documents to ensure consistency and completeness

- More attention to formally defining a product technical strategy, against which to weigh candidate requirements, to ensure that the evolving product maintains its goals over time

- Improved methods for obtaining user participation in validating that the defined requirements correctly meet true user needs

- The definition of well-formed and formal data bases in which to catalog and store requirements.

- Tools to facilitate retrieval, analysis, and prioritization

At the same time, there has been a recognition that some user needs will change as soon as a product becomes visible, leading to attempts of rapid prototyping and incremental implementation as ways of meeting dynamic user needs.

This topic of Requirements Engineering is treated in detail in Chapter 4 of this book.

1.6.2 Human Factors

With advances in the sophistication of computer applications, it became an absolute necessity for designers and architects to focus on the human-machine interface. As a result, advances have been made in both the ease with which humans can interact with computers, as well as in obtaining assistance from the system when problems or questions arise. Modern techniques are being applied in increasing degree to tutorial materials, users' guides, and reference materials. More information is available to aid the information developer in making decisions as to which information should best be made available in hard copy tutorial or reference manuals, and which should best be provided by means of on-line HELP facilities [SCHN80]. The human factors topic is addressed in more detail in Chapter 5.

1.7 Defect Detection and Prevention Related to Software Reliability

When you as a consumer buy a product such as an appliance or automobile, you expect it will perform consistently and without failure according to some expectations. For software products, these expectations might be represented in the product specifications. There is an implied, if not stated, contract between the seller and the purchaser of any product. Wherein, if the product meets specifications for the designated purchase price, then both parties are satisfied with the exchange. This basic aspect of the marketplace applies to all exchanges of products for money. When you buy an appliance, you have certain expectations of function. People are less interested or motivated to buy appliances with known faults or defects.

Software is a different type of product, but new buyers might assume it follows the same marketplace scenario. However, with software, known and documented defects and restrictions are often shipped with the product. Furthermore, it is culturally "accepted" by experienced buyers that defects yet to be discovered exist in shipped software products. It is known that software is not as reliable as users would like, but since it is accepted by the user community, why change the reliability requirement? After all, there are billions of dollars of software product licenses sold every year despite the presence of defects.

This is an unfair description of the software industry, for much has been done, is in plan to be done, and will be done continuously to increase the reliability of software products. No software producer wants to ship a product with known or anticipated defects. Both industry and academia are focused on how software reliability might be improved. Nonetheless, we still have a reliability issue with software in the industry at large, and we, in general, ship products with defects. User satisfaction which determines the success of products is clearly affected by reliability.

While we are not currently able to remove all defects from the software products that we create and deliver to our user, we are making good progress towards that end. Given where we are in the technological maturity of the industry, certain choices of processes, tools, practices, and methodologies will help to produce a higher level of reliability. This is to say that in any one environment some processes, tools, practices, and methodologies work better than others. A goal of this book is to present a view of some of these present preferred choices. In our definition of an industrial view we include all software programs which must stand the tests of time, reliability, and maintainability whether they are products developed as application, embedded, or system programs.

1.7.1 Defect Detection and Prevention

It is generally accepted in the industry today that quality and productivity gains may be effectively realized by improving defect detection methods and by preventing the introduction of defects in the first place.

Defect detection is often associated with formal testing activities. During the last decade, detection has also been applied at the design and early implementation stages by means of rigorous design and code *Inspections* [FAGA86]. Testing as one form of defect detection will be treated in a subsequent volume to this book.

Defect *prevention* is generally accepted as offering greater efficiency gains per unit of investment than improvements in defect detection methods. Software Engineering approaches to defect prevention are beginning to include analyzing each defect detected to determine in what process stage it was introduced, what caused the defect to be introduced, and what permanent change could be instituted in the process to prevent that type of defect from ever occurring again. A technique for doing this, called *error cause analysis*, is to have the programmer evaluate his own errors, make such analysis part of the ongoing normal day to day process, and establish permanent feedback mechanisms between the discovery point for each defect and the point at which it was introduced [JONE85]. This view of prevention implies changing something in the environment which previously was a cause of error. Thus, once the cause is removed, the defect type is prevented from occurring again. Effective prevention requires understanding the history of product development in a production environment. Defect prevention will be addressed in more detail in a subsequent volume.

We discuss techniques for defect detection in Chapter 8 of this volume. The techniques include inspections, reviews, walkthroughs, peer reviews, and proofs of correctness. Another and broader software engineering approach to defect prevention depends upon reusing defect-free parts, as discussed in 1.8, "Capital Investment for Software."

1.7.2 Design Methodologies

Design is where the solution is determined for the requirements statement that defines the users' needs. It is also the development phase that introduces the most difficult errors to isolate and fix. Additionally, it is reputed to be the phase which introduces the highest volume of errors for some product development efforts. One might suspect that not all design methodologies are equally good for all software projects, and that one methodology might be better than others at preventing error injection. While the issue of which design methodology, in general, is best is still debated, we believe that some methodologies are better for certain types of software projects than they are for other projects. We explore design, the prevalent methodologies existent today, and our preferred choice in Chapter 7, Chapter 9, and Chapter 10.

1.8 Capital Investment for Software

Analogies have been drawn between the current state of evolution of Software Engineering and that of the industrial revolution during the 19th century [WEGN84]. For example, the technology that fueled the industrial revolution was highly labor-intensive initially, becoming capital-intensive as it matured. Economists use the term capital to refer to reusable industrial resources. The software industry has not yet fully exploited the economic advantage of reusable resources. Additionally, product enhancement, which is a form of capital reuse, typically builds on predecessors where the design basis often does not fully represent the actual code. This inconsistency between two views (design and code) of what the product should be doing leads to problems during the enhancement stage in the development cycle, and often to mistakes. The inconsistency is the cause of the old-code problem.

1.8.1 The Old-code Problem Prevention

It is the unfortunate situation in much of the software industry today that the actual specification and design documents used during the program synthesis process are not saved. If saved, these documents are not maintained adequately to convey the design rationale to one who was not a part of the original development effort. Thus, those who must diagnose and fix defects during the maintenance stage, or those who must enhance the product with features for a new release or version of the product often have to recreate the design, and in so doing make assumptions which at times lead to design errors.

The term used in software for extracting or abstracting the essence of the design from a software product is *reverse engineering*. Through reverse engineering an attempt can be made to get back what was lost, specifically the design documentation. Reverse engineering is usually costly, and not technically or economically feasible for most existing software. This problem is especially visible when old code needs to be enhanced or maintained, because it adds to the costs by making the job more difficult, slows productivity, inhibits quality, and consumes an increasingly large percentage of scarce programming talent. How one might prevent the old-code problem is addressed in the chapters on design and implementation. Whenever practices in the past have created a situation where reverse engineering is necessary, something of the design will almost always be irretrievably lost [SNEE84]. This is because the design abstraction is not explicit in the code. Furthermore, even when the design is visible, it may not carry with it the original or implicit requirements [ROMA85]. Two points are to be made here:

1. A loosely run design process can become one of the major contributors to propagating the old-code problem.

2. There is increasing recognition in the industry that a significant portion of the software must be developed as if it were a capital investment, that is, that it will be reused. Reusable, rather than throw away parts, are required, thus bringing the old-code problem to the foreground for resolution.

The old-code problem is addressed in Chapter 11 and in more detail in Volume 2 of this series.

1.8.2 Reuse

While we will not be discussing the subject of reuse in software in depth until a subsequent volume, there are some introductory concepts that should be mentioned in this volume, since reuse is an important solution for the software crisis.

A machine tool such as a lathe, or a resource such as an assembly line, is a capital good because it represents an investment in a reusable resource. This concept may be extended to include, for example, today's operating systems, compilers, and some programming development tools.

A factor that enabled early industry to make the transition from labor-intensive to capital-intensive goods was *standardization*. For example, the adoption of standard machine screw sizes and thread dimensions by the Society of Automotive Engineers permitted universal use of millions of mass-produced machine screws in thousands of diverse applications.

Also significant was the standardization of concepts to define properties of materials, such as viscosity of lubricants, octane rating of fuel for reciprocating engines, or the behavior of motive machines, such as brake-horsepower. It is interesting to note that this type of standard is defined in terms of repeatable procedures for measuring the behavior of an object. From these we can deduce that the specified property does indeed exist, rather than measuring the intrinsic property itself.

Another example was the extensive standardization of commonly used or needed functions, such as universal standards for certain industrial buildings regarding entries, exits, fire escapes, and sprinkler systems that apply to a generic class of building, without describing a specific building.

It is not difficult to draw several software analogies to the above examples. A few examples are reusable program macros, standard performance benchmark tests, and design abstractions. Capital formation in software is highly dependent on the implementation of concepts and models, rather than physical goods and machines. In both the conceptual and physical media, however, a key common denominator is reusability.

Reusability is a long-standing, general engineering principle stemming from a need to avoid duplication and to capture commonality for classes of inherently similar tasks [WEGN84].

In the late 1950s and early 1960s, the basic economic motivation for the development of the stored program computer was the reusability of computer hardware which could have different stored programs as contrasted to the relatively special-purpose computers and accounting machines then in existence. Thus, exploitation of stored program concepts in hardware marked a major advance toward general-purpose computers. The current economic posture of software in the industry bears some similarities to the factors that were affecting hardware of the 1950s. Except perhaps for the major general-purpose operating systems and subsystems, much software of today consists of special-purpose, nonreusable components. The changing economic balance between hardware and software is resulting in changed perceptions of what is capital-intensive, and on the importance of exploiting reusability in the future [FREE83].

Types of Software Reuse

Discussions of reuse can be complicated by the fact that software components are reused in several different forms, circumstances, and environments. A subroutine that is called repeatedly at execution time is being reused. So is a major component that is "lifted" from one system and "plugged in" to another.

If the scope of software reusability is extended to include resources that are used to produce the software product, then reusable components include software development tools, environments, concepts, and the people that design and produce the software. Peter Wegner, in his discussion on capital-intensive software technology, suggests that reusable components fall into two major categories [WEGN84]. These are:

1. Resources used in building a variety of structures, such as

   - macros
   - design concepts
   - data abstractions
   - function abstractions
   - user interfaces

2. Resources used in performing the tasks of designing and building software products, such as

   - compilers
   - editors
   - program libraries
   - data bases
   - programming standards and conventions
   - programming process definitions

Wegner further classifies reusable software components into these four types:

1. Software components reused in a variety of independent applications
2. Components reused in successive versions of a given program
3. Those reused whenever programs containing the component are executed
4. Those reused by being repeatedly called during program execution

The first two types directly affect the cost of program development and service. The third depends upon how integral the program is in its customers' day-to-day process, thus demonstrating the reusability of the hardware. The last affects how efficiently the software utilizes the hardware resource and the degree to which maximum functionality can be achieved with the minimum amount of newly written code.

Most of the current software engineering work on reusability focuses on the first two types. The first type of reuse, reusing software components in different applications or in different major components of an operating system, has long been intriguing to many but has been fraught with difficulties. This is perhaps due to the following two major reasons:

1. It is difficult to define a component that is generalized enough to be potentially reusable across two or more applications and specific enough to be efficient.

2. It is difficult to communicate the existence of the reusable candidate component to the developers of other applications. In real-world practice, there is a vast difference between designing and implementing a component to be reusable and actually having it reused. Solutions to these problems range from a library of reusable parts, designs, or even ideas, to generalized partial applications that can be copied to start a new application [POLS86].

The second type of reuse, reusing a component in successive versions of a software product, is the most common type in practice today. Almost all software projects currently under development are enhancing existing products. Very few are complete replacements of existing products, and fewer still are completely new products for which no predecessor exists. This type of reuse is also the most capital-intensive of the four types. The major reasons are:

1. The number of versions, sometimes called releases, of a product over its lifetime can be in the tens, or even possibly in the hundreds.

2. It is seldom cost effective to completely replace a component with a new rewritten one in a new product release; therefore, enhancement and reuse are the general rule rather than the exception.

It is important to note here that as software development begins to exploit reuse, that the software process will of necessity have to change. We will discuss the change to the software process and reuse in detail in a subsequent volume.

1.9 Types of Software

While we are exploring the different issues in software engineering, we should ask which software has these issues. Is all software the same? Should all software be developed with the same process or the same rigor? This book is interested in industrial quality software. This does not mean it is limited to systems software. Embedded and application software is a larger and growing part of the industry also.

Some software is developed for a narrow marketplace. The software for the NASA Space Shuttle System, for the Social Security Administration, for the

Federal Aviation Administration (FAA), or the Strategic Defense Initiative (SDI) are examples of some user products which require as high if not a higher level of reliability than do many products marketed by large software manufacturers for unlimited commercial use. This is not to suggest that other types of software can afford to be unreliable, but the consequences of unreliable software for some products is certainly more catastrophic.

This book is intended for programmers and managers of those software products which (1) require high quality and reliability, (2) need to survive through maintenance and enhancement, (3) involve more than a handful of programmers working together, and (4) need to have control over project costs and schedules. This book is also intended for students who want to understand the problems facing the development of large software projects.

1.10 Outlook for the 1990s

Many of the activities for improving the software process of the current decade focus on the requirements and design stages. As the results of these efforts come to fruition in the 1990s, one can visualize an evolving Software Engineering process advancing in such fields as artificial intelligence and automatic programming and spurred by two economic motivations:

1. To meet the growing demand for the application of computers in the world's society

2. To increase the use of programs, program materials, and algorithms for creating programs as reusable capital resources

1.10.1 Knowledge Engineering

In the next decade, software technology will increasingly emphasize knowledge organization and reusability by both people and computers. Wegner's previously cited work [WEGN84] equates the computer revolution we are now undergoing with the Industrial Revolution of the last century and suggests that computer knowledge engineering will fundamentally amplify people's ability to manage information just as the Industrial Revolution amplified our ability to manage physical phenomena.

Wegner describes knowledge engineering as a body of techniques for managing the complexity of knowledge, just as Software Engineering is a body of techniques for managing the complexity of software. He relates knowledge engineering in the computer age to historical examples of knowledge engineering such as Euclid's Elements that provided the basis for managing geometrical knowledge and Linnaeus's classification techniques that manage knowledge of botany and biology. These works for classifying and managing knowledge were as important a contribution to science as the contribution of the knowledge itself, and so will the computer's contribution to the management of knowledge be as important a contribution as the knowledge itself.

Here are some example targets for knowledge engineering of the future:

- Electronic Books - restructuring of existing knowledge repositories, such as the Library of Congress, and making them accessible through retrieval systems.

- Knowledge Support Environments - just as programming support environments assist the software engineer of today, so might knowledge support environments assist students, authors and researchers in creating, learning, and using a body of knowledge. For example, a university of the future might be engineered to provide such a total knowledge support environment through a network of distributed knowledge bases accessible from around the world [SHUE86].

- Dynamic documents - providing the ability at the terminal to navigate easily between different levels of abstraction and different views of conceptual objects to gain a more complete understanding of the domain of discourse.

- Computer authoring technology - creating computer textbooks that organize large knowledge domains into nonsequential knowledge structures and frames designed in a special way to be read only on-line.

1.10.2 Artificial Intelligence and Knowledge-Based Systems

It is popular to say that artificial intelligence and knowledge-based systems will play a role in Software Engineering of the 1990s. But what specifically does this mean? Will the user be able to converse with a system in natural language for advice on how to state a problem to be solved and then be presented with the results? Probably not in the foreseeable future [SIMO86]. However, what is achievable in the next decade is to learn enough about that part of the human problem-solving process that takes us from the formal specification of a program to a running program. To be able to do that completely and automatically, that is, to go from a state description of what we want to create as a solution, to the actual procedures which are the solution will not be achievable by means of a typical compiler approach. Instead it will require a knowledge base and the heuristic search capabilities of artificial intelligence systems.

1.10.3 Programmerless Programming

In the not too distant past, the users of the telephone were required to place each call with the assistance of a trained operator at a central switchboard. The advent of the dial telephone provided the end user the capability to place the call without the aid of the trained operator. Thus, through automation the task of making phone calls became markedly easier, and with the ease of use came a rapid increase in the number of phone calls made.

Problem solving with the use of computers is now accomplished by grade school children, high school and college students, attorneys, engineers, and finally, the professional programmer who creates programs for use by others. "Programmerless programming" is a coined phrase implying automated support for solving problems using a computer without the use of programming-like languages or the assistance of a programmer trained in these languages and approaches.

1.10.4 Automatic Programming

The term *automatic programming* has at least three definitions. These are:

1. Programming in a higher level language than a Fourth Generation Language. This is sometimes called automatic code generation

2. Automated assistance in acquiring specifications, validating them against requirements, and then translating them to formal specification form for automatic compiling

3. Automating the total *programming environment* such that scheduling, process controls, configuration management, and Software Engineering principles are embodied in the automated process

The rationale for the first definition is based upon history. A very early tool to automatically punch holes in a paper tape from higher level statements was in its day performing automatic programming. In today's terms, the tool would have been called an assembler. Similar early instances of automatic programming resulted in compilers such as FORTRAN and ALGOL. Therefore, the argument goes, automatic programming has always been a euphemism for programming with a higher level language than was then available to the programmer; and therefore, future research in automatic programming will simply be research in the implementation of higher level programming languages [PARN85].

The second definition treats programming as more than just compilation. It includes, for example, the automated assist process of acquiring the specification, the validating of the specification against its external requirements, and some interactive means for translating this high level, informal specification to a lower but formal one which can be automatically compiled. The problem thus defined has been called the extended automatic programming problem [BALZ85]. Balzer shows that the first two definitions above give rise to two complementary approaches to automatic programming.

1. In the first approach, the state-of-the-art advances bottom-up by the addition of optimizations that can be automatically compiled and by the creation of a specification language which relates those optimizations to a specification.

2. In the second approach, full automation is given up, a desired specification language is adopted, and the gap between it and the level that can be automatically compiled is bridged interactively, by human beings, from the top-down.

The second approach builds upon advances in the first approach by extending its applicability to situations which cannot be handled automatically, but which can be handled interactively.

The third definition of automatic programming suggests the integration of a set of programming process tools, such as programming libraries, change control support, data collection and analysis, and management data bases into a single, automated environment.

We view automatic programming as encompassing all three definitions, and will discuss this subject in Chapter 2 when we address automating the process of software development.

1.11 Technology Transfer

It is not uncommon for a new technology to take 10 to 20 years before it becomes widely used in software development. For example, widespread use of a higher-level language, rather than assembler language, for IBM's System/370 operating system development gradually evolved over a period of ten years from the point at which a running higher-level language compiler for systems programming was first available in the late 1960s. Many other promising methods and ideas seem to never achieve implementation in the real world of software development.

Why do new and better ways of doing things take so long to become a part of the software development culture? The answer lies in examination of the motivational systems at work in the developer's pragmatic world and in the world of the methodology pioneer. The developer is severely constrained to deliver the product on time and within budget. A primary consideration in doing this is to use only tools and techniques that have been proven in the past to deliver products. When new tools are implanted in the current process, they are usually of the "homegrown" variety. Such tools usually serve to automate bits of the conventional process without significantly changing the process itself. Such homegrown tools abound in software and are usually highly tailored to a particular project or locale and consequently not portable to other projects. The methodology pioneer, on the other hand, deals in new methods and tools which are perceived by the developer to be either:

1. Not addressing a real problem

    The new method or tool proposes a change in the process that is not recognized as needed by current practitioners in the process. This is the "solution looking for a problem" syndrome. While such proposed solutions may indeed exist in a few cases, as perhaps from a research environment, all too often the problem addressed is real from an overall pragmatic Software Engineering view, but not perceived as such at the local level where older and safer methods may have become entrenched.

2. Addressing a real problem but with an inappropriate solution

    The solution embodied in the proposed methodology or tool may conflict with local philosophy as to the best way to develop software, or it may be so encompassing that only parts of the solution would be applicable locally even though it was successful elsewhere.

3. Addressing a real problem and with an appropriate solution

    This is the situation where a new tool conforms nicely to the local philosophy, appears to be directly portable from other projects where it has been amply proven successful, but requires additional unplanned resource to make the conversion.

These are some of the reasons why technology transfer can be a slow process if allowed to just "happen by osmosis." Therefore, technology transfer into the 1990s requires additional overall focus and a strategy applied now to accelerate the transfer [MUSA83]. Current day examples are IBM's central focus on evaluating its software development process and identifying the real problems [RADI85B], defining an overall process architecture for the 1990s [RADI85A], and defining an overall architecture for automating the management of and tools for the future process [HOFF85].

Another example of focus on technology transfer into the 1990s is work in progress by the Microelectronics and Computer Technology Corporation (MCC) under the direction of Laszlo A. Belady, vice president and program director of the Software Technology Program. In an interview [MYER85], Belady cites three principles being applied for development and transfer of technology into several client companies:

1. Solutions need problems: Only those research solutions that match a real problem in the workaday world get transferred.

2. The human element: There is at least as much sociological component in technology transfer as there is technical component. The people affected must be involved in the advance of the technology transfer and should be involved in the development of the technology itself.

3. Tools: It is easier to transfer and establish tools and make them consistent than it is to transfer methods.

1.12 The Software Engineer's Task

The computer is basically a problem-solving tool. As in real life, the real task in problem solving is not in the solving of the problem at all, but rather in defining the problem such that an appropriate solution can be chosen from a knowledge base, human or computer, of many possible solution approaches.

The Software Engineer of today is

- A problem definer who analyzes user needs and then defines user problems in the context of the user's current process. In some environments this is the role of the systems analyst.

- A solution definer, who selects a general approach in the context of a proposed new user process, develops technical solutions, validates the proposed solution against the defined problem, establishes a design within practical constraints, and selects the best development and testing process for developing the software.

The task of the Software Engineer in the foreseeable future will be to bring the state of the art to a point where the user defines the problem space and specification with the help of the computer; the computer's role with the Software Engineer will select appropriate technical solutions and then deliver them.

1.13 Summary

Before we make a transition into the content of this book, it needs to be restated that, as an industry, we have much to do to evolve to a higher plateau where reliability is not an issue; where the user population is vastly larger; where what is learned by developing one product can be easily propagated into the next product; where we can repeatedly set and meet goals for schedules, productivity, and quality; and where software can play its rightful role in the larger evolution toward a better world and toward worldwide peace through industrial and economic relationships. We believe that a well defined software process can lead to a higher industrial maturity level for software at large, and that it offers the avenue to meet these challenges.

1.14 References

[BALZ85] R. Balzer, "A 15 Year Perspective on Automatic Programming," *IEEE Transactions on Software Engineering*, Vol. SE-11, No. 11 (November 1985), pp. 1257 – 68.

[BOEH83] B. W. Boehm, "Software Life Cycle Factors," *Handbook of Software Engineering*, Van Nostrand Reinhold Company (1983), pp. 494 – 518.

[BOEH84] B. W. Boehm, "Verifying and Validating Software Requirements and Design Specifications," *IEEE SOFTWARE Magazine*, Vol. 1, No. 1 (January 1984), pp. 75 – 88.

[FAGA86] M. E. Fagan, "Advances in Software Inspections," *IEEE Transactions on Software Engineering*, Vol. SE-12, No. 7 (July 1986), pp. 744 – 51.

[FLAH85] M. J. Flaherty, "Programming Process Productivity Measurement System for System/370," *IBM Systems Journal*, Vol. 24, No. 2 (1985), pp. 168 – 75.

[FREE83] P. Freeman, "Reusable Software Engineering: Concepts and Research Directions," "Tutorial on Software Design Techniques—4th Edition," *IEEE Computer Society Press* (1983), pp. 63 – 76.

[HOFF85] G. F. Hoffnagle and W. E. Beregi, "Automating the Software Development Process," *IBM Systems Journal*, Vol. 24, No. 2 (1985), pp. 102 – 20.

[HUMP85] W. S. Humphrey, "The IBM Large Systems Software Development Process: Objectives and Directions," *IBM Systems Journal*, Vol. 24, No. 2 (1985), pp. 76 – 8.

[JONE85] C. L. Jones, "A Process-Integrated Approach to Defect Prevention," *IBM Systems Journal*, Vol. 24, No. 2 (1985), pp. 150 – 67.

[MUSA83] J. D. Musa, "Stimulating Software Engineering Progress—A Report of the Software Engineering Planning Group," *ACM Software Engineering Planning Notes*, Vol. 8, No. 2 (April 1983), pp. 29 – 54.

[MYER85] W. Myers, "MCC: Planning The Revolution in Software," *IEEE SOFTWARE Magazine*, Vol. 2, No. 6 (November 1985), pp. 68–73.

[PARN85] D. L. Parnas, "Software Aspects of Strategic Defense Systems," *Communications of the ACM*, Vol. 28, No. 12 (December 1985), pp. 1326–35.

[POLS86] F. J. Polster, "Reuse of Software Through Generation of Partial Systems," *IEEE Transactions on Software Engineering*, Vol. SE-12, No. 3 (March 1986), pp. 402–16.

[RADI85A] R. A. Radice, N. K. Roth, A. C. O'Hara, Jr. and W. A. Ciarfella, "A Programming Process Architecture," *IBM Systems Journal*, Vol. 24, No. 2 (1985), pp. 76–8.

[RADI85B] R. A. Radice, J. T. Harding, P. E. Munnis, and R. W. Phillips, "A Programming Process Study," *IBM Systems Journal*, Vol. 24, No. 2 (1985), pp. 91–101.

[ROMA85] P. Roman, "Taxonomy of Current Issues in Requirements Engineering," *IEEE COMPUTER Magazine*, Vol. 18, No. 4 (April 1985), pp. 14–21.

[SCHN80] B. Schneiderman, *Software Psychology: Human Factors in Computer and Information Systems*, Winthrop Publishers (1980).

[SHUE86] R. Shuey and G. Wiederhold, "Data Engineering and Information Systems," *IEEE COMPUTER Magazine*, Vol. 19, No. 1 (January 1986), pp. 18–30.

[SIMO86] A. Simon, "Whether Software Engineering Needs To Be Artificially Intelligent," *IEEE Transactions on Software Engineering*, Vol. SE-12, No. 7 (July 1986), pp. 726–32.

[SNEE84] H. M. Sneed, "Software Renewal: A Case Study," *IEEE SOFTWARE Magazine*, Vol. 1, No. 3 (July 1984), pp. 56–63.

[WEGN84] P. Wegner, "Capital-Intensive Software Technology," *IEEE SOFTWARE Magazine*, Vol. 1, No. 3 (July 1984), pp. 7–45.

[WOLV83] R. W. Wolverton, "Software Costing," *Handbook of Software Engineering*, Van Nostrand Reinhold Company (1983), pp. 469–93.

Additional Recommended Reading

Bauer, F. L., *Software Engineering*, Springer — Verlag (1975).

Evans, M. W., P. Piazza, and J. B. Dolkas, *Principles of Productive Software Management*, Wiley (1983).

Fairley, R., *Software Engineering Concepts*, McGraw-Hill Book Company (1985).

Jensen, R. W. and C. C. Tonies, *Software Engineering*, Prentice Hall, Inc. (1979).

Naur, P. and B. Randell, Editors, *Software Engineering: Report on a Conference Sponsored by NATO Science Committee, Garmish, Germany, 7th to 11th October 1968*, NATO Scientific Affairs Division, Brussels, Belgium (January 1969).

Pfleeger, S. L., *Software Engineering: The Production of Quality Software*, Macmillian Publishing Company (1987).

Pressman, R. S., *Software Engineering: A Practitioner's Approach*, McGraw-Hill Book Company (1982).

Shooman, M. L., *Software Engineering*, McGraw Hill-Book Company (1983).

Sommerville, I., *Software Engineering*, Second Edition, Addison-Wesley Publishing Company (1985).

Chapter 2. The Process of Software Production

2.1 Introduction

What is a software process and why do we care? Beginning with basics, a "process" is a way of doing something. We commonly speak of the process of moving, or the process of building a house, or the process of baking a cake, or the process of manufacturing, or even the process of aging. Most processes of a defined type have degrees of variability, but they also have for each of their respective domains something they hold in common, namely, a similar end product. A specific process type leads to a specific end, but the implementation of the process may vary depending on a multiplicity of variables. Thus, there is more than one way to develop a product within any defined process.

It is intuitive and by all means important to note that while there is more than one way to do something, that there is always at any given time only one best way within the constraints of the problem. This one best way or process can remain true, if and only if the environment is held constant. When the environment changes, the process will need to change if it is to continue to vie for the claim of the "best way." Thus, a process must be flexible if it is to continue to deliver the best value we expect of it.

The reader can probably best accept this claim by an example. Let us suppose you are a maker of books, a publisher. As a publisher, you would make the best use of all the tools, tasks, and methods available to you to get to a large volume production as inexpensively and as fast as possible. This would assure the highest profit. What if, however, your goal were the highest quality rather than the highest profit? How would the process of making books be different? What if you were Benjamin Franklin in the 1730s? How would his process compare to yours today as a high volume, high profit publisher? We think you would agree in these two cases that the processes would be different. Thus, a process is determined by (1) goals or objective, and their priorities, and (2) the available technology. Additionally, the process will probably change over time and the constraints of the available technology. Thus, a process will need to change as the technology on which it is based changes.

Process applies to the making of software, also, and in fact that is what the rest of this chapter is about; that is, the software process -- what it is, what it will help us do as software engineers, and how it is controllable to meet our goals.

For now let us suggest that a good process can repeatedly lead to good products, a better process can lead to better products, and a best process offers us the ability to repeatedly deliver superior products. Thus, our motivation should be to find a superior process to help us deliver superior software products.

2.2 An Evolution of Process in Software

During the evolution of software development discussed in Chapter 1, a defined process slowly emerged. Some of the early approaches that led to the current state of process discipline are described in this section of process evolution.

2.2.1 Cut and Run or Code and Go

During the 1950s, before programmers began to think seriously about a process for producing software, a simple model was followed. Basically, it went something like this: Code a solution to the problem statement and test it. Plain and simple, cut and run, code and go; then if it works, use it. If it works well, keep using it until something better is needed. Then, when something better was needed, repeat the process. In some few situations, a rough design might actually have been produced prior to the code being produced, but this was more an exception than it was a rule. Where there might have been a design, it was even more rarely kept for future reference.

Soon this "process" was destined to evolve into a more orderly approach. Primarily, this was driven by three demands: (1) the problems to be solved with software were becoming more complex, that is, they were harder to visualize without a lot more advance work in the thinking or design stage; (2) managers and users were becoming disenchanted with late delivery dates of promised code; and (3) users were dissatisfied with the quality of the delivered products. Thus, as the needs of a more complex problem which had to be solved within a more prescribed time frame became more demanding, so too did the need to define a better software process.

The example of the cut and run process prevalent in the 1950s is overly simplistic and in that vein is unfair. We are sure some programmers did more than is implied here. Those who had a more disciplined process we would venture to say probably had better programs as a result. In fact, it was these very people who had found a discipline in their own work, who added to the evolution towards a better software process. Those who practiced a less disciplined approach produced a solution which failed to perform reliably or map to the original user requirements. It is unfortunate, but true, that there are still some who practice software development today as it was practiced in its infancy.

2.2.2 Design—Code—Test—Maintenance

The next process evolution step was quickly reached but incomplete even in its evolution. The literature of programming in the late 1950s and early 1960s speaks of software production as being composed of four basic stages: Design — Code — Test — Maintenance. From a global view, these stages do indeed exist, but when the business of making software recognizes only these stages, then it needs also to accept the concomitant problems that come with this limited view. Among these problems are: user requirements that are missed or misinterpreted, delivery of a product the user does not want, late delivery of the product, quality overruns in the delivered product, and cost overruns in building the product. The results of these types of problems are not acceptable in any mature industry, but in the early 1960s software was not yet a mature industry.

2.2.3 The Staged or Phased Process (the Product Life Cycle)

The next step in process evolution was to take a full view of the product life cycle and to account for all major transitions which the product experiences. This birth to death view of the product was dubbed the *product life cycle* and was typically divided into six phases. These phases carried the somewhat descriptive titles of (1) Planning, (2) Architecture, (3) Specification, (4) Design and Implementation, (5) Installation and Packaging, and (6) Service.

This life cycle definition was certainly a refinement of its predecessor and was in many ways the first disciplining of the software production cycle by suggesting that at some level all software products do have a homogeneous structure in common in their development. It also admitted via the planning phase to a stage where one actually planned out the full project through service.

Product life cycle definitions with discrete phase definitions became evident in the software production houses of the 1960s and, although the model itself has remained basically the same at a global view, there have been some refinements over time. Where writers speak of the product life cycle today it usually means more than it did in its early definitions.

2.2.4 Waterfall Model

The waterfall model of the software life cycle, although originally presented publicly in 1970 [ROYC70], did not become popular in the software industry until Boehm brought attention to it later in the 1970s [BOEH73]. It has remained somewhat unchanged since that time. Figure 2 on page 32 is an illustration of the waterfall concept.

There are four parts to this model [BOEH81]:

1. Each phase is required and ends with a verification, validation, or test activity to ensure that the objectives of each phase are satisfied.

2. The product goes through each phase sequentially from system feasibility through phase out and produces ever improving *baselines* or intermediate products.

3. Interactions within a phase occur until it is verified or validated to be satisfactory.

4. The baseline, once achieved, is put under formal change control process, where no changes are made to the baseline unless all interested parties agree.

Boehm, in *Software Engineering Economics*, gives two economic rationales for the waterfall model.

1. In order to achieve a successful software product, we must achieve all of the subgoals within each phase at some stage anyway.

2. Any different ordering of the phases will produce a less successful software product.

The first rationale has been proven time and time again by projects which have not adhered to it. These projects have overrun costs and schedules, misinterpreted user requirements, or delivered an unacceptable product. In all these cases of failure, subgoals within phases were compromised. There is no documented case of a large project ignoring subgoals within a phase and meeting the initial objectives of cost, schedule, and function. If there has been one, the case has never been publicly made. We have seen examples, however, where high risk projects, such as those called *skunk works* or *rugby teams* have intentionally compromised subgoals of different phases in order to capture a market position, and

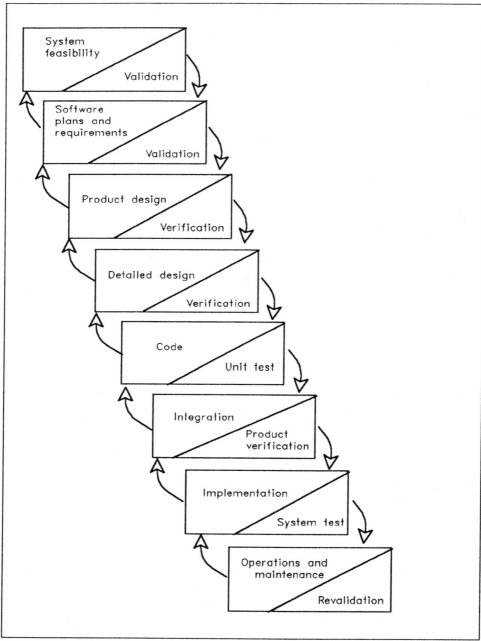

Figure 2. The Waterfall Model of the Software Life Cycle

in some cases this type of project is successful in its initial release. Subsequent releases or upgrades to the product, however, are not always so successful, especially when the subgoals continue to be suboptimized. The second rationale has been proven by data from various sources: IBM [FAGA76], GTE [DALY77], TRW [BOEH81], and ATT [STEP76]. The data shows that it costs more to remove defects later in the development cycle. By not focusing on earlier phases, that is, by attempting to skip phases or reorder them, more errors become manifest in the later phases of product development.

2.2.5 Incremental Development

The waterfall model implies a sequential approach to building a product. For many reasons this is impractical on large projects. The waterfall model imposes an arbitrary order on how the project should unfold over time, and it implies a nonparallel schedule of subparts and parts of the product under development. Additionally iteration is not visibly evident in the waterfall model.

The next logical process evolution is, therefore, to break the one sequential approach into a series of increments or parts which in aggregate run in parallel but which individually can proceed sequentially. Basically, it requires that, during the design phase, the product should be divided into increments with a predetermined order of implementation. These increments are later regrouped or synchronized into the product in aggregates until finally the product is fully built.

2.3 Recommended Process Approach

The Programming Process Architecture [RADI85A] describes required activities for an operational process to develop software. The Programming Process Architecture (PPA) includes a rigorous definition of all product development tasks, definitions of process management tasks, mechanisms for analysis and evolution of the process, and product quality reviews to be used during the various stages of the development cycle. The PPA as described in Radice et al. [RADI85A] requires explicit entry criteria, validation, and exit criteria for each task in the process. When combined, these four parts form a fundamental, repeatable paradigm of the Architecture.

The PPA is the highest representation of the software process relative to any specific project instance of a defined process. In conjunction with the PPA are various lower level project process definitions which implement the necessary levels of detail relevant to any one product environment. This book will not address these lower levels of implementation as the details of the description do not add to the points we want to make. In fact, we can only give an abstraction in these chapters of what a full PPA is in itself. Nonetheless, enough will be addressed for the reader to get a full understanding of all concepts integrated in the PPA and how these concepts can be applied to form a specific project process definition.

While there have been many efforts to describe a software engineering environment (SEE), few have used process as the focus and driving force to the extent called out in the PPA approach. The SEEs have typically focused on tools and methodologies first. It is only recently that the solutions for Software Engineering tools and environments have been understood to require "a solid and formal theoretical base, a unifying conceptual framework and a coherent programming process" [LEHM84].

The PPA requires that a process be defined before the tools and methodologies are defined to automate the process; to do otherwise is to put the cart before the horse. This focus on defining the process first, then integrating the tools and methodologies, marks a key aspect of the PPA. The definition of a software engineering environment can then proceed in an orderly manner, and two desired results can be brought about. First, the integration of tools and methodologies can be done on a defined economic priority basis. Second, the process defines the tools needed and not vice versa. Without a clearly defined and accepted Programming Process Architecture, the tools and methodologies may come together in a loosely coupled manner with reduced effectiveness. The primary and specific focus on process allows for a tightly coupled process-tools-methodologies-practices structure on which a SEE can be built and evolved. The SEE goal is a software engineering environment which will permit zero defect results within a highly productive development cycle, and the PPA supports this goal.

We believe the PPA defined in this book is a necessary and orderly step in the progression of process for the software industry. We fully expect that the PPA as currently defined and used will evolve, and in so doing, lead to yet better process definitions for individual products developed with the PPA approach.

The PPA assumes a homogeneous structure for software development, providing a well-defined process that can be used to:

1. Accommodate easier transfer of product development between groups
2. Assist in the process management of the product
3. Aid in a set of development practices
4. Most importantly, increase both quality and productivity in software products

Thus, the Programming Process Architecture defines a basis from which an orderly evolution in the business of developing software can begin. To achieve this, the PPA as it exists today: (1) ensures a repeatable and simple paradigm at all levels of the software process, (2) contains the means for self-improvement by basing itself on the need for statistical quality control, (3) requires a validation mechanism for any work item produced during the development cycle, (4) is based on what already exists in the software industry, drawing only from the best proven alternatives, (5) addresses the complete life cycle of software production, and (6) does not require a complete set of tools in its first iteration. It is expected that the PPA may be incrementally refined as tools become available and integrated for the process definitions refined from the PPA. For example, as code generators become practical, we would expect that the Code stage would be modified, if not deleted.

2.3.1 Problems in Previous Process Approaches

It is our belief that the PPA represents a meaningful step towards an improved and future process definition and approach to building large software products. Unfortunately, it is sometimes necessary to demonstrate that a proclaimed improvement is indeed better than those it succeeds by showing their faults. It is not our intent to suggest that other approaches in the software business have not included some of the same premises in their process definitions as those which are embedded in the PPA but rather to show what is necessary for inclusion in a process definition.

The approaches to defining a process life cycle model which preceded the PPA exhibited one or more of the following problems. In today's software business these problems limit effective industrial software production:

1. All major product stages are not defined.

2. Entry and exit criteria at stage transitions are not defined.

3. Ability to refine the implemented process definition is not built into the model.

4. The process definition is not based on and evolved from data generated from the process itself.

5. Validation of all completed work items or changes in their state are not required.

6. Change control for modifying work items is not clearly defined.

7. Parallel process paths are not defined or supported.

8. Iteration is not addressed.

9. Work ahead is not addressed.

We will see shortly how these problems are addressed in the PPA.

2.3.2 Process Management Principles

Before we show how stages and activities are defined in the PPA, it is necessary to understand that a good process may lead to good results, and it is our belief that a well-managed and well-defined process can lead to superior results. Therefore, the Programming Process Architecture has been defined to support the following process management principles:

- The process must be defined.

- The process must be actively, continually, and consistently managed to consistently improve quality and increase productivity.

- Consistent management of a process requires that the process:

    - Be decomposed into parts (process stages)

    - Have entry criteria, tasks, validations, and exit criteria defined for each part

    - Have process data regularly reviewed, analyzed, and used for process improvement (statistical control)

    - Have for each work item a quality plan which is certifiable and allows any necessary changes to be validated before being included in the product or its associated documentation

    - Have problems with the product or process recorded and analyzed for cause, effect, and improvement

    - Have changes to the product or process controlled (they should be recorded, tracked, and evaluated for effectiveness)

    - Have goal setting, data capture, analysis and feedback, performed for improvement of both the product and the process

2.3.3 Entry—Task—Validation—Exit:
A Paradigm in the Programming Process Architecture

The PPA employs rigorous structure in controlling the execution of the process for each activity within each stage of the process. This structure calls for a predefined set of of entry criteria, tasks, validations, and exit criteria for each activity or stage. This recurring paradigm structure of entry criteria, tasks, validations, 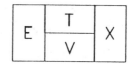 and exit criteria is formally defined an *activity* in the PPA and is illustrated in Figure 3 on page 37. This paradigm is referred to as the ETVX model.

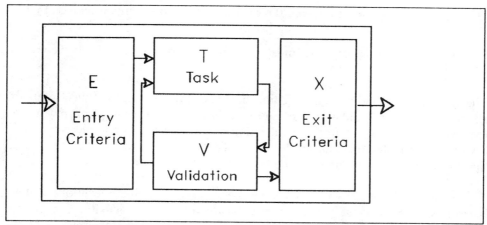

Figure 3. The ETVX Paradigm

ETVX represents the notion that at any level of abstraction or refinement for a work item activity, that there must be entry (E) and exit (X) criteria, that there is a task to be done (T), and that what is done needs to be validated (V). Without these four basic building blocks the model is incomplete and there is no assurance of the product subparts being developed as required.

Although the ETVX model is used at a stage level, it does not imply that all activities or tasks in a later stage must wait for completion of predecessor stages. The later stages may be functioning in parallel with previous stages. Any one ETVX activity grouping may begin execution once the state conditions described in the entry (E) part have been satisfied. If the entry criteria have been satisfied, then the task can begin execution. When the task is completed, then the validation can begin. However, in order for a stage to be fully completed, all exit criteria must be satisfied at some time in the product life cycle. When the exit criteria is not yet satisfied, the completion must wait until all required state conditions are brought about. This waiting can optionally occur at entry to a stage or activity. The model not only permits but encourages that asynchronous processing occurs during a product development cycle.

For example, the Module Level Design stage assumes that many modules are being designed in parallel. When these designs are validated, and exit criteria are satisfied, the modules may independently be implemented during the Code stage and unit tested during the Unit Test stage. However, function test may not begin until all the required modules are available based on predefined entry criteria to the Function Verification stage. Thus, for a given activity within a stage or for the stage itself, there is a predefined

1. list of entry criteria that should be satisfied before beginning the tasks

2. set of task descriptions that specify what is to be accomplished

3. validation procedure to ensure the quality of the work items produced by the tasks

4. checklist of exit criteria that must be satisfied before the activity is viewed as complete.

The ETVX model indicates the relationships and flow among the four aspects of an activity. If a validation procedure determines that change or rework is required within a task before the validation can be viewed as complete and successful, then the iterative loop of task and validation is repeated until it is resolved that the work items produced by the task are satisfactorily completed.

The paradigm displayed with ETVX can be applied to as fine a level of detail as is required to control the process; that is, at the lowest level activity, since activities can be nested. It can also be applied at the process stage level. Thus, ETVX is a process management control structure to prevent problems or defects from moving forward from one stage or activity of the defined process to another related stage or activity.

As noted earlier an underlying theme of the PPA is the focus on process control through process management activities. Each stage of the process includes explicit process management activities that emphasize product and process data capture, analysis, and feedback. Through a required quality plan and quality reviews, the product is monitored and managed at every stage and activity in the process. Through process *postmortem* meetings and analysis, the process is additionally monitored at the end of each stage. This allows a high degree of control including corrective action to achieve quality goals as the product evolves, rather than waiting until testing is completed to determine the quality level.

We want to acknowledge here that much of the early definition of the ETVX model is based on the work of Norman C. Folden, Norman K. Roth, Almerin C. O'Hara, Jr., and Willian A. Ciarfella [RADI85C].

Task Refinement

In its simplest form the ETVX model applies to all levels of definition whether it be an abstraction as broad as the entire the life cycle process, the next level of refinement called *stages*, or the next level of refinement called *activities*. If the process definer chooses to refine tasks into *subactivities*, the ETVX model would apply at this level also. The nesting of subactivities can continue to any level of refinement. Thus, the essence of the ETVX model remains the same regardless of the level at which it is viewed.

The notion of these levels of refinement for the design stages is represented in the stage labeled Component Level Design (CLD). In this example there are two subtasks contained in the upper level task. One of these subtasks shows another level of subtasking, and the other shows two levels of subtasking. This tells us that before the highest level task is completed, the two sublevels need to be completed within the ETVX time sequence for this major task. See Figure 4.

Prototyping and Work-Ahead

Prototyping, a form of work-ahead, is also representable within the ETVX model. Figure 5 on page 40 shows that prototyping, or work-ahead, for some portion of the Product Level Design (PLD) is handled with the same paradigm stipulated for any other set of activities.

In this example, some portion of the design will have proceeded into Code and Unit Test, then Product Level Design is re-entered before the validated design proceeds into the product. Thus, we have gone outside of the sequential ETVX definition for this level of design activity. We are moving into code and unit test for a period of time and thus are working ahead of the process definition. The prototyping may have been necessary to verify that a tricky algorithm is going to work as specified, and it is desirable to know the answer before completing the Product Level Design. Nonetheless, all task results for the entire PLD must be validated and all exit criteria must be satisfied before the activity can be marked as work completed for later stages. Basically any activity can be started even if the entry criteria have not been satisfied, but an activity cannot be exited until all criteria have been satisfied.

Task Repetition

Task repetition is a form of iteration and needs to be addressed within the ETVX paradigm. Sometimes it will be necessary to repeat a task within an activity because the validation shows that the task has not completed satisfactorily. This repetition is important as it allows us to integrate information about the physical task as it was completed with our predetermined expectations of what that completion should be. We ensure the satisfaction of the task completed through validation, as we repeat or loop through the task-validation sequence until the validation is satisfied. This repetition is shown in Figure 6 on page 41 with the dotted lines between T and V. Once the validation is satisfied the process continues on into the X part of the paradigm as shown by the solid line between V and X.

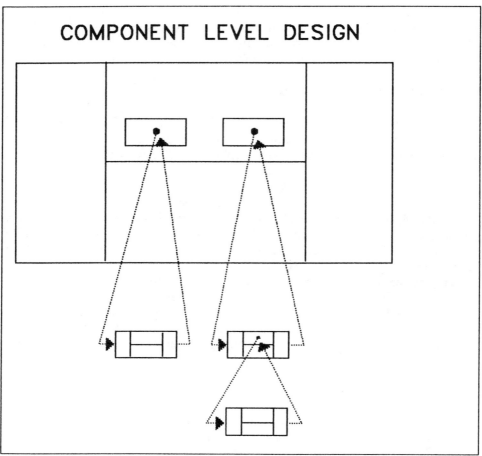

Figure 4. Example of Design Task Refinement

Rework

Rework is yet another form of process iteration in the life-cycle mode. Figure 7 on page 42 shows how this might look graphically. In this example the dotted line represents leaving the task part because of some predetermined reason such as an error found during Unit Test and returning to a higher level in the process such as Model Level Design to resolve the error. Once the design is corrected for the module error, the Code stage can be re-entered for this module error, and once code is completed the Unit Test stage is re-entered for this module error. Note, that the Unit Test task is still processing as long as it has work to do while the iteration for the error is resolved.

If the error fix now resolved is validated as correct, then the ETVX grouping for this Unit Test may continue on to its own validation. Assuming all other work

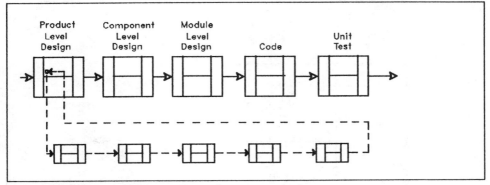

Figure 5. Work-ahead Process Example

items in this module Unit Test have been validated, the process will continue on into the exit criteria evaluation. Otherwise, the looping between task and validation will continue until all of the validation has been satisfied.

Suppose a defect is found during the Functional Verification Test (FVT) stage and it requires rework starting with activities of the Component Level Design (CLD) stage. The PPA allows for the various activities of this test stage to continue uninterrupted, while the required activities of the design stage iterate to resolve the found problem. This overlap of activities from different stages is natural and necessary. The CLD stage activities, when finally completed, then lead to those required in the Module Level Design, Code, Unit Test, and Functional Verification Test stages. This allows for a smooth, managed, change-controlled process to resolve the problem while other process activities continue undisturbed. Another example would be the parallelism of design, code, and testing of different product parts. This is evident as at any point in time groups of modules or functional units exist in different project states. Although this level of product parallelism is necessary for schedule and productivity efficiencies, for any one atomic module the design, code, and test will of course be serial.

2.4 Process Stages

The PPA partitions the process into 12 stages of development. Each of these stages may be viewed as a state of evolution of the product. Each stage is named for the major activity that occurs during that time frame. However, many other activities will be occurring in the same time frame. For example, although a stage is named Code, it contains concurrent activities for testing, marketing, service, publications, process management, and other aspects of program development. These activities are part of the work performed from the other viewpoints necessary to deliver a software product. The 12 process stages described in the PPA are shown in Figure 8 on page 43.

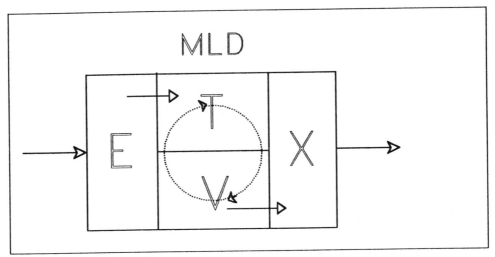

Figure 6. Activity Repetition

Implementation or application of the PPA to any single development project can result in variations of stage definitions from the one shown. For example, the development of a particular product might show that two design stages are being used rather than three. This is within the bounds of a PPA implementation. Nonetheless, the essence of the tasks within the three defined design stages would be performed under the definition of the two design stages. Therefore, while the segmentation of the process and the stage names might be different, the essential work to be done to complete the project is the same. We know of no way to skip or delete development activities which are necessary to evolve a product from Requirements through General Availability without causing quality problems. Refer to Boehm's argument as noted in section 2.2.4.

The segmentation of the process into 12 process stages in the Architecture is somewhat arbitrary and is primarily meant to demonstrate how partitioning of the process is accomplished and not to restrict product process implementations or operational processes to exactly 12 stages. We know of projects with more than 12 stages as well as projects with less.

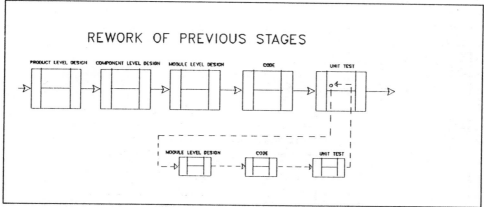

Figure 7. Example of Rework in Previous Stages

2.4.1 Stage Definitions

We as programmers all believe we know what is meant by the terms *code* or *design*. Nonetheless, sometimes these terms are used differently. Here then are our definitions of the 12 stages defined in the PPA. They are similar to terms used in the Software Engineering culture, but in any event, when referencing the PPA where a term is used, the meaning is as indicated in these following definitions:

1. Requirements and Planning:

   During this stage two sets of activities occur:

   - Product and system level requirements are documented and entered into a tracking system.

   - Product and project planning are begun with appropriate process and product activities including creation of a product quality plan.

   Product planning consists of many activities (reference Chapter 3) including:

   - Documentation of the process to be used.

   - Completion of a business proposal, and defining the business reasons for going into software production. Project planning includes the identification of the process to be used, and selection and implementation of a management support system for collecting of process data; planning and tracking; and analysis, evaluation, and feedback of process and product data.

   The PPA assumes a specific methodology wherein requirements are gathered, problem analysis is carried out, documented, and used to create a solution

FAMILY	STAGE	
REQUIREMENTS AND PLANNING	Requirements and Planning	(R&P)
DESIGN	Product Level Design	(PLD)
	Component Level Design	(CLD)
	Module Level Design	(MLD)
IMPLEMENTATION	Code	(C)
	Unit Test	(UT)
TESTING	Function Verification Test	(FVT)
	Product Verification Test	(PVT)
	System Verification Test	(SVT)
PACKAGING AND VALIDATION	Package and Release	(P&R)
	Limited Availability	(LA)
GENERAL AVAILABILITY	General Availability	(GA)

Figure 8. Process Stages Grouped into Families

that describes new or enhanced function as a response to a problem. The solution is then coordinated and transformed into a Product Level Design. This procedure is carried out first at the system level if that view is relevant to the problem and then for specific products within the system.

2. Product Level Design (PLD):

PLD represents a definition of the product functions that will satisfy the requirements produced during the previous stage. This is the first or highest level of design statement which is developed as part of the product solution. Performance and usability objectives are identified and publications planning begins. Prototyping may be employed in this stage to assist in exploring usability of design approaches or to make visible the capability of the product to meet user requirements.

3. Component Level Design (CLD):

A partitioning of functions into substructures with hierarchical relationships representing the product occurs during this stage. These substructures represent an intermediate decomposition of the Product Level Design statement but do not include a level of definition which will exist in the Module Level Design. The set of module names are defined. The principal data structures and control paths specified for each module in the hierarchy are also defined.

4. Module Level Design (MLD):

This includes detailing of each module into a specific logic solution. Each logic path is detailed to denote specific procedural activities. Data structures are defined to the lowest level of detail. Installability and serviceability walk-throughs are held. A plan is completed to enable the product to be used from more than just the English language view. The first drafts of product documentation are made available.

5. Code (C):

The transformation of the Module Level Design representation into a compilable language with resultant object code is completed. All test plans are completed and test cases for the Functional Verification Test and Product Verification Test are completed.

6. Unit Test (UT):

The testing of each module's logic occurs here to assure that all logic paths are covered and operate according to the Module Level Design specifications. In some cases, groups of modules may be executed as a unit.

7. Function Verification Test (FVT):

The execution of all product functions in an integrated product with respect to the product specification is completed. When this level of testing is complete, the product functions will have been proven to work in a simulated and constrained environment.

8. Product Verification Test (PVT):

This stage includes execution of all product functions in a real and unconstrained environment. This test will be executed from a user perspective, but it will not necessarily and intentionally force the functions to execute in a stressed or loaded environment. Performance and usability capabilities are measured as a total product set. When this test is complete, product delivery dates are at minimal risk and the product can therefore be announced to the marketplace.

9. System Verification Test (SVT):

This is execution of all product functions from the user perspective in an integrated hardware and software environment which will stress the system from performance, reliability, availability, usability, and capability viewpoints. When this test is complete, the product will successfully perform to the requirements statement and the user perspective.

10. Package and Release (P and R):

During this stage, the various parts which define the full product set, including product tapes, feature tapes, product publications, and installation guides are brought together as a unified product and are used as the users will see them. The results of this test will demonstrate that a user can install the product and bring it to successful operation.

11. Limited Availability:

This stage calls for execution of the product in a set of actual customer or user environments prior to releasing the product for general availability. This stage is a validation of the marketing and field support for the product and will additionally have demonstrated that the product functions to the users' expectations in actual user environments.

12. General Availability:

This stage starts with delivery of the product to the marketplace. All manuals, products, field service, market education materials, support, and distribution channels must be in place and working satisfactorily.

2.5 Stage Attributes

We have found that there are 11 attributes in each stage which must be addressed if process effectiveness and efficiencies are to be understood and managed. The degree to which these attributes are evident defines a level of maturity about the process stage. In fact, the maturity of the stage can be measured against these attributes on a scale of one to five, where one is high. Then stages with attributes evaluated at lower levels of maturity can be viewed as candidates for change to improve effectiveness and efficiency. These 11 attributes and their definitions have been discussed in more detail in an *IBM Systems Journal* issue to which the reader is referred [RADI85B]. The attributes and definitions are:

1. *Process*:

   The systematic flow and relationships of tasks and information to produce a product within a stage

2. *Methods*:

   The systematic procedures and techniques to accomplish a task

3. *Adherence to Practices*:

   A properly defined, proven, and commonly understood process ethic that is adhered to by the product development team members, and the consistency with which the process ethic is followed

4. *Tools*:

   The automated support of tasks, methodologies, and practices

5. *Change Control*:

   The methodology by which all changes to the product are controlled

6. *Data Gathering*:

   The collection of appropriate data and information which illustrates the process performance

7. *Data Communication and Use*:

   The effective analysis and communication of process data and information to improve the process

8. *Goal Setting*:

   The establishment and use of quantifiable goals or targets for the purpose of improving the process

9. *Quality Focus*:

The pursuit and achievement of product excellence in every process task, including understanding and action on what must be changed in the process to accomplish product excellence

10. *Customer Focus*:

   The achievement of customer needs and requirements in the product at each process stage. Customer is viewed as both the end user of the product and the next person to work on the development of the product during its life cycle.

11. Technical Awareness:

   The technical knowledge of the state-of-the-art products and processes used in the profession

Each of these attributes describes the effectiveness, efficiencies, and completeness of the stages and activities as executed during execution of an actual development project. Each of the attributes must be addressed and understood by the product manager in order to achieve high function, quality, and productivity. Now that we have a view of 12 stages in the PPA and 11 attributes that can be measured against each of these stages, we can decompose the focus on software development into a matrix of 12 by 11 cells. Each of these cells can be separately viewed and separately evaluated for its contribution to the product under development. Each cell can be evaluated on a scale of 1 to 5, and necessary actions can be taken based on these evaluations to improve the activities affected. Some cells have more of an effect on the business and, therefore, should assume a priority focus. Nonetheless, all cells have an effect on the final product, and all should be considered as candidates indicating where the software production process can be improved. See Figure 9 on page 49.

2.6 Viewpoints across the Programming Process Architecture

While we may normally think only in terms of product development when we speak of process for software production, there are many activities in the project that are under execution simultaneously by different groups of people. These related activities are called *viewpoints* and include the following:

- Build and Integration, which address how the different parts are controlled during the project life cycle

- Testing, which has planning activities that begin as early as the PLD stage

- Program Development, which results in the software function seen by the user

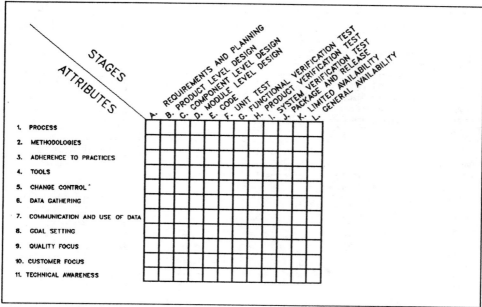

Figure 9. Matrix of States and Attributes

- Publications, which includes all text the user may see for the product

- Marketing and Service, which includes all activities required to sell and service the product

- Process Management, which includes all activities to manage the work in the other viewpoints

See Figure 10 on page 50 for a representation of the relationship of tasks with stages and viewpoints (VP).

2.6.1 An Example of Viewpoints Within the FVT Stage

An example of some work that occurs in these viewpoints for one stage of the development process, Functional Verification Test, is shown in this section:

1. Program Development

   Problems found during formal testing are reported and documented with an appropriate data base. A programmer then analyzes each problem and works with others to determine a solution. The analysis and resolution determines at which stage in the development cycle rework should start. While other testing continues, the activities of the earlier stages required to resolve the problem are formally executed until the problem is closed. If the solution involves design and code changes, then appropriate design documents are

	RP	PLD	CLD	MLD	C	UT	FVT	PVT	SVT	PR	ESP
VP-PROGRAM DEVELOPMENT:											
Initial Business Proposal	—										
Programming Objectives	—	—									
Performance Objectives		—									
Initial Programming Specs	—										
Prog. System Structure		—	—	—							
Final Programming Specs			—								
Program Logic Specs			—	—							
Product Workbook		—	—	—	—	—	—	—	—	—	—
VP-TESTING:											
Comprehensive Test Plan		—	—	—	—						
Installability Ckpt. Plan	—			—							
Performance Test Plan		—	—								
Unit Test Plan			—								
FVT Plan		—	—								
PVT Plan			—								
SVT Plan					—						
Unit Test Cases					—						
FVT Cases					—	—					
PVT Cases					—		—				
SVT Cases					—						
VP-PUBLICATIONS:											
Information Objectives	—	—									
Information Specs		—	—								
Info. Measurement Plan		—	—	—							
Multiple End User Language Support Plan		—	—	—							
Information Products			—	—	—	—	—				
VP-BUILD & INTEGRATION											
Build Plan		—	—	—	—	—	—	—	—	—	—
VP-MARKETING & SERVICE:											
Service Education Training Requirements	—										
Service Plan		—		—					—		
Service Training Plan		—		—							
Distribution and Support Plan		—			—		—	—			
Customer Education Materials		—				—			—		—
Initial Plan for LA			—	—							
VP-PROCESS MANAGEMENT:											
Process Definition	—										
Concurrences List	—										
Disaster Recovery Plan	—										
Project Plan	—	—	—	—	—	—	—	—	—	—	—
Quality Plan	—	—	—	—	—	—	—	—	—	—	—
I/S Support Plan		—	—	—	—	—	—	—	—	—	
High Risk Module List		—	—	—	—	—	—	—	—	—	—
Process Postmortem	—	—	—	—	—	—	—	—	—	—	—

Figure 10. Example of Work Flow across Stages by Viewpoint

updated and code is written, inspected, and unit tested prior to integrating it into the driver or package of modules being used for the functional verification test. This is all done using a defined automated change control process. Documentation is updated and kept current for all changes.

2. Testing

Running the functional verification test cases is the key test activity at this time. The test cases themselves were created prior to beginning this stage. Concurrently, a usability test appropriate for this part of the development cycle may take place. Any problems or suggested changes are documented as the first step in a formal configuration management process.

Preparation for Product Verification Test is completed. This includes the writing, inspecting, and testing of test cases as well as the organization and training of test team and problem determination team personnel.

3. Publications

Drafts of associated publications and any other information development materials continue to be refined. Reviews of any language support materials for nondomestic markets are completed.

4. Build and Integration

The Build Plan, a dynamic document detailing the management and control of all the product parts, is kept current, test drivers are built and regression tested to support the testing efforts.

5. Marketing and Service

The final plan for limited availability of the product is created and the distribution and support plan is refined to reflect any changes. The product announcement package is distributed for review. A serviceability walkthrough is completed.

6. Process Management

Several process management activities occur during this and every stage. Refinement of the quality plan and continual monitoring and assessment of the Functional Verification Test progress are, of course, key activities here. Others include the product quality review and process postmortem meeting mentioned earlier. They each have specific tasks that are directed by the data gathered during this stage of the process when compared to the product and process goals established earlier in the project cycle.

This completes the example for the FVT stage. Each other stage has for each viewpoint its own set of concurrent activities.

2.6.2 Streamlining

The PPA was developed with the intent of improving IBM large systems software development. However, projects with short development schedules, or with few programmers may elect to use a *streamlined process*. For those projects which qualify for a streamlined approach, the basic principles of the PPA still apply, and must be retained in the streamlined process:

- Segment the process into well-defined stages.

- Segment the different viewpoints necessary to produce a finished product set.

- Adhere to the essence of the PPA at the stage and activity level by defining task descriptions, entry criteria, validation procedures, and exit criteria.

- Establish appropriate process activities including a quality plan, periodic quality reviews, and process postmortem meetings.

2.7 Summary

In this chapter we have discussed the evolution of the software process. During this evolution improvements were made to the model and definition of process in software development, culminating in the Programming Process Architecture (PPA). This PPA is our recommended approach. Since it is an architecture, it represents the highest level of process definition for product development. Specific products adhering to the PPA will have their own implementation or instantiation of the process for their environment. Key to the PPA is the Entry-Task-Validation-Exit (ETVX) paradigm which applies at all levels of process definition; for example, the life cycle, the stages of the process life cycle, and the activities within the stages. The ETVX paradigm ensures that work items produced during the product life cycle are developed within predetermined entry/exit criteria and with a validation of all work performed during a task subsection of an activity. The process in the PPA define 12 stages of product development. These stages were discussed as were 11 attributes which apply to each stage, which help identify the strengths and weaknesses which may be inherent in a specific product process definition. The major part of the PPA is the process management principle which states that the process should be defined prior to deciding on tools and methodologies to be used during the product development.

2.8 References

[BOEH73] B. W. Boehm, "Software and Its Impact: A Quantitative Assessment," *Datamation*, Vol. 19, No. 5 (May 1973), pp. 48–59.

[BOEH81] B. W. Boehm, *Software Engineering Economics*, Prentice-Hall (1981).

[DALY77] E. B. Daly, "Management of Software Engineering," *IEEE Transactions on Software Engineering* Vol. SE-3, No. 3 (May 1977), pp. 229–42.

[FAGA76] M. E. Fagan, "Design and Code Inspections to Reduce Errors in Program Development," *IBM Systems Journal*, Vol. 15, No. 3 (1976), pp. 182–211.

[LEHM84] M. M. Lehman, "A Further Model of Coherent Programming Processes," Proceedings Workshop, Runnymede, England (February 1984).

[RADI85A] R. A. Radice, N. K. Roth, A. C. O'Hara, Jr., and W. A. Ciarfella, "A Programming Process Architecture," *IBM Systems Journal*, Vol. 24, No. 2 (1985).

[RADI85B] R. A. Radice, J. T. Harding, P. E. Munnis, and R. W. Phillips, "A Programming Process Study," *IBM Systems Journal*, Vol. 24, No. 2 (1985).

[RADI85C] R. A. Radice, N. K. Roth, A. C. O'Hara, Jr., and W. A. Ciarfella, "A Programming Process Architecture," *IBM Systems Journal*, Vol. 24, No. 2 (1985).

[ROYC70] W. W. Royce, "Managing the Development of Large Software Systems: Concepts and Techniques," *Proceedings*, WESCON (August 1970).

[STEP76] W. E. Stephenson, "An Analysis of Resources Used on the SAFEGUARD System Software Development," Bell Labs (August 1976).

Additional Recommended Reading

A Software Engineering Environment for the Navy, Report of the NAVMAT Software Engineering Environment Working Group, Report AD-A1311941/7, Naval Material Command (NAVMAT), Washington, DC (March 1982).

Aron, J., *The Program Development Process—The Programming Team, Part 2*, Addison-Wesley Publishing Co. (1983).

Deming, W. E., *Quality, Productivity, and Competitive Position*, MIT, Center for Advanced Engineering Study, Cambridge, MA. (1982).

Evans, M. W., P. H. Piazza, and J. B. Dolkos, *Principles of Productive Software Management*, John Wiley and Sons (1983).

Madden, W. A., and K. Y. Rone, "Design, Development, Integration: Space Shuttle Primary Flight Software Syst em," *Communications of the ACM*, Vol. 27, No. 9 (September 1984).

Mills, H. D., D. O'Neill, R. C. Linger, M. Dyer, and R. E. Quinnan, "The Management of Software Engineering," *IBM Systems Journal*, Vol. 19, No. 4 (1980), pp. 414−477.

O'Neill, D., "The Management of Software Engineering, Part II: Software Engineering Progra m," *IBM Systems Journal*, Vol. 19, No. 4 (1980).

Proceedings of the 3rd International Software Process Workshop, IEEE Computer Society Press (1986). Workshop theme was Iteration in the Software Process.

Proceedings 9th International Conference on Software Engineering, IEEE Computer Society Press (1987). Conference theme was Software Process.

Radice, R. A., "Large Systems Software Implementation,," *Application Development Systems: The Inside Story of Multinational Product Development*, Tosiyasu L. Kunii, editor, Springer-Verlag (1986).

Part 2. The Software Product

Chapter 3. Planning the Product

3.1 Introduction

In Chapter 2 we defined the first stage of the software engineering process as the Requirements and Planning stage. This chapter deals with the first part of the Requirements and Planning stage, in which an initial business case is made for going ahead with the development of a proposed software product. The next chapter, entitled "Requirements Engineering" covers the second part of the Requirements and Planning stage, in which the requirements are refined to a point suitable for input to the Product Level Design stage.

3.1.1 Requirements and Planning Viewpoints

Several planning activities take place at once during the Requirements and Planning stage. In addition to the initial product planning activities, and the Requirements Engineering activities taking place during this stage, other planning activities are underway from the viewpoints of related organizations. For example:

1. **Test Planning:** The testing organization begins developing an overall test plan, sometimes called a *Comprehensive Test Plan (CTP)*. The CTP defines the entry and exit criteria for each planned testing stage, and the acceptance criteria for delivery of the product to customers. Initial sizing of the required testing effort, and preliminary start and end dates for each test stage are also provided.

2. **Product Publications:** Objectives are written for the various publications that are to become a part of the product offering.

3. **Usability Objectives** Usability objectives are written during the Requirements and Planning stage. These objectives document the characteristics assumed about the product's end-users. Usability goals are developed to better enable product designers and product publication developers to make proper design decisions.

4. **Marketing and Service:** Product education and requirements for training service personnel are initiated. Reliability and maintainability objectives are established, and initial estimates of service costs are also made.

5. **Project Planning:** The overall project plan, including schedule dates, organizational aspects, and resources required is initiated during this stage, to be completed during various other stages during the life-cycle. (Refer to Chapter 6, Planning the Project).

3.2 Key Concepts of This Chapter

It is not within the scope of this text on Software Engineering to treat the subject of software business planning exhaustively. However, since this activity results in the key set of work items needed to begin the software life cycle, we will focus on:

1. The *content* of the business case resulting from the product planning activity

2. The *relationship* of the business case to the Requirements Engineering and project planning activities, (covered in Chapter 4 and Chapter 6 respectively)

3. The *rationale* behind making a business case

Additional details on product planning can be found in Pressman's text on Software Engineering [PRES82] and in Birrell's and Ould's handbook [BIRR86].

Product planning activities initiate a development project. These are the very first activities at the inception of a product and result in a proposal that defines the need for a product and in some cases establishes the overall system strategy and business case for the product. Sometimes the results are called the *systems proposal*, the *project inception proposal*, or the *business case*. We will call the work item resulting from the product planning activities the *business proposal* in this text.

3.2.1 Relationship to Requirements Engineering Stage

The Requirements Engineering process starts when product planning activities have established an acceptable business case for a particular product. The business proposal in commercial systems is usually defined within an established *business strategy* for a given line of products, or market segment. When completed, it contains a high-level set of requirements. Some of the requirements will be of a long-range strategic nature, derived from formal growth studies looking five to ten years into the future. The creation of the business proposal actually requires an initial pass through the Requirements Engineering process and the project planning process at a high-level to establish initial sizings and schedules for input to the feasibility and decision portions of the business case.

Detailed project planning (see Chapter 6) also takes place during the Requirements and Planning stage. The relationship between product planning, Requirements Engineering, and project planning activities is shown in Figure 11 on page 59. The upper portion of the figure shows product planning to include a "mini-cycle" through parts of the Requirements Engineering and project planning activities. The resulting business proposal shown as output of the product planning cycle enables a decision to go ahead, or not to go ahead, with the project. The decision is based upon an assessed desirability of the product from the standpoint of the customers' needs and an initial sizing of the organization's capability to produce the desired product on the needed schedule and within a targeted cost range.

At this point, the Requirements Engineering and project planning activities begin. The figure shows Requirements Engineering producing Programming Objectives documents and Requirements and Product Level Design documents. Project planning relies on input from this process also, and produces the project plan under which the execution of the project will be managed.

3.3 Entry Criteria

What usually initiates a business proposal for a particular product? Planning of a software product must always be done within the context of business and technical strategies A *business strategy* defines the domain of a particular product, or group of products within a 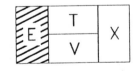 software market place and establishes policies governing business and technical direction for the product.

The market place can be defined in *segments*. Market segments are sets of prospective customers that share common needs: for example, home computer applications, commercial banking, word processing, military applications, retail sales.

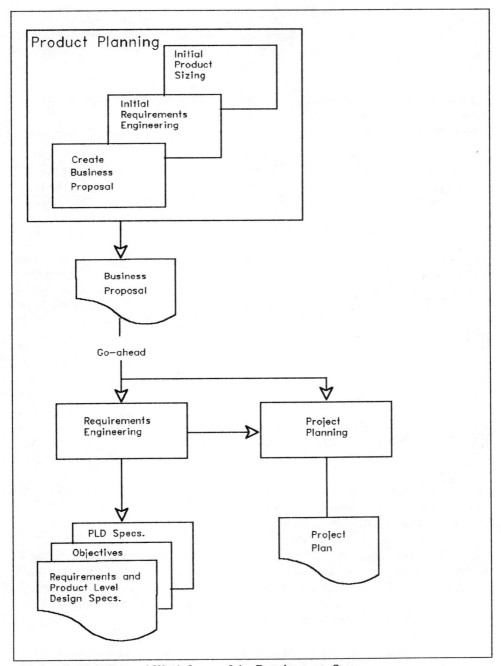

Figure 11. Activities and Work Items of the Requirements Stage

The business strategy depicts how the product is targeted to grow in that market place over time. Business strategies are based on market studies, customer requests, analysis of competitive products and strategies, analysis of economic factors, and dependence on a technology base.

A *technical strategy* defines the anticipated technology base upon which the product will grow. A statement of a technical strategy found in an business proposal might be,

> This product will strive to evolve from its use of current data base technology to artificial intelligence (AI) and knowledge based system approaches, as the industry technology base matures

The criteria for when to initiate a business proposal for a particular product can include both business and technical strategy reasons. For example, the initiation of a business proposal for electronic funds transfer system for commercial banking might be triggered by a marketing analysis, while the proposal for a product line of digital wrist watches might be triggered by breakthroughs in chip technology, or the proposal for a new military weapons aiming system by advances in laser technology.

3.4 Creating the Business Proposal

This initial product planning phase is not as rigorous as the ensuing stages of the development process that we normally include in the domain of Software Engineering. Indeed, many consider this activity outside of what we usually define as Software Engineering. It is a 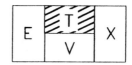 highly judgmental activity involving many business risk factors and requires experienced individuals with ability to perceive many business factors and take intuitive leaps. Nonetheless this part of the product life cycle has activities which are necessary to complete the work within product planning and can be modeled by the ETVX paradigm.

Figure 12 on page 61 shows the major topics covered in a typical commercial system business proposal. The following sections discuss the tasks required for each topic in turn.

```
┌────────────────────────────────────────────────────────────────────┐
│                                                                      │
│    1. High-level and strategic requirements analysis                 │
│                                                                      │
│    2. Business opportunity                                           │
│                                                                      │
│    3. Competitive analysis                                           │
│                                                                      │
│    4. Description of proposed product                                │
│                                                                      │
│    5. Cost and price objectives                                      │
│                                                                      │
│    6. Initial sizings                                                │
│                                                                      │
│    7. Projected profit and loss                                      │
│                                                                      │
│    8. Risk Factors                                                   │
│                                                                      │
│    9. Work plan                                                      │
│                                                                      │
│   10. The Decision                                                   │
│                                                                      │
└────────────────────────────────────────────────────────────────────┘
```

Figure 12. Topics Covered in a Typical Business Proposal

3.4.1 High-Level and Strategic Requirements Analysis

High-level requirements analysis is done in the context of the defined business and technical strategies. It involves a high-level pass through the Requirements Engineering process defined in Chapter 4. The basic outputs are:

1. **Definition of the product environment:** This includes the market segments that will be addressed by the product and describes in a fair amount of detail the type of users that will interact with the product, that is, their characteristics, roles, training, and skill levels.

2. **The set of problems that are being addressed:** Problem categories are defined from overall problem statements, such as "Productivity is low," "The users' process is error-prone," "Existing products exhibit poor human factors," or "System performance is unsatisfactory." Specific problems and the causes associated with each of these problem statements are described in a level of detail sufficient to suggest meaningful solutions in the next step.

3. **Proposed solutions:** General solutions derived from the problem analysis are outlined, such as "The error-prone portions of the user's process need to be

automated." This is followed by details on what those error portions are, and how the automated process might differ from the current manual process.

3.4.2 Business Opportunity

Basically, business opportunity is expressed in terms of the market penetration and revenues that could be anticipated if a product were to be introduced that solves the stated problems. In commercial software, market penetration is expressed in a sales estimate we shall call a *preliminary sales estimate* in this text. The preliminary sales estimate forecasts sales over a designated time period for the proposed product, across various market segments and operating environments specified in the business and technical strategies for the product.

Business opportunities are optimally valid through a specified window of time in the market place, and so the required availability date for the product is another key ingredient in specifying business opportunity.

3.4.3 Competitive Analysis

Competitive analysis is critical to the business proposal. Here are some reasons for its importance:

1. It provides valuable insights into types of solutions to the users' problems that have proven successful in the past and those that have not.

2. It gives indications of parts of the market that may become saturated, or dry up, in the future. There is no need to market a better mousetrap if (1) the world already has a ten-year supply of mousetraps on hand, or (2) there won't be any mice due to some other external cause.

3. It can show the anticipated shifts in the industry technological base. Should you plan to market a new line of buggy whips, or should you switch part of your enterprise to marketing automobile accelerator pedals? Both are devices that make vehicles go faster, but each work on a different technological base.

A thorough competitive analysis can have a significant effect on the validity of the preliminary sales estimate as well as on the business and technical strategies.

3.4.4 Description of Proposed Product

To this point in the business proposal, we have established a market domain and strategies for our product, characteristics of the users of the product, the problems it will set out to solve, its market penetration, and an assessment of how predecessor products have addressed similar problems. We are now ready to form a high-level description of the required product with respect to its function and a number of attributes.

1. **Required Functional Capabilities:** This is a high-level description of what the product must do to support the user's new way of doing business. It is in response to the proposed solutions that resulted from the requirements analysis activity described earlier.

2. **Product Attributes:** These state a desired, or required, property of the proposed product. One way to remember the kind of properties we are talking about for a software product is with an acronym *CUPRIM*. CUPRIM is derived from the first letter of the words:

   - Capability
   - Usability
   - Performance
   - Reliability
   - Installability
   - Maintainability

   Most of the contemporary literature and methodologies for requirements focus on defining functional capability. Attributes other than capability are sometimes called *constraints* [ROMA85] because they restrict the kinds of solutions the designer might consider. We will continue to call them *attributes* in this book because, although they do represent constraints on the designer, they also represent desired characteristics of the resultant product itself.

Statements of the desired product capabilities and attributes in the business proposal, as well as schedule and resource constraints from other sources, all serve to establish boundaries for the possible solutions leading to the proposed product. The solution that can exist within a set of constraints has been called the *solution space* for a problem [YEH80]. Definitions of the product attributes in the business proposal are later refined during the formal Requirements and Planning stage. Precise definitions of the required properties, such as the CUPRIM attributes, are essential because they establish the foundation on which the future design is validated, on which the implementation is tested, and on which customer feedback through use of the finished product can ultimately be obtained.

3.4.5 Cost and Price Objectives

Price objectives are basically a projection of "what the market would be willing to pay" for the solution to the problems outlined in the proposal. Competitive pressures on pricing also effect price objectives. Cost to develop the product is a constraint which has a direct effect on meeting price objectives and delivering a competitive product.

Setting cost boundaries or targets is an essential ingredient in the business proposal. Particularly in software, the possible solutions available for the defined problems are many and varied. For this reason, some software proposals have literally priced themselves out of the market, by offering overly costly or sophisticated solutions, or solutions that cannot be produced in time to match within a cost constraint to meet a business opportunity time frame. Another reason cost targets are essential is that sometimes the technology base in the industry is just not capable of providing a cost effective solution that could be offered at a price commensurate with the buyer's real needs or willingness to pay.

Cost objectives may be broken into categories and addressed independently in the resulting cost estimate, such as subparts for marketing, for development, for product distribution, and for service.

Sometimes the difference between a cost competitive product and one that is not competitive is difficult to perceive. This is especially true during the project development. In fact, it is too easy to lose sight of the cost and price objectives when the development comes under difficult times. There are times when it is most important that all participants in the project understand the cost, schedule, and price objectives.

3.4.6 Initial Sizings

This portion of the business proposal is basically a statement of the capability of the enterprise to produce the required product. The basic parameters estimated are product size, the resource required, and the projected availability date. The initial estimates for the parameters are derived by taking a high-level pass through the project planning activity, described in Chapter 6, and as illustrated in Figure 11 on page 59.

3.4.7 Projected Profit And Loss

A projected profit and loss statement is also part of the business proposal. This includes a planned payback schedule, and shows the anticipated effect that the proposed product would have on the total business enterprise, if it were to be developed. Often, a new addition to the product line of an enterprise can affect the projected sales of other related products already offered by the company, requiring the planner to investigate the market posture and forecast assumptions of these products as well.

3.4.8 Risk Factors

The decision factors are basically a sizing of the risks associated with all the variables that could endanger the success of the project once under way. Figure 13 on page 66 lists some of the types of risk factors likely to play a part in a business proposal.

In real life practice, at the time of making the business proposal we can divide the risks into two categories:

1. What may we have already estimated incorrectly?
2. What could go wrong as the life cycle unfolds?

In the first category, we can place the initial sizings, the description of the user environment for the proposed product, the pricing objectives, the competitive analysis, and the projected profit and loss. This is why there are *estimating contingencies*. A "contingency" is usually expressed as a percentage of the total estimate added to the estimate. In practice, each of the above named variables is estimated within a contingency band-width: for example, plus or minus 25 percent. The amount of contingency is based upon historical experience and other rationale. Contingency of this kind is usually built into the committed figures. An accurate assessment of the amount of contingency included in each variable, and its rationale, is essential input to making the final business decision to go ahead with the project.

In the second category are variables outside the direct control of the project, and which are subject to change during the course of the project. Examples of such variables would be changes in competitive posture due to an unexpected announcement of a competitive product, inability of vendors to deliver committed software parts on time, and unanticipated swings in the economy.

- Dependencies on hardware development schedules
- Dependencies on components under development by other software projects
- Estimating contingencies
- Business risk factors
- Technical risk factors
- Legal factors

Figure 13. Some Types of Risk Factors Covered in a Business Proposal

3.4.9 Work Plan

The business proposal usually contains an initial work plan, including the organization targeted for doing the work, required staffing buildup, and skill levels needed. The business proposal would also include a detailed work plan for getting to the next step in the event the decision is made to go ahead with the project.

3.5 Validation

Before the completed business proposal is ready for use as a decision-making tool, it must be validated for completeness, consistency, and correctness. Validation for completeness and consistency means checking to see that all topics are covered and that all facts, assump-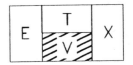
tions, and conclusions are logically consistent with one another. "Correctness" in the case of a business proposal is highly subjective, and validation of it requires several internal reviews where all assumptions are reevaluated for reasonability, and all conclusions checked for plausibility.

3.6 Exit Criteria

How do business planners know when the business proposal is complete? Perhaps the most common method is simply to end the initial planning activity when the business proposal is "finished," meaning that all the necessary elements have been included. This is usually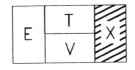
accomplished through internal reviews validating that all sections are covered, and all assumptions are consistent with each other.

In the final analysis, the proposal is considered complete when, after considerable review and discussion, those making the business decision are comfortable that the appropriate amount of decision-making information is present. An additional boundary may also be expressed in terms of a fixed dollar ceiling. Sometimes for government or military projects, a specific contract is issued, covering only a fixed cost for submitting the initial proposal.

3.7 The Decision

When the business proposal is complete, who participates in the decision to go ahead with, or kill, the proposed project? The players include representatives of the sponsoring organization, such as an executive or product manager, frequently supported by a project review committee consisting of representatives from financial control, legal, software development, and marketing or user representatives.

During the decision-making process, initial sizings, projected profit and loss, and risk factors are weighed against cost and price objectives to establish the feasibility of the business proposal.

The decision choices are basically:

1. Go ahead with the project
2. Reject the proposal
3. Proceed to the next major checkpoint in the work plan and reevaluate the decision

Whatever the decision, it should be documented in the business proposal along with the rationale for making it.

3.8 Summary

Product planning starts with the inception of the *idea* for making a software product, and ends when initial feasibility of the proposed product has been explored to where a decision to take, or not to take, the business risk can be made.

Product planning, while less well defined, is a part of the development process. It has far-reaching effects on the efforts in later development stages and on the organization's ability to deliver a quality product on time and within cost. In the final analysis, every product must have a plan based on a business analysis. To do otherwise leads to project management problems throughout the development life cycle.

The Requirements Engineering activity described in the next chapter can be viewed as a natural extension of the product planning that created the initial business proposal.

3.9 References

[BIRR86] N. D. Birrell and M. A. Ould, *A Practical Handbook For Software Development*, Cambridge University Press (1986), pp. 47 – 109.

[PRES82] R. S. Pressman, *Software Engineering: A Practitioner's Approach*, McGraw-Hill Book Company (1982) pp. 31 – 93.

[ROMA85] G. Roman, "A Taxonomy of Current Issues in Requirements Engineering," *IEEE COMPUTER Magazine*, Vol. 18, No. 4 (April, 1985), pp. 14 – 21.

[YEH80] R. T. Yeh and P. Zave, "Specifying Software Requirements," *Proceedings of the IEEE*, Vol. 68, No. 9 (September, 1980), pp. 1077 – 85.

Additional Recommended Reading

Boehm, B. W., *Software Engineering Economics*, Prentice-Hall (1981).

Evans, M. W., P. Piazza, and J. B. Dolkas, *Principles of Productive Software Management*, John Wiley and Sons (1983), pp. 141 – 218.

Jensen, R. W., and C. C. Tonies, *Software Engineering*, Prentice-Hall (1979), pp. 24 – 63.

Shooman, M. L., *Software Engineering*, McGraw-Hill (1983) pp. 438 – 83.

Wolverton, R. W., "Software Costing," *Handbook of Software Engineering*, Van Nostrand Reinhold (1984), pp. 469 – 93.

Chapter 4. Requirements Engineering

4.1 Introduction

In Chapter 3 we depicted product planning as the first part of the Requirements stage. An initial pass through the Requirements Engineering process provides technical feasibility information. When combined with the initial marketing estimates, this pass completes the business case, enabling the decision to proceed or not with detailed Requirements Engineering, design, and implementation of the target product. This chapter presents detailed *Requirements Engineering*, the principal activity of the Requirements stage.

Basically, the Requirements Engineering process transforms the description of the product found in the business proposal to a much more refined description needed for the Product Level Design stage. Thus, after the decision to go ahead with the project has been made, Requirements Engineering activities bridge business planning or contract bid activities at project inception to Product Level Design activities.

In this chapter, we first introduce the concepts of Requirements Engineering, then address some of its current problems, and describe some promising solutions. We then explore Requirements Engineering methodologies and languages in more depth, analyzing such questions as:

Why do the methodologies described in this chapter work?

What are their relative merits and disadvantages? Do formatted specification languages help? If so, why?

We will also explore one methodology in depth and conclude with an example of its use. Additionally, we discuss the relationship between Requirements Engineering and design methodologies.

4.2 Key Concepts of This Chapter

After completing this chapter, the reader will understand that:

1. Requirements Engineering is considered today by many in the industry as the weakest part of the entire software development process.

2. There is a growing focus on the problem by software engineers in industry, government, and academia.

3. There are a number of successful solutions to some of the basic problems in Requirements Engineering. Achievable improvements are in sight based on some simple methodologies that can be applied now.

4. Perseverance in the use of formal specification techniques may provide a more rigorous bridge from requirements to design, building a foundation for additional automation of the software development process.

4.2.1 Requirements Engineering Domain

Figure 14 on page 71 depicts Requirements Engineering as a process for transforming the overall requirements in the business proposal into the detailed requirements necessary for the Product Level Design.
In the figure, the results of the Requirement Engineering process are shown as a set of documents that (1) specifies the detailed requirements for the product, (2) defines the programming objectives, and (3) documents the initial design considerations, sometimes called *design directions*.

In this text we will refer to the above collection of documents as the *Requirements and PLD Specifications*, or *RPLD Specifications*.

The arrow labeled "T" in the figure represents tasks necessary to translate the "nebulous cloud" of requirements to the RPLD Specifications. The arrow labeled "V" represents the subsequent validation activities essential for ensuring that the defined requirements truly state the customers' needs, and subsequently that the Product Level Design correctly satisfies the requirements as defined.

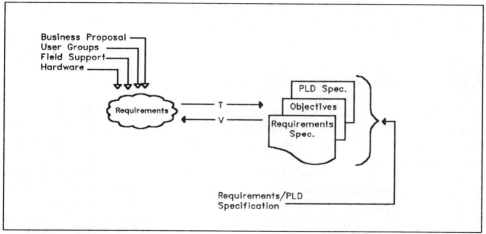

Figure 14. Requirements Engineering Domain

4.2.2 What Is a Requirement?

A *requirement* conveys an essential property that the system must or should satisfy. A complete set of requirements would cover the needed product's *capability, usability, performance, reliability, installability*, and *maintainability*, or the CUPRIM attributes described in Chapter 3, Planning the Product .

Requirements may be stated with varying degrees of constraints on the designer. These constraints can be *mandatory* (e.g., "The response time **shall** not exceed two seconds"); or *desired* (e.g., "Menus displayed at the terminal **should** present no more than six choices for human factors reasons"); or *optional* (e.g., "Parsing **may** be done through a subset of the standard 'XYZ Parser,' or an equivalent new component, at the discretion of the developer").

Some government and military requirements specifications assign specific meanings to words like *shall, should*, and *may*. Each occurrence of the word "shall" in a requirements specification is considered an instance of a unique requirement, and counts of the number of "shalls" provide a sort of metric for monitoring increases in the number of requirements placed on the contractor of the software. Requirements are usually not as formally classified as this in commercial software development enterprises.

In general, no matter what the enterprise, requirements are statements of functional capabilities for the proposed product, and the attributes it must exhibit.

4.2.3 Sources of Requirements

Requirements come from a number of sources. For example, in commercial systems software, requirements are engendered both by the need to support new hardware devices and by the needs of the end users of existing software products for enhancements in any of the CUPRIM attributes. Some software requirements are of a long-range, strategic nature, derived from formal studies that look five to ten years into the future. This is the type of requirement generally defined at the business proposal level. Most other requirements are shorter range, more specific, and almost always in the context of an existing system or product line. Such requirements are generated by individual users, field personnel, and user groups. These requirements take the form of specific suggestions for enhancing the functional capability, the performance, or other attributes of a product currently in use.

4.3 Some Problems with Requirements Engineering

Software has certainly come a long way since its early role as collections of simple procedures to make the hardware run. Today, the users' dependence upon highly sophisticated systems applications again and again makes painfully evident the critical need for understanding and articulating to the software designers the true requirements, correctly and completely.

Equally important is to be able to accurately trace the proposed design and implementation back to the requirements. As an industry, we have a pervasive difficulty in doing these things with any noteworthy degree of precision. This, in the eyes of many practitioners, places the Requirements stage in the foreground as one of the weakest parts of Software Engineering [BELL76], [MAYS85], [ROMA85], [SIMO86].

To help understand this problem we will examine it from two viewpoints: first, from a composite view of ways in which past products have failed to meet important user requirements; and second, from the software engineer's view of problem areas in the development process that might have contributed to such failures to meet the requirements.

4.3.1 Typical Problems from a Product Perspective

When products fall short of meeting user requirements, the problem can usually be traced to one or more of the following types of causes:

1. The requirements, as initially defined, do not accurately account for the customers' real problems:

   For example, an incorrectly stated requirement that solves a non-problem, is propagated throughout the development cycle because of failure to adequately verify its correctness with prospective users at the outset of the project.

2. Requirements not properly prioritized:

   There are always more requirements than can be satisfied in a single release or version of a software product. Therefore, prioritization must be done. Adequate prioritization takes into account both the aggregate priorities of the prospective users and the level of technical difficulty and cost of satisfying each requirement. When this prioritization is not done properly, functions and features that are of less importance to the majority of users can appear in a release at the expense of other features needed more urgently.

3. Design does not match defined requirements:

   In this case, the requirements are properly defined, but the design is not completely traceable to them. Lack of backward traceability between design and requirements results in products that either (1) fail to implement planned requirements, or (2) solve requirements that do not exist.

4. Lack of a business strategy to keep product evolution on-track:

   A strategy is essential for establishing the target domain within which the product can evolve. Without it, problems are bound to develop. Here is an example of what can happen: assume you are the owner of a very clean and popular text editing program. Sales are doing well, and ample revenue is available to implement almost any user suggestion as it comes in. If all user suggestions for improvement of the editor were implemented on an ad hoc basis, the editor could quite likely grow over time into an awkward file control system; the file control system in turn might evolve to a poorly constructed library control environment; the library control environment could then become a totally inadequate solution for a full process support environment; and so on. Unlike the amoeba, products that extend their domain on an ad hoc basis cannot easily be split into two parts and continue to survive. Thus, they risk becoming extinct like dinosaurs.

Suppose on the other hand, your editor is an integral part of a business strategy which establishes it as a part of a planned word processing environment. In this case, prioritization of incoming user requirements would be much more to the point and effective, enabling your editor to grow in concert with other equally well-integrated components.

Thus, a business strategy is essential for prioritizing requirements effectively, and for having a product survive and remain competitive in its segment of the software market.

4.3.2 Typical Problems from a Process Perspective

We will now look into some typical development process characteristics that can contribute to the types of product problems described previously.

1. Lack of a coordination point when multiple functions within an organization gather requirements:

   It is not unusual in a large commercial project to find requirements planners, designers, and testers consulting with various customer representatives and obtaining requirements input. It is indeed desirable to maintain direct customer contact with many individuals in the development organization. However, serious problems occur when the individuals contacting the customers do not communicate with each other. Consider this case: a designer of a product having many users gets a suggestion for an additional feature from a user and incorporates it in the design without consulting the requirements planner. The result is that the finished product may have a feature in the next release for which there is no business justifiable requirement, and which may even conflict with the product business strategy.

2. Lack of a reliable method for capturing the true user needs:

   The large scale software products we are dealing with in this text typically have thousands, and sometimes tens of thousands of users. In addition, particularly in generalized commercial software like operating systems and many of the more popular personal computer software packages, the variety of possible applications can run into the hundreds or thousands. It is therefore not possible to know the total set of true requirements. In addition to not knowing all of the needed product functional capabilities for large numbers of customers, essential usability needs can also be easily overlooked. Finally, reviewing and validating Requirements and Product Level Design material with actual customers is not practiced consistently.

3. Inappropriate level of specification:

There may be overspecification, or imbedding of unnecessary design constraints in the requirements specification. There may be underspecification, overlooking of requirements, or incomplete definition of requirements.

4. Lack of rigor for conveying the true requirements to the designer:

All design efforts include informal discussions of requirements and perhaps foil presentations by requirements planners. This is essential dialog. However, when the dialog is not tied down by a more rigorous specification of the requirements, then ambiguities and misconceptions can go undetected until far into the design cycle, sometimes never to surface until delivery of the product to the customer.

5. Lack of a systematic method for validating the resultant design against specified requirements:

Backward traceability from the design to the requirements specification that engendered it is essential. The more complex and voluminous the specification, the more difficult this is to accomplish.

6. Late requirements force-fitted into the development cycle:

Sometimes, for good business reasons, new requirements are imposed on the product during the design stages, during coding, or even as late as the formal testing stages. This can be disruptive to everyone involved. Designs have to be modified, test plans and test cases need to be adjusted, product publications need to be changed, and so on. Can this be prevented?

The Requirements Engineering stage is unique in that it has continuous input and output. Even if one could somehow capture the true set of requirements for an instant, it would only be for a fleeting moment. This is because the true user requirements themselves are constantly changing. Why is this true? Here are perhaps two principal reasons:

a. Ongoing use of computers continues to suggest new applications that were not perceived initially.

b. The users' actual environment and needs of the business are constantly changing.

Thus, the elusive "true requirements" is a moving target. Requirements are ever-changing —never ceasing to come from all sources. The challenge then for a successful Requirements Engineering process, is to capture, prioritize, and freeze requirements at points in time, as would a photographic snapshot freeze continuous motion, so that a specific release or version of a product can be designed, implemented, and delivered.

The problem, therefore, is not how to prevent late requirements, but rather how to set up a flexible and responsive process whereby such requirements can be accommodated, or at least where the impact of late-coming and critical requirements can be minimized and managed.

7. Lack of a central repository for communication, control, and tracking of requirements:

The process for transforming requirements into a set of feasible system solutions, and subsequently into design, is frequently informal, human intensive, and error prone. As currently practiced in most organizations, collecting, cataloging, and prioritizing requirements is typically a "paper" process, that is, requirements are kept informally in notes, memos, and foil presentations in people's desk drawers rather than organized and cataloged under database tools to facilitate orderly retention and retrieval. Consequently, critical documentation, original rationale, and the "big picture" behind the Requirements Engineering and Product Level Design decisions is for the most part lost to those destined to follow the product through design, through implementation, through maintenance, and into the enhancement stages of the product.

Problems mount when lack of requirements and design documentation forces maintenance and enhancement activities to focus only on the source code. Balzer points out in his article on automatic programming

> All the programmer's skill has already been applied in optimizing this form (the source code). These optimizations *spread* information; that is, they take advantage of what is known elsewhere and substitute complex but efficient realizations for what originally were simple abstractions.

[BALZ85] The system is much harder to understand when one has only the source code to use. The maintainers will have an even more difficult time servicing the product if the available high level design specification material cannot be easily traced back to the underlying user requirements.

4.3.3 Some Typical Requirements Inputs

Overall requirements inputs originate with the business proposal. These requirements are usually at a very high level and serve to bound the scope of the proposed product undertaking. It is necessary to obtain requirements inputs at a much lower level of granularity to complete the Requirements Engineering activity. Such detailed requirements come in many forms. The next few pages show a series of example requirements inputs such as might be received on a large commercial system product with a variety of users.

In the first example, Figure 15 on page 77, the requirement is actually stated as a suggested solution, leaving the underlying problem only to be deduced by the reader. Another common type of requirements statement encountered are those that convey too little information, as in Figure 16 on page 78, or make ambiguous requests, as in Figure 17 on page 78. Sometimes too much information masks out the true requirement as well, as in the requirement phrased as a suggested design in Figure 18 on page 79, or as in the "laundry list" of dozens of unprioritized requirements illustrated in Figure 19 on page 79.

Requirements can come to the requirements planner through the "back door" too—that is, from the ongoing design effort itself. Frequently, exploratory design activities are begun in parallel with refinement of the requirements. If the planners hold the Requirements Engineering activity in the state of foil presentations, memo writing, and informal discussions too long for a product without aggressively bringing it to closure, a situation all too often develops where the design is rapidly becoming firm while the requirements specifications are not.

One recourse open to the design manager in such a situation is to make the dilemma visible by presenting the growing design material as a supplement to, or in place of, the long awaited, approved version of the requirements and programming Objectives documentation, as illustrated in Figure 20 on page 80. Regardless of whether technical or organizational problems allow the requirements to float in this manner for too long a time in the project, the effect is that the design effort actually drives the requirements definition in many respects, and the product ultimately suffers.

Requirement Statement 1

"Please allow abbreviations for the keywords of the TRACE command. For example: L= for LINE=; N= for NODE=; EV= for EVENT=."

This requirement is stated as a *solution*.

- What is the underlying problem? What is its impact?

- Who is the end user and what user tasks are involved with the use of the TRACE command?

- Does the solution fit within the product developer's long-range plan for the product?

- Is there a better alternative to solving the problem?

Figure 15. A Solution Statement

And finally, Figure 21 on page 80 illustrates a case early in the Requirements and Planning stage when the business proposal is complete and the decision has been made to go ahead with Requirements Engineering on the product. The figure suggests some of the checks that must be made to ensure that the information provided is adequate to effectively begin the activity for the product. This figure suggests that there is an *entry criteria* for the Requirements Engineering activity that should be examined early. This topic is discussed in more detail in the next section, 4.4, "Entry Criteria" on page 81.

Requirement Statement 2

"The customer does not get adequate support from the system for problem determination on telephone line problems."

This requirement is stated as a *problem*, but

- Is the customer the same as the end user?

- What specific user tasks are involved with the problem determination referred to by this requirement?

- What is the impact of this problem on the user or on the vendor of the problem determination support?

- What is the "system" referred to in the problem statement?

Figure 16. Not Enough Information

Requirement Statement 3

"Provide the Communications Help Desk Operator with a single system image."

This requirement is *ambiguous*.

- What does "single system image" mean?
- What is the underlying problem?
- What is the impact of the problem?

Figure 17. An Ambiguous Request

> **Requirement Statement 4**
>
> "Add a function to the module CXBRSCNW to set the TASKEXT
> bit in the CXBTSK control block whenever a task has been
> restarted. This will allow the customer to implement a user
> exit to monitor task execution."

This requirement is stated as a *design solution.*

- What is the underlying problem or need?
- Do other users have the same need?
- Is the "CXBRSCNW" module the appropriate place to put this function?
- Is there a better way to meet the customer need?

Figure 18. A Design Request

> **Requirement Statement 5**
>
> "Following is a list of 137 new features and functions requested
> by our users as derived by our last search of the User Request
> Database. All are classified as high priority by our Marketing
> Organization. Please respond with your plan."
>
>   1. ....
>   2. ....
>   . ...
>   137. ....

- What *tasks* are the users who requested
  these solutions trying to accomplish?
- What are the underlying problems with these tasks?
- Are there perhaps better solutions to the problems?
- How do these requests map to our long-range *technical strategy?*

Figure 19. The Laundry List

Requirement Statement 6

"Pending receipt of completed Programming Objectives for
Product XYZ, we are circulating the attached initial design
document for your comments."

A design is being undertaken without formal requirements documentation:

- What user tasks are being supported *explicitly*?

- What user tasks are being supported by *implication*?

- Are *all* required user problems being addressed?

- Are any *nonproblems* being solved in the design?

- Why are the requirements specifications late?

Figure 20. A Stake in the Ground

Requirement Statement 7

"Attached is the preliminary sales estimate and business proposal
for our entirely new Product_X. Please complete the RPLD documentation
for completion of the Product Level Design Stage."

How complete is the documentation provided, really?

- Are the user needs, characteristics and environment adequately
  defined?

- Is there an adequate description of the current user process?

- What specific problems are to be resolved by the target product?

- Is there adequate
  information given to describe the target user process?

- Are all the stated problems resolved by the target process?

Figure 21. A New Product

4.4 Entry Criteria

Requirements Engineering activities start when a business case, like the business proposal discussed in Chapter 3, or a contract for bid, is underway for a particular product. Once the business proposal has been completed, and the decision made to go ahead with the 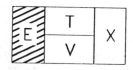 project, detailed Requirements Engineering activity may commence. The essential information to be extracted from the business proposal for Requirements Engineering includes:

1. Definition of the product environment: this includes the market segments that will be addressed by the product and types of users that will interact with the product, that is, their characteristics, roles, training, and skill levels.

2. The set of problems that are being addressed: specific problems and the causes associated with each of these problem statements described in a level of detail sufficient to suggest meaningful directions for further refinement.

3. Proposed solutions: general solutions derived from the problem analysis in terms of how the process for the user of the new product might differ from the current process.

4. Competitive analysis: this indicates similar solutions to users' problems that have proven successful in the past, and those that have not.

5. The required functional capabilities of the product: a high level description of what the product must do to support the users' new way of doing business.

6. Statements of the desired product attributes, such as the CUPRIM attributes, suitable for further refinement: thorough specification of these attributes provides the essential foundation on which all future design is validated, the implementation is tested, and customer feedback from the finished product is obtained and evaluated.

7. Cost boundaries or targets: this includes subparts for marketing, development, product distribution, and service.

4.5 Requirements Engineering Tasks

Some promising solutions have emerged on the requirements problems outlined previously. Along with an
increasing general awareness of how integral the
Requirements Engineering process actually is to the
success of software development enterprises, advances
are being made in three major areas:

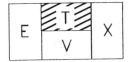

1. Increasing applications of local data bases for cataloging, retaining, and
   retrieving requirements.

2. The development of systematic methodologies for requirements analysis and
   solution definition, leading to more effective product designs.

3. Increased application of Requirements Engineering tools.

In the following sections, we will discuss a recommended Requirements Engineering approach and some of the more popular tools that have been applied
successfully in the industry.

4.5.1 The Requirements and PLD Specification

In this text, the set of documents that specify the requirements and the high level
design input for meeting the requirements, is called the *Requirements and Product
Level Design Specifications*, or *RPLD Specifications*. In total, the RPLD set of
documents represents the transformation of user needs to high level design. In
them, the following topics must be addressed:

1. Relevant assumptions about user characteristics and environment.

2. A description of *tasks* in the current user process that are to be replaced or
   improved. This results in a task-oriented description of what the user currently does.

3. A description of the problems associated with the current process.

4. A task-oriented description of the desired solution to the stated problem, in
   terms of a new target process that would replace the current process.

5. A description of the desired attributes (e.g. CUPRIM) to be exhibited by the
   new product during the execution of the tasks in the target process.

6. A high-level design description of the product that is to perform the tasks of
   the required target process.

4.5.2 A Basic Requirements Engineering Approach

Considering that a typical set of requirements inputs consists of massive amounts of apparently unrelated, diverse bits of information, it would be humanly impossible to assimilate it all at once and then converge on a solution as a single task. A well known problem solving approach for dealing with such complexities is to separate the concerns of the problem, and then focus on each concern, one at a time. In this text we separate Requirements Engineering concerns into *activities*, *perspectives*, and *aspects* (Refer to Figure 22 on page 84). The three activities shown in the figure are defined as:

1. *Synthesis*, or constructing the appropriate work item from the initial information collected.

2. *Analysis* of the product description thus constructed for consistency, completeness, and adherence to the methodology.

3. *Communication* of the product description to both internal and external reviewers and approvers.

Each activity, in turn, may be approached from different *perspectives*, enabling the planner or designer to focus on the activity from several different perspectives, one at a time. Example perspectives are phrased as questions in Figure 23 on page 85. When applied to the synthesis activity, they suggest separate tasks that must be performed in creating the Requirements Engineering work items. When applied to the analysis activity, they serve as a checklist for verifying the completeness and consistency of the work items, and for the communication activity, they help organize the information into discrete exhibits that aid the reviewer in understanding and evaluating the work items.

The perspectives are then further decomposed into various *aspects* of the target product. For example, some aspects associated with the environment perspective are shown in Figure 24 on page 86.

Thus, in an activity-perspective-aspect structure, aspects may be considered as "building blocks" that are collected together to form perspectives, which in turn are synthesized, analyzed, or communicated during the three activities.

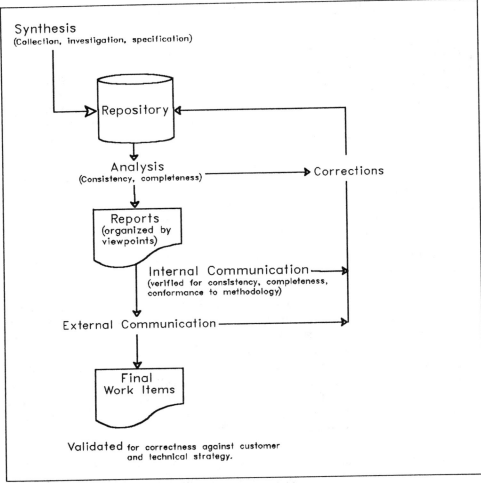

Figure 22. Requirements Engineering Process Activities

4.5.3 Planning and Design Methodology (PDM)

A Requirements Engineering approach called *Planning and Design Methodology (PDM)* has been used for parts of IBM's large scale commercial software systems development, as described by Mays, Ciarfella, Orzech, and Phillips [MAYS85]. It is similar to approaches used in other software development communities as well, especially where new software development consists of adding functions and features to an existing software product baseline.

PDM incorporates the notion of separation of concerns, as described in 4.5.2, "A Basic Requirements Engineering Approach" on page 83. In addition, it consists of four discrete steps, each with its own set of resultant work items: *Require-*

```
Perspectives:

 • What is the environment with which the current and
   proposed system will interact?

 • What is the current user process and tasks?

 • What specific problems are associated with the current
   process that need to be solved at this time?

 • What are the proposed target user process and tasks?

 • How will the previously defined problems
   be addressed and resolved by the proposed target process?

 • What are the design implications for the target product that
   will support and perform the tasks of the target process?
```

Figure 23. Example Perspectives for Separating Concerns

ments Collection, Problem Analysis, Solution Definition, and *Product Level Design Direction*.

Each of the four steps produces a set of work items, shown in Figure 25 on page 87:

1. The Requirements Collection activity produces *requirements input* documentation containing initial statements of "raw" requirements as received from various sources.

2. The Problem Analysis activity produces *problem definition* documentation describing the problem, or set of problems, in terms of the existing user process and system.

3. The Solution Definition activity produces *solution definition* documentation describing solutions to the previously described problems in terms of required new or enhanced function from the external, user view of the system. These are the requirements statements.

4. The Product Level Design Assessment activity produces *design direction* documentation. While not a complete design statement or design solution, this work item makes up a part of the Product Level Design information, including suggested placement of the design n the affected areas of the product or products.

Now we will show an example application of the PDM principles just described. The example is based on one shown in an article about PDM in the IBM Systems Journal [MAYS85]. It will show a sequence of three documents, illus-

```
Aspects of the Environment Perspective:

 •  User Enterprises

 •  Human Interfaces

       - End Users

       - Operators

       - System Support Personnel

       - Service Personnel

 •  Systems Interfaces
```

Figure 24. Example Aspects Associated with the Environment Perspective

trating a systematic transition from raw *requirements input*, through *problem analysis*, and finally to a *solution definition*.

Example Input Document

Figure 26 on page 88 represents an extraction of one requirements input from many cataloged in a requirements data base. After some preliminary control information that helps to classify the requirements input and track its progress, the submitter suggests a specific solution to a problem with a "communications trace facility" on a particular system. The document illustrates one type of requirement statement typically received: it suggests a specific solution to a problem that is implied but not defined.

Example Problem Analysis Document

Several Requirements Input documents such as the one illustrated in Figure 26 on page 88 will be collected and combined to create a statement of a general class of problems associated with the trace facility. In our example, assume a class of problems has been generalized to the statement "the communications trace function is too complex to use and is error prone." The problem analysis detail and problem statement appears in Figure 27 on page 89. In addition to the general problem statement, four specific additional problem statements have been extracted after analysis of the various other requirements inputs (not shown in the example).

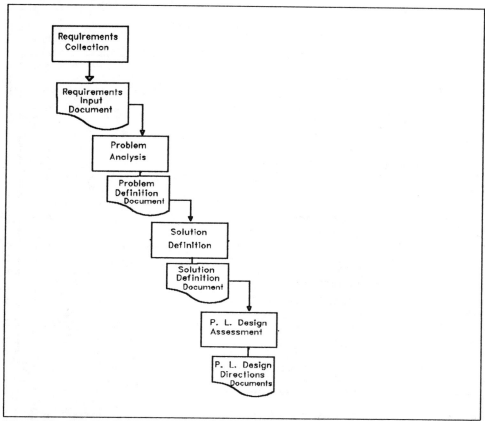

Figure 25. Overview of a Requirements Engineering Process

At this point, individual requirements suggestions, such as the one in Figure 26 on page 88, can be viewed in context of the complete "problem space," as pointed out by Yeh [YEH80]. Of all the tasks in this systematic Requirements Engineering process, problem definition is by far the most difficult, since it requires a full understanding of the user characteristics and skills (e.g., the operators and the system programmers), and an understanding of the actual process the users go through to accomplish their tasks (e.g., under what circumstances are the trace commands used, and what is actually happening in the process at that time?).

Example Solution Definition Document

In the example solution in Figure 28, a full screen facility is proposed that will enable the operator to enter trace commands, complete with help facilities and improved messages.

```
REQUIREMENTS INPUT DOCUMENT

┌─ Control Information ─────────────────────────────────

   o  Input Requirement number    PR0102
   o  Source Reference            PASR N187723
   o  Submitter information       J. Duncan, B.O. 245
                                  Chicago, Il
   o  Submitter's priority        Medium
   o  Author (person recording)   R. G. Mays, Raleigh
   o  Assigned priority           High
   o  Status                      Problem Analysis level
   o  Response to submitter       Accepted, 2/18/85
   o  Category/Subcategory        Problem Management/
                                  Problem Determination
   o  Search Keywords             Trace, Operator Commands
   o  Problem Definition Doc.      PR1071

┌─ Abstract ────────────────────────────────────────────

  Allow keyword abbreviations in the trace command

┌─ Requirement Text ────────────────────────────────────

  It is very difficult to key in the long trace commands to start up a
  communications trace.  Customer desires the ability to use one- or
  two-character abbreviations for the command keywords.  For example:
  L- for LINE-, N- for NODE-, EV- for EVENT
```

Figure 26. Example Requirements Input Document

Notice in the example under "Problem Conditions Addressed," that the four specific problems are restated, followed by the proposed solution. This aids in the critical validation step to ensure that:

1. All problems have proposed solutions

2. All proposed solutions solve recognized problems

What happened to the initial suggestion in (Figure 26) that the trace commands be abbreviated? That was not adopted as part of the solution. Will the proposed solution solve the underlying problem in a different way? Yes, most definitely. It

```
┌─────────────────────────────────────────────────────────────────┐
│                                                                   │
│       PROBLEM ANALYSIS DOCUMENT                                   │
│   ┌─ Control Information ──────────────────────────────────────┐  │
│   │                                                            │  │
│   │   o  Problem Definition number    PR1071                   │  │
│   │   o  Category/Subcategory         Problem Management/       │  │
│   │                                   Problem Determination     │  │
│   │   o  Author                       R. G. Mays                │  │
│   │   o  Status                       Customer review completed │  │
│   │   o  Input Requirements addressed PR0085, PR0102            │  │
│   │   o  Solution Definition document PR2045                    │  │
│   └────────────────────────────────────────────────────────────┘  │
│                                                                   │
│   ┌─ Abstract ─────────────────────────────────────────────────┐  │
│   │                                                            │  │
│   │ The communications trace function is too complex to use    │  │
│   │ and is error                                               │  │
│   │ prone.                                                     │  │
│   └────────────────────────────────────────────────────────────┘  │
│                                                                   │
│   ┌─ Current Function ─────────────────────────────────────────┐  │
│   │                                                            │  │
│   │ The trace function consists of trace commands entered at   │  │
│   │ the oper-                                                  │  │
│   │ ator console that control the starting and stopping of     │  │
│   │ line traces                                                │  │
│   │ and formatting and printing of the traces for output.      │  │
│   └────────────────────────────────────────────────────────────┘  │
│                                                                   │
│   ┌─ User Tasks ───────────────────────────────────────────────┐  │
│   │                                                            │  │
│   │ The trace commands are generally entered by the system     │  │
│   │ programmer.                                                │  │
│   │ The operator does not enter them because the commands are  │  │
│   │ complex                                                    │  │
│   │ and a significant level of expertise is required to enter  │  │
│   │ them prop-                                                 │  │
│   │ erly.  The system programmer generally looks up the        │  │
│   │ command, writes                                            │  │
│   │ it out, enters the command at the console, and waits for   │  │
│   │ an indi-                                                   │  │
│   │ cation that the desired communications event has occurred. │  │
│   │ He or                                                      │  │
│   │ she then enters commands to format and print the trace.    │  │
│   └────────────────────────────────────────────────────────────┘  │
│                                                                   │
└─────────────────────────────────────────────────────────────────┘
```

Figure 27 (Part 1 of 2). Example Problem Analysis Document

also solves the problem of the operator frequently having to call on the system programmer to use the trace commands.

In summary, the approach shown in the preceding examples illustrates a simple and effective application of a very basic problem solving approach to systematically transform a myriad of raw requirements and suggestions into a set of sol-

```
┌─────────────────────────────────────────────────────────────────┐
│           PROBLEM ANALYSIS DOCUMENT (CONTINUED)                   │
│  ┌── Problem Conditions ───────────────────────────────────────  │
│                                                                   │
│   1. The trace facility requires too high a skill level:  Only expe- │
│      rienced  system  programmers  can  reliably  do  communications │
│      traces.   The  impact  of  this  is  that  some  customers  who  do  not │
│      have  an  experienced  staff  are  unable  to  do  adequate  problem │
│      determination.                                               │
│                                                                   │
│   2. Trace commands are frequently keyed in erroneously:  If an error │
│      is  made,  the  only  recourse  is  to  rekey  the  command.   This  can  be │
│      very  frustrating.                                           │
│                                                                   │
│   3. There is no on-line help facility:   The  user  must  frequently │
│      reference  the  trace  manuals  and  often  guesses  at  actions  and │
│      command  formats.                                            │
│                                                                   │
│   4. The system programmer must guess whether the desired communi- │
│      cations event has occurred: The  impact  of  this  is  that  often │
│      large  quantities  of  excess  trace  data  are  collected,  formatted, │
│      and  printed  needlessly.                                    │
│                                                                   │
└─────────────────────────────────────────────────────────────────┘
```

Figure 27 (Part 2 of 2). Example Problem Analysis Document

ution definitions, ready for input to the design directions step (not shown in the examples).

4.5.4 RPLD Model

The recommended approach to Requirements Engineering in this text is derived by combining the methodology for separation of concerns in 4.5.2, "A Basic Requirements Engineering Approach" on page 83, with the discrete process steps and work items described in 4.5.3, "Planning and Design Methodology (PDM)" on page 84.   The resultant methodology is depicted in a model, called the *Requirements and Product Level Design (RPLD) Model.* eight *perspectives,* and the four PDM work items. The model includes Figure 29 on page 93 names the perspectives and associates them with the resultant PDM work items. For each of the work items, Synthesis, Analysis, and Communication activities are performed from the appropriate perspectives.

```
SOLUTION DEFINITION DOCUMENT

┌─ Control Information ─────────────────────────────────────────────┐
│                                                                    │
│   o  Solution Definition number    PR2045                          │
│   o  Category/Subcategory          Problem Management/             │
│                                    Problem Determination          │
│   o  Author                        R. G. Mays                      │
│   o  Status                        In internal review              │
│   o  Problem Definition addressed  PR1071                          │
│   o  Design Direction              Not started                     │
│                                                                    │
└────────────────────────────────────────────────────────────────────┘

┌─ Abstract ────────────────────────────────────────────────────────┐
│                                                                    │
│  Improve the communications trace ease of use.                     │
│                                                                    │
└────────────────────────────────────────────────────────────────────┘

┌─ Proposed Function ───────────────────────────────────────────────┐
│                                                                    │
│  The proposed trace function will consist of a full screen facility│
│  for entering trace commands at the operator console.  An additional│
│  trace function will be provided to specify communications events to│
│  be associated with the trace.  The trace will then monitor communi-│
│  cations events and, when the specified event is detected, give an │
│  indication to the user and/or terminate the trace.   The trace    │
│  command and all of the corresponding specifications can be saved in│
│  a disk dataset and called up and modified prior to running.  A help│
│  facility will be provided to explain specific fields on the screens│
│  and their possible values.                                        │
│                                                                    │
└────────────────────────────────────────────────────────────────────┘

┌─ User Tasks ──────────────────────────────────────────────────────┐
│                                                                    │
│  The trace commands will now be entered by filling the appropriate │
│  fields on the screen.  The user may be either a system programmer or│
│  an operator.  He or she will need to refer to the trace manual only│
│  if a detailed explanation of the trace command, with examples, is │
│  needed.                                                           │
│                                                                    │
└────────────────────────────────────────────────────────────────────┘
```

Figure 28 (Part 1 of 2). Example Solution Definition Document

```
┌─────────────────────────────────────────────────────────────────┐
│         SOLUTION DEFINITION DOCUMENT (CONTINUED)                  │
│  ┌─ Problem Conditions Addressed ──────────────────────────────┐ │
│  │                                                             │ │
│  │  1. The trace facility requires too high a skill level:     │ │
│  │     With the on-line interface and help facility, less      │ │
│  │     experienced system programmers will be able to enter    │ │
│  │     the commands. With the "canned" trace commends,         │ │
│  │     operators will be able to run preliminary traces for    │ │
│  │     PD without having to call in a system programmer.       │ │
│  │                                                             │ │
│  │  2. The trace commands are frequently keyed in erroneously: │ │
│  │     This is addressed by the full-screen prompting.         │ │
│  │                                                             │ │
│  │  3. There is no on-line help facility: This will now be     │ │
│  │     provided.                                               │ │
│  │                                                             │ │
│  │  4. The system programmer must guess whether the desired    │ │
│  │     communications even has occurred: The event monitoring  │ │
│  │     function addresses this.                                │ │
│  │                                                             │ │
│  └─────────────────────────────────────────────────────────────┘ │
└─────────────────────────────────────────────────────────────────┘
```

Figure 28 (Part 2 of 2). Example Solution Definition Document

Environment-to-Process Bridges

Figure 30 on page 94 is a picture of the RPLD Model itself. In it, the perspectives are shown as partitions, or parts, connected to each other by relationships, or "bridges."

Two sets of bridges are shown in Figure 30 between the Environment perspective and the Process perspectives:

1. Environment-to-Current and Target Processes: Common characteristics that bind these two together are:

   a. Inputs
   b. Outputs
   c. Usability attributes

2. Current Process-to-Target Process: Common characteristics of these are:

   a. Current Process problem statements
   b. Target Process solution statements

RPLD PERSPECTIVE	PDM WORK ITEM

Environment
 	
Current User Process
 	
Problem Statements
	Input Requirements
	    Document
	
	Problem Definition
	    Document

Solution Statements Target Process	Solution Definition Document

Current Product
    Specification
 	
Target Product
    Design
 	
Dynamics
	Design Direction
	    Document

Figure 29. RPLD Model Perspectives Relative to PDM Documents

Process-to-Product Bridges

In addition to the two sets of environment-to-process bridges listed above, the model indicates that the Current and Target Processes *utilize* the Current and Target Products respectively. It may also be said that the Current and Target Products are *utilized by* the Current and Target Processes.

In the RPLD specification model, the solution statements and target process constitutes the *requirements specification* and the target product constitutes the *design direction*. This is an important distinction between requirements and design. In practice, the Requirements Engineering activity continually bridges the requirement and design domain in both directions. Most methodologies of today do not crisply define such a requirements-to-design bridge, and hence do not clearly point out when it is being traversed. This leads to problems of either underspecification or overspecification in the resultant design. This is understandable because not much is known, or articulated with precision in industry or

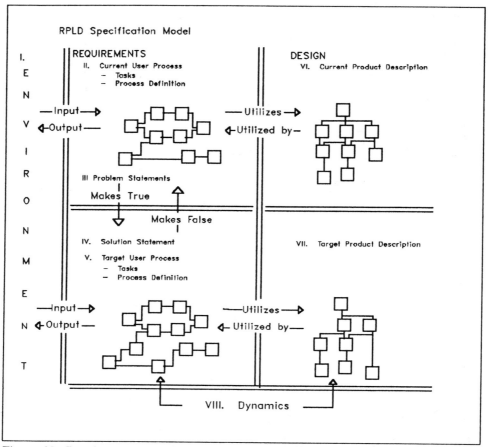

Figure 30. Requirements and Product Level Design (RPLD) Model

academia, about the differences in information content and level of detail between "requirements" and "design" documents.

Requirements specifications state the desired functional capabilities and other attributes of the product. Design specifications are a response as to how these capabilities and attributes will be achieved. Design is the conceptualizing and selection of technical choices or alternatives for implementing the specified requirements and includes the subsequent verification that the design will truly satisfy the requirements specification. We can help to distinguish between the requirements domain and the Product Level Design domain by characterizing these properties as in Figure 31 on page 95.

```
    REQUIREMENTS VIEW              PRODUCT LEVEL DESIGN VIEW

  . User view of the world       . Designer view of the world

  . Defines target process       . Defines target product
      tasks                          components and functions

  . Conceptual model             . Functional model

  . The what                     . The how

  . Task-oriented description     . State machine representation

  . Target process tasks         . Target product functions
      "utilize" target               "utilized by" target
      product functions              process tasks

  . E-R representation            . Procedural design language
                                     representations
```

Figure 31. The View from Opposite Ends of the Requirements-Design Bridge

Relationship of Environment to Product

It can be noted in the prior discussion of bridges between perspectives in the RPLD Model, the Process perspectives exist as a layer between the Environment and the Product. The semantic implications of this model are key to the Requirements Engineering approach we are presenting in this text:

1. From the Environment view (i.e., the user), capabilities and other attributes (e.g., CUPRIM) required of the *product* are expressed independent of the *tasks* the user needs to perform and the *process* for performing them. In this way, the user is free to express problems and solutions in terms of what the product "must do," and not what it "must be," or how it must do it.

2. From the Product view (i.e., the designer), the structural properties, functions, and other attributes to be utilized by the users' task-oriented process description can be expressed in terms of what the product "will be," and tested (validated) against the users' task-oriented description of what the product "must do."

4.6 Use of E-R Languages for Requirements Engineering

Historically, Requirements and Product Level Design Specifications have been expressed in natural languages. This carries the implicit expense of ambiguity in communication, making it difficult to validate the specifications to the true requirements. Use of an *entity-relationship-attribute* language, commonly called an *entity-relation (E-R)* language, can reduce communication expense by bringing precision of expression and elimination of ambiguity to this critical set of high level specification documents [BALZ78], [BALZ79], [TEIC77].

Later in this chapter, we have an example of using an E-R language to solve a sample Requirements Engineering problem. Let us briefly discuss E-R languages, and how to interpret the upcoming example:

- An *entity* is something, real or abstract, about which we may store data.

  Examples: John Smith, Sue Jones

- An *entity type* names a class of entities that share the same attributes.

  Example: PROGRAMMER is an entity type

- An *attribute* is a single class of information about an entity type.

  Example: NAME is an attribute of entity-type PROGRAMMER.

- An *attribute value* is a symbol denoting some quality or quantity that describes an instance of the attribute.

  Example: John Smith and Sue Jones are instances (values) of the attribute, "NAME." Since NAME is an attribute of the entity-type PROGRAMMER, then John Smith and Sue Jones are instances of the entity-type PRO-GRAMMER, or they are ENTITIES of type PROGRAMMER. Thus, an entity is described by attribute values.

- A *relationship* is an association between two entity-types.

  Example: Suppose in addition to PROGRAMMER, we have defined an entity-type CODE-LISTING. We can now state that "PROGRAMMER RECEIVES CODE-LISTING." The term "RECEIVES" is now a *relation*.

An advantage of writing specifications in E-R languages is that they lend themselves readily to machine-assisted checking for consistency and completeness.

A disadvantage of machine-processable E-R languages is that they at first appear to humans as very terse and difficult to comprehend. This apprehension soon goes away as familiarity develops. However, the realities of the software environment are that, while Requirements Engineering practitioners who write in formatted, E-R languages are quite comfortable with them, most individuals who must review, understand, and approve the documents, are not. This represents a challenge for developers of E-R language processing tools. One approach is to make all input and output appear in natural language form, as narrative, to be encoded and decoded in the E-R form internally.

4.6.1 PSL/PSA Tutorial

PSL, or *Problem Statement Language*, was developed at the University of Michigan under the *ISDOS* Project. A set of analysis programs, called the *Problem Statement Analyzer (PSA)* is also provided under license by the ISDOS Corporation of Ann Arbor, Michigan [TEIC77]. This section describes PSL and how to interpret it when reading a Requirements and Product Level Design specification that has been written in PSL.

Example PSL Expressions

PSL uses a predefined set of entity-types and relations. PSL uses the term *object* to mean *entity*, and so shall we in the examples of this text. The examples that follow are extracted from a subset of PSL similar to what has been used for requirements definition in some IBM systems programming projects. The subset of PSL object-types and relations we are using in the examples is shown in Figure 32.

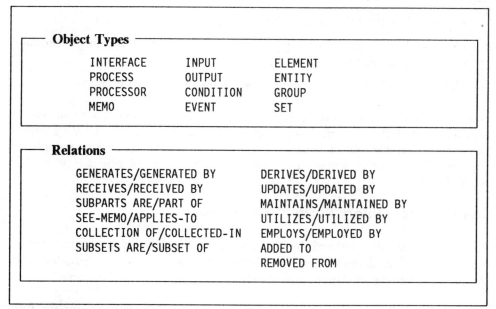

Figure 32. Example PSL Object-Types and Relations

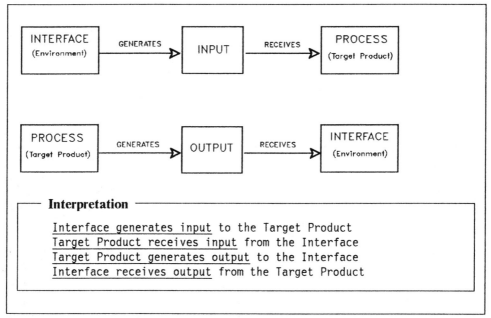

Figure 33. PSL Expressions. Example statements about the target product and its environment.

A simple expression in PSL syntax is illustrated in Figure 33 on page 98. The way we are using PSL in this example is:

PROCESS is an entity-type in the domain of the target product

INTERFACE is an object-type outside the domain of the target product, called the *environment*

INPUT and *OUTPUT* are object-types shared by the two domains.

Another type of relation is the hierarchy, denoted by the *subparts are* and *part of* expressions in PSL. Figure 34 on page 99 illustrates that hierarchical structures can be defined for object types. Figure 35 on page 100 is an example of expressing a hierarchy within the entity *Compiler_Users* of object-type *ENVI-RONMENT*.

The Complementary Form of Expression

For every expression entered by the user of PSL, there is a complementary expression. For example, the complement of the expression, "programmers receive compiler output" is "compiler output is received by programmers."

The Problem Statement Analyzer (PSA) is a set of analyzer programs for PSL

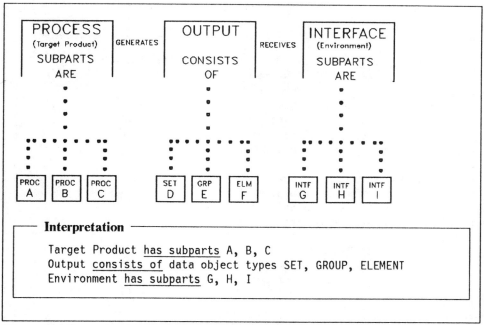

Figure 34. Expressing Hierarchical Structures with PSL

that automatically generate the complement of every expression originally entered, and can show both forms on various PSL reports. Thus, additional relationships can be automatically *derived* beyond what the PSL user explicitly entered. Some examples of these complementary expressions are shown in Figure 36 on page 101 as pairs of complementary expressions. For any pair, the user may explicitly state one expression, and the PSA language processor will generate the other and place it in the output report in the context of other objects named in the expression. For example, if you entered as part of the description for "Output_B" the expression, "Output_B is GENERATED BY Product_X," a machine-generated complementary expression would appear in the description of the object "Product_X" saying that "Product_X GENERATES Output_B." In addition, PSL is a *context sensitive* language, meaning that words and phrases take on additional meaning depending on the context in which they are used. This can be used to generate still more information. Suppose for example we want to define John Smith and Sue Jones as instances of of object-type INTER-FACE; Source_Code as an instance of object-type INPUT; and code listing as an instance of object-type OUTPUT; and connect them via the GENERATES/RECEIVES relationships. Figure 37 on page 102 illustrates the initial definition of these relationships and the additional information generated by PSA.

```
        DEFINE INTERFACE                 Compiler_Users ;
          SUBPARTS ARE   Engineers,
                         Programmers;
            GENERATES    Engineering_Algorithms,
                         Source_Code ;
            RECEIVES     Engineering_Results,
                         Code_Listings ;

        DEFINE INTERFACE                       Engineers ;
              PART OF    Compiler_Users ;
            GENERATES    Engineering_Algorithms;
            RECEIVES     Engineering_Results ;

        DEFINE INTERFACE                     Programmers ;
              PART OF    Compiler_Users ;
          SUBPARTS ARE   John_Smith,
                         Sue_Jones ;
            GENERATES    Source_Code;
            RECEIVES     Code_Listings;
```

Interpretation:

Everything above may be viewed as a paragraph containing information about the subject, *Compiler_Users.*

The paragraph may be broken down into the following sentences:

- *Compiler_Users* may be either Engineers or Programmers.

- *Engineers* generate Engineering_Algorithms.

- *Engineers* receive Engineering_Results.

- *Programmers* generate Source-Code.

- *Programmers* receive Code-Listings.

Figure 35. Examples of Generates/Receives Relationship

The generation of complementary and context sensitive information is a powerful feature of the PSA language processor because it makes analysis of the PSL-encoded description easier. Often, relationships are made visible that were not initially perceived by the person creating the specification, leading to the discovery of incorrect assumptions or inconsistencies.

```
Interface_1  SUBPARTS ARE   Interface_2,...Interface_n
Interface_2,...Interface_n   PART OF    Interface_1

Interface_1  GENERATES       Input_A
Input_A      GENERATED BY    Interface_1

Interface_1  RECEIVES        Output_B
Output_B     RECEIVED BY     Interface_1

Output_B     GENERATED BY    Product_X
Product_X    GENERATES       Output_B
```

Figure 36. Examples of Complementary Expressions

Data Structures and Derivation

Figure 38 on page 103 shows an example of how data structures are expressed in PSL, and Figure 39 on page 104 illustrates how data derivation is expressed.

Product Dynamics

Product Dynamics denotes expressions of the *conditions* under which the target product is to perform its functions. The generic form of expression is shown in Figure 40 on page 105, and a PSL encoded example is shown in Figure 41 on page 106.

Assigning Properties and Characteristics

Properties and characteristics may be attributed to objects by means of *key words, synonyms,* and *attributes* statements.

Key words and synonyms may be employed in PSL expressions to assist in machine analysis. For example, the expression

```
    KEYWORDS ARE   'unresolved'
```

could facilitate a machine search for all objects that as yet have unresolved issues outstanding against them.

Synonyms are used as name qualifiers, such as for example:

```
    SYNONYMS ARE    The_Compiler,
                    Compiler,
                    FORTRAN_Compiler,
                    Cmpl            ;
```

```
┌─ Input ──────────────────────────────────────────────────┐
│                                                            │
│       DEFINE INPUT                     Source_Code ;       │
│             GENERATED BY     John_Smith,                   │
│                              Sue_Jones ;                   │
│              RECEIVED BY     Compiler ;                    │
│                                                            │
│       DEFINE OUTPUT                    Code_Listings ;     │
│             GENERATED BY     Compiler ;                    │
│              RECEIVED BY     John_Smith,                   │
│                              Sue_Jones ;                   │
│                                                            │
│   Interpretation:                                          │
│                                                            │
│       Source code, generated by John Smith and Sue Jones, │
│       is received by the compiler.                         │
│                                                            │
│       Code listings, generated by the compiler, are       │
│       received by John Smith and Sue Jones.                │
│                                                            │
└────────────────────────────────────────────────────────────┘
```

```
       DEFINE INTERFACE             John_Smith ;
             GENERATES     Source_Code ;
              RECEIVES     Code_Listings ;

       DEFINE INTERFACE             Sue_Jones   ;
             GENERATES     Source_Code ;
              RECEIVES     Code_Listings ;

       DEFINE  PROCESS             Compiler ;
             GENERATES     Code_Listings ;
              RECEIVES     Source_Code ;
```

Interpretation:

John Smith and Sue Jones generate source code and receive
code listings.

The compiler receives source code and generates code listings.

Figure 37. PSL Example Using Generates/Receives Relationship. The original input is
shown in the box. The complementary expressions generated by PSA are
shown outside the box.

```
DEFINE SET                 Program_Library ;

COLLECTION OF    Source_Code ,
                 Compiled_Modules ;

ORDERED BY       Module_Types,
                 Module_Names,
                 Module_Owner_Names ;
```

Interpretation:
The paragraph enclosed in the box above contains the following
information:

1. The *Program Library* is a collection of Source_Code
   and Object_Code.
   (These data objects are defined elsewhere as either INPUTS, OUTPUTS,
   or ELEMENTS.)

2. The *Program Library* may be ordered (arranged, sorted,
   cataloged) by Module Types, Module Names, or Module Owner Names.

Figure 38. Example of Data Structure Expression

Attributes for PSL objects may be explicitly assigned by the "ATTRIBUTES
ARE" expression. For example, when describing a PROCESS, the expression

```
ATTRIBUTES ARE  Object-Code-Performance
                        'Primary importance',
                Compiler-Performance
                        'Secondary importance';
```

implies that object code performance is to be given priority over compiler performance during the design process.

Prose Descriptions

PSL objects may have a prose description, or commentary, assigned by means of
the keyword "DESCRIPTION." Such descriptions can add clarity for the reader
of the PSL reports. The narrative descriptions can also be retrieved and printed
separately in a structured order, without the accompanying PSL statements, to
create a more or less conventional looking description for the casual reviewer.

```
DEFINE ELEMENT                    Compiled_Modules ;

        DERIVED BY    Compiler
             USING    Source-Code,
                      Assembler-Instruction-Set ;

        ADDED TO      Program_Library  BY  Compiler ;
    REMOVED FROM      Program_Library  BY  Testing_Process ;
```

Figure 39. Example of Data Derivation and Use Expressions

References to External Documents

Documents external to the PSL data base are referenced by the "SEE MEMO" expression. For example, the statement

```
        SEE MEMO    'ANSI-Standards' ;
```

points to a document containing further information related to the object being described.

4.6.2 SREM

Software Requirements Engineering Methodology (SREM) was originally developed in the mid-1970s by M. W. Alford and others to assist in requirements definition for the United States Ballistic Missile Defense Weapons System [ALFO80]. SREM is owned by TRW, and has been used in various enterprises including Martin Marietta Denver Aerospace and the USAF Rome Air Development Center [SCHE85].

A system of supporting tools for the SREM approach was also developed in the mid-1970s called the *Requirements Engineering And Validation System* (REVS) [ALFO85]. REVS uses an entity relationship language called *Requirements Specification Language* (RSL) to describe the requirements as a network of paths between system inputs and outputs, along with the functions necessary to transform the data along these paths from input to output states. The conditions under which the data transforms are to be made are also shown in the same network. The REVS functions can then analyze the networks described in RSL for consistency, completeness, and backward traceability to the higher level system requirements statements.

During their evolution, the SREM techniques were extended to encompass the definition of system level requirements. This extension is called *System Requirements Engineering Methodology* (SYSREM). Starting with SYSREM, one follows a systematic process of decomposing system level requirements into the

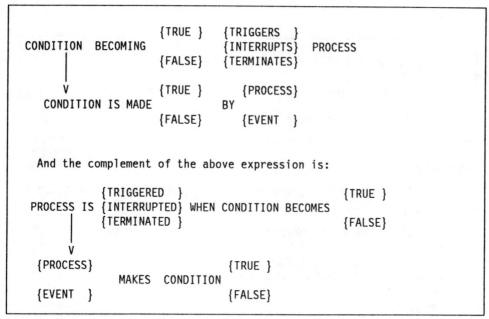

Figure 40. Example of PSL Syntax for Dynamics Expressions

subsystem level, and through further decomposition via SREM to software functional specifications.

As with PSL/PSA, the RSL/REVS combination has been used with good results as a verification tool for requirements. The semantic model on which RSL is based carries the notion of processing paths expressed as the inputs required to produce a specified set of responses, or outputs. Networks of these paths relating outputs to their inputs constructed in RSL are called *requirements networks*, or *R-NETS*. An advantage of R-NETS is that they associate all necessary processing paths and outputs with each unique input. Thus each processing path resulting from an input can be viewed as a *requirement*. Also, specific *validation* points may be assigned along each path to ensure that all requirements are being met.

In addition, as with PSA, the REVS provides a number of static analysis checks for consistency when RSL statements are added to the data base.

```
    DEFINE CONDITION              Programmer_Is_New ;

      BECOMING  TRUE  TRIGGERS    New_Progr_Orientation ;

          IS  MADE  TRUE  BY      Hiring-Process ;
```

Interpretation:

1. The existence of new programmers triggers a new employee orientation process.

2. The existence of new employees is made possible by a hiring process

Figure 41. Example of Product Dynamics Expression

4.6.3 SADT

Structured Analysis and Design Technique (SADT) is a methodology developed by Douglass T. Ross beginning in 1974 [ROSS77] [ROSS85] that is useful for system planning, requirements analysis, and system design. It was developed to provide a rigorous, disciplined approach for reaching an understanding of user needs prior to providing a design solution. Of significance is that SADT did not evolve from a design technique, but rather was developed by examining the problems associated with defining system requirements. It is generally not used for module or low-level design, since the constructs necessary for module design of sequence, selection, and combinatorial logic interaction are not easily expressed in SADT. SADT is most suited to defining requirements and high level design specifications.

The principal feature of SADT, that sets it apart from other methods, is its diagramming notation and technique for structuring the results of the analysis and high level design activities. Because of its ability to communicate ideas by graphical means, it has been characterized as a requirements blueprint language [ROMA85]. In addition, a systematic approach has been developed by its practitioners that involves frequent review and capitalizes on the benefits of the graphic notation to make the evolving refinements visible at all steps along the way.

Two basic types of models are employed in SADT: the *activity model* and the *data model*. The activity model is oriented toward decomposition of activities and the data model is oriented toward the decomposition of data. While each model references both activities and data, the difference lies primarily in the focus.

The SADT data model is illustrated in Figure 42 on page 108. The box in the figure depicts a data object, and the arrows show relationships between the data and the environment that creates and uses it. The left side of the box shows the activity which generates the data. The right side of the box shows the activity which uses the data. The top of the box shows the controls which constrain the generation and use of the data. The bottom of the box shows the storage mechanism for the data.

In the SADT activity model the box depicts function, and the arrows depict relationships to data and control. In Figure 43 on page 109, the *mechanism* arrow indicates the agent which will actually transform the input to the output. The mechanism might be a device, such as a printer; a tool, such as an editor; or even state data, such as a data dictionary. The *control* arrow depicts the commands or conditions which will cause the activity to begin, or otherwise govern its behavior.

The left side of an activity box is used to show input data and the right hand side shows output data. In addition, the SADT notation allows one to describe control and supporting mechanisms: the top of an Activity box is used to show the control data that triggers, or constrains, the operation of the activity. This allows explicit distinction between control data and input/output data, permitting the analyst or designer to better view the functional cohesiveness of all the boxes on the diagram. This is advantageous because, if only input/output relationships could be illustrated, then procedural coupling would be the only degree of strength that could be evaluated. When control flow can be superimposed upon the the diagrams, then the dynamics of the process being specified can be better visualized, and in addition, varying degrees of binding can be evaluated during decomposition.

Activity and data models may be used in networks to describe a process, as shown in Figure 44 on page 110. The figure depicts a process in which a document is to be created, refined, and printed, based upon an initial request for the document, and later on a successful review of the document's contents before printing. In the interim, the document is updated and refined using an editor that displays the evolving document at a terminal.

SADT diagrams may also be refined in hierarchies that decompose a problem into its parts. When organized in a hierarchy, each box may be a parent summarizing the diagrams below it or a child giving details of the parent above it. One of the noteworthy properties of SADT is that both its analysis techniques and its notation constrain the user to express a given part of the solution (i.e., a box) in terms of only a few simple aspects (e.g., inputs, outputs, mechanism, control). If a box cannot be expressed in these simple terms, it is too complex, and the definer is required to decompose the box into subparts until all boxes in the diagram can be expressed in these simple terms.

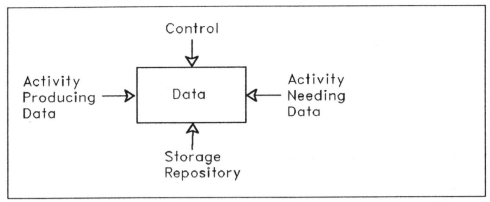

Figure 42. SADT Data Model

4.6.4 An Example E-R Language Application of RPLD Model

If you were given a multitude of apparently unrelated requirements, how would you formulate a precise statement of what is to be designed and implemented to satisfy them? Where would you begin? How would you prioritize, selecting some and rejecting others? How would you know when you are finished? The example given in this section is designed to walk you through the systematic approach described earlier, and to familiarize you with the use of an E-R language at the same time.

We will call our E-R language *A Specification Language* and use the acronym *ASL*. A complete description of the ASL syntactic forms appears in Appendix A of this text. The set of documentation resulting from the application of the methodology we are going to use will be called the *Requirements and Product Level Design Specification*, and we will refer to it from now on as the *RPLD Specification*.

The Goal of the Example

Assume we are to perform Requirements Engineering on an existing customer process for the purpose of automating it. Since this is a chapter on Requirements Engineering, we have chosen as our imaginary client in this example a customer in the business of developing software and in particular need of automating the Requirements Engineering portion of the process. Thus, in this example we will perform Requirements Engineering on the problem of automating the Requirements Engineering process itself.

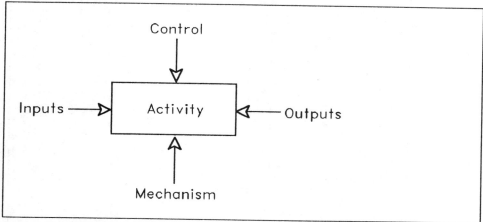

Figure 43. SADT Activity Model

The Approach

We will define a high level framework on which to solve the problem in ASL. We will refine the Requirements stage into descriptions of the *current* Requirements Engineering process used by our client, *problems* associated with the current process, propose some *solutions*, define a *target* process that supports our solutions, and finally a Product Level Design description of the *target product*.

We will call the target process the *Automated Requirements Engineering Process*, and the target product, the *Requirements Engineering Work Station*. This example will be performed in five systematic steps:

1. *Step 1:* Define an overall problem-solving framework in ASL.

2. *Step 2:* Define the users' environment and overall data flow between it and the Current Product.

3. *Step 3:* Describe the current Requirements Engineering process and define the problems associated with it.

4. *Step 4:* Define solutions to the current problems and a resulting target process that supports the solutions.

5. *Step 5:* Define target product and data flow between it and its environment.

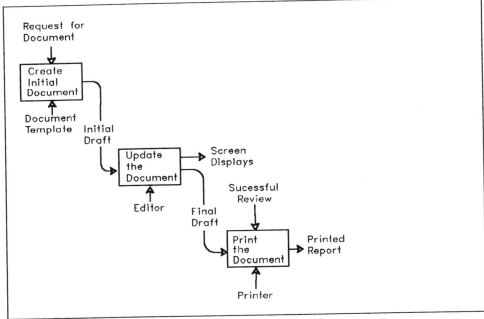

Figure 44. Example SADT Activity Diagram

Step 1: Overall Problem-Solving Model

We will pattern our problem-solving technique after the RPLD Model described in 4.5.4, "RPLD Model" on page 90. The four ASL objects defined in Figure 45 on page 111 depict the beginning of an RPLD Specification by establishing the root nodes for subsequent definition of the current users, the current product, the current process, and problems associated with the current process.

Next we turn our attention to defining the root nodes of the *target* process and system, as illustrated in Figure 46 on page 112, electing this time to explicitly define the input and output flow between the domains of the environment and target product.

To this point in the example, we have provided enough information to view the structure of the basic RPLD problem solving model. Our perception of what has been stated will be enhanced if additional information could be generated by inference from the information that was explicitly stated. For example, in Figure 45 on page 111, it is stated that current users generate current product inputs, and current product functions receive them. It follows then, that "current product inputs are generated by current users and received by current product functions."

```
TYPE: ENVIRONMENT                    Current_Users ;
        GENERATES    Current_Product_Inputs ;
        RECEIVES     Current_Product_Outputs ;

TYPE: FSM (Finite State Machine) Current_Product_Functions ;
        GENERATES    Current_Product_Outputs ;
        RECEIVES     Current_Product_Inputs ;
     UTILIZED BY     Current_Process ;

TYPE: CURRENT ACTIVITY               Current_Process ;
         CREATES     Current_Process_Work_Items ;
         CHANGES     Current_Process_Work_Items ;
        VALIDATES    Current_Process_Work_Items ;

TYPE: PROBLEM                        Current_Problems ;
      MADE TRUE BY   Current_Process ;
      MADE FALSE BY  Target_Process ;
```

Interpretation:

Current_Users generate inputs to and receive outputs from the current product.

The *Current_Product_Functions* receive the inputs and generate the outputs.

The *Current_Process* creates, or changes, or validates *work items*.

Some *Current_Problems* are made true by the current process and made false by target process.

Figure 45. Initial Input Describing Current Process and Product

Let us now assume we have available a specification analyzer utility that can generate the complement of these ASL expressions and perform other checks for consistency, completeness, and conformance to methodology. We will call the utility *A Specification Analyzer (ASA)*. By running ASA against our ASL description completed thus far, the result can be used to

1. review what has been explicitly stated.

2. view what has been *inferred* from the direct statements by means of the generated complementary expressions.

```
┌─────────────────────────────────────────────────────────────┐
│  ┌──────────────────────────────────────────────────────────┐│
│  │                                                          ││
│  │  TYPE: SOLUTION                 Solutions_To_Current_Problems ; ││
│  │         RESOLVES      Current_Problems ;                 ││
│  │                                                          ││
│  │  TYPE: TARGET ACTIVITY              Target_Process ;     ││
│  │     MAKES SOLUTION    Solutions_To_Current_Problems   TRUE ; ││
│  │         UTILIZES      Target_Product_Functions ;         ││
│  │                                                          ││
│  │  TYPE: WORK ITEM                Target_Process_Work_Items ; ││
│  │        CREATED BY     Target_Process ;                   ││
│  │        CHANGED BY     Target_Process ;                   ││
│  │      VALIDATED BY     Target_Process ;                   ││
│  │                                                          ││
│  │  TYPE: INPUT                    Target_Product_Inputs ;  ││
│  │      GENERATED BY     Target_Users ;                     ││
│  │       RECEIVED BY     Target_Product_Functions ;         ││
│  │                                                          ││
│  │  TYPE: OUTPUT                   Target_Product_Outputs ; ││
│  │      GENERATED BY     Target_Product_Functions ;         ││
│  │       RECEIVED BY     Target_Users ;                     ││
│  │                                                          ││
│  │  TYPE: FSM                      Target_Product_Functions ; ││
│  │      PERFORMED BY     Tools_And_Procedures ;             ││
│  │                                                          ││
│  └──────────────────────────────────────────────────────────┘│
└─────────────────────────────────────────────────────────────┘
```

Interpretation:

Target_Product_Inputs received by the target product will be generated by target users.

Target_Product_Outputs generated by the target product will be received by the target users.

The *Target_Process* will make current problems false, and their solutions true. It will also utilize some functions of the target product.

Target_Process_Work_Items can be created, changed, or validated by the target process.

Solutions_To_Current_Problems resolve current problems.

Target_Product_Functions are performed by tools and procedures.

Figure 46. Initial Input Describing Target Process and Product

In Figure 47 on page 114 and Figure 48 on page 115 the statements we entered directly are shown in boxes, and the complementary expressions generated by ASA are shown outside the boxes.

It can be noted in these figures that ASA generated some new object names in addition to the complementary expressions. For example, in Figure 45 on page 111, it was stated that Current_Users generate Current_Product_Inputs. Even though the object "Current_Product_Inputs" was not defined explicitly at that time, ASA was able to define the object as type INPUT. This is possible because, as with PSL described previously, ASL is a context-sensitive language, and words or phrases take on additional meaning due to the context in which they appear. Thus, "Current_Product_Inputs" is generated by ASA as an object of type INPUT because, in the semantics of ASL, only an object of type ENVIRONMENT can generate it (see "Current_Users" in the figure), and only objects of type FSM can receive it (see "Current_Product_Functions") in the figure.

Likewise, "Tools_And_Procedures" referenced but not defined in Figure 46 on page 112 was generated by ASA as an object of type AGENT in Figure 48 on page 115 because an object of type FSM can only be performed by an AGENT.

This completes the overall root structure for the ASL model we will now use for defining the automated Requirements Engineering process and the Requirements Engineering Work Station.

Step 2: Environment and Data Flow

In this step we will focus on the detail for the *environment*, the *inputs* to the current and target product that are generated by members of the environment, and the *outputs* that are received by members of the environment.

In Figure 49 on page 117 the environment is depicted from the perspectives of the user enterprise, the system environment, and the requirements engineer users themselves. Information such as characteristics of the user enterprise, the system environment, and user skills would have been obtained through interviews and other studies of our client's business. In Figure 50 on page 119 we have identified specific inputs and outputs of the current product. Let us also assume that, through additional interviews with our client, we have identified a specific function named *Doc_Distribution_Process* that is part of the current product. For the time being, except for this function, we will treat the current product as a monolithic "black box," since at the moment we are interested in it only to the extent of its inputs and outputs.

```
┌──────────────────────────────────────────────────────────────────────┐
│                                                                        │
│  ┌─ Input ─────────────────────────────────────────────────────────┐  │
│  │  TYPE: ENVIRONMENT            Current_Users ;                     │  │
│  │           GENERATES     Current_Product_Inputs ;                  │  │
│  │            RECEIVES     Current_Product_Outputs ;                 │  │
│  │                                                                   │  │
│  │  TYPE: FSM                    Current_Product_Functions ;         │  │
│  │           GENERATES     Current_Product_Outputs ;                 │  │
│  │            RECEIVES     Current_Product_Inputs ;                  │  │
│  │          UTILIZED BY    Current_Process ;                         │  │
│  └───────────────────────────────────────────────────────────────────┘  │
│                                                                        │
│     TYPE: INPUT                  Current_Product_Inputs ;              │
│         GENERATED BY    Current_Users ;                               │
│          RECEIVED BY    Current_Product_Functions ;                   │
│                                                                        │
│     TYPE: OUTPUT                 Current_Product_Outputs ;             │
│         GENERATED BY    Current_Product_Functions ;                   │
│          RECEIVED BY    Current_Users ;                               │
│  ┌─ Input ─────────────────────────────────────────────────────────┐  │
│  │  TYPE: CURRENT ACTIVITY       Current_Process ;                   │  │
│  │            CREATES     Current_Process_Work_Items ;               │  │
│  │            CHANGES     Current_Process_Work_Items ;               │  │
│  │           VALIDATES    Current_Process_Work_Items ;               │  │
│  └───────────────────────────────────────────────────────────────────┘  │
│                                                                        │
│       MAKES PROBLEM    Current_Problems    TRUE ;                     │
│           UTILIZES     Current_Product_Functions ;                    │
│                                                                        │
│     TYPE: WORK ITEM              Current_Process_Work_Items ;          │
│         CREATED BY     Current_Process ;                              │
│         CHANGED BY     Current_Process ;                              │
│         VALIDATED BY   Current_Process ;                              │
│  ┌─ Input ─────────────────────────────────────────────────────────┐  │
│  │  TYPE: PROBLEM               Current_Problems ;                   │  │
│  │      MADE TRUE BY    Current_Process ;                            │  │
│  │     MADE FALSE BY    Target_Process ;                             │  │
│  │       RESOLVED BY    Solutions_To_Current_Problems ;              │  │
│  └───────────────────────────────────────────────────────────────────┘  │
│                                                                        │
└──────────────────────────────────────────────────────────────────────┘
```

Figure 47. Composite Report of Current Process and Product. Statements in boxes were entered explicitly. Statements not in boxes were automatically generated.

```
┌─ Input ──────────────────────────────────────────────────┐
│                                                           │
│  TYPE: SOLUTION            Solutions_To_Current_Problems ; │
│         RESOLVES      Current_Problems ;                  │
│                                                           │
└───────────────────────────────────────────────────────────┘


      MADE TRUE BY     Target_Process ;

┌─ Input ──────────────────────────────────────────────────┐
│                                                           │
│  TYPE: TARGET ACTIVITY      Target_Process ;              │
│     MAKES SOLUTION     Solutions_To_Current_Problems  TRUE ;│
│         UTILIZES     Target_Product_Functions ;           │
│                                                           │
└───────────────────────────────────────────────────────────┘


           CREATES     Target_Process_Work_Items ;
           CHANGES     Target_Process_Work_Items ;
         VALIDATES     Target_Process_Work_Items ;
     MAKES PROBLEM     Current_Problems     FALSE ;

┌─ Input ──────────────────────────────────────────────────┐
│                                                           │
│  TYPE: WORK ITEM            Target_Process_Work_Items ;   │
│        CREATED BY     Target_Process ;                    │
│        CHANGED BY     Target_Process ;                    │
│      VALIDATED BY     Target_Process ;                    │
│                                                           │
└───────────────────────────────────────────────────────────┘


  TYPE: ENVIRONMENT              Target_Users ;
          GENERATES     Target_Product_Inputs ;
           RECEIVES     Target_Product_Outputs ;

┌─ Input ──────────────────────────────────────────────────┐
│                                                           │
│  TYPE: INPUT                Target_Product_Inputs ;       │
│      GENERATED BY     Target_Users ;                      │
│       RECEIVED BY     Target_Product_Functions ;          │
│                                                           │
└───────────────────────────────────────────────────────────┘
```

Figure 48 (Part 1 of 2). Composite Report of Target Process and Product

```
┌─ Input ──────────────────────────────────────────────────────┐
│                                                                │
│  TYPE: OUTPUT                    Target_Product_Outputs ;      │
│        GENERATED BY     Target_Product_Functions ;             │
│         RECEIVED BY     Target_Users ;                         │
│                                                                │
└────────────────────────────────────────────────────────────────┘

┌─ Input ──────────────────────────────────────────────────────┐
│                                                                │
│  TYPE: FSM                      Target_Product_Functions ;     │
│        PERFORMED BY     Tools_And_Procedures ;                 │
│                                                                │
└────────────────────────────────────────────────────────────────┘

         GENERATES      Target_Product_Outputs ;
         RECEIVES       Target_Product_Inputs ;
       UTILIZED BY      Target_Process ;

  TYPE: AGENT                        Tools_And_Procedures ;
         PERFORMS       Target_Product_Functions ;
```

Figure 48 (Part 2 of 2). Composite Report of Target Process and Product

Step 3: Current Process and Problem Definition

Now let us focus on the *process* that causes the current product "black box" to generate the defined outputs from the inputs received. It is important to note that we are still not going to be concerned with *how* the black box produces the outputs. Our concern is strictly with what tasks the users of the black box are performing that require results to be produced.

The current process will be defined in terms of *Activities* and *Work Items*. In Figure 51 on page 120 we have defined an overall Requirements Engineering activity that names subactivities for writing the initial and final programming Specifications documents, reviewing them, and getting them approved.

Let us now turn to the RPLD_Specifications as a work item and define the allowable *states* and *operations* that can be performed on it. Figure 52 on page 121 shows that the RPLD Specifications can be transformed from creation through approval by various activities.

While defining the RPLD work item, we referenced two new activities, shown in Figure 53 on page 122.

Having defined the current process and a key work item that it produces, we focus in Figure 54 on page 123 on defining a set of *problems* associated with the

```
TYPE: USER ENTERPRISE              Software_Product_Development ;

      DESCRIPTION ;

User enterprises are assumed to be the development of software products
for sale to consumers and contracters. The particular market segment is
users of personal computers, who are generally not experienced in pro-
gramming skills. Competition is keen in this segment of the software
business, and many software vendors who will use this Requirements
Engineering Work Station will be undercapitalized and in need of high-
volume, short-term cash flow customers for their software products.

Additional detail will be found in the RADLIPS Market Analysis Report.
;

          DEFINER IS      'Jason Jones' ;
        ATTRIBUTES ARE    Competition 'Highly Competitive',
                          Capitalization 'Low',
                          Cash_Flow 'Short Term',
                          Market_Segment 'PC_Applications',
                          Customer_Skill_Level 'Non-Programmers' ;
          REFER TO        RADLIPS_Market_Analysis_Report ;




TYPE: REFERENCE                    RADLIPS_Market_Analysis_Report ;

      DESCRIPTION

The referenced document is a market analysis available under file
number XYZ123 ;

          DEFINER IS      Market_Research_Corp ;
       OBJECT OWNER IS    RADLIPS_Corp ;
          APPLIES TO      Software_Product_Development ;
```

Figure 49 (Part 1 of 2). Input Describing Environment Detail

current Requirements Engineering process and an overall solutions place-holder
to be refined later.

```
TYPE: SYSTEM ENVIRONMENT          Development_Support_Systems ;

     DESCRIPTION ;

The current support environment for potential users of the Requirements
Engineering Work Station already includes other PC work stations,
various office communication systems, and systems for testing or proto-
typing their products under development.     ;

          HAS PARTS    PC_Work_Stations,
                       Office_Communication_System,
                       Test_Environment_System ;

TYPE: USER                        Requirements_Engineer ;

     DESCRIPTION ;
Requirements Engineers who will use the new work station are generally
assumed to be using traditional methods for requirements analysis, and
will not be conversant in E-R languages or methodologies.

          PART OF    Current_Users ;
     ATTRIBUTES ARE   Skill_Level 'Unfamiliar With E-R Lang.',
                      Methodology_Experience 'Not Experienced' ;
```

Figure 49 (Part 2 of 2). Input Describing Environment Detail

Step 4: Solutions and Target Process Definition

Let us assume that after analysis, we have determined that the important solutions to incorporate in the new Requirements Engineering process are to put the
requirements input in a data base, to institute a systematic requirements analysis
technique including the use of graphic analysis aids, to ensure traceability from
requirements to design, and to improve the review process. These solutions are
defined and related to the problems they address and to the target activities that
will achieve them in Figure 55 on page 124.

The activities to be incorporated in the target process are named as subparts of a
root activity called "target requirements engineering activities" illustrated in
Figure 56 on page 125. The figure also shows that a *Doc_Distribution_Process*
has been identified to cause the approved RPLD Specifications document to
become output from the target product.

```
TYPE: INPUT                         Requirements_Input ;

     DESCRIPTION ;

The basic inputs to the Requirements Engineering process are generated
by the Requirements Engineer from communication with users and the
market.

          PART OF      Current_Product_Inputs ;
     GENERATED BY      Requirements_Engineer;
     RECEIVED BY       Current_Product_Functions ;

TYPE: INPUT                         Design_Considerations ;

     DESCRIPTION ;

Another type of inputs are various design considerations derived from
working with designers during the Requirements Engineering process.

          PART OF      Current_Product_Inputs ;
     GENERATED BY      Requirements_Engineer;
     RECEIVED BY       Current_Product_Functions ;

TYPE: OUTPUT                        RPLD_Specs_Document ;
          PART OF      Current_Product_Outputs ;
     GENERATED BY      Doc_Distribution_Process
                            USING  RPLD_Specs
                                        IN STATE  Approved ;
     RECEIVED  BY      Requirements_Engineer ;

TYPE: OUTPUT                        Design_Direction_Documents ;
          PART OF      Current_Product_Outputs ;
     GENERATED BY      Current_Product_Functions ;
     RECEIVED  BY      Requirements_Engineer ;

TYPE: FSM                           Doc_Distribution_Process ;
          PART OF      Current_Product_Functions,
                       Target_Product_Functions ;
```

Figure 50. Inputs Describing Current Process Inputs and Outputs. This describes data
flow between environment and current product.

```
TYPE: CURRENT ACTIVITY          Reqmts_Engn_Activities ;

     DESCRIPTION  ;

The  two  basic  activities  of  the  current  Requirements  Engineering
process are writing RPLD Specifications and getting them validated and
approved.   The process starts when the business proposal is completed
and ends when the approved RPLD Specifications have been completed and
included in the product baseline documents.

        PERSPECTIVE     'Current Process' ;
        HAS PARTS       Write_RPLD_Specs,
                        Approve_RPLD_Specs ;
          UTILIZES      Current_Product_Functions   ;
          VALIDATES     RPLD_Specs ;
     ENTRY ENABLED WHEN  Business_Proposal
                           IN STATE  Completed  BECOMES TRUE ;
     EXIT  ENABLED WHEN  RPLD_Specs
                           IN STATE  Baselined  BECOMES TRUE ;
          CREATES       RPLD_Specs ;
          CHANGES       RPLD_Specs  TO STATE  Baselined ;
     MAKES  PROBLEM     Reqmts_Engineering_Problems   TRUE ;
```

Figure 51. Initial Input for Overall Requirements Engineering Stage

Step 5: Data Flow and Target Product Design Directions

In Figure 57 on page 126 the characteristics of the target requirements engineer
are defined, and the inputs and outputs generated and received by these users are
also identified.

At this point, the detailed activities that accomplish the named state transitions of
the target process work items would be defined (not shown in this example).

A number of candidates for design considerations would also have have appeared
as Finite State Machines (FSMs) in the target product section of our RPLD
model. Some of those candidates may have been carryovers from existing functions identified in the current product. Others are new additions, obtained by
following a rule that while defining the target process any activity which could be
reused two or more times in the target process network becomes a candidate for
consideration as an FSM in the target product. This feature of ASL helps bridge
the requirements to the design. The ASL semantics are such that Activities
cannot be used in more than one node in the process definition network—they
can only *utilize* FSMs to get reusable function. Thus, as the target process defi-

```
TYPE: WORK ITEM                      RPLD_Specs;

     CREATED BY    Reqmts_Engn_Activities ;
     CHANGED TO STATE   Baselined  BY  Reqmts_Engn_Activities ;
  BECOMING TRUE  IN STATE  Baselined
                  ENABLES EXIT FROM  Reqmts_Engn_Activities ;
```

┌─ **Inputs** ───┐
```
  ATTRIBUTES ARE    Allowable_States 'Created',
                                     'Final_Draft',
                                     'Approved',
                                     'Baselined',
      CHANGED TO STATE   Final_Draft  BY   Write_RPLD_Specs
                  USING RPLD_Specs  IN STATE Created ;
    VALIDATED TO STATE   Approved   BY  Approve_RPLD_Specs
                  USING RPLD_Specs  IN STATE  Final_Draft ;


  BECOMING TRUE  IN STATE  Created
                  ENABLES ENTRY TO   Write_RPLD_Specs ;
  BECOMING TRUE  IN STATE  Final_Draft
                  ENABLES EXIT FROM  Write_RPLD_Specs ;
  BECOMING TRUE  IN STATE  Final_Draft
                  ENABLES ENTRY TO   Approve_RPLD_Specs ;
  BECOMING TRUE  IN STATE  Approved
                  ENABLES EXIT FROM  Approve_RPLD_Specs ;
  BECOMING TRUE  IN STATE  Approved
                  ENABLES ENTRY TO   Do_PLD_Stage ;
```
└──┘

Figure 52. Initial Description of RPLD Specifications.   Statements in boxes were
entered explicitly. Statements not in boxes were generated by ASA from previous definition of Reqmts_Engn_Activities.

nition is refined, a number of FSMs will accumulate on the target product "side
of the fence," suggesting the emergence of building blocks for the designer's consideration, as separate and distinct from user tasks defined from the requirements
perspective.

In Figure 58 on page 127, a reusable document distribution process, document
update facility, and Specifications approval process has been identified for consideration by the designer of the target product.

Figure 59 on page 128 shows more detail of the three components and suggests
the invocation of *agents* to perform some of the tasks. Thus, to the designer, this
scheme presents a very high level view of candidate components in the system,

```
TYPE: CURRENT ACTIVITY              Write_RPLD_Specs ;
        PART OF    Reqmts_Engn_Activities ;
    ENTRY ENABLED WHEN
            RPLD_Specs IN STATE  Created BECOMES  TRUE ;
     EXIT ENABLED WHEN
            RPLD_Specs IN STATE  Final_Draft BECOMES TRUE ;


TYPE: CURRENT ACTIVITY              Approve_RPLD_Specs ;
        PART OF    Reqmts_Engn_Activities ;
    ENTRY ENABLED WHEN  RPLD_Specs
                IN STATE   Reviewed   BECOMES TRUE ;
     EXIT  ENABLED WHEN  RPLD_Specs
                IN STATE   Baselined  BECOMES TRUE ;
```

Figure 53. Detailed Requirements Engineering Activities. All the above statements were generated by ASL from previous description of RPLD_Specs and Reqmts_Engn_Activities.

which are executed by agents that are a combination of automated facilities and human procedures. Two tools and the role of a person are depicted as agents in Figure 60 on page 129.

Summary

In this example, we have illustrated the use of an E-R language applied in a systematic Requirements Engineering process.

The example attempted to bring out two principal benefits in using an E-R language, and in particular a strongly typed E-R language such as ASL, for creating requirements and high level design specifications:

1. The encoded specification can be machine-analyzed for consistency, completeness, and conformance to a methodology.

2. The automatic generation of the complementary relation aids in human comprehension of the specification, providing a better foundation for communicating and validating the correctness of the specification.

```
TYPE: PROBLEM                      Reqmts_Engineering_Problems ;
        HAS PARTS     Insufficient_Reqmts_Detail,
                      Reqmts_Inputs_Not_Visible,
                      Incomplete_PO_Reviews,
                      Many_Unresolved_Rqmts_Issues,
                      Many_RPLD_Specs_Non_Concurrences,
                      Lack_Change_Control_On_RPLD_Specs ;
     MADE TRUE BY     Reqmts_Engn_Activities ;
    MADE FALSE BY     Tgt_Reqmts_Engn_Activities ;
      RESOLVED BY     Reqmts_Engineering_Solutions ;


TYPE: SOLUTION                    Reqmts_Engineering_Solutions ;
        RESOLVES      Reqmts_Engineering_Problems ;


TYPE: PROBLEM                      Reqmts_Inputs_Not_Visible ;
          PART OF     Reqmts_Engineering_Problems ;
     MADE TRUE BY     Write_RPLD_Specs ;


TYPE: PROBLEM                      Insufficient_Reqmts_Detail  ;
          PART OF     Reqmts_Engineering_Problems ;
     MADE TRUE BY     Write_RPLD_Specs ;


TYPE: PROBLEM                      Many_Unresolved_Reqmts_Issues ;
          PART OF     Reqmts_Engineering_Problems ;
     MADE TRUE BY     Approve_RPLD_Specs ;


TYPE: PROBLEM                      Many_RPLD_Specs_Non_Concurrences  ;
          PART OF     Reqmts_Engineering_Problems ;
     MADE TRUE BY     Approve_RPLD_Specs ;


TYPE: PROBLEM                      Lack_Change_Control_On_RPLD_Specs ;
          PART OF     Reqmts_Engineering_Problems ;
     MADE TRUE BY     Reqmts_Engn_Activities ;
```

Figure 54. Initial Input for Problems and Solutions

```
TYPE: SOLUTION                    Reqmts_Engineering_Solutions ;
       HAS PARTS      Put_Reqmts_Inputs_In_A_Database,
                      Do_Systematic_Problem_Analysis,
                      Provide_Graphic_Analysis_Aids ,
                      Provide_Traceability_To_Design,
                      Provide_Effective_Review_Process ;
     MADE TRUE BY     Tgt_Reqmts_Engn_Activities ;
        RESOLVES      Reqmts_Engineering_Problems ;


TYPE: SOLUTION                    Put_Reqmts_Inputs_In_A_Database ;
       PART OF        Reqmts_Engineering_Solutions ;
     MADE TRUE BY     Catalog_Requirements_Inputs ;
        RESOLVES      Reqmts_Inputs_Not_Visible,
                      Insufficient_Reqmts_Detail ;


TYPE: SOLUTION                    Do_Systematic_Problem_Analysis ;
       PART OF        Reqmts_Engineering_Solutions ;
     MADE TRUE BY     Analyze_Problems ;
        RESOLVES      Many_Unresolved_Reqmts_Issues ;


TYPE: SOLUTION                    Provide_Graphic_Analysis_Aids ;
       PART OF        Reqmts_Engineering_Solutions ;
     MADE TRUE BY     Analyze_Problems ;
        RESOLVES      Reqmts_Inputs_Not_Visible  ;


TYPE: SOLUTION                    Provide_Traceability_To_Design ;
       PART OF        Reqmts_Engineering_Solutions ;
     MADE TRUE BY     Define_Design_Directions ;
        RESOLVES      Lack_Change_Control_On_Specifications ;


TYPE: SOLUTION                    Provide_Effective_Review_Process ;
       PART OF        Reqmts_Engineering_Solutions ;
     MADE TRUE BY     Define_Solutions,
                      Tgt_Write_RPLD_Specs,
                      Tgt_Approve_RPLD_Specs ;
        RESOLVES      Many_Unresolved_Reqmts_Issues,
                      Many_RPLD_Specs_Non_Concurrences ;
```

Figure 55. Requirements Engineering Solutions

```
TYPE: TARGET ACTIVITY              Tgt_Reqmts_Engn_Activities ;
       PERSPECTIVE       'Target Process' ;
         HAS PARTS       Catalog_Requirements_Inputs,
                         Analyze_Problems,
                         Define_Solutions,
                         Define_Design_Directions,
                         Tgt_Write_RPLD_Specs,
                         Tgt_Approve_RPLD_Specs ;
          UTILIZES       Doc_Distribution_Process ;
     MAKES PROBLEM       Reqmts_Engineering_Problems   FALSE ;
     MAKES SOLUTION      Reqmts_Engineering_Solutions TRUE   ;
     ENTRY ENABLED WHEN  Business_Proposal
                         IN STATE  Completed  BECOMES TRUE ;
      EXIT  ENABLED WHEN  RPLD_Specs
                         IN STATE  Approved   BECOMES TRUE ;
           CREATES       New_RPLD_Specs ;
          VALIDATES      New_RPLD_Specs  TO STATE  Approved ;
           CHANGES       New_RPLD_Specs  TO STATE  Baselined ;
```

Figure 56. Target Requirements Engineering Process

4.7 Validation

Validation of the RPLD specification set focuses on the correctness with which the problems and corresponding solutions have been defined. In complex projects, this is usually done by means of formal review meetings and work groups involving customer representatives, requirements planners, and product designers.

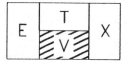

4.7.1 Key Validation Checkpoints

There are two important validation checkpoints in the Requirements Engineering process (refer to Figure 61 on page 130):

1. Validation of problem/solution definition with users: The critical turning point that marks an effective definition of requirements is

   a. the precision with which problems with the current process have been defined

   b. validation from the users' view that the problem definition is indeed accurate and complete

   c. verification that the defined solutions map precisely to the defined problem set, ensuring that (1) all problems have solutions and (2) all solutions have problems

```
TYPE: USER                        Tgt_Requirements_Engineer ;
    ATTRIBUTES ARE    Skill_Level 'Familiar With E-R Lang.',
                      Methodology_Experience 'Experienced' ;
        PART OF       Software_Developers ;
      GENERATES       Reqmts_Input,
                      Tgt_Process_Definition,
                      Problem_Statements,
                      Solution_Statements,
                      Target_Process_Definition,
                      Target_Product_Definition,
                      Design_Considerations ;
       RECEIVES       Requirements_Summary_Listings,
                      Consistency_Analysis_Reports,
                      Tgt_Process_Pictures,
                      Problem_Definition_Documents,
                      Solution_Definition_Documents,
                      Target_Process_Pictures,
                      Target_Product_Pictures,
                      RPLD_Specs_Document,
                      Design_Direction_Documents ;
```

Figure 57. Target Requirements Engineer

    d. validation that the proposed solutions are viable from the users' view

2. Validation of solution definition and design direction with technical strategy involves

    a. validation that the proposed solutions are correct relative to the defined technical strategy for the product line

    b. verification that the design direction and the solution definition map to ensure that (1) all solutions are forward-traceable to the proposed design and (2) all design statements are backward-traceable to specific solution statements

4.7.2 Characteristics of a Good Requirements Specification

According to an IEEE Standards Committee [IEEE84], a good Requirements Specification is:

1. Unambiguous: Every requirement stated has one and only one meaning. For example, each characteristic of the final product must be described by a single unique term.

```
TYPE: FSM                    Target_Product_Functions ;
     HAS PARTS       Document_Distribution_Process,
                     Document_Update_Facility,
                     Specifications_Approval_Process ;
     UTILIZED BY     Reqmts_Engn_Activities ;
     GENERATES       RPLD_Specs_Document
                           USING RPLD_Specs IN STATE Approved,
                     Initial_Progr_Specs_Document,
                           USING Initial_Specs IN STATE Approved,
                     Final_Progr_Specs_Document ;
```

Figure 58. Target Product Overview

2. Complete: All significant capabilities and attributes of the target process are addressed. Conformity to applicable standards are specified. All references and terms are fully defined.

3. Verifiable: For every stated requirement, some finite and cost effective method must exist with which a person or a machine can check that the requirement is satisfied. For example, requirements statements such as "The product should have a good human interface" is not verifiable because the term "good" is vague.

4. Consistent: No set of individual requirements conflict. There are four types of inconsistencies commonly found in requirements specifications:

   a. Reference to an object by two or more names

   b. Conflict in specified characteristics of an object. For example, a report might be described as "tabular" in one instance and "textual" in another

   c. Logic or temporal conflicts between two specified actions. For example, stating that A must always follow B in one instance, and that A and B may occur simultaneously in another

   d. Conflict in the actions that can be performed on a particular object type. For example, stating that an Input is *received by* the target product in one instance, and is *generated by* the target product in another.

5. Modifiable: The structure and style of this requirement specification should allow changes to be made easily, completely, and consistently. For example, the document should have a coherent organization with a table of contents, an index, and explicit cross-referencing. Also, the specification should not be redundant; that is, the same requirement should appear once, and only once, in the document.

6. Traceable: A set of conventions and organizations should be applied that facilitates both backward traceability of each requirement to its sources and

```
TYPE: FSM                          Document_Update_Facility ;
        PART OF      Target_Product_Functions ;
        UTILIZED BY  Tgt_Write_RPLD_Specs ;
        PERFORMED BY XYZ_Editor,
                     Document_Formatting_Tool ;
        CHANGES      RPLD_Specs,
                     Initial_Progr_Specs,
                     Final_Progr_Specs,
                     Program_Logic_Specs,
                     Source_Code ;

TYPE: FSM                          Doc_Distribution_Process ;
        PART OF      Target_Product_Functions ;
        UTILIZED BY  Reqmts_Engn_Activities ;
        GENERATES    RPLD_Specs_Document
                        USING RPLD_Specs IN STATE Approved,
                     Initial_Progr_Specs_Document
                        USING Initial_Progr_Specs IN STATE Approved,
                     Final_Progr_Specs_Document ;

TYPE: FSM                          Specifications_Approval_Process ;
        PART OF      Target_Product_Functions ;
        UTILIZED BY  Tgt_Approve_RPLD_Specs  ;
        PERFORMED BY Specifications_Approvers ;
```

Figure 59. Target Product Components

forward traceability to all documents spawned by the requirements specification.

7. Usable during the operation and maintenance phase: The requirements specification should address the future needs of operation and maintenance. For example, maintenance is usually carried out by personnel not associated with the original development. While local changes and corrections can be made by means of well-commented code, changes of a wider scope require a level of design and requirements specifications documentation. Knowledge of this type may be taken for granted in the developing organization, but is frequently missing in the maintenance organization. If the reason for, or origin of, the function is not understood, it is nearly impossible to perform adequate maintenance.

```
TYPE: TOOL                          XYZ_Editor  ;
         PERFORMS      Document_Update_Facility ;

TYPE: TOOL                          Doc_Formatting_Tool ;
         PERFORMS      Document_Update_Facility ;

TYPE: PERSON                   Specifications_Approver  ;
         REFER TO      PO_Review_Distribution_List ;
         PERFORMS      Specifications_Approval_Process ;
```

Figure 60. Target Product Agents

4.7.3 The Four Cs

When validation is performed, one way to think about the properties that a good RPLD Specification must possess is in terms of *Four Cs*, which are:

1. **Consistency:** The specification must be consistent within itself. For example, devoid of ambiguity, conflicting references, or contradictory statements.

2. **Completeness:**

   a. Functional capability and all other necessary product attributes must be addressed in the specification.

   b. The specification must be stated at the proper level of detail to meet the needs of those who will use it as their input.

3. **Conformance** to methodology:

   a. The specification is developed according to accepted practices

   b. The resultant product conforms to externally imposed standards and internally defined conventions (e.g., ANSI Standards, or internal conventions for register use).

4. **Correctness:** The specification must correctly satisfy the true requirements of the user.

4.7.4 Verification and Validation

The *IEEE Standard Glossary of Software Engineering Terminology* [IEEE85] defines "verification" and "validation" as follows:

> *verification:* The process of determining whether or not the products of a given phase of the software development cycle fulfill the requirements established during the previous phase.

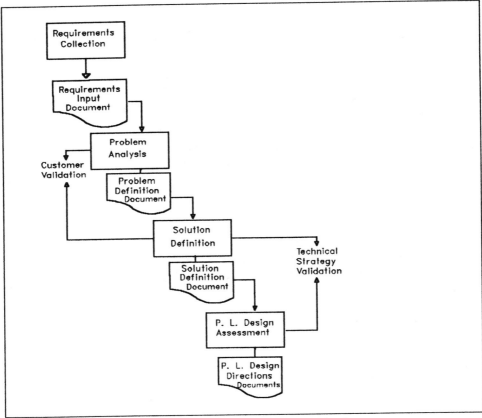

Figure 61. Key Requirements Engineering Validation Checkpoints.

> *validation:* The process of evaluating software at the end of the software development process to ensure compliance with software requirements.

To apply this definition to the notion of the "Four Cs" discussed above, note that a specification has both *intrinsic* properties and *extrinsic* properties. Refer to Figure 62 on page 131: Consistency, Completeness, and Conformance to methodology are shown in the figure as *intrinsic* because they refer to properties in and of the specification itself. Such properties may be verified independently of the product described in the specification; for example, against a set of standards for all specifications. These are properties such as described in 4.7.2, "Characteristics of a Good Requirements Specification" on page 126. We use the term "verify" when talking about ensuring the presence of these intrinsic properties.

Correctness is *extrinsic*, because it refers to a property external to the specification itself, that is, to required attributes of the product being described, such as for

```
    INTRINSIC              EXTRINSIC
    (VERIFY)               (VALIDATE)

  . Consistency          . Correctness

  . Completeness

  . Conformance
    to Methodology
```

Figure 62. The Four Cs of Requirements Specification. Intrinsic properties are *verified* internally. Extrinsic property is *validated* externally.

example CUPRIM attributes. Correctness can only be achieved through external communication and validation to true requirements of the customer.

We use the term *validate* when talking about ensuring the *truth* of the specification as viewed from its external requirements. A shorthand rule [BOEH84] to help remember the difference between *verify* and *validate* is:

- Verification: "Am I building the product right?"

- Validation: "Am I building the right product?"

4.8 Exit Criteria

The completion of the Requirements and Planning stage overlaps the beginning of the Product Level Design stage because the Requirements Engineering activity includes the creation of some of the initial Product Level Design documentation, as requirements planners 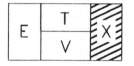 and product level designers work together to understand the true requirements, perhaps producing prototypes and user scenarios, and finally producing the design directions documentation that assesses the effect on overall product design.

As mentioned earlier, in 4.3.2, "Typical Problems from a Process Perspective" on page 74, it is essential that requirements planners and designers aggressively bring the Requirements Engineering activity and resulting RPLD Specifications to closure so the design does not speed ahead without benefit of a crisp set of reviewed, understood, and approved requirements. This goal is easy to talk about and difficult to achieve, due in part to the fact that requirements inputs are continually being received, and in part to the basic motivations of the planner to hold the requirements definition somewhat open-ended, allowing for the possibility of "one more requirement just around the corner," and the designer to close the door and "pull the train away from the platform" to get on with the design.

In current day state of the art, human judgment prevails in place of a precise set of *exit criteria* to tell when the requirements are properly finished. However, our "Four Cs" may help again here, by separating the concerns of the exit criteria into *intrinsic* and *extrinsic* properties as described in 4.7.4, "Verification and Validation" on page 129. At a minimum, the RPLD Specification documentation can be evaluated on the basis of its intrinsic properties (i.e., Completeness, Consistency, Conformance to methodology) before declaring the Requirements and Planning stage complete. This leaves only "Correctness" open for debate and subjective judgment. Toward this end, the designer should evaluate the correctness of the RPLD information provided in terms of "Is information adequate for the design job ahead?" and the planner should be asking, "Am I willing to accept *any design* based upon the information transmitted by these documents?"

4.9 Conclusions

The reader should now have an appreciation of why many practitioners consider the Requirements stage to be the weakest part of the entire software development process, and how some of the key Software Engineering problems in this area are being addressed by an emerging Requirements Engineering discipline. The growing focus on the problem in industry, government, and academia has brought forth some promising examples of successful solutions to the basic problems. Evidence exists that significant improvements are attainable through use of simple and practical methodologies, such as in 4.5.3, "Planning and Design Methodology (PDM)" on page 84 and 4.5.4, "RPLD Model" on page 90, and supported by structuring techniques such as SADT and by E-R languages and analysis tools such as SREM and PSL/PSA.

4.9.1 Effects of Using Rigorous Requirements Process

Experiences have shown that when a systematic Requirements Engineering approach is introduced in a process not already using them, visible benefits occur.

For example, the Software Requirements Engineering Methodology (SREM) was applied in a controlled study to an imbedded system project for the U.S. Air Force in 1979 [SCHE85]. The conclusion of the experiment was that, even though some difficulties had to be overcome, overall the structured approach of SREM was of great value in identifying inconsistencies and ambiguities in the requirements and high level specifications.

Likewise, when the Planning and Design Methodology (PDM) was initially applied to two pilot projects in an IBM System Development division, similar results were realized, as reported by Phillips and Ciarfella in [MAYS85]. These projects were undertaken to evaluate the effectiveness of the concepts of the formal Activities, Perspectives, and Aspects similar to those described previously in 4.5.2, "A Basic Requirements Engineering Approach" on page 83.

The first project was for the development of a new version of a compiler, and the second project involved the development of a major new addition to the IBM Multiple Virtual System (MVS) control program. In both projects, the then already existing or partially completed requirements and design documents were transformed to PSL constructs, and PSA was used to analyze the resultant specification for consistency.

In a series of review meetings, the results were presented and discussed jointly with requirements planners and designers. The meetings generally ended with many issues clarified and resolved, as well as with newly identified issues that had not been articulated previously. At the conclusion of both projects, the participants agreed that the structure and formalism of the resultant specifications helped to raise important requirements issues that normally would not have surfaced until much later had a traditional process been employed.

Subsequent experiences with this and other similar methods continue to provide evidence that applying increased structure and rigor in the Requirements Engineering stages greatly accelerates early identification and resolution of critical requirements issues.

4.9.2 Achievable Process Goals Today

One way to gauge the leading edge of the current state of the art in a Requirements Engineering process is to depict one that would result if all the techniques and practices proven to be beneficial in at least one project across the industry were combined into one "ideal" process. Such a "best-of-breed," composite process would represent the best requirements process proven to be achievable with the current-day proven techniques, tools, and disciplines. Following are some characteristics that could depict such an ideal Requirements Engineering process:

- A systematic Requirements Engineering approach is in place that supports:
  - Effective gathering of requirements
  - Rigorous user problem analysis
  - Solution definition that maps to the problems defined
  - Proper design placement of solutions
  - Realistic prioritization of requirements

- Requirements are controlled in a central repository.

- Entry criteria are clearly defined for each Requirements Engineering activity.

- Exit criteria are defined for each requirements work item produced in terms that ensure proper scope and depth of specification.

- A long-term technical strategy, or direction statement, exists against which to weigh each requirement request.

- A process exists to facilitate verification of consistency, completeness, and conformance to accepted standards and conventions for each document produced.

- The process supports validation for correctness through effective use of

  - Usability, installability, maintainability reviews
  - Customer reviews of both Requirements and Product Level Design specifications and prototypes

- A method for controlling changes to requirements specifications is in place to ensure that

  - Requirements changes are processed through the normal Requirements Engineering process
  - Design changes are evaluated for possible effect on the agreed-to requirements

- The Requirements Engineering process itself is documented and understood to ensure repeatability.

- A criteria for minimum acceptable hardware specifications exists to ensure

  - Completeness
  - Timeliness
  - Adequate description of software implications

- Adequate knowledge of competitive or related products and strategies is maintained.

4.9.3 Future Requirements Engineering Goals and Trends

Perseverance in the use of formal specification techniques currently emerging from the Requirements Engineering field may someday attain the essential, rigorous bridge between requirements and design, and thereby provide a foundation for additional automation of the software development process.

When employed in the past on actual projects, the various Requirements Engineering techniques described in this chapter have shown encouraging progress in this direction, through separating concerns and by following systematic problem-solving scenarios to transform a myriad of user suggestions into quasi-formal specifications.

Such quasi-formal specifications in turn add one more span in bridging from Requirements to Design stages. For example, E-R languages such as used in the examples for this text, are derived from an internal set of constructs or model. Such constructs might someday be translated to an executable design language, thus adding the final connecting span in an automatic specification-to-design bridge.

We will probably not be conversing in natural language directly with the computer for solving problems in the foreseeable future. What does seem within our grasp, however, is to be able to automatically transform the formal state description of what we want into actual machine procedures [SIMO86]. This means that the Requirements Engineer of the future would analyze user requirements to the point of specifying the problem as a state description of the desired results in a language understandable to the machine. Then the computer could perform a search of a knowledge base for possible solutions, select the best solution, make the chosen solution visible to the prospective user for validation, and execute the solution if authorized by the user.

What effect might automation of the specification-to-design bridge as just described have on this part of the process in terms of our Entry, Task, Validation, Exit (ETVX) paradigm? In addition to obvious changes in the Task and Validation procedures, methodologies and tools must change too. For example, in describing Requirements Engineering activities in this chapter, we expressed the Validation/Verification function of the ETVX paradigm in terms of the "Four Cs" (*consistency, completeness, conformance to a methodology*, and *correctness*). Automation as just described will undoubtedly relieve humans of much burdensome verification chores for the first three.

Validation for the Fourth C (*correctness*) however, remains essentially a human activity. Regardless of how successful we are at providing such automated assistance in the Requirements Engineering process, the essence of the process will remain focused on dialog between user and analyst and on human insight and judgment to understand and articulate the problem to be solved and to validate the correctness of the solution relative to human perceptions of the "true" requirements.

4.10 References

[ALFO80] M. W. Alford, "Software Requirements in the 80s: From Alchemy to Science," *Proceedings Of The Annual Conference,* ACM 80, Nashville, TN, October 27 − 29, 1980; ACM Baltimore, MD (1980), pp. 342 − 49.

[ALFO85] M. W. Alford, "SREM at the Age of Eight: The Distributed Computing Design System," *IEEE COMPUTER Magazine,* Vol. 18, No. 4 (April, 1985), pp. 36 − 46.

[BELL76] T. E. Bell and T. A. Thayer, "Software Requirements: Are They Really a Problem?," *IEEE Proceedings, 2nd Annual Conference on Software Engineering,* San Francisco, CA (October 13 − 15, 1976), pp. 61 − 8.

[BALZ78] R. Balzer, N. Goldman, and D. Wile, "Informality in Program Specification," *IEEE Transactions on Software Engineering,* SE-4, No. 2 (March, 1978). pp. 94 − 103.

[BALZ79] R. Balzer and N. Goldman, "Principles of Good Software Specification and Their Implications for Specification Languages," *Proceedings of Specifying Reliable Software Conference* (April, 1979), pp. 58 − 67.

[BALZ85] R. Balzer, "A 15 Year Perspective on Automatic Programming," *IEEE Transactions on Software Engineering*, Vol. SE-11, No. 11 (November, 1985) pp. 1257 − 68.

[BOEH84] B. W. Boehm, "Verifying and Validating Software Requirements and Design Specifications," *IEEE SOFTWARE Magazine*, Vol. 1, No. 1 (January, 1984) pp. 75 − 88

[IEEE83] *IEEE Standard Glossary of Software Engineering Terminology*, IEEE Standard Number 729 − 1983, IEEE − CS order number 729, Los Alamitos, CA, 1983.

[IEEE84] *IEEE Guide to Software Requirements Specifications*, ANSI/IEEE Standard Number 830 − 1984, available from the IEEE Service Center, 445 Hoes Lane, Piscataway, NJ 08854.

[MAYS85] R. G. Mays, L. S. Orzech, W. A. Ciarfella, and R. W. Phillips, "PDM: A Requirements Methodology for Software System Enhancements," *IBM Systems Journal*, Vol. 24, No. 2 (1985), pp. 134 − 49.

[ROMA85] G. Roman, "A Taxonomy of Current Issues in Requirements Engineering," *IEEE COMPUTER Magazine*, Vol. 18, No. 4 (April 1985), pp. 14 − 21.

[ROSS77] D. T. Ross and K. E. Schoman, "Structured Analysis for Requirements Definition," *IEEE Transactions on Software Engineering*, Vol. SE-3, No. 1 (January 1977), pp. 6–15.

[ROSS85] D. T. Ross, "Applications and Extensions of SADT," *IEEE COMPUTER Magazine*, Vol. 18, No. 4 (April 1985), pp. 25–34.

[SHCE85] P. A. Scheffer, A. H. Stone, W. E. Rzepka, "A Case Study of SREM," *IEEE COMPUTER Magazine,* Vol. 18, No. 4 (April 1985), pp. 47–54.

[SIMO86] H. A. Simon, "Whether Software Engineering Needs to Be Artificially Intelligent," *IEEE Transactions on Software Engineering,* Vol. SE-12, No. 7 (July 1986), pp. 726–32.

[TEIC77] D. Teichroew and E. A. Hershey, "PSL/PSA: A Computer Aided Technique for Structured Documentation and Analysis of Information Processing Systems," *IEEE Transactions on Software Engineering,* SE-3, No. 1 (January 1977), pp. 41–8.

[YEH80] R. T. Yeh and P. Zave, "Specifying Software Requirements," *Proceedings of the IEEE,* Vol. 68, No. 9 (September 1980), pp. 1077–85.

Additional Recommended Reading

Bass, L. J., "An Approach to User Specification of Interactive Display Interfaces," *IEEE Transactions on Software Engineering,* Vol. SE-11, No. 8 (August 1985) pp. 686–98.

Berzins, V., and M. Gray, "Analysis and Design in MSG.84: Formalizing Functional Specifications," *IEEE Transactions on Software Engineering,* Vol. SE-11, No. 8 (August 1985) pp. 657–70.

Borgida, A., S. Greenspan, J. Mylopoulos, "Knowledge Representation as the Basis for Requirements Specifications," *IEEE COMPUTER Magazine,* Vol. 18, No. 4 (April 1985), pp. 82–91.

Chi, U. H., "Formal Specification of User Interfaces: A Comparison and Evaluation of Four Axiomatic Approaches," *IEEE Transactions On Software Engineering,* Vol. SE-11, No. 8 (August 1985), pp. 671–85.

Chandrasekharan, M., B. Dasarathy, Z. Kishimoto, "Requirements-Based Testing of Real-Time Systems: Modeling for Testability," *IEEE COMPUTER Magazine,* Vol. 18, No. 4 (April 1985), pp. 71–80.

Heninger, K.,"Specifying Software Requirements for Complex Systems: New Techniques and Their Application," *IEEE Transactions on Software Engineering,* Vol. SE-6 (January 1980), pp. 2 – 13.

Meyer, B., "On Formalism in Specifications," *IEEE SOFTWARE Magazine,* (January 1985), pp. 6 – 14.

Orzech, L. S., "PSA: A Computer Aided Tool and Technique for Specification and Analysis of Product Level Designs," *IBM/FSD Software Engineering Exchange,* Vol. 2, No. 1 (October 1979), pp. 2 – 9.

Scharer, L., "Pinpointing Requirements," *Datamation,* (April 1981), pp. 139 – 42.

Sievert, G. E. and T. A. Mizell, "Specification-Based Software Engineering with TAGS," *IEEE COMPUTER Magazine,* Vol. 18, No. 4 (April 1985), pp. 56 – 65.

Sneed, H. M., "Software Renewal: A Case Study," *IEEE SOFTWARE Magazine,* Vol. 1, No. 3 (July 1984), pp. 56 – 63.

Chapter 5. Human Factors and Usability

5.1 Human Factors and Usability: What Do We Mean?

As the need for more software products increases or continues at the present compound growth rate, so too will the number of users of the ensuing software products increase. This increase will most likely be seen in users with little or no computer expertise. However, this demand for more software is typically softened because of problems with using the software. Users are frequently intimidated by many aspects which product programmers find easy, comfortable, or assume should be obvious. However, in the eyes of the product user it is not always so easy, comfortable, or obvious. It is this gap in the view of usability between the programmers and the users of their programs that we need to more successfully bridge. Software usability and how it can be improved are the subjects of this chapter.

Sometimes the problem of usability is also referred to as a human factors issue. Addressing human factors in this sense means factoring into the development of the software those product aspects and relationships between the user and the product that will make the user more productive and more likely to be satisfied with the product. *Usability* in this book will mean the ease of use of a product to include all interactions of the user with the product. *Human factors* are those aspects accounted for in the product which lead to usability. We will focus on (1) the issues of usability as seen and experienced by the endusers who come in contact with the software after it has been produced, and (2) the consideration of human factors by the development group while it is producing the product. The programmer must address human factors to increase usability.

During the course of the chapter we will see that usability is a consideration which must be focused during the Requirements stage just as any other functional requirement is addressed for a product. Additionally, we suggest that if the usability objectives defined during Requirements are met, that the users will be satisfied, the quality of the product will be higher, and the defects in human factors of the product will be reduced.

5.1.1 What Products Are We Talking About?

Basically, when a product or subproduct has a user interface allowing the user to make functional choices through a response or a request, then this product is a candidate for human factors or usability consideration. We include all documentation which a user may have to read to successfully use the product. This applies to all communication with the user, whether it is in a printed document form or it appears in interactive use with the software program.

Are all software products subject to usability considerations? Schneiderman, who has written one of the best treatises on software usability, although he called it software psychology, states that:

> Frequently mentioned topics for software psychology include programming languages, operating system control languages, data base query facilities, editors, terminal interactions, computer-assisted instruction, personal computing systems and terminal usage by non-skilled users. [SCHN80]

Later in the same book he states that usability

> encompasses all human use of computers but concentrates on software development, query facility usage and interface design.

These quotes are interesting to us for two reasons: (1) what they indicate about the domain of software human factor interest, and (2) what they leave out. We agree with the products or subparts of products that Schneiderman's list includes. A number of others could be added, including the vast majority of applications, games, and spreadsheet programs, among others. Additionally, subparts of products, which in many cases could be products in and of themselves, for example, dispatchers, resource managers, access methods, or functional algorithms, are also candidates in our thinking.

When we finally net the candidate products list, more program types are included for usability consideration than are excluded. Indeed, any program or program part that interfaces with the user is subject to human factors analysis. Programs that only interface to programs or to hardware are not of interest.

5.1.2 Are All Users the Same?

All people are not the same, therefore, we must assume that for any given program not all users will be the same. The questions are: (1) how different can we expect the users of a program to be? and (2) how different are the users from the general population? Alphonse Chapanis in his lectures somewhat jocularly states that 50 percent of all people are below average intelligence. This is fact. It is irrefutable. All populations of reasonable size take on a normal or bell-shaped distribution for a measured attribute. Intelligence is one such attribute. Some users will be exceptionally capable, some will have extreme difficulties, and most will be about as capable as we expected. We need to account for user differences in our program interface, otherwise we should not be surprised if some users do things which we never anticipated or for which we never designed. The results in these instances may be problems which work against the user's interests.

The earliest users of software were actually the people who developed the software; that is, engineers, mathematicians, and scientists. Their programs were complex, and, in our terms, probably difficult to use, but these people were comfortable with the complex interfaces to the products they developed. Unfortunately, many of these early habits were carried over to the programmers who inherited unusable programs as their base and who learned from their predecessors' difficult-to-use programs.

Martin [MART73] lists a number of major categories of operators, that is, users, who may use terminals for interactive dialogs. Unless the software designer is aware of which user or set of users may engage in a dialog with a product, the opportunity of satisfying usability requirements, stated or not, will be decreased.

For example, the needs of an experienced operator are different from those of a casual operator who spends most of the day doing something other than using the terminal. An operator who has programming skills will be more comfortable with certain operations than would a nonprogrammer. Martin makes a point in stating that "when a programmer is designing the terminal dialog, he must be careful not to associate his own skills with those of the proposed operator."

An operator or user with high intelligence will perform differently, and, in turn, will be more at ease with certain tasks and operations than would a less qualified user. This may be a sensitive issue, but it is real. Likewise, an operator who has had detailed training will undoubtedly perform better and probably expect a different dialog structure than one who is untrained.

The focus of control in an operator-computer relationship depends on who initiates the work. Martin suggests that if the operator initiates the work, then the operator may be classed as "active." If the operator is present only to serve the machine, then he is a "slave" operator. Some operators have other things to do, but do take some actions initiated by the computer. These operators are classified as "passive." Still other operators intercept invalid, unprocessable, or questionable transactions. Martin classes these as "intercept" operators. Finally, there are operators who are present to bridge a gap between the computer and an end user, such as management, through a telecommunications link. These are classed as "intermediary" operators. In some environments the operator will function in a number of these classes. Key here is that the different operators or user types have been identified. This is an important step in human factors analysis.

All of these operators have different needs which must be satisfied through the dialog facility provided to them. Figure 63 on page 143 shows a summary of these categories. Unless the operators are clearly identified, the dialog designer might either overdesign or underdesign a solution, either of which outcome might cause irritation or problems to the users. The first step in designing a dialog is to determine the category of operators who will use it. Successful dialogs will differ between a "dedicated" and "casual" operator, between a trained and untrained operator, between an operator with or without programming skills, and between high and average IQ operators. Knowing who the user is in specific terms is important to human factors analysis and the usability of the product.

5.1.3 The Objectives of Usability

In a nutshell, the objectives of usability are to ensure that the product is easy to learn, easy to use productively, easy to recover when an error is made by the user, and finally more likely to leave the user satisfied with the product.

This suggests four main aspects of usability that must be addressed for a product.

1. The effort to learn or relearn a task

2. The effort to perform a learned task

3. The effect of errors while doing a task

4. User satisfaction

These four aspects may have detailed specific objectives based on the product under analysis. Schneier suggests that the following need to be addressed [SCHN85]:

1. The effort to learn or relearn a task should be minimized.

   a. The number of concepts the user must understand in order to use the system should be minimized.

   b. Communications to and from the system should be self-evident.

			Operator with programming skills		Operator with high IQ		Operator without high IQ		
			With detailed training	With little training	With detailed training	With little training	With detailed training	With little training	Totally untrained operator
			1	2	3	4	5	6	7
Dedicated	Active	A							
	Passive	B							
	Slave	C							
	Intercept	D							
	Intermediary	E							
Casual	Active	F							
	Passive	G							
	Slave	H							
	Intercept	I							
	Intermediary	J							

Figure 63. Categories of Terminal Operators (from Martin)

c. The product should be as similar as possible to other system products used by the user.

d. The amount of documentation that must be read to use the system should be minimized.

e. The documentation should be understandable to the user, retrievable when it is needed, and sufficient for the task at hand.

2. The effort to perform a learned task should be minimized.

   a. It should be easy to remember what was learned about using the system from session to session.

   b. The user interface should be as convenient to the user as possible.

   c. Program outputs should be readily available when needed.

   d. Program outputs should be readily understandable by the intended users.

3. The effect of errors while doing a task should be minimized.

   a. It should be difficult to make errors.

b. When errors are made, it should be easy to recover.

4. The user should find the system pleasant to use and feel productive.

a. The user should feel positively about the product.

b. The user should feel productive.

Figure 64 on page 145 encapsulates these aspects of usability in a simple chart checklist form. Here it is suggested that first it is important to identify who the users are, then it is necessary to define the tasks which these users will perform with the product. Only after these two steps have been accomplished can further usability analysis be done on the product. This chart once completed for a product should be used as input to all usability verifications.

5.1.4 New Versus Existing Products

Just as it is sometimes easier to create a new building than to repair an old one, it is easier to apply usability objectives to a new product than it is to try to add usability to an existing product. This is not to suggest that it cannot be done for old or existing products. It can. It simply may cost more than if it had been done right the first time.

User feedback on existing products should be used to determine how evolutionary usability enhancements will be made. Other factors such as cost, migration difficulty, or performance may militate, even from the users perspective, against the overhauling of a product's external interface. Once a user has made an investment in working with a product as it was originally designed, it may be difficult to change to a new external interface.

If a product cannot be dramatically changed in the interest of usability, there are smaller or evolutionary changes which can be made [SCHN85]. For example:

- Provide additional documentation which might prove beneficial to certain user sets.

- Rewrite messages.

- Reduce the number of steps to perform a task.

- Change defaults to match what most users do repeatedly.

- Make defaults user controllable.

- Remove potential error situations or make it more difficult for the user to make a mistake.

- Provide a full panel front-end for an existing command.

- Provide more help capabilities.

ASPECT / PRODUCT or PRODUCT PART	WHO IS THE USER	TASKS	EFFORT REQUIRED TO LEARN A TASK				
			HOW MANY NEW CONCEPTS	HOW MUCH INFORMATION TO LEARN	HOW EASY TO UNDERSTAND	HOW SIMILAR IN COMMUNICATION	HOW NATURAL TO COMMUNICATE

ASPECT / PRODUCT or PRODUCT PART	EFFORT REQUIRED TO PERFORM A TASK					EFFORT TO MAKE RECOVERY FROM ERRORS		
	HOW MUCH INPUT TO ASSIMILATE	HOW MUCH OUTPUT PRODUCED	HOW LONG WILL IT TAKE	HOW MANY STEPS/ ACTIVITIES/ DECISIONS	WHAT SKILL LEVEL	HOW DIFFICULT TO MAKE	HOW OBVIOUS IS ERROR	HOW CONVENIENT TO RECOVER

Figure 64. Usability Aspects and Evaluation Criteria

5.1.5 Cause of User Error

A primary cause of user error is providing the wrong interface to the user. For example, Martin [MART73] lists 23 techniques to consider for alphanumeric keyboard displays as shown in Figure 65 on page 146. If the systems analyst who leads the design of a product incorrectly chooses one of these techniques for the products' intended audience, then it should not be a surprise to learn that the users are having difficulty with realtime terminal conversation or that they are incurring a high incidence of error. The best choice is dependent on identifying the user types for the product.

Murphy's law states, if it can happen, it will; that is, if the user can make an error, the user will make an error. We cannot prevent the user from blatant misuse, but we can develop a product which will help the user to recover. Some potential user error aspects to which we should pay particular attention are [SCHN85]:

1. Making it difficult for a user to make a critical error. For example on DELETEs or CANCELs, we should not allow abbreviations, and we should reverify with the user after each of these commands has been initiated.

```
 1. Simple query

 2. Mnemonic techniques

 3. English language techniques

 4. Programming-like statements

 5. Action-code systems

 6. Multiple action-code systems

 7. Building up a record on the screen

 8. Scroll technique

 9. Simple instruction to operator

10. Multiple instruction to operator

11. Menu selection

12. Multiscreen menu

13. Telephone directory technique

14. Multipart menu

15. Multianswer menu

16. Use of displayed formats

17. Variable-length multiple entry

18. Multiple-format statements

19. Form filling

20. Overwriting

21. Panel modification techniques

22. Text editing techniques

23. Hybrid dialog
```

Figure 65. Techniques for Alphanumeric Keyboard Displays (from Martin)

2. Typing errors should be correctable without retyping the complete line.

3. Error messages should suggest a recovery action.

4. Consider highlighting error messages for easy identification.

5. Error messages should be issued as soon as the error is made and detected after the user has completed a request.

6. User confusion should be anticipated at every level of interface, and the user should in all cases have a way to get help, recover, or exit safely to a known point.

7. The user should always know what state his session is in and the state name should imply how he got there.

5.2 How to Approach Usability

There are two primary requirements that need to be fulfilled if the problem of usability is to be addressed and successfully achieved for a product. First is managing for usability, and second is designing for usability. Managing for usability requires a continued and directed focus for the life of the development project. Designing for usability is equally important because, of all the process stages where usability can go astray, the most likely is here.

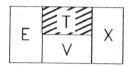

5.2.1 Managing for Usability

It is nearly impossible to add in or retrofit usability to an existing product in such a way as to be competitive and satisfy customers. It is more effective to manage and design it in from the start.

Nickel [NICK82] states that usability must be explicitly managed throughout the development of a product, and that lack of usability is generally due to the following causes:

1. Lack of awareness by developers

2. Lack of front end planning

3. Lack of a consistent strategy

4. Lack of design techniques

5. Lack of evaluation during development

Schneier suggests that these causes can be effectively addressed by doing the following:

1. Define usability for the product.

2. Get a management commitment to usability.

3. Sensitize the developers to usability.

4. Plan for usability.

5. Design for usability.

6. Evaluate usability throughout product development.

Let us explore each of these briefly.

Define usability for the product.

As the term "usable" is somewhat open to interpretation, it becomes mandatory that there be a clear definition for the product and that it be made visible to all members of the product team early in the development cycle. It should be written into the product objectives so it cannot be debated later, and it should be measurable. For example, it is one thing to say that the product is easy to learn and another to state that the user as defined in the product specification should be able to learn the product and successfully use it after ten hours of study or training. Be specific; be quantitative.

Get a management commitment to usability.

Management is often more committed to a function if there is a market requirement for it. However, usability is often not viewed as function. Treat usability as any other product function. The first step is to determine what the product's usability requirements may be. These should then be compared and ranked for value against other functions or product requirements. If usability has a high priority, then the product manager must assign responsibility to a specific individual or group to make it happen. If this is not done, then it is "no one's" responsibility and it will be relegated to the back burner of things to do for the product. Eventually it may fall off the burner of things included in the product release contents.

Sensitize the developers to usability.

Not all the programmers on the project will be involved with user interfaces, but of those who will be, the following should be made available to them:

1. Classes in usability and human factors techniques.

2. Hands-on experience with similar products.

3. Contact with existing or potential users.

Plan for usability.

It is one thing for a development team to say they want usability in their product, and another to make it happen. Two essential major process tasks must be completed in order to make it happen as desired.

First, there must be a usability statement in the objectives document and it must be carried forward through all of the design specification documents. At a minimum, this statement should include the following: the user sets, the tasks they will perform with the product, how usability by task will be measured, and against which criteria each task will be measured.

Second, there should be a separate usability plan which should describe [SCHN85]

- The usability organization, that is, who has the responsibility to ensure and measure the product's usability?

- Sensitivity/awareness plan, that is, how will the product organization be made aware of and educated in usability?

- Product externals definition plan, that is, what are the checkpoints for the user interface to be defined and refined?

- Usability measurement plan, that is, what and how will the product usability be measured?

- Schedules, checkpoints, and key dependencies on other product development activities

Design for usability.

A good, usable product must be designed from the users' perspective and that perspective must be designed into the product from the very beginning. This does not mean it will not change. Indeed, the users' perspective may change in different ways and degrees throughout the project cycle, but in so doing, each change should add to the ease of use of the product. The designers must be aware of the practical usability goals and must ensure the design is working within those goals.

Evaluate usability throughout product development.

Even though usability is defined at the beginning of the product, its evaluation must continue throughout the development cycle. To do otherwise would be to assume that the first impressions of the required user interfaces were complete and correct. This initial insight is rarely fully correct. We will address in 5.3, "How to Evaluate Usability" on page 153 of this chapter a number of ways to evaluate usability.

5.2.2 Designing with Usability in Mind

Just as with any other function in a product, usability will evolve from the "what needs to be done" stage during requirements analysis to the "how it will be done" stages of design. Therefore, given that we have a statement of the user characteristics and an enumeration of tasks the user will perform while using the product, we can then proceed to evolve our design with usability in mind.

We will need to define the sequence of steps which the user must follow to accomplish each task. These steps should be validated with users. Next, we need to determine how each type of user will interact with the product at each step and evaluate the decision requirements along these lines for design [PETE80].

If there is more than one form in which the user can interact with a product type, as in the case of dialogs, this will have to be decided at design time, as each form carries with it different design constraints. For example, different types of display hardware require different design decisions and capabilities. Which of the previously mentioned 23 dialog interfaces is chosen will determine different design constraints.

Once all the relevant decisions have been made on the design or "how it will be done," the designers should get their view validated by a user review or through a prototype. Thus, we see that the ETVX paradigm is a part of the usability function, also. These reviews will offer new insights which will then have to be incorporated into the design. For example, Martin [MART73] gives a more detailed view of the possible steps which might be used in a dialog design. Note that there are iterative steps during this design, suggesting that it is unlikely to get it all right the first time in the design. See Figure 66 on page 151.

The key factor to keep in mind during the Design stages is that the user involvement with the product and the steps the user must follow to complete a task *must* be appropriate to the intended user. To design a task sequence for a sophisticated or expert user when most users will be naive to the product can only lead to failure for the product or to serious user dissatisfaction. In terms of being appropriate, the users' working language should be used, not the programmers.

The best laid plans of mice and programmers often go astray, so it is important to understand and admit that users will make some errors. Some will use the product only for the reasons it was developed and will use it as documented, but many will evolve their own sequence of steps in performing a task. Some of these users will cause the program either to fail or to work other than expected, other than designed, or other that the initial requirements stated. In these situations, the product must be tolerant of errors. This is a design decision. How fault tolerant the product will be is ultimately determined by other factors such as

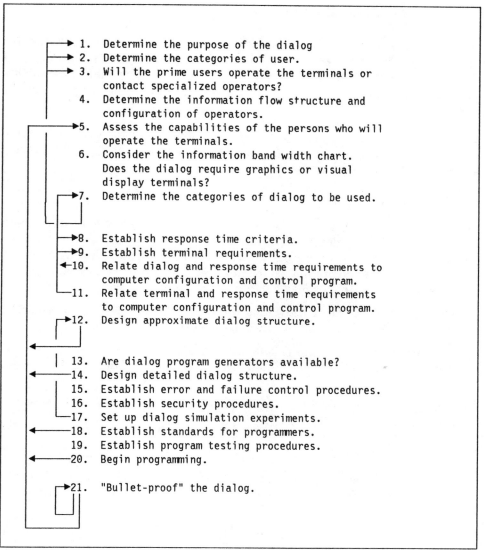

1. Determine the purpose of the dialog
2. Determine the categories of user.
3. Will the prime users operate the terminals or contact specialized operators?
4. Determine the information flow structure and configuration of operators.
5. Assess the capabilities of the persons who will operate the terminals.
6. Consider the information band width chart. Does the dialog require graphics or visual display terminals?
7. Determine the categories of dialog to be used.

8. Establish response time criteria.
9. Establish terminal requirements.
10. Relate dialog and response time requirements to computer configuration and control program.
11. Relate terminal and response time requirements to computer configuration and control program.
12. Design approximate dialog structure.

13. Are dialog program generators available?
14. Design detailed dialog structure.
15. Establish error and failure control procedures.
16. Establish security procedures.
17. Set up dialog simulation experiments.
18. Establish standards for programmers.
19. Establish program testing procedures.
20. Begin programming.

21. "Bullet-proof" the dialog.

Figure 66. Possible Steps in Dialog Design (from Martin)

cost and performance, but the question needs to be asked during design. There are various techniques that the designer can choose from to improve fault tolerance, including:

- checking for valid input

- designing recovery routines for detected errors

- continuing to operate in a degraded mode

5.2.3 Measuring Usability

As we set the objectives for usability in a product, it helps to quantify how the objectives will be measured. If we do not quantify the usability objectives, we cannot be assured we have satisfied them. If we cannot quantify the usability objectives, they may be vague or fuzzy objectives which need to be restated or clarified.

The three aspects of usability noted in the section on the Objectives of Usability (5.1.3) need to be addressed to bring quantification to our objectives [SCHN85]. Some examples of areas in which objectives may be set are:

Effort required to leave a task

- How many new concepts must the user learn? The percentage of pages in the documentation describing conceptual information is one way to measure the volume of new concepts. Fewer pages may indicate fewer concepts to learn. Another indication is the number of options needed to use the product. Fewer options may indicate fewer concepts to learn.

- Length of training time: How long will it take the average user to be able to use the product? This is best measured with real users.

- Automatic use time: How long will it take the average user to use the product with proficiency, without hesitation, and without dependence on documentation?

- Information to be read: How many pages of documentation must be read in order to accomplish a task.

Efforts required to perform a task

- Number of irrelevant actions required: How many activities must a user perform which are irrelevant to the task? An example would be deciphering a message that is not clearly stated.

- Time and frequency to warm up: How long will it take a casual user to relearn the skill to perform a task?

- Decision-making time: How long does it take to respond to status which requires a decision?

Effort to recover from errors

- Number of errors: How many errors might the average user be expected to make per unit of time? The more complicated the interface, the higher the probability of error.

- Cost to recover from errors: How much time, how many operations, and what is the cost in resources for the user to recover from an error? Common errors should have a minimum recovery cost.

These are only examples. Specifics of what should be measured for usability of a product are particular to the product. Key is that some measure of usability is planned and executed. If it is not planned, it probably will not occur.

5.3 How to Evaluate Usability

If a decision has been made to focus on usability in a product, then it is essential that the chosen way to achieve this usability must be validated or verified, otherwise, all might have been for naught. The following paragraphs describe ways for evaluating product usability. We will explore each in detail in subsequent chapter sections.

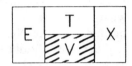

Of the major ways to evaluate usability in software, user involvement is first and foremost. In the long run this is the least costly and to many extents the most valid approach as it involves the user in the product objectives. The user involvement should be structured, valid user representation should exist, and the data from the user review does require analysis.

Prototyping can be a valuable technique for obtaining user feedback on a proposed design. In some environments it might also be fairly expensive, but this really depends on the complexities of the product. Not all products can be easily prototyped, so economics and alternatives need to be evaluated. The key to prototyping is not to be tempted to convert it into the product, but rather to use it as a part of the process in developing the product.

Usability laboratories are typically expensive because they require special facilities and equipment. In some cases a fair amount of evaluation can be accomplished with a less sophisticated laboratory environment.

Testing for usability also can be expensive. The cost to perform usability testing is determined by the type of product. The user should be involved in the test where possible. Testing for usability is the last possible time in the development cycle to verify for usability, and it is usually too late to fix all but trivial unanticipated problems. It should be used in conjunction with other validation and verification methods rather than as the only method.

In the area of documentation, there are various readability indices which are immediately applicable to evaluate usability.

Let us now discuss each of these approaches to evaluating usability.

5.3.1 User Involvement

To ensure that the product will meet the users' needs once it has been determined that a need for the product exists, the product development process should be structured to allow for as much user interfacing as can be managed prior to product delivery.   This basically means that the user should be involved throughout the development cycle, if it is possible for the user to participate.

Prior to the Requirements stage, user comments will be analyzed to determine what requirements, usability or otherwise, are needed to be satisfied in the product.   Once these have been determined, the ranked list of the product's requirements should be verified with a valid subset of users.   In some situations, as with new product types, this may not be as fruitful to the product since the user market may not be fully prepared to assess the product.   For the vast majority of products, the users have some feelings about what they want or would like to see in the product.   In some instances, the product development team may have to establish legal nondisclosure agreements with the users to protect proprietary product information.

Users should be involved in viewing and reviewing the prototype.   The prototype is the first time the user gets to see something that looks like the product.

User guides for products should be reviewed by the users as soon as they are available which should be as soon as possible after closure on the Requirements stage.   In some instances the user guides may not be available until design is well under way.   The reviews will validate that the users and developers are in agreement on the problem to be solved and how it is proposed to be solved.

Later, when the product is in test, users can be invited to see how the product actually performs.   Although this is late in the cycle, it is better to catch a problem here than after the product is shipped to the users.

Finally, the product, after it has completed all tests and validations inside the product shop, should be installed in actual user environments prior to general availability to a larger population of users.

While it is important to involve users where appropriate to ensure the product will meet user needs, the product team must be in control of the development, and should not allow the user to cause indiscriminate changes to product directions, or allow the user to become involved to the point where there is product development interference such that the commitments can not be satisfied. In some situations this is a fine line and must be watched continuously.

5.3.2 Usability Prototyping

A *usability* prototype is a stripped down functional representation of the product. It mimics the external view of the product, but typically has different internals. It is not the product, it should not evolve directly into the product, and it is done as fast as possible with minimal resources. If this premise is accepted, then it must also be accepted that the prototype will not handle most run time aspects, such as error situations. As designers, we will have to make the decision on how much function will be implemented in the prototype for error processing. For example, we will probably not allow all possible input conditions, nor will all inputs be checked for validity.

The prototype for usability is concerned with the "what" aspects of the product, not the "how" aspects. This is to say that as long as the interfaces between the user and the product are visible, we do not really care what mechanisms are used to hold those external manifestations together. Certainly the prototype internals may affect response time or performance in a degraded fashion, but if we can ignore this for the time being, we can treat the prototype exactly as if it were functionally the product. Therefore, it can be determined early in the product cycle whether particular user interfaces through commands, messages, PF keys, screen formats, and HELP facilities are doing what we and the user expect and want.

Additionally, the prototype can help us to evaluate alternatives in the design of a user interface where we do not know which is a better or preferred way of interfacing to the user. This is especially important in new products, but is also useful where we want to make evolutionary changes in existing products but want to minimize user disruption.

5.3.3 Usability Laboratories

Usability laboratories have been designed such that a volunteer user can be observed and monitored while using a product. Typically this requires an isolation room with cameras, other recording equipment, and one-way mirrors to allow the observer to have immediate but disconnected involvement with the subject user.

Hirsch [HIRS81] describes procedures used at one usability laboratory to evaluate human factors for hardware and software products. Important to note, as Hirsch does, is how complex and considerable in time it is to effectively establish a good experimental mode in which to evaluate a software product. The example he addresses is a programming language. "It took nearly a year of program development to reach the point where evaluation could begin, even on an elementary level." We can suspect that much of this is part of the learning curve on how to apply usability evaluations to software in a controlled laboratory environment, but the cost of the laboratories is still nontrivial.

Another primary factor leading to this high start-up cost for laboratory evaluation is that alternatives must be built into the evaluation process in order to determine which of a series of approaches might work best for a product.

Usability laboratories and the procedures used during evaluation in those environments still are in their early stages of maturity. Despite great progress, much is yet to be documented and much more is yet to be learned on how best to use this approach.

5.3.4 Testing

Usability testing is best performed during the System Verification Test stage, although some testing can effectively be done in the Functional Verification Test stage and with a prototype if one is available. As with other functions that will be tested, it is essential that exit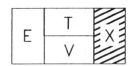
criteria in the form of acceptable levels of usability be defined in the test plans and based on the objectives documented at the beginning of the project. Test criteria in general must have the aspect of measurability, otherwise the interpretation of success or failure is debatable, and, therefore, vulnerable to dynamic change during the development cycle.

There might be a separate usability test plan if it is warranted, but there is most certainly a usability section to the general test plans for each of the test stages.

Chapanis [CHAP81] states that usability testing must be carefully planned in advance to ensure valid results, and that the following should be included:

- Define what you mean by usability.

- Define the target populations.

- Select a random, or representative, sample of test subjects from the target population.

- Decide on the purpose of the test.

- Select an appropriate testing methodology.

- Determine what tasks the subjects should perform.

- Decide on the appropriate usability measurements.

- Set up the testing facilities.

- Do a pilot test.

- Conduct the test.

- Analyze the results.

If test subjects are more "user-like," the results are likely to be more meaningful. The three main populations in descending order of preference are [SCHN85]:

1. End users or customers of the product

2. Programmers not familiar with this product

3. Screened programmers who role-play as users

There is no one way to completely test usability for all products. The methods chosen should be documented and justified in the test plan and validated as the best approach during the test plan inspection. Since some of these methods require considerable lead time, this is an important reason why the test plan needs to be completed early in the Product Level Design stage.

Methods which have been successfully used during Function and System Verification Tests include:

1. Attitude questionnaires—this is highly subjective, but can serve to highlight issues when a repeated problem is noted across various users.

2. Controlled experiments—this is the most scientific approach but comes with a high lead time and cost.

3. Task level reviews which map the user and tasks against what the user and the product do in completing a task function [THOR81].

4. Walk-throughs—here the "testers" performing the walk-through try to play the user role.

5. User-oriented testing—this is most real when it takes place in an actual user environment, but at best can happen only at the end of System Verification Test, which may be too late if there is a major usability problem. A prototype will permit some earlier testing with the user. Together with other early approaches, System Verification Test offers the most accurate data to completely evaluate usability.

5.3.5 Readability Indices

Up to this point we have been primarily concerned with product programs. However, the first thing the user typically sees is documentation, not the actual product. Most user documentation leaves much to be desired, and one can rightfully wonder whether there are any repeatable ways to make it easier to read. There are a number of existing indices and methods that can be used to measure reading difficulty of a document or even a written passage. These include:

1. Flesch Reading Ease Score [FLES75]

   The procedure to measure readability is:

   a. Select three samples of 100 words each.

   b. Count the number of complete sentences in each 100-word sample. (The last sentence in the sample is the one that ends closest to the 100-word mark, for example, on the 94th word or the 107th word.) Compute the average sentence length over the three samples.

   c. Count the total number of syllables in each sample, and again average it over the three samples.

   d. Mark the average sentence length and the average number of syllables on the Flesch Reading Ease Chart Figure 67 on page 159 and draw a straight line to connect the two points. The intersection of the line with the center line on the chart gives the reading ease score and its corresponding reading grade level.

2. Fry Readability Score [FRY77]

   The procedure is as follows:

   a. Select three samples of 100 words each.

   b. Count the number of sentences in each sample, estimating the length of the fraction of the of the last sentence to the nearest one-tenth. Compute the average sentence length over the three samples.

   c. Count the total number of syllables in each sample and again average it over the three samples.

   d. Use the Fry Readability Graph Figure 68 on page 160 to plot the intersection of the average sentence length with the average number of syllables. The area of the graph in which this intersection point falls will give the approximate reading grade level.

3. Forecast Reading Level Formula [SCHN85]

   The procedure is:

   a. Select a 150-word sample.

   b. Count the number of one-syllable words in the example.

   c. Divide this number by 10.

   d. Subtract the result from 20 to obtain the estimated reading grade level.

4. The Fog Index [SCHN85]

   a. Take a sample of at least 100 words. Determine the average number of words per sentence.

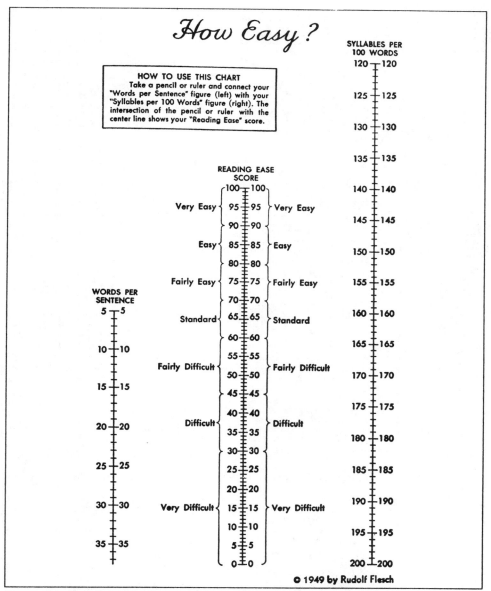

Figure 67. Flesch Reading Ease Chart

b. Count the number of polysyllables (words of three syllables or more) per 100 words. Omit capitalized words, combinations of short easy words like *manpower* and verbs made into three syllables by adding *-es* or *-ed*.

c. Add the average number of words per sentence to the pollysyllable count and multiply the sum by 0.4. Round to the nearest integer. Since few

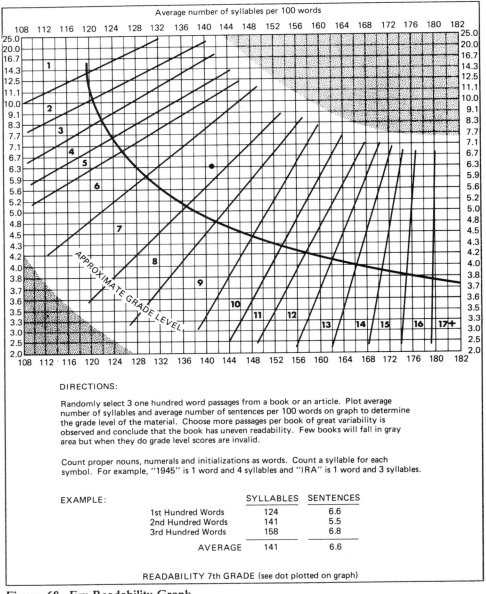

Figure 68. Fry Readability Graph

The image above contains the following labels and text:

Average number of syllables per 100 words

Top/bottom axis: 108 112 116 120 124 128 132 136 140 144 148 152 156 160 164 168 172 176 180 182

Left axis: 25.0 20.0 16.7 14.3 12.5 11.1 10.0 9.1 8.3 7.7 7.1 6.7 6.3 5.9 5.6 5.2 5.0 4.8 4.5 4.3 4.2 4.0 3.8 3.7 3.6 3.5 3.3 3.0 2.5 2.0

Right axis: 25.0 20.0 16.7 14.3 12.5 11.1 10.0 9.1 8.3 7.7 7.1 6.7 6.3 5.9 5.6 5.2 5.0 4.8 4.5 4.3 4.2 4.0 3.8 3.7 3.6 3.5 3.3 3.0 2.5 2.0

Curve labels: 1 2 3 4 5 6 7 8 9 10 11 12 13 14 15 16 17+

APPROXIMATE GRADE LEVEL

DIRECTIONS:

Randomly select 3 one hundred word passages from a book or an article. Plot average number of syllables and average number of sentences per 100 words on graph to determine the grade level of the material. Choose more passages per book of great variability is observed and conclude that the book has uneven readability. Few books will fall in gray area but when they do grade level scores are invalid.

Count proper nouns, numerals and initializations as words. Count a syllable for each symbol. For example, "1945" is 1 word and 4 syllables and "IRA" is 1 word and 3 syllables.

EXAMPLE:		SYLLABLES	SENTENCES
	1st Hundred Words	124	6.6
	2nd Hundred Words	141	5.5
	3rd Hundred Words	158	6.8
	AVERAGE	141	6.6

READABILITY 7th GRADE (see dot plotted on graph)

readers have more than 17 years of schooling, a passage yielding a number greater than 17 is assigned a Fog index of 17 plus.

5.4 User Interfaces

We will explore here some of the interfaces between a user and a software product. These interfaces are the primary usability concern with most users as it is through these interfaces that the user works with the product.

5.4.1 Commands

Commands are the means by which the user is given authorized access to the facilities provided by a program. Commands initiate an action or set an environment parameter or state, and as such the frequently required commands should be easy to initiate. Likewise, actions which may cause abnormal and undesired situations should be difficult to initiate, if not prevented.

It is easier for a user to remember a small number of generic commands than many specific commands [MILL77]. It is preferred, for example, in the order shown, to provide the interfaces as shown in Figure 69.

```
1.  Single command:
        LIST, where the system determines the data set type
                to be listed.
2.  Single generic command with parameters:
        LIST POS or CAT or SEQ, where a choice of data set types is
                under user control through one command name.
3.  Separate commands
        a.  LISTPOS
        b.  LISTCAT
        c.  LISTSEQ
                where three different commands are required.
```

Figure 69. Three Different Forms for a LIST Command

There are natural user aspects that commands should address, for example [SMIT81]:

1. Users remember meaningful mnemonics better for commands.

2. Frequently used commands should have one to two character abbreviations.

3. Commands with serious or nonrecoverable effects should not have abbreviations.

4. Make abbreviations as distinctive as possible from other abbreviations, to avoid confusion.

5. For abbreviations, drop end letters rather than front or middle letters unless another abbreviation is commonplace (for example, MGR vs. MAN; CPU vs. COM).

5.4.2 Messages

Messages function as the primary way the product responds to user actions or informs the user of status of product processing. Yet messages are often relegated to a class of trivial function and as a result are given improper focus which leads to poor communication with the user. The end result is an unsatisfied user. We were once told by a large account user's operator, "If your programmers had told me what they really meant in this message (an example) we would not have had to work until three this morning trying to fix a problem."

Messages, while typically short, can carry a big effect, and therefore, we should want them to present our products always in the best of light to the users. Some aspects which we should be very mindful of are shown in Figure 70 on page 163.

Messages in general should tell the user what to do next rather than only what is wrong.

5.4.3 PF Keys

Program function keys allow, with a single keystroke, the entry of a function request. To our minds, there are not enough of them. They are quick and one cannot misspell them; however, they can be misused. Thus, if it is too easy to hit the wrong key to invoke a function, then a usability problem exists.

The following guidelines should be considered [SMIT81]:

1. PF keys should be used for fast frequent commands.

2. PF key definitions should be consistent with other products.

3. PF key definitions should be located easily on the screen.

4. PF keys should be user definable for experts.

PF keys should be used for frequent commands and never for infrequent commands.

1. Messages should be self-explanatory.

   EXAMPLE: XX 000I AE1, I0E, 03, 0200,400000000000,,,TCAMBLOC

   may have all the information needed, but it is unreadable and
   intimidating, and therefore, not a good message for communication
   with the user.

2. Messages should help the user with the task he is trying to do.
   Do not give too much or too little information for required
   actions to be taken by the user.

3. Messages should be sent only to those who need to see them.

4. Messages should describe unique situations. Do not mix or clump
   several situations into one message.

5. A message should be explicitly accurate for the conditions under
   which it is sent. For example:

   IXX730 Data Set XXXXXXXXX NOT FOUND

   should only be issued under not found conditions, not
   under conditions where the data set could not be read
   for some reason.

6. Consider multiple level messages for multiple skill users.

7. Message format should be consistent across the product.

8. Error messages should tell the user what is wrong and should
   suggest the next action for the user to take.

9. Message style should be factual and nonthreatening.

10. Message length should be balanced with the frequency of its display.

11. Message should be self-contained or explicitly refer to a manual
    for further explanation.

12. Messages should use the language of the user, that is, English,
    French, and so on.

Figure 70. Aspects to Consider for Messages

5.4.4 Screen Formats

Screen formats are what the user sees more than any other part of the product, and therefore, they should present the product in its best light to the user. A consistent user interface should be presented to the users across products. To this end, there are some guidelines that will help [SCHN85] [PETE80]:

1. The screen should have a title.

2. Provide context information, if the screen is part of a larger body of information.

3. Make it obvious what to do on the screen.

4. Screens should have consistent layouts across panels.

5. Screens should be simple and uncluttered.

6. Menus should clearly list all possible responses.

7. Text paragraphs should be separated by at least one blank line.

8. There should be a maximum 50 to 55 characters per line of running text.

9. Formats should be organized to minimize cursor movement.

10. Scrolling functions should refer to the user's view of the data.

11. Highlighting should be

    a. used to help the user.

    b. consistent.

    c. used for objective reasons, not because you like it.

    d. used conservatively.

12. Capitalization should be avoided unless necessary.

13. Fast paths should be available to expert users.

14. Color should be used to help communicate with the user.

5.4.5 Computer Assisted Instruction (CAI)

Computer assisted instruction has been around since 1966, and while it is not an aspect of user interface similar to others we have discussed, it is relevant because the increasing population of people who are receiving instruction through this type of facility.

There are five major types of CAI programs [MART73]:

1. *Tutorial*—where material is presented and then questions are asked of the user.

2. *Drill and Practice*—where skills are taught through repetitive actions.

3. *Problem Solving*—where a student user can discuss results to assigned problems through various levels of help capability.

4. *Socratic Dialog or Expert Systems*—where the program "behaves" with near-human intelligence during a question dialog.

5. *Simulation*—where student users interact with a program which simulates some physical environment.

In all of these situations, the user requires immediate feedback. The responses should be complete, nonthreatening, and not cute or irritating to the user. Depending on the mode of input/output, the guidelines noted in earlier sections should be followed for CAI programs.

5.4.6 Response Time

Response time is an important attribute of most user interfaces. It represents the interval between the last user keyed input and the system response to that input.

A number of studies have demonstrated that as the response time improves, so too does the user's productivity [THAD81] [MILL67] [SCHN85].

Clearly not all keyed input should receive the same response. Indeed, the user does not expect the same response time for all requests, but the user does have a level of expectation which is determined by the type of requested function. An acceptable response for different types of requests follows [MILL67] [MART73]:

Maximum Acceptable Response Times

- 0.1 second

  - Response to key press—there should be feedback to the user that the system has understood the physical activation of a key, switch, or other movable part of a control panel. The click of a typewriter key when pressed, or the movement of a crosshair on a screen when a joystick is manipulated should be almost instantaneous.

- 0.1 second

  - Drawing with a light pen—as a light pen is drawing lines, the image should immediately appear on the screen.

- 0.5 second

- Trivial transactions—a request for a simple action (for example, many editing subtasks) should be responded to almost immediately. If the user notices, the response is too slow.

- 0.5 to 1 second

  - Request for next page—if the user is searching for an item which may occur on any of several pages, it should take no longer than 0.5 second to turn pages. If the user is reading text from a page, it should take no more than one second for the first few lines of the next page to appear on the screen. The user should be able to skip several pages with the same response time as skipping to the next page.

- 1 second

  - Entry selection via light pen—since it is easier for a nontypist to select an entry from a list of choices with a light pen, the user will expect a fast response from the system. If the user is creating graphics by selecting forms from a menu of acceptable choices, response time of one second is acceptable.

- 1 to 2 seconds

  - Response to "Can the system do work for me?"—a simple or routing request should be completed in normal conversational speed, about a second (two seconds maximum).

- 1 to 3 seconds

  - Response to "Is the system listening?"—a telephone dial tone tells the user that the system is able to provide service, and should respond with the selected information within three seconds.

- 2 seconds

  - Response to selection from a list of information—if the user has selected a record, or choice from a list or menu, the system should respond with the selected information within two seconds.

  - Response to simple status inquiry. The user usually has a simple question in mind, for example "What is the time?" Response should be given as if in normal conversation, within two seconds.

- 2 to 4 seconds

  - Error feedback following completion of input. It is disturbing to the user to be interrupted in mid-thought. If the system is scanning user input as it is being entered, it should allow the user to complete the line (for example, press the enter key) before notifying the user of the error. The user should be informed of his error after two seconds and before four seconds.

— Complex inquiry response in tabular form. A complex inquiry requires the system to collect information and construct the answer based on input from the user. A query from a relational data base is an example, "Display the names of people working in department D84." The response from the system should be within the normal conversational range of two seconds, with a maximum of four seconds.

- 2 to 10 seconds

— Graphic response to complex inquiry should begin in two seconds and be complete in twenty seconds.

- 4 seconds

— Complex response to status inquiry—If the user understands that the response will involve accessing and manipulating data, it can take a little longer; up to four seconds. An example of this type of query might be, "Give me the current order status of inventory part FG 375 258."

- 5 seconds

— A complex task involving a large degree of closure should be complete within five seconds. If the system is driving the dialog (for example, during computer assisted instruction), and the user has completed a topic or assignment, the system should provide information about the next procedure or assignment within five seconds.

- 15 seconds

— Response to "Load this program"—the loading of programs or data requested by the user should be completed within 15 seconds, (60 seconds maximum). Similarly, restarting a program or session from where the user left off the day before should be completed within 15 seconds (60 seconds maximum).

— Response to "Run this problem"—if the user has input programming statements that are processed by another component or system, the response time is variable. For example, a user has written a short program to solve a problem, or has entered formatting statements for a text processing program. Acceptable response time is influenced by how long it took to write and enter the input statements and associated data. The user will be more impatient if the results from this process are needed to continue work in a larger process.

In most applications the very short response times are predominant and account for 95 percent or more of the activity [HOGS67].

5.4.7 Help Facilities

Help facilities provide a user with access to additional information, which can be optionally selected. When it is invoked by the user, there is usually a particular immediate need, therefore, HELP should have as an objective to quickly and efficiently answer the users' questions [CLAR81A].

There are some specific aspects which HELP should provide as a capability [SCHN85] [CLAR81B]:

1. The user should always be able to invoke HELP no matter where he is in the program execution.

2. The user should be able to exit HELP with a single command and return to the environment where the user last was working.

3. HELP information should be task oriented.

4. HELP information should be located quickly and easily.

5. HELP information should be nondisruptive to the sequence execution where it is not invoked.

6. HELP PF keys should be consistent with mainline processing.

7. HELP information should be in the language of the user.

8. It should be verified that HELP is helpful.

5.4.8 Summary

Usability should be considered an essential property of the product, beginning with the Requirements stage, especially for products that have a direct interface to the user. Since not all users are the same, the product may have to be designed recognizing different user populations. The tasks which the different user types will perform should be identified. The product objectives should address (1) the effort to learn or relearn a task, (2) the effort to perform a learned task, (3) the effect of errors while doing a task, and (4) user satisfaction. Since usability is most determined by user interfaces, it is important that we choose the best interface from alternatives for any user set.

Two primary focuses must be maintained throughout the product development cycle: managing for usability and designing for usability. If we ease up on either, we may find erosion in the usability level of the product.

Usability, like any other function can be validated and verified There are a number of approaches being practiced. These include user involvement in the product, prototyping, usability laboratories, and testing for usability. For documentation there are a number of accepted readability indices used in the industry.

The dominant user interfaces we discussed in the chapter include commands, messages, PF keys, screen formats, CAI, response time, and HELP facilities.

The focus on usability must never stop during any stage of the development cycle. It is a part of the job for all programmers and managers working on and delivering products to users.

5.5 References

[CHAP81] A. Chapanis, "Evaluating Ease of Use," *Proceedings of the Software and Information Usability Symposium*, Vol. 1, Poughkeepsie, NY (September 1981), pp. 105–20.

[CLAR81A] I. A. Clark, "How to Help 'Help' Help," *Technical Report HF022*, IBM United Kingdom Laboratory, Ltd., Hursley Park, Winchester, Hampshire, United Kingdom (December 1981).

[CLAR81B] I. A. Clark, "Software Simulation as a Tool for Usable Product Design," *IBM Systems Journal*, Vol. 20, No. 3 (1981), pp. 272–93.

[FLES75] R. Flesch, *The Art of Readable Writing*, Harper and Row (1975).

[FRY77] E. Fry, "Fry's Readability Graph: Classifications, Validity, and Extensions to Level 17," *Journal of Reading* (December 1977).

[HIRS81] R. S. Hirsch, "Procedures of the Human Factors Center at San Jose," *IBM Systems Journal*, Vol. 20, No. 2 (1981).

[HOGS67] G. R. Hogsett, D. A. Nisewanger, and A. C. O'Hara, Jr., "An Application Experiment with On-Line Graphics-Aided ECAP," *Proceedings 1967, International Solid State Circuit Conference*, pp. 72–3.

[MART73] J. Martin, *Design of Man-Computer Dialogs*, Prentice-Hall (1973).

[MILL67] R. B. Miller, "Response Time in Man-Computer Conversational Transactions," *Technical Report TR00.1660*, IBM Corporation, Systems Development Division, Poughkeepsie, NY (October 1967).

[MILL77] L. A. Miller and T. C. Thomas, "Behavioral Issues in the Use of Interactive Systems," *International Journal Man-Machine Studies*, Vol. 9 (1977), pp. 509–36.

[NICK82] P. K. Nickel, S. B. Sager, and P. M. Soutter, "Usability and You—A Guide for Product Management," IBM SCD, Kingston, NY, 12401 (April 1982).

[PETE80] D. E. Peterson, "Screen Design Guidelines," IBM GSD, Rochester, MN (1980).

[SCHN80] B. Schneiderman, *Software Psychology—Human Factors in Computer and Information Systems*, Winthrop Publishers (1980).

[SCHN85] C. A. Schneier, "Usability Guidelines for Interactive Software," *IBM TR 52.001* (1985).

[SMIT81] S. L. Smith, "Man-Machine Interface Requirements Definitions and Design Guidelines," *MTR-8134*, The MITRE Corporation, Bedford, MA (February 1981).

[THAD81] A. J. Thadhani, "Interactive User Productivity," *IBM Systems Journal*, Vol. 20, No. 4 (1981), pp. 407 – 23.

[THOR81] J. H. Thornley, "Assuring the Human Factor of Software at Design Time," *Software and Information Usability Symposium Proceedings*, Vol. 2, September 15-18, 1981, Poughkeepsie, NY, pp. 69 – 76.

Additional Recommended Readings

Chapanis, A., *Man-Machine Engineering*, Brooks/Cole Publishing Company, (1965).

DeGreene, K. B., *System Psychology*, McGraw-Hill Book Company, (1920).

Dreyfuss, H., *Designing for People*, Simon and Schuster, (1955).

Gilb, T., and G. M. Weinberg, *Humanized Input — Techniques for Reliable Keyed Input*, Winthrop Publishers, (1977).

"The Humanization of Computer Interface," Special Issue, *Communications of the ACM*, Vol. 26, No. 4, (April 1983).

Meister, D., *Human Factors: Theory and Practice*, John Wiley and Sons, (1971).

Rubinstein, R., and H. Hersch, *The Human Factors*, Digital Press, (1984).

Part 3. Software Engineering Methods

Chapter 6. Planning the Project

6.1 Introduction

Planning the project begins when the feasibility of the product has been established. Once the decision to go ahead with the software development project has been made, more detailed plans are made to enable actual execution of the project and to ensure the stated product cost, schedule, and quality goals will be met. The activity occurs during the Requirements and Planning stage in our life-cycle model (see Chapter 2).

In this chapter, we will define *project planning* and identify some current planning problems in relation to the roles of various individuals involved in the planning and management process. Recommended planning methodologies and tools will be discussed. And finally, characteristics of a good project planning process will be presented.

6.2 Key Concepts of Project Planning

The basic variables involved in project planning are:

1. The end date
2. The resources available, which include consideration for
   - productivity goals
   - quality goals
3. The size and scope of the required work product

All planning starts from the assumption that any two of the above three variables are known. The planner solves for the third. Consider the following examples:

Case 1: You are given the required end date and the size of the required work product: What resources will be required to complete the job? For example, suppose a specified set of new functions were needed for delivery in a certain release of a system. How many developers would be needed on the project?

Case 2: You are given the size of the required work product and the resources available: What is the projected end date? For example, a product of known size is to be developed within a fixed resource. Will its delivery date meet the market opportunity within the time specified in the preliminary sales estimate?

Case 3: You are given the end date and the available resources: Solve for the size or scope of the work product that can be produced within those constraints. For example, a given product has accumulated a prioritized list of requirements that in total would keep the developers busy for several years. For the next release, given a fixed resource available, how many and which of the many requirements can be satisfied?

6.3 Planning Viewpoints

Planning for a project is done from several different viewpoints. For example, the planned project structure must be tailored to meet the needs of the customer requirements, business needs, technical constraints, and internal development and support capabilities. Ten basic elements were identified by Evans et al. [EVAN83]. They are shown in Figure 71 on page 174. The ten elements are in the center of the figure, starting with "Project purpose and scope," and ending with "Quality assurance provisions." Typical documents and plans that play a direct role in the planning are illustrated around the periphery.

Some secondary elements, also represented by documents, are illustrated in Figure 72 on page 175. These planning elements address the validation, testing, and project control aspects of the development process.

Another way to depict a project plan is in terms of our development process model described in Chapter 2. The total project planning spectrum encompasses all stages, activities, and viewpoints in the process. This means there are subparts of the total plan that cover one or more major activities in the process. Planning for all the subparts is initiated during the Requirements and Planning stage. Completion of each subpart depends upon the stage in which it applies or is needed. Examples of the key plan subparts are shown in Figure 73 on page 176.

In addition to each of the process stages shown in the figure, the total project plan covers the viewpoints of product publications, marketing and service, and process management.

This text discusses planning for the Requirements and Planning stage, the Design stages, and the Code stage. A subsequent volume of this text book series will discuss planning for the remainder of the development stages.

6.4 Some Typical Planning Problems

"NO MATTER WHERE YOU GO, THERE YOU ARE."

This indisputable statement is the only thing that can be said with certainty about planning. Difficulty begins when the thought is extended, as suggested by Pressman:

> If you don't know where you're going, it's exceedingly difficult to get there and nearly as difficult to determine that where you are is where you want to be. [PRES82]

A trait shared by many successful project managers and planners is the ability to anticipate where the project is going to experience trouble before it happens. In their text *Software Engineering*, Jensen and Tonies [JENS79] identify three levels of awareness in project planning and management. The levels are expressed in terms of one's ability to assess the type, amount, and structure of resources that will be required to complete a project successfully.

1. A first-level planner would define the resources needed to accomplish a task under generally ideal conditions - that is, under the assumption that planned resources will be applied efficiently, no subsequent changes will occur in the initial task definitions, and no mistakes will be made.

2. A second-level planning job will take into account some of the unavoidable uncertainties and inefficiencies in all project environments, such as allowing for sick leaves, training start-up time, lead time in acquiring needed resource and people, and finally a blanket contingency for anything that might go wrong.

3. The third, and most sophisticated, level of planning encompasses all the above, but also includes an analysis of all those things that might go wrong. The analysis is based on experience with similar situations. This level of planning makes it possible to recognize potential risk areas and trouble spots, and to apply resource and management attention to the task as it will actually manifest itself.

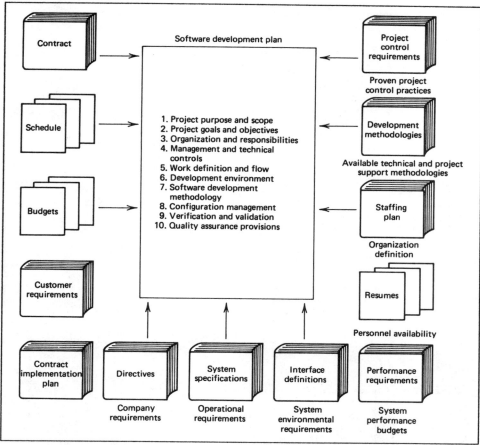

Figure 71. Software Development Plan. Reprinted with permission from *Principles of Productive Software Management [EVAN83], p. 178.*

The major cause of large project failure is inadequate planning. When programming project plans go awry, one or more basic causes show up again and again. These causes are discussed in the following sections.

6.4.1 When Size Estimates Are Inaccurate

A principal cause of project failure is failure to accurately estimate the size and scope of the project; and in turn a principal cause of this problem is lack of historical data for similar projects from which lessons can be extracted. It is essential to retain the ability for quantitatively assessing reasons why prior projects deviated from their plans. Without this, it is not possible to anticipate with any degree of confidence what might go wrong on the project currently being

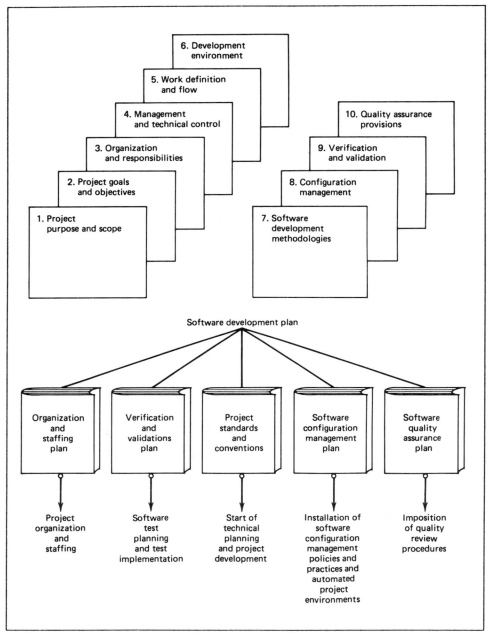

Figure 72. Second-level Planning Documents. Reprinted with permission from *Principles of Productive Software Management [EVAN83], p. 179.*

planned, why it might go wrong, and what should be built into the plan to account for the eventuality.

176   Part 3. Software Engineering Methods

- Product planning:

  - User requirements analysis
  - Product capabilities
  - Usability objectives
  - Performance objectives
  - Other CUPRIM objectives
  - Product publications objectives

- Project planning:

  - Product size estimates
  - Project resource estimates
  - Schedules
  - Staffing and skills
  - Product publications development plan
  - Process definition and management
  - Reporting and controls

- For design stages (product level, component level, module level):

  - Updated product size estimates
  - Usability review checkpoints
  - Inspection checkpoints
  - Design change control process

- For implementation stages (coding and unit testing):

  - Schedule dates for delivery of coded functions for testing
  - Inspection checkpoints
  - Unit test plans

- For testing stages (function level, product level, system level):

  - Test plans
  - Test case development staffing
  - Machine resources needed for test execution
  - Test plan review checkpoints
  - Test case Inspection checkpoints

Figure 73 (Part 1 of 2). Planning Tasks During the Requirements and Planning Stage

An inadequate tracking system on prior projects is the principal cause of these problems. An inadequate tracking system in turn is usually attributable to any of three deficiencies:

1. Insufficient use of process metrics, that is, not enough types of data are specified for collection during the project

2. Adequate metrics specified, but data is inconsistently collected during the project

```
• For Package and Validation stages (package and release, limited
  availability):

  - Release content plan
  - Program distribution plan
  - Limited availability installation and test plan

• For General Availability:

  - Service process
  - Defect reporting process
  - Fix validation process
  - Product training plan
```

Figure 73 (Part 2 of 2). Planning Tasks During the Requirements and Planning Stage

3. Inconsistent analysis and feedback of data for improving the process for the
   next project

Once underway, an early indicator that a project might be heading for trouble is a
change in the estimated size or scope of the product at each successive stage. It is
not uncommon in large commercial system projects for the number of the lines
of code actually implemented to exceed the very early size estimates by 50 percent
to 100 percent. It is critical that size projections be reevaluated and revised at
every design stage and other appropriate project checkpoints so as to converge as
rapidly as possible on sizings that will prove accurate when the code is implemented.

This lack of estimating precision can usually be traced to one or more of the following causes:

1. The magnitude of code that will be required to handle exception conditions is
   grossly underestimated in the initial product specification.

2. Requirements are not completely understood.

3. Technical complexity of the solution is not completely understood.

4. Existing design of the base product (old code) is not visible.

5. New requirements are introduced after the start of the project.

In the book, *The Mythical Man Month,* Brooks [BROO74] points out that, when
we are uncertain of our estimates, we often lack the "courteous stubbornness to
make people wait for a good product." He goes on to say that, as when a chef
makes an omelet, the urgency of the patron may govern the scheduled completion of the task, but it cannot govern the actual completion:

An omelet promised in ten minutes may appear to be progressing nicely. But when it has not set in ten minutes, the customer has two choices-- wait or eat it raw. Software customers have had the same choices. The cook has another choice: he can turn up the heat. The result is often an omelet nothing can save—burned in one part, raw in another.

6.4.2 When the Project Plan is Inadequate

Of the three basic planning variables described in 6.2, "Key Concepts of Project Planning," (i.e. the completion date, the resources available, and the size of the product), the usual consequence of poor planning is that the project completion date is placed in jeopardy, or it slips. A typical recovery response is to apply more resources or to try to push the project through anyway by shortcutting the process. All too often, the first shortcuts to be taken are to reduce or eliminate the time allocated for the validation steps, such as reviews, Inspections, and testing. Shortcuts taken in project planning, like those taken in cooking an omelet, inevitably result in compromising quality.

Inadequate planning can usually be traced to one or more of these causes:

1. Dependencies within the product, and on other products, are not accounted for in the plan.

2. Plans lack sufficient detail and granularity.

3. Inadequate time is allowed for validation and rework of work items during the project.

As a poorly planned project progresses, a further level of degeneration can be indicated during the Code and Unit Test stages when a growing amount of scrap and rework is experienced due to discovery and fixing of design and coding defects. When a project is experiencing excessive rework, the cause can usually be traced to one or more of the following:

1. Requirements are not completely understood at design time

2. Requirements are changing in mid-stream

3. Inadequate design specifications have been passed on from prior stages

4. Short cuts in validation are being taken at critical points in the process (e.g., reviews, Inspection, testing)

And finally, the poorly planned project can degenerate past its point of no return when the rework volume exceeds a critical mass, that is, when people "no longer have time to do it right, just to do it over." At this point it is usually too late even to apply extra help because the scheduled end date can no longer accommodate the necessary learning curve for the newcomers. At this point, not only has the product quality been compromised, but the schedule has now been missed, and the project needs to be scrapped, or redefined and restarted at an earlier stage.

6.5 Entry Criteria for Project Planning

Initial project planning starts as input to the business proposal, followed by more extensive planning when the decision to go ahead with the project has been made, and Requirements Engineering activities are underway. At the outset, the inputs required before beginning the 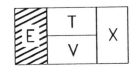 project plan are the three basic planning variables of completion date, project resources, and product size. Initial values for all three of these basic factors will be obtained from the completed business proposal (see Chapter 3).

6.6 Planning Tasks and Methods

When considered in total, project planning in software development can appear as a complicated, amorphous mass of detail with endless plan documents, schedules, and checklists. The problem becomes more manageable 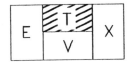 when one can separate the concerns into discrete perspectives. In this section we discuss software project planning first, in terms of estimating size and resources, and second, in terms of methods for dividing the project into manageable chunks of responsibilities and tasks. In addition, we present the latter topic in terms of two methods: one, a widely used method called *work breakdown structure*, and two, a recommended method we shall call the *project process definition* in this text.

Basically, all software resource estimating methods involve variations on the following steps:

1. Understanding what properties are required for the product, such as its capabilities, usability, performance, and reliability (refer to Chapter 3, Planning the Product and Chapter 4, Requirements Engineering)

2. Estimating the size, scope, and complexity of the needed work items

3. Defining the tasks required to produce the needed work items

4. Determining the resources needed to perform the defined tasks

5. Identifying dependencies between tasks

6. Determining availability of needed resources and assigning a schedule to the tasks accordingly

6.6.1 Resource Estimation

Estimating the resource required for a given project is usually done with the aid of tools that embody *resource estimation models.* There are two basic approaches to creating resource estimation models:

1. Perform empirical analysis of data from the history of several projects, and extrapolate the empirically derived correlations to predict the future.

2. Hypothesize a set of presumed cause-effect relationships, and derive predictive algorithms from the hypothesis.

In practice, resource estimation models are defined and calibrated by iterating between the two approaches: that is, they are defined by algorithms representing cause-effect relationships assumed to exist between development tasks and the resultant work products and are calibrated by substituting values in the algorithms that are derived from empirical analysis of historical data from similar prior projects. Analysis of the results in turn provides further insight into the assumed cause-effect relationships and refined algorithms, and the process repeats [BOEH81], [WOLV84].

Resource estimation models can be classified as follows [BASI80]:

1. Static Single and Multiple Variable Models

   These models derive resource required as a function of some property of the work product, for example, lines of code. This then is multiplied against a constant calculated from empirical analysis of past projects to produce the estimate. The term "static" means that the model is not designed to spread the estimate over time.

2. Dynamic multi-variable models

   Dynamic models add time series to the equations and therefore can project resources required over time. Dynamic multi-variable models are used for most resource estimating. Basically, they weigh time against the size of the effort according to an empirically derived distribution, which is used in turn to make a projection of resource required over time. In sophisticated multi-variable models, the time variable may be expressed in other than calendar or clock time, such as power-on hours, person-months (number of persons times number of months), or user-months (number of users times number of months). Some tools use multi-variable models to perform regression analysis on historical data for the same or similar product being estimated. The actual historical distribution function derived is in turn used to make the projection.

A typical application of this principle is illustrated in the Putnam Estimation Model [PUTN80], which assumes a specific distribution of effort across the various stages of the software life cycle. The Putnam model was derived from analysis of workload over time for several large-scale projects, and suggests that effort on a project reaches its peak during the implementation stages and then declines during testing. The shape of the distribution in the Putnam model is close to that described earlier by Lord Rayleigh and substantiated by data collected by P. Norden [NORD80]. Hence, the curve is generally called the Rayleigh-Norden curve.

Curves of similar shape were also reported by Boehm [BOEH81] in Figure 74 on page 183. The curves shown plot percentage of development schedule completed against percentage of average staffing.

They were derived from analysis of several projects, which were categorized as operating in *organic mode, semidetached mode,* and *embedded mode.* Projects operating in "organic mode" were those in which small teams developed enhancements to familiar systems in familiar environments. Projects in "embedded mode" were complex and embedded in highly constrained sets of hardware and software requirements and regulations. "Semidetached mode" projects were those of intermediate complexity and having a mixture of organic and embedded project characteristics. Projects in organic mode generally were able to become productive and staff earlier than the embedded projects.

3. Theoretical models

These models use built-in algorithms, based upon a hypothesis, to produce a prediction, instead of dynamically analyzing history to derive a function that is in turn used for projection, as in the dynamic multi-variable models above. An application of theoretical models are the so-called "predictive" models because they purport to predict future behavior via the algorithms embedded in them. Such models have little practical use in software resource estimation. They are useful, however, for setting boundaries or goals and targets for estimators, based upon the constraints implicit in their built-in algorithms.

One of the more sophisticated estimating approaches is B. Boehm's *COnstructive COst MOdel (COCOMO)* [BOEH81]. Basically, this approach models a set of assumed cause-effect relationships between attributes of the desired software product, constraints of its run-time environment, its capabilities, and experience levels of the people on the project, and attributes of the process required to produce it. Figure 75 on page 184 shows a sample list of parameters used in the model.

The planner calibrates the model to the particular project being estimated by assigning a rating of "very low, low, normal, high, very high, extra high" to each of the parameters. In addition, each parameter has a unique set of multipliers for

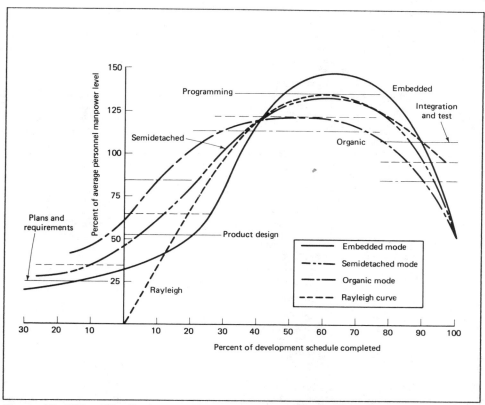

Figure 74. Effort Distribution on Three Types of Projects. Reprinted with permission from *Software Engineering Economics* [BOEH81], p. 93.

the increments above, derived by statistical analysis of several past projects. For example, the multiplier for very low use of modern programming practices might be 1.24, and for very high use, 0.82. These multipliers in turn cause the model to estimate larger or smaller amounts of resource required for the project.

6.6.2 Work Breakdown Structure

A widely used technique for separating a large project into manageable tasks is called a *work breakdown structure*. Evans et al. in their text *Principles of Productive Software Management* [EVAN83], describe a work breakdown structure as a "a product-oriented division of hardware, software, services, and other work tasks that organize, define, and graphically display the work to be accomplished in order to develop a specified product."

Figure 76 on page 185 is an illustration of a very high-level work breakdown structure that depicts the tasks of an overall program planning process.

```
• Product Attributes

    - Required software reliability
    - Data base size
    - Product complexity

• Computer Attributes

    - Execution time constraint
    - Main storage constraint
    - Computer turnaround time

• Personnel Attributes

    - Analyst capability
    - Applications experience
    - Programmer capability
    - Programming language experience

• Project Attributes

    - Use of modern programming practices
    - Use of software tools
    - Required development schedule
```

Figure 75. Example COCOMO Parameters

At lower levels of refinement, a work breakdown structure points to *work package instructions*, as illustrated in Figure 77 on page 186. A work package instruction is a detailed description of a specific piece of work to to accomplished. According to Evans et al. a work package

- describes a manageable piece of work

- is unique and clearly distinguished from all other work packages

- is scheduled with a start and completion date; has defined, documented scope; and is controlled by budgets

- assigns responsibility for performing the work to a single organizational element with any suballocation of work done by the assigned organization

- is integrated with detailed engineering, manufacturing, and other schedules as applicable

If defined to a low enough level of granularity, work packages offer the advantage of being unique, self-contained definitions of work that will remain relatively stable, even if the overall project definition or schedules shift during the course of the project.

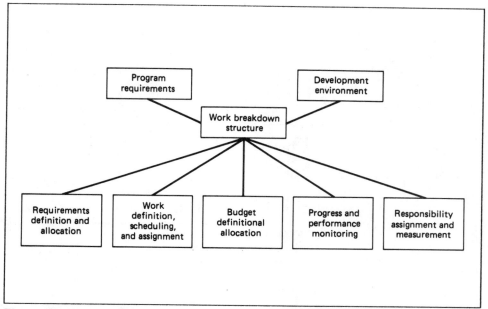

Figure 76. Work Breakdown Structure of the Programming Planning Process. Reprinted with permission from *Principles of Productive Software Management [EVAN83], p. 124.*

6.6.3 Project Process Definition

In this text we recommend a level of planning beyond the work breakdown structure, one that relies upon an operational description of the specific project superimposed over a generic definition of a process, such as that presented in Chapter 2. The result is an operational description of the intended development process for a particular product. We shall call this operational description a *project process definition,* and define it as the instantiation of a Programming Process Architecture, such as the one describing the life-cycle model of this text [RADI85].

The planning method we describe focuses on the dynamics of the process when applied to the conduct of a given project. There are at least three separate systems at work during the course of a development project, each of which must be planned for:

1. A process management system that defines the process and provides controls

2. A change management system that controls design changes, code changes, changes to test cases, and changes to the development process itself

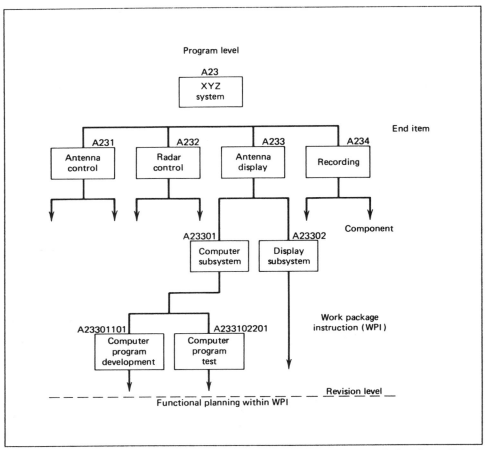

Figure 77. Sample Work Breakdown Structure. Reprinted with permission from *Principles of Productive Software Management [EVAN83], p. 123.*

3. A project management system for setting quantitative goals and tracking progress

Other systems are at work too, such as people and organization dynamics. The effect of these will be discussed in a subsequent volume of this text series.

Planning the Process Management System

When an operational description of the specific project being planned is applied to the generic process definition, the result is the process management system for controlling the project. Such a description will include:

• Specific names of the work items to be produced during the project

- Stages and activities that produce the work items, showing tasks, entry criteria, validation procedures, and exit criteria
- Identification of rework activities that will result from review and validation activities
- The sequential and concurrent order of execution of activities
- Methodologies, practices, and tools to be employed for each activity
- Event and data recording points to be used in the project management system
- Organizational and individual responsibilities for each activity

The operational representation of the development process described in Chapter 2 is based upon the notion of *work items*, and the changes in state that these work items undergo from the beginning to the end of a project.

Work items may be divided into two types: *product work items* and *process work items*. Examples of product work items include programming objectives, specifications, design documentation, product publications, and code. Process work items are those not directly part of the shipped product, such as project plans, test plans, change requests, trouble reports, and product quality analysis reports. Each product and process work item may be further divided into parts for ease and control. For example, design work items are divided by product, component, subcomponent, specification chapters, and code modules.

To control the project, a data base is required that will track the following information about each work item:

- *Attributes* that describe the work item
- *Relationships* to show interdependencies between work items
- *States* to show evolution of work items through the process

Elements of the project process definition that the planner will use to define the process management system are *attributes, relationships, states, activities, and entry/exit criteria.* The following sections describe how these are used:

Attributes: These describe a work item, and can include:

- Type (e.g., a product work item, a planning document, a change request document)
- Creation date and name of the work item
- Level (e.g., system, version, release to which the work item applies)
- Security authorization level and access control

Relationships: These depict the work item in the context of other work items and the activities that produce them. For example, relationships might be used to declare that one work item is a subpart of another work item, such as a section in a larger specification document, or that a work item is created by a certain named activity in the process or authored by a certain individual programmer.

States: These define levels of completion for work items. They are used as control points governing the evolution of each work item in the plan. Allowable states for a work item may be defined in terms of the activities that can be performed on the work item. Figure 78 on page 189 shows an example of the allowable states that might be designated at a high level for an overall product. The states designated coincide with the completion of various stages in our process life cycle model (described in Chapter 2). States defined at this high level would be useful, for example, as reporting control points for high level management in an organization that has several projects underway at the same time.

At a lower level than the previous example, allowable states might be designated for a specific type of work item in the project. Figure 79 on page 190 illustrates some possible allowable states for a Final Programming Specification (FPS) document. States tracked at this level for the FPS could play a useful role as control points in the entry and exit criteria of various activities that either act upon, or depend upon, the existence of the Final Programming Specification in a given state. For example, if you were a test planner for a new product, you might need to know when its FPS document reaches Final Draft state before starting your test planning activity, and later knowing when the specification reaches the Approved state, enabling you to complete the test plan.

Your test plan on the other hand might have the allowable states illustrated in Figure 80 on page 191. These in turn will become control points enabling still other activities to take place in the process, such as writing the test cases.

Activities: Having defined the work items and their allowable states, the planner will add to the process definition the activities that will achieve each of the defined state transitions.

As discussed in 6.6.2, "Work Breakdown Structure" on page 183, activities thus defined will include such information as:

- The name of the individual, organization, or automated tool that will perform the state transition on the work item
- Scheduled start and completion dates for the activity
- Resources allocated to the activity

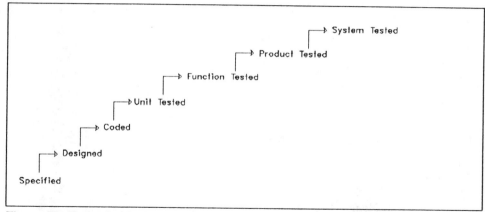

Figure 78. Example of Allowable Product States for High Level Reporting

In addition to the above work breakdown structure parameters, descriptions of the activities in a project process definition include the notion of *validation, entry criteria,* and *exit criteria,* as described for the ETVX Paradigm in Chapter 2.

The planner defines validation steps for the project at every point in the process definition where work item state transitions will occur. The validation steps identified in the plan can range from a reminder on a programmer's checklist to review the code commentary one last time before submitting a module for test, to specifying the resources and schedules for a series of formal code Inspections.

The exit criteria for an activity is expressed in terms of the work item states that will be achieved upon successful completion of the activity.

Entry criteria are the prerequisite states that must exist before the activity can begin. When the entry and exit criteria have been completely defined for all activities in the process, that is, when all prerequisite and resultant states have been identified, the process definition is complete, and all work item dependencies in the project will have been identified.

The completed process management system definition: To summarize, definition of the process management system is part of a project process definition for a specific project plan. In it are defined the following:

1. Work items and their allowable states

2. Activities that will accomplish the state transitions

   a. People, organizations, tools that will perform the state transitions
   b. Planned start and end dates for the activities
   c. Resources allocated

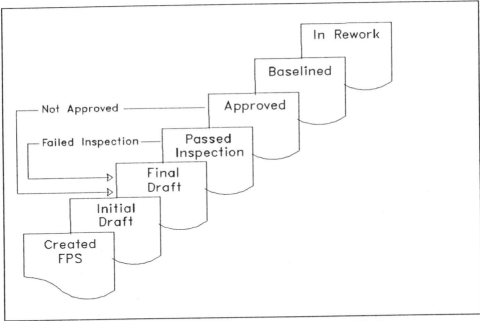

Figure 79. Example of Allowable States for a Programming Specification.

3. States that must be achieved upon successful completion of each activity (i.e., the exit criteria)

4. Prerequisite states that must exist to start each activity (i.e., the entry criteria)

By defining the process as a network of work items, activities, and states as above, the planner creates a management tool to focus on the expected overall dynamics of the project as the controlling mechanism, rather than on disconnected collections of lower level procedures often found embedded in tools and techniques.

Planning the Change Management System

The second aspect of a project process definition is the *change management system*. Change management is a process management discipline for controlling changes to the product throughout the life cycle. A subpart of a larger topic called *configuration management* (discussed in Volume 2 of this text series), change management is the process of identifying the structure of a product for the purpose of systematically controlling changes to its parts. A change management plan defines the goals, structure, responsibilities, and degree of change control to be exercised in the project.

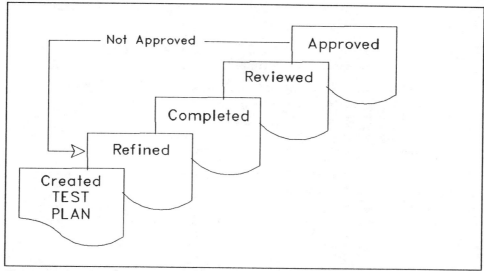

Figure 80. Example of Allowable States for a Test Plan

Change management relies upon the concept of *baselines*. Baselines are made up of those completed work items against which all subsequent changes are to be controlled. Once the work item has been included in the baseline, nothing may be added to it or modified without appropriate authorization. A baseline establishes the basis for communication and negotiation among all groups with an interest in the software.

Baselines evolve as completed product and process work items increase in number and detail, and changes are made. A comparison of baselines from one time to another makes the evolution of the software product visible and traceable. Identifying completed work items in a baseline is a continuing activity for all process stages. All work items should be included or the rationale for not including a work item should be documented.

In addition to the product work items, baselines include descriptions of the agreed-to process for developing the product. A change management plan defines

1. The number of baselines to be established, and when they are to be established

2. The product and process work items to be included in each baseline

3. The data base, library scheme, and tools to be used to manage change

The change management process is followed for all product and process work items in the baseline. This process includes four basic activities:

1. Submitting the appropriate change request, defining the problem and possible solutions. Types of change requests include

   - a design change request (DCR) for suggested changes to requirements, objectives, specifications, design, or test cases.

   - a trouble report for problems found during test stages that require corrective changes to the code or to the product publications Such a trouble report will be converted to a design change request if a work item other than code or product publications must also be changed to correct the problem

   - a trouble report for problems found during customer use of the shipped product. As with internal trouble reports during test stages, these reports must be converted to a design change request, if the design documentation must also be changed to correct the problem

   - a plan change request for changes to plans after they are approved and baselined

   - a process change request for changes to the agreed-to development or service process

2. Evaluating the change requests and recording their status, such as authorized, rejected, or deferred. Evaluation and authorization responsibilities may be assigned to

   - a design review board to evaluate and authorize all design change requests

   - a central coordinator for all trouble reports submitted during testing stages

   - a joint development and service review function to certify the correctness of all fixes for customer reported problems.

   - an appropriate level of management for approval of changes to the plan

   - an appropriate level of management for approval of all changes to the development process

3. Implementing the authorized changes. This includes ensuring that all affected work items in the baseline are changed. A flagging scheme is used to identify change areas in all affected documents, for example, change bars on documents, or code change flags on source code lines. Later these flags can be analyzed to determine the reasons that changes were made to the product over time.

4. Integrating the changes into the baseline. This includes testing or otherwise verifying that the baseline has not regressed with respect to its previous functions and capabilities.

Planning the Project Management System

The third aspect of a project process definition is the *project management system*. A project management system defines the project tracking data that will be captured, how it will be analyzed, and how it will be fed back to control and improve the development process. Integral to the project management system is a data base capable of recording all project information throughout the development and service life cycle. Such a system must support

- collecting and archiving of a complete set of process data to support decision making, quality reviews, and error causal analysis during the development cycle.

- planning and tracking of resources, schedules, and dependencies throughout the development cycle for the product.

- analysis and feedback of product and process data to product management and staff during the development cycle.

- evaluation of the cost and effectiveness of activities and stages in the development process.

- ability to analyze and set product quality goals that are related to specific properties of the defined process.

- ability to analyze and set process productivity goals.

Quality-Productivity Planning: A quality-productivity plan is essentially a set of product and process goals with a rationale for what will be done in the development process to meet each goal. The purpose of the quality-productivity plan is to provide a focus for goal-directed product development and to ensure that the measurable quality of the shipped product is superior to that of its predecessors and competitors. For new products that have no specific predecessor, the quality bench mark is based upon the observed quality of similar products.

Both management and technical staff should participate as a team in setting goals and determining which process actions at a team level will affect the goals, and to what degree. For example, the quality-productivity plan for a typical IBM large commercial system development project might include:

1. A project overview of the planned release content, functional capability, or size in terms of lines of code and pages of documentation

2. Goals and projections:

   Defect prevention and detection goals, stated quantitatively for each major product work item, estimate the number of defects to be introduced at each stage, the number to be detected, and the number remaining (i.e., the *quality level*) at the exit from each stage. An analysis structure is defined that will trace each defect to its point of introduction during the course of the project and derive estimates of incoming and outgoing quality levels for each development and test stage.

Projections are made for the number of defects that will escape to field use. This becomes one of the major factors considered in setting the quality goal for the product. Once set, this goal becomes the baseline goal for the entire development process. During development, the outlook for making the shipped quality level goal is periodically reassessed. If the project begins to track off target from its established goal, corrective action can be taken immediately.

Another type of quality goal that can be established is in terms of the CUPRIM attributes defined in Chapter 3, (i.e., Capability, Usability, Performance, Reliability, Installability, and Maintainability). How the product fares relative to the customers' expectations in terms of these attributes can be sampled over the long term by periodically surveying representative numbers of customers.

3. Methods by which all stated goals will be met:

A description is made of the historical rationale and methods used for establishing the goals for each process stage and work item.

Definitions are given for the measurement parameters, counting methods, tools, and validation procedures that will be used to track progress toward achieving the committed quality and productivity goals.

A description of any process changes that have been instituted to better achieve the goals is included, and individuals responsible for each goal are identified.

The plan also includes a schedule of planned quality-productivity reviews. This is a recurring activity, at a minimum held upon completion of each process stage. The quality-productivity goals are analyzed based upon current data collected about the progress of the work items covered. Actions are put in place to correct for deviations from the planned quality-productivity status at each review.

Data Analysis and Reporting: In planning for project data analysis and reporting, the planner must determine what types of analyses are necessary for controlling and improving the product and the process. It is easy for the planner at this point to simply propagate the measurements and reports from past projects into the one currently being planned. However, the problems with this approach are that (1) obsolescent reports, now ineffective as project management tools, will continue to be propagated into the current project, and (2) opportunities for identifying and instituting permanent improvements in the process for this and the next project, through analysis and feedback of data, are missed.

Thus, the existing analysis and reporting structure should be reexamined and fine-tuned at the outset of every new project, no matter how much like the last project it seems to be on the surface. An effective approach for doing this is:

1. Determine the audience for each analysis or report.

2. List the objectives for using the analysis or report in terms of how it will satisfy the needs of its selected audience.

3. Determine how often, or under what circumstances, the analysis or report should be produced during the course of the project.

   • Identify exception indicators for the selected display. Determine how much variation will be allowed before flagging for special attention.

   • Anticipate in advance the types of action most likely to be called for when a measurement value deviates beyond its clip point.

4. Define the data items needed for the analysis or report.

5. Determine how the results will be presented or displayed most effectively from a human factors perspective for the selected audience of the analysis or report.

An effective way to determine what measures will be needed to support the required analysis and reporting structure is to divide them into two categories: *product measures* and *process measures.*

Product measures include parameters that indicate some intrinsic property of the product being developed. Examples of product measures are:

• Estimates made at each process step of the projected number of lines of code in the product at the time of general availability to users.

• Projected product quality levels which are identified at entry to and exit from each process stage and which are derived from

   — estimates of new defects to be introduced at each process stage
   — estimates of defects to be detected and removed at each process stage

Process measures indicate some characteristics of the development process, such as how productively or how efficiently a particular test activity is running. Examples of process measures are:

• Accuracy of size estimating: indicated by measuring the difference between the old and revised size estimates made at each process step. Recording and analyzing the reason for each variance can lead to improvements in estimating methodology for the product area.

- Detection efficiency: measurements are made of the ratio of estimated incoming defect levels to outgoing defect levels at each inspection or test stage. This measure is used to determine where the verification and testing process can be improved.

- Escape analysis: analysis of the reason why each defect escaped from a given verification or test stage. This is used to determine what permanent improvements can be instituted in the test or inspection stages to prevent the same type of escapes in future work.

- Causal analysis: analysis of each defect discovered during Inspections, test stages, and field use, to determine what caused it to be introduced, in what stage it was introduced, and how it could have been prevented. Permanent process changes are then implemented to prevent the same type of defect from occurring in the future. Experiences in applying causal analysis techniques have shown this to be an effective method for identifying and making specific process improvements. [JONE85]. This topic will be covered in more detail in Volume 2 of this textbook series.

- Measurements of response time for diagnosing and fixing defects discovered during inspections and testing.

- Measurements of the efficiency of the detection process itself. For example, Inspection preparation time, or defects discovered per hour of Inspection time.

Data Collection: Once the planner has determined the types of data analysis and reporting that are to be done for the project, he or she is in a position to define the data to be collected during the course of the project. Following are some types of data typically collected in a large project to support the analysis and reporting needs determined previously:

1. Product size data

   - Projected new and changed source instructions and total source instructions, to be reestimated at the completion of the following process stages:

     - Requirements and Planning
     - Product Level Design
     - Component Level Design
     - Module Level Design

   - Actual counts of code at the completion of

     - Code and Unit Test
     - Function Verification Test
     - Product Verification Test
     - System Verification Test

   All projected lines of code and actual counts should be kept at a low level of granularity. For example, by function, by module, by Design Change Request, and even by defect fixed.

   Regardless of whether the new size estimate made at each design stage is the same or different from the previous one, the rationale for why it is the same or why it is different should be documented and maintained for analysis. The same applies to actual code counts as the product progresses through successive testing stages. If this practice is continued over several projects, new insights will emerge, eventually leading to an estimating methodology that becomes increasingly more repeatable and reliable.

2. Data from Inspections and reviews

   The types of data that should be collected from each Inspection or review of specifications, design, code, test cases, product publications, and project plans are:

   - Names of the work items reviewed or inspected
   - Major errors found (i.e., those that would probably result in a reported defect)
   - Minor errors (i.e., errors that would probably not result in a reported defect—example: a punctuation error in code commentary)
   - Actual new and changed lines of code inspected
   - Actual total lines of code inspected (including old code)
   - Work items that are being reinspected
   - Individual participants' preparation time and inspection time

3. Data from testing stages

   Defect data is collected from Unit Test, Functional Verification Test (FVT), Product Verification Test (PVT), and System Verification Test (SVT). Each defect must be tracked through to the integration of the fix. Records kept for each defect should include:

- Defect description
- Date and time the problem was reported
- Severity of the problem in terms of impact to the project
- Source (for example, code, product publication, test case)
- Causal analysis data

Data that would enable analysis of the testing process itself must also be collected. Examples are:

- Number of test cases successful by test stage
- Person months by test stage
- Escape analysis data

4. Defect data from field use:

- Report of the defect
- Number of customers experiencing problems from the defect
- Number of hours to resolve the problems
- Date first reported, answered, fixed
- Reported release
- Release causing the error
- Releases in which fixed

5. Causal analysis and escape analysis data (refer to discussion in "Data Analysis and Reporting" on page 194):

- Type of errors analyzed (e.g., Inspections, DCRs, reported from testing, reported from field use)
- Error description
- Work item where found
- The stage and activity in the process where it was found
- The stage and activity where it could have first been found, given an "ideal" detection process
- Type of error (e.g., interface, register usage, standards)
- Category of cause, for example, lack of education on a new function, on base code, or in some other manner; communication breakdown; oversight; or transcription error
- The stage and activity in the process where it was introduced (e.g., design, code, test, fixing another defect)
- Number of errors analyzed
- Number of suggested actions
- Number of participants
- Session duration in hours
- Process prevention change recommended

6. Design change requests

  - Description of requested design change
  - Disposition (e.g., approved, rejected, deferred to a future release)
  - Dates submitted and closed
  - Estimated and actual code integration dates
  - Cause (e.g., requirements change, design error, performance improvement)
  - Estimated and actual lines of code associated with the change.

7. Resources and schedules

  - Programmer-months

    - by stage
    - by work item
    - for problem determination
    - for rework activities

  - Projected and actual beginning and end dates for project activities

8. Product publications data

  - Retrievability, readability, index ratings, if appropriate

  - For each product publication inspected:

    - Inspection date
    - Estimated or actual pages and/or screens
    - Major errors (that is, those that would probably result in a field reported defect)
    - Minor errors (that is, other recorded errors)
    - Number of pages and/or screens being reinspected
    - Number of pages and/or screens that need reinspection
    - Preparation time and inspection time

  - For human factors testing:

    - Time to find and set up the publication or help screen, read it, use it to do a key task, and complete the task
    - Total task time
    - Total number of errors
    - Number of errors due to publication or help screen
    - Total number of assists
    - Number of assists required due to publication or help screen
    - Test-subject satisfaction

  - Data from field surveys on publications or interactive help-screen facilities

6.7 Validation of a Project Plan

The project plan is validated by cross checking against the history of similar projects, and is subjected to exhaustive technical and management reviews before committing to it. According to the "Four Cs" from Chapter 3, desirable properties of a project plan are 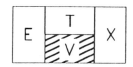 completeness, consistency, conformance to a methodology, and correctness. The first three of these properties are validated by studying the documented set of plans. In this type of validation, our goal is to ensure the following:

- Work scope is completely identified

  Input to project planning calls for a thorough understanding of the technical content of the product to be developed and is obtained during the Requirements stage. Often this is not completely achievable, but the work scope, to the extent it can be defined, must be developed. A set of tasks is defined for all who will contribute work to the project. The tasks include reviews, Inspections, and the resulting rework.

- Quantitative goals are stated

  The quality-productivity plan should include goals for defect levels, performance evaluation, usability at every appropriate stage in the process. Wherever possible, the plan should show quantitative links that relate specific aspects of the process to desired properties of the product that is to be developed.

- Resources estimates

  All plans should include estimates for people and supporting resources needed for every task. All estimates of resources needed should be commensurate with stated quality and productivity goals.

- Adequate time for validation and rework

  Plans should be examined carefully to ensure that ample time has been allowed for reviews, Inspections, and rework. A review or Inspection should be planned for at every point in the process where a task operates on a work item to change its state.

- Events scheduled at an adequate level of granularity

  Dependencies between tasks are identified, and a realistic schedule in terms of events and checkpoints should exist in sufficient granularity for managing the project.

- Data collection and analysis:

  Data collection and the means for analyzing and reporting progress must be specified thoroughly in the plan. Types of analysis specified should allow for continual revalidation and adjustments of the planning assumptions in the plan as actual events transpire.

- Assessment of risks and available options:

In the final analysis, the plan is validated for the fourth C (Correctness) by human judgment. There are no specific criteria for knowing when a plan is "correct." Thoroughness of the planning effort, the availability of accurate data for analysis from similar past projects, the amount of review and validation that the plan has been subjected to, and the experience level of the planners are all key factors.

For example, resource estimates are a critical part of the project plan. How much confidence can be placed in the estimate given in a particular plan? Statistical models are often used to estimate resources required, and inexperienced planners frequently assign too much responsibility for the accuracy of an estimate to the model and not enough to their own good judgment. These models are tools, not crutches. They are fallible.

An experienced pool or billiards player will modify the behavior of the shot by putting a spin, or "English," on the cue ball when necessary to ensure success. An experienced planner will take the time to thoroughly understand the rationale and assumed cause-effect relationship inherent in the model and then apply some "English" before accepting the output as is. Validation of the plan requires extensive review and discussion of all its aspects to ensure that all assumptions are consistent with one another and that all conclusions drawn are as rational as possible.

6.8 Exit Criteria

A total project plan has a number of subparts. All are started during the Requirements and Planning stage, and each is finished in time to take effect for the particular stage to which it applies. Each planning activity that creates a plan subpart should be viewed as having exit criteria definable in terms of the required properties of the plan.

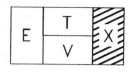

In general, the exit criteria for any of these planning activities would include verification that the validation steps outlined in the previous section have taken place. In addition, a re-check of the entry criteria should be made to see that all elements of this criteria are met. Finally, a plan subpart would be considered complete when those needing it to manage their part of the process are comfortable that the plan has undergone sufficient reviews to ascertain that the plan is complete, consistent, was done according to the best methodologies, and is "correct" in the judgment of its reviewers and authors.

6.9 Summary

In this chapter, we defined project planning and identified some current planning problems relative to the goals of various individuals involved in the planning and management process. Some planning methodologies and approaches were discussed.

1. We discussed interactions between the three basic parameters involved in project planning:

   a. The end date

   b. The resources available, which include:

      • Productivity goals
      • Quality goals

   c. The size and scope of the required work product

   Planning starts from the assumption of any two of the above three parameters; one can solve for the third if it is unknown.

2. A good plan has five basic ingredients:

   a. The work scope is completely identified.
   b. The resources needed for every task are estimated.
   c. Events are scheduled at proper levels of granularity.
   d. Data collection and analysis are built into the plan.
   e. Assessment is made of risks and available options.

3. Proper management of a complex project must be exercised above the level of procedures embedded in tools and techniques. This is done through an operational description that focuses on the dynamics of the project (called the *project process definition* in this text). In it are defined:

   a. Work items and their allowable states

   b. Activities that will accomplish the state transitions

      1) People, organizations, tools that will perform the state transitions
      2) Planned start and end dates for the activities
      3) Resources allocated

   c. States that will be achieved upon completion of each activity (i.e., the exit criteria)

   d. Prerequisite states that must exist to start each activity (i.e., the entry criteria)

6.10 References

[BASI80] V. Basili, *Models and Metrics for Software Management and Engineering*, IEEE Computer Society Press (1980), pp. 4 – 9.

[BOEH81] B. W. Boehm, *Software Engineering Economics*, Prentice-Hall (1981).

[BROO74] F. P. Brooks, Jr., "The Mythical Man-Month: Essays on Software Engineering," Addison Wesley (1974).

[EVAN83] M. W. Evans, P. Piazza, and J. B. Dolkas, *Principles of Productive Software Management*, John Wiley and Sons (1983), pp. 141 – 218.

[JENS79] R. W. Jensen and C. C. Tonies, *Software Engineering*, Prentice-Hall (1979), pp. 24 – 63.

[JONE85] C. L. Jones, "A Process Integrated Approach to Defect Prevention," *IBM Systems Journal*, Vol. 24, No. 2 (1985), pp. 150 – 67.

[NORD80] P. Norden, "Useful Tools For Project Management," *Software Cost Estimating And Life Cycle Control*, IEEE Computer Society Press (1980), pp. 216 – 25.

[PRES82] R. S. Pressman, *Software Engineering: A Practitioner's Approach*, McGraw-Hill Book Company (1982), pp. 31 – 93.

[PUTN80] L. Putnam, "Software Cost Estimating and Life Cycle Control," *IEEE Computer Society Press* (1980), p. 15.

[RADI85] R. A. Radice, N. K. Roth, A. C. O'Hara, Jr., and W. A. Ciarfella, "A Programming Process Architecture," *IBM Systems Journal*, Vol. 24, No. 2 (1985), pp. 79 – 90.

[WOLV84] R. W. Wolverton, "Software Costing," *Handbook of Software Engineering*, Van Nostrand Reinhold (1984), pp. 469 – 93.

Additional Suggested Reading

Boehm, B. H., M. H. Penedo, E. D. Stuckle, R. D. Williams, A. B. Pyster, "A Software Development Environment for Improving Productivity," *IEEE Computer Magazine*, (June, 1984), pp. 30–42.

Shooman, M. L., *Software Engineering*, McGraw-Hill Book Company (1983), pp. 438–83.

Williams, R. D., "Management of Software Development," *Handbook of Software Engineering*, Van Nostrand Reinhold (1984), pp. 456–68.

Chapter 7. Design of Software

7.1 The Role of Design in Software Engineering

Design is the bridge between a validated set of requirements and the implementation of a solution to satisfy those requirements. However, unlike the solidity of bridges such as the Golden Gate or the Brooklyn, this requirements-to-design bridge is conceptual rather than substantial. It is abstract rather than real. We may represent the design in various forms such as graphic trees, data flow diagrams, pseudo-code, or design languages, but these representations are only carriers of the essence of the design. That essence is the conceptual solution to the requirements statement or problem. The actual solution will become visible only when we have implemented the design in some source code which can be compiled and then executed on a processor. The transition from design to code causes the solution which is understood by humans to be transformed to an equivalent solution used by a machine to produce a desired result.

The conceptual solution, however, if not properly completed, can lead to failure in the implementation. We do not want to belabor the analogy of a bridge, but an improperly designed bridge cannot be implemented successfully or inexpensively. This was evident in the Tacoma Narrows Bridge incident where the compounding force of a harmonic frequency during a storm caused the bridge to literally fall apart. The flaw in this case was in the design, which did not fully account for the effects of the harmonic frequency. If it were understood after the bridge was completed, it would not have been an easy solution to correct the problem. This is to say, by example, that the flaws of design cannot be corrected, at least not easily corrected, in the implementation. There are exceptions, but they are few rather than typical. Although in comparison it is easier to change a software implementation than a hardware implementation, it is nonetheless more costly to repair software after its implementation that in its design stage.

We can reduce the density of design flaws by discovering and removing them prior to implementation, or by not introducing them into the design in the first place. The former can be addressed through various verification techniques such as Inspections at an informal level or through design proofs of correctness at a more formal level. We should not assume that defect removal techniques eliminate all the defects. Therefore, software is always vulnerable to having problems discovered which might cause an implemented solution to fail at the most undesirable moments while it is in use. We should, however, ardently strive to accomplish a defect-free design.

Defect inhibition or prevention is limited by the design representations and methodologies we have in our arsenal of choices. L. J. Peters says that

> our advances in software design are a direct result of our increased capacity to deal with systems as abstractions. [PETE81]

What is required, then, is a design methodology that permits flexibility to resolve problems from various domains and that can be easily implemented, so that the resulting product is very close to being defect free. We want a methodology that does not "help" us to make errors while we are creating a conceptual or abstract solution. We will address a recommended methodology in Chapter 9.

To help us better understand the role of design in software engineering, Peters and Tripp have developed a morphological model, or organizational scheme, of software engineering and its relationship to design [PETE78]. The model consists of three mutually orthogonal axes which show the relationships and intersections of three different conceptual approaches to software engineering: time, logic, and formalism (Reference Figure 81 on page 207). The time dimension is the development cycle we addressed in Chapter 2. The logic dimension categorizes the generic activities that take place within each stage of the development cycle. The formalism dimension addresses the notion that the product is developed through continual construction and intellectual refinement of a succession of models: mental, structural, and linguistic.

The relationships between these axes for design defines which alternatives we might use or solutions we might yet require in order to completely bridge between requirements and implementation. In this and in Chapter 9 and Chapter 10 we shall explore some alternatives seen through this morphology and indicate a recommended approach.

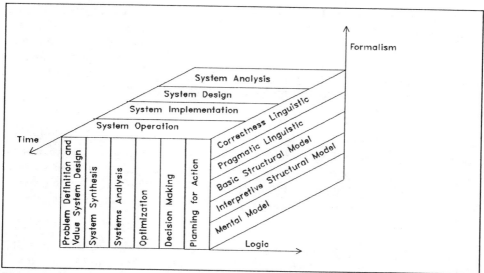

Figure 81. A Morphological Model for Software Engineering

Finally, it is important to note that not only are design errors made, but they account for the majority of errors made while developing a software product. Additionally, these design errors are persistent in withstanding removal [BOEH75]. Furthermore, if the design is not adequately verified against the requirements, the errors from the Requirements stage will be propagated into Code.

7.2 What Is Design?

First and foremost when we speak of design in the context of software engineering, we do not mean design as in the arts where it loosely means composition, style, or decoration. It would be hard to argue, however, that design for software does not require creativity. It indeed does. Therefore, we accept that design even in software engineering seems to work best when creative insight leads to a solution that can later be manifested in the implementation.

Typically in engineering design means to create a concise and complete record of the concepts and relationships that embody a solution to some stated problem. In software engineering, this is equally true, and it also is true that the design is not the "thing" itself. We do not want to dwell on philosophy, but let us resolve for our purposes in this book that design while not the "thing" itself, is indeed the "idea" of the "thing."

This idea may be achieved in any of a number of different ways, and we will define these ways as being *methodologies*. Additionally, the idea may be communicated or shown in a number of different ways, which we call *representations* of the design idea. We will briefly explore the essence of both design methodologies and design representations in this chapter and dwell in more detail on some selected alternatives to both in Chapter 9 and Chapter 10. We will also suggest that an arsenal of specific concepts is required for a designer to be repeatedly successful, and we will give our recommended approach among the prevalent methodologies.

Before we proceed, and since we do not want to mislead the reader, it should be understood that the software industry has not yet settled on a universally accepted approach to design. Indeed, the scope and definition of design in general is debated. Ultimately, we may come to accept that since there are many types of software, there may be many appropriate methodologies to accomplish design of software.

One way of looking at design is to ask, "What does it produce?" It is not sufficient in a business world to suggest that design produces ideas only. Certainly it does, but these ideas are more particularly solutions to the problem posed in the requirements statement, which we can view as directing us towards a solution target or functional goal. Therefore, the solution, that is, the design, will be only as good as the statement of the goals, that is, the requirements. Thus, the effort and discipline to achieve a consistent and complete set of requirements becomes paramount to the whole process. Freeman states:

> It is a fundamental characteristic of designing that we are permitted the opportunity to achieve any set of desired goals. If we want a system to be very user centered, we have the opportunity to design it that way (or, at least to emphasize that goal within our existing constraints). On the other hand, if we do not pay attention to all of our goals during design, there is usually little that can be done later to incorporate them into the system. [FREE83]

Freeman suggests that not only do we need a complete and consistent set of requirements, but that they must all be accounted for, integrated, and interrelated in the design statement. There is many a slip between the cup and the lip, and we must be sensitive to this fact of human nature. Not only must we understand that programmers in fact do make errors, but more importantly, better solutions are possible when we acknowledge and account for human fallibility.

We probably cannot completely satisfy all readers with a definition of design. Then, perhaps we should approach this definition problem from the other end, that is, stating what design is not. First, design, is the analysis of a number of potential solutions to the problem itself, it is not analysis of the problem, which is relegated to the Requirements and Planning stage. In practice the analysis aspect for the Requirements does not end at a discrete point prior to beginning design, that is, additional requirements or refinements of requirements undoubtedly continue during the design stages.

Second, design is not the implementation or coding of the solution. Unfortunately, some practitioners in the software industry may leap from requirements or problem statements directly into the coding of the solution only to learn that such a barnstorming approach typically leads to product disasters.

Thus, we must accept that design is a stage or sequence of stages unto itself, occurring between the analysis of a problem and the implementation of its solution. The way we proceed through these stages and the way we capture the work items of these stages is the subject of our remaining discussions on design.

Finally, we recognize that design is a human activity, which supplies the HOW part to the requirements analysis WHAT part in the problem-solution relationship.

7.3 Designing: What We Do

Some programmers may be prone to jump into the implementation level much too soon, yet the history of our industry is replete with examples of poorly written programs that have resulted from such a process. This desire to leap into implementation occurs for a number of reasons including both the toy-like fascination with playing the coding game, the apparent difficulties of performing a disciplined design, and the sometimes real need to see some critical function execute before we can verify design closure.

Given the orderly progression within a good design methodology, we should be able to make design as immediately ego satisfying as is coding, while at the same time removing the apparent difficulties of following a disciplined design. The many cases we have seen convince us that this is true. In the cases where some work-ahead requires a partial implementation before design has established closure, the methodology should allow for both a work-ahead implementation and a feedback into the design to establish design closure.

There are three basic steps to any problem-solving approach: analyze, hypothesize, and validate. Thus we analyze all the information we have about a problem, then we select from alternatives our hypothesized solution to the problem, and, finally, we validate whether we are solving the problem correctly. This loosely translates in software engineering to: requirements, design, and test. We have previously addressed how to perform analysis in the Requirements Engineering chapter. We discuss a number of approaches to design in this book. Test is be addressed in Volume 2 of this series.

Enos and Van Tilburg suggest that people who describe problem solving for software in terms of discrete stages leading to solutions tend to mix the design process with the management of the process. This mixing leads to an inconsistency because the human creative process of design as an individual act to reach a solution.

> Committees and design teams cannot conceive overall solutions; only individuals can. The issue that has evolved is: we tend to confuse the microsteps of individuals solving problems in the data processing world with the macrosteps of managing people on a project. The design methodologies and formalized procedures of design and programming allow committees and design teams to effectively integrate individual creativity in problem solving. This provides for solutions of problems beyond the ability of a single individual. We often increase individual creativity with teams by using formal methodology. [ENOS79]

We do not debate this statement, but do suggest that the understanding of how we can best integrate the creative act into software design is still an open area of discussion.

Peters states that there are three phases to design: divergence, transformation, and convergence [PETE81]. We will shortly see how this division relates to our three different stages of design.

During the divergence phase, the designer must assimilate all input as raw material in order to determine the true operating characteristics or objectives of the product. The requirements may in fact be restructured and changed as a result. The problem has been redefined. Some level of instability has therefore been added. It is important to note that if the Requirements Engineering was not validated to be complete, then the designer will have to do the requirements analysis prior to completing the divergence phase.

In the transformation phase several alternative solutions to this redefined problem are posed. A decision as to which of these alternative solutions should be used is made and therefore this phase can be viewed as the most critical: "The transformation phase is not only critical but the most demanding for designers since it requires delicate balancing of contending design factors" [PETE81].

In the final phase, convergence, the selected or combined alternatives are refined for eventual implementation. This is to say that the design is completed. See Figure 82 on page 211.

We can break design down into more granular activities and Freeman offers a good list of intellectual activities performed during design.
He notes, as did Enos and Van Tilburg, that it is important to differentiate between the managerial concerns that are focused by the life-cycle view of design

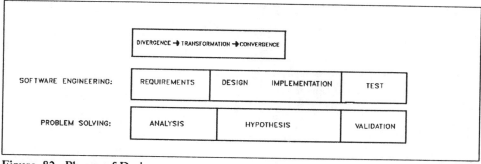

Figure 82. Phases of Design

and the technical concerns or activities that are carried out during design [FREE83]. Freeman lists these technical activities hierarchically as shown in Figure 83 on page 212.

If we map these activities against Peters' phases of divergence, transformation, convergence we see where the different design tasks are performed as shown in Figure 84 on page 213.

Let us now establish the basic definitions for these items. In a number of cases we have extended or modified Freeman's definitions for his set of activities. See Figure 85 on page 214.

This classification allows us to begin understanding where time may have to be spent doing design and the sequence and relationship between these activities. Important to note at this time is that the divergence phase is not adequately addressed with this set of activities, and Freeman does state that the activities "described here do not form a complete and consistent model of the design process." We have added two activities to this set, as shown in Figure 84 on page 213 which are included in the divergence phase: acquisition and problem resolution.

Acquisition as Belady states in his preface to Peters' book is the gathering "of a repertoire of alternatives, the raw materials for design: components, component solutions, and knowledge, all contained in catalogs, textbooks, and the mind."

Problem resolution is the reworking of the original requirements such that they are now bounded and are believed to be achievable under constraints of the solution environment.

Thus, we now have two more activities which are particular to the divergence phase, but just as Freeman indicated, we also do not know that this enhanced set is necessarily complete. Nonetheless, it does afford us a way to better understand what choices we need to make in using and understanding the many alternatives

```
                        DESIGN ACTIVITIES


     1.  Construction activities
            2.  Creation activities
                   3.  Decomposition
                       Translation
                       Abstraction
                       Elaboration
                       Evaluation
                       Decision making
            2.  Reflection activities
                   3.  Search
                       Reconstruction
                       Change identification
     1.  Control activities
            2.  Verification activities
                   3.  Comparison
                       Corruption identification
                       Representation quality control
            2.  Validation activities
                   3.  Prediction
                       Control
                       Extraction
```

Figure 83. Design Activities (from Freeman)

in design methodologies and representations. It also should indicate by its length of activities that design is not a stage that can be easily or quickly passed through.

7.4 Design Levels

We will show shortly that there are three levels within the design layer of the product life cycle. It is important to note, however, that not all three levels are required for all projects. In fact, it could be argued that for trivial programs design need not be a visibly discrete activity. We must tread carefully with this thought, however, as the trap of extrapolating to no or minimal design for other programs would result in project disasters. How then do we determine when we need any or all specific design levels?

The three design levels are labeled *Product Level Design*, *Component Level Design*, and *Module Level Design*. If the product were small enough to be contained within one module, then the need for a Product or Component level could be questioned. Again, however, we need to be wary of quicksand waiting for the

ACTIVITY/PHASE	DIVERGENCE	TRANSFORMATION	CONVERGENCE
Decomposition	X	X	X
Translation		X	X
Abstraction	X	X	X
Elaboration			X
Evaluation	X	X	X
Decision making	X	X	X
Search		X	X
Reconstruction		X	X
Change identification	X	X	X
Comparison		X	X
Corruption identification		X	X
Representation quality control		X	X
Prediction		X	X
Control		X	X
Extraction		X	X
Added Activities			
Acquisition	X		
Problem Resolution	X		

Figure 84. Mapping of Design Activities to Design Phases

naive. What is a module? At one perspective it is a separately compilable and self-contained functional entity. This, however, leaves the domain open to modules of minimal size in terms of lines of code to modules literally of tens of thousands of lines of code. The latter can be more in the nature of products than subparts of a product. We will more specifically address the idea of modules later in Chapter 9 and Chapter 10.

Decomposition---breaking a larger part into smaller

Translation---converting from one representation into another

Abstraction---generalizing, removing irrelevant details, separating the
essentials from the inessentials, or conceptualizing a general
quality which is unrelated to any particular concrete object or
refinement

Elaboration---detailing or adding features

Evaluation---determining on a dynamic and continuous basis that a
progression in the design process satisfies previously
determined criteria

Decision making---generating alternatives, evaluating those
alternatives, and choosing one alternative

Search---looking for specific representations which could satisfy the
solution

Reconstruction---producing the representation for the solution which
has been determined to satisfy the problem

Change Identification---identifying specific changes to a solution
representation or objective set

Comparison---examination of the consistency of meaning between two
or more representations

Corruption identification---denoting the difference in meaning
between two representations

Representation quality control---comparing the design representation
to a set of external quality criteria

Prediction---determining if a specification, if implemented, will
meet the objectives

Control---determining if representations of the design meet the
objectives

Extraction---revising the objectives based on inconsistent but
acceptable specifications or representations

Figure 85. Definition of Design Activities (from Freeman)

The problem appears to be one of scope and more specifically one of scope of control as we progress from requirements through design and on to implementation. If the problem is large enough to be decomposed into discrete subparts, then we have a Product Level Design (PLD). But is there a next level of design? Again, it becomes a question of scope of control. If the subparts derived during the PLD stage are small enough and discrete enough to stand as entities, then we may be done with design. If the designer has intellectual control over the part, then further decomposition may not be necessary. More important, however, is whether the implementer who receives the design agrees with the design in its final level of refinement.

Thus we have four basic design solution paths we could follow as shown in Figure 86 on page 216.

Let us now look at how we might make the choice as to which is appropriate to the problem we are trying to solve. Clearly, if we do more than is needed, we will waste resources, and if we do less, we will probably develop an inferior solution or miss schedules or require more resources later to complete the solution.

Before moving to Product Level Design, we should understand how the levels of design relate to the phases which Peters defines (reference Figure 87 on page 217). We suggest that divergence and transformation are fully contained within the highest level of design, here shown as PLD, and that convergence fully contains the activities of Component Level Design (CLD), Module Level Design (MLD), and additionally some activities within PLD.

One caution: all models are abstractions and work best when they remain simple. It is not intended to suggest either that the boundaries shown in Figure 87 on page 217 are firm or that some activities are not revisited in lower levels of design, nor is it suggested that work-ahead or iteration of activities is disallowed.

7.4.1 Product Level Design (PLD)

Let us begin by looking at an example. Reference Figure 88 on page 218. The product that we are addressing in this example is a programmer's workbench: a facility to help programmers perform their tasks and activities more productively and with higher quality output. It is not suggested that this is a complete definition of what is needed to satisfy the many programming tasks and activities: it is a definition for example purposes only.

We are suggesting here that the example product (The Programmer's Workbench) is composed of six, discrete subparts, or components of the product entity. This chart does not show the relationships, requirements or dependencies

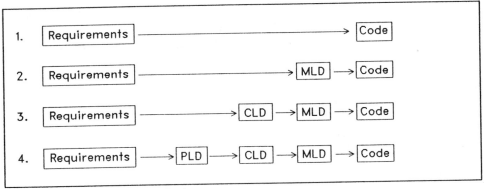

Figure 86. Problem Solution Paths

between these components. It only shows that the components relate as subparts of the product. It does not show the tasks that the product supports nor how these tasks relate. These were defined during the Requirements stage (Chapter 4). We would expect that tasks identified during the requirements analysis are allocated across these subparts.

It is not the intent here to show how the PLD is represented nor the method used to transform the Requirements Statement into a PLD representation. We will address this transformation specifically in Chapter 9. We are only representing by example the conceptual relationship of a product and its components. Now that the components have been selected, the design refinement into modules can begin.

7.4.2 Component Level Design (CLD)

If we continue with The Programmer's Workbench as an example, and select the component of the Test Case Generator, we might have a parts decomposition which looks as shown in Figure 89 on page 219. The parts in this example are modules. The component designs may proceed in parallel as much as the components are separable.

Again we are not showing any relationship except hierarchy towards the component of these modules within the Test Case Generator. Not shown is how these modules relate to the programming tasks or activities that are performed during the test stage of the product cycle. These we will address in Chapter 10 when we discuss Module Level Design.

This example only serves to represent the decomposition of a component into a set of modules which define that component. It does not show the relationships, requirements or dependencies between these modules. We will discuss in more

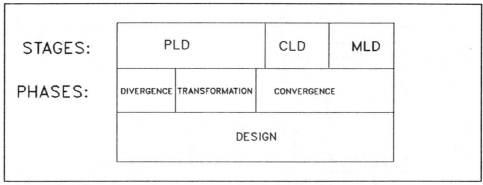

Figure 87. Design Stages Mapped to Design Solution Phases

depth how we evolve in an orderly and controllable manner from PLD to CLD when we discuss CLD in Chapter 9.

For now we should understand that when we have completed CLD we will have identified and assigned all of the tasks to the component subparts, and we will have addressed the need for specific modules to solve the requirements to complete the tasks identified during the requirements analysis. We have not addressed how the modules support meeting these requirements.

7.4.3 Module Level Design

The final stage is Module Level Design. It is during this stage that we will have many more parallel efforts proceeding during the same time frame. Each effort will address how the functional need of the specific module will be solved. During PLD there are minimal to no parallel design efforts, since the product is being addressed as an entity. During CLD we may have fanned out into parallelism for Component Level design statements. During MLD we fan out into even more parallelism.

When we have completed MLD for any one module, we will have everything we need to enter implementation as the next orderly step in the product life cycle. From a conceptual view the parts of the product life cycle are related as shown in Figure 90 on page 220.

We have fanned out into module parts and we will fan in by putting the parts together and testing them as an entity at different merged levels until we have one product part which is delivered to the user. Note that modules may have a relationship and affect more than one component or function.

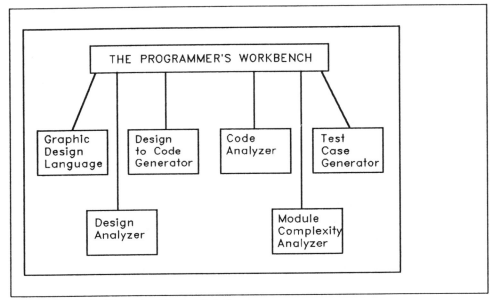

Figure 88. PLD View of a Design Solution

7.5 Models and Conceptual Views

In his 1978 ACM Turing Award Lecture, "The Paradigm of Programming," Robert W. Floyd called for the need to identify the paradigms we use in programming, since change in any discipline can only come about as change in the dominant paradigms is made evident. This is to say that if we have only one way to think about problems that we attempt to solve, then we are limited to the power of the paradigm we use or the way we think. If we wish to expand our solutions, then we must expand our base of paradigms, or ways to address problems. As Floyd says,

> if the advancement of the general act of programming requires the continuing invention and elaboration of paradigms, advancement of the act of the individual programmer requires that he expand his repertory of paradigms. [FLOY79]

Furthermore, not only do the concepts and paradigms we know affect how we may think about solving a problem, but they determine the processes, practices, tools, and methodologies we will develop to support us in our pursuits of software solutions. Thus, a methodology, for example, based on a specific paradigm may have solutions limited to a set of specific problems for which it works very well, but when used with a different set of problems the methodology may either constrict the solution or cause a less desirable solution to become manifest. We will explore how design methodologies relate to problem characteristics in

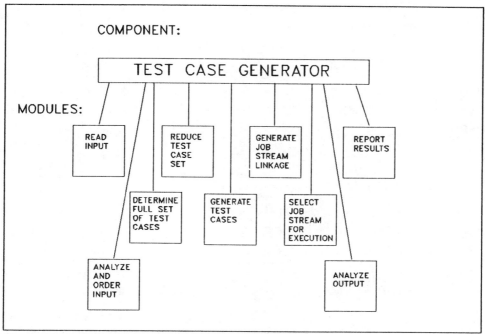

COMPONENT:

TEST CASE GENERATOR

MODULES:

READ INPUT

REDUCE TEST CASE SET

GENERATE JOB STREAM LINKAGE

REPORT RESULTS

DETERMINE FULL SET OF TEST CASES

GENERATE TEST CASES

SELECT JOB STREAM FOR EXECUTION

ANALYZE AND ORDER INPUT

ANALYZE OUTPUT

Figure 89. An Example of a CLD View of a Design Solution

Chapter 9 and Chapter 10. The software concepts in the following list are viewed as necessary but are not necessarily complete or sufficient for the programmers' working paradigm set. Nonetheless, as some of the more significant paradigms, they will allow us to better understand the methodologies we discuss later and will especially have relevance to the preferred methodologies we will recommend.

1. Structure
2. Hierarchy
3. Networking
4. Function
5. Finite State Machine

7.5.1 Structure

As mentioned earlier we can have subparts of a program. These subparts and their relationships we call the structure of a program. When we have a program composed of only one part, that is, the program itself, then we do not speak of the structure of the parts for indeed there is none. This was especially evident in the early days of programming. As program size and complexity grew, the need for ordered subprograms or subparts also grew. Over time, these parts became

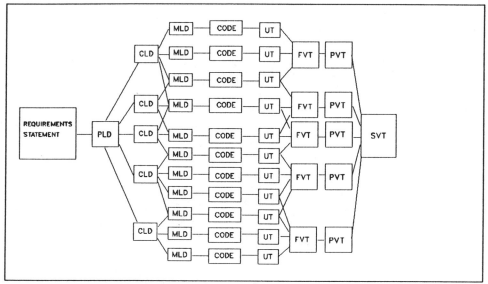

Figure 90. Conceptual Solution Parts View of the Product Life Cycle

known as modules and contained logical clusters of function, data, or both. Interfaces between these modules allowed the subparts to function as a whole unit.

Although this was a necessary advance in programming concepts, it evolved haphazardly, so that the order of the structure left much to be desired. For example, Figure 91 on page 221 shows the *structure* of a program's subparts and their calling relationships. For those of us today who use concepts such as structured programming and hierarchy, Figure 90 is an unacceptable structure. Yet its representative haphazardness was normal operating procedure within many design structures. There are two basic forms of structure which are of interest in programs: hierarchy and networks.

7.5.2 Hierarchy

When we view a program's structure as having layers progressing in abstraction where each layer is a decomposition of a previous layer into the lower level layer's constituent parts, we then have employed a *hierarchical decomposition*, and the hierarchical structure shows the relationships of this decomposition. Thus, in the previous example of the Programmer's Workbench we have a hierarchical decomposition structure showing decomposition, since the product at level one is divisible into components at level 2 which are in turn divisible into modules at level 3. We could proceed further to show how the segments or subparts of the modules exist at yet the fourth level of refinement in our solution.

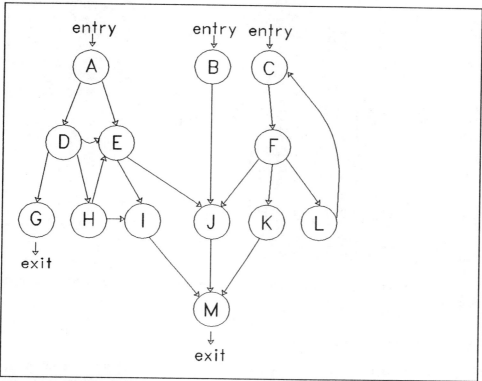

Figure 91. Example of Unstructured Program Structure

Another type of relationship in a hierarchical structure is stated by the the direction of flow between entities. This flow can be either progressively up or down depending on perspective, but it is always consistent in its progression. Thus, in Figure 92 on page 222, if the flow direction is shown by the arrows, we are always progressing down towards the final level. In this example module A can only call modules B or C. Module A is at a higher level than either modules B or C in a calling sequence hierarchy. Here, unlike the hierarchy showing decomposition relationships, we have a relationship of flow of control. This type of hierarchy is typically shown in organizational charts, where, for example, a group of managers report to a director. We would hardly think in this case that the director is decomposable into the managers, but we would think in terms of a flow of control from the director to the managers. The hierarchy is further defined as shown by the control flow relationships in Figure 92 on page 222. Level 5 represents modules which are four levels removed from the topmost level in execution sequence. As Fairley notes, hierarchical decomposition can result from a number of different criteria. "These include decomposition into processing steps and substeps, decomposition to reinforce information hiding, coupling and cohesion, data encapsulation, and/or problem modeling" [FAIR85].

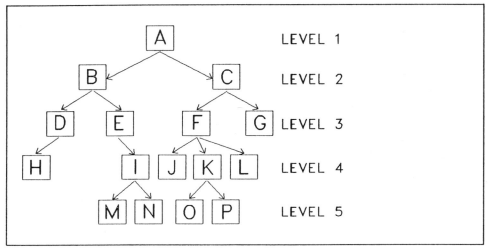

Figure 92. Example of Hierarchy Control Flow

We will see more of hierarchy when we discuss top down design and structured programming.

7.5.3 Networking

When we represent a structure as a network, the flow in the structure takes the direction of flow initiated by the nodes in the network structure. There is no one top view. For example, IBM's Virtual Telecommunication Access Method (VTAM) supports network communication. As shown in Figure 93 on page 223, the flow can be from any application or terminal to any other application or terminal.

Network relationships in design are particularly relevant to Entity-Relationship-Attribute (ERA) and to data flow design based methodologies and representations. The nodes in a network typically represent processors or transformers of data and the arcs between the nodes represent data flow or data links between the processors.

7.5.4 Function

A function is the model that can be used for algorithms packaged as programs or modules. The basis for this model is mathematics [LING79]. As a model, it is defined as a set of ordered pairs where each first element is unique. The set of all the first elements is called the domain; the set of all second elements is called the range. The function rule maps the domain to the range. Reference Figure 94 on

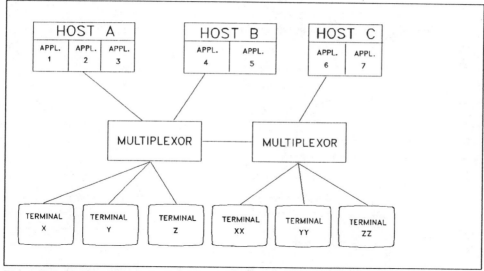

Figure 93. A Telecommunication Network

page 224 where the function module is shown graphically and in different representations of a mathematical function statement.

We commonly apply this model as a procedure where specific input values are expected to always produce the same output value each time the procedure is executed with the same input. Functions are necessary for us to build libraries of procedures from which we get packaged solutions rather than having to re-invent one every time a functional capability is needed. We will also see later how the function model plays a very essential role in helping us to develop proof of correctness methodologies.

7.5.5 Finite State Machine (FSM)

The concept of the finite state machine or FSM is another model which allows us to view how inputs are processed into outputs. The important difference as reflected in Figure 95 on page 225 is the introduction of the internal state of the machine. There are a finite number of states for any machine and the relationships or transition rules for external inputs, internal machine states, and external outputs must be explicitly defined within the machine. With each transition, the output derived from both the input and the existing state of the machine is changed to one that is predefined under the executing conditions defined in the FSM. Thus mathematically the state machine is a set of ordered pairs (such that no two pairs have the same first element) of ordered pairs.

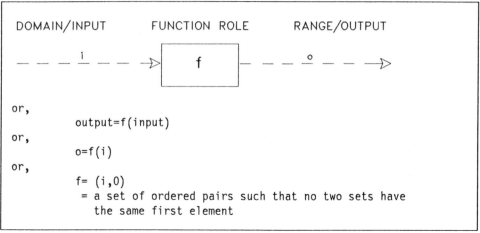

DOMAIN/INPUT   FUNCTION ROLE   RANGE/OUTPUT

or,
          output=f(input)
or,
          o=f(i)
or,
          f= (i,0)
            = a set of ordered pairs such that no two sets have
              the same first element

Figure 94. Function Representation

We can show FSM processing in a tabular form that fully defines the allowable inputs, outputs, and new state transformations based on the inputs and current state at the time of the input. Reference Figure 96 on page 226.

Here we see that the same external inputs (3s and 4s) produce different external outputs (1 and 6, 2 and 8, respectively). A function always would return the same output for any one same input. Therefore this would not appear to an external observer to be a function since the same inputs derived different output. In an FSM the output is determined by both the input and the current state of the machine. To an observer inside the machine, it would be a function, and the set of ordered pairs for this example are:

$$((1,3)(3,1)), ((3,4)(4,2)), ((4,4)(4,8)), (4,3)(3,6)), ((3,6)(6,3))$$

We will make use of FSMs when we discuss the topic of design and data abstractions in Chapter 10. As with functions that can be decomposed within a program, FSMs can also exist at different levels [SALT76].

7.6 Design Methodologies

There are five basic groupings that encompass the many existing design methodologies used in software engineering. These are: functional decomposition, data structure, data flow, prescriptive, and object oriented. We will explore each of these in more detail here and in later chapters.

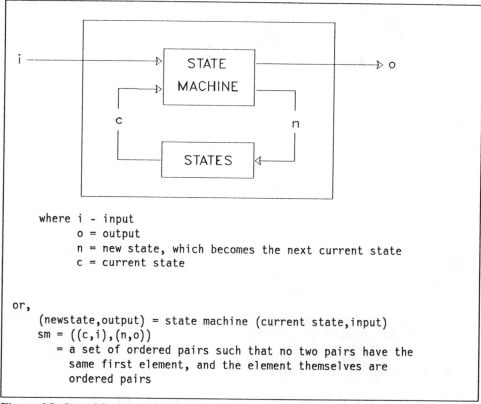

```
        where i - input
              o = output
              n = new state, which becomes the next current state
              c = current state


or,
        (newstate,output) = state machine (current state,input)
        sm = ((c,i),(n,o))
            = a set of ordered pairs such that no two pairs have the
              same first element, and the element themselves are
              ordered pairs
```

Figure 95. State Machine Representation

First we should understand what we mean when we speak of a software design methodology. Simply stated, it is a way of doing the design. Freeman offers three aspects which a design method must address: (1) what decisions are to be made, (2) how to make them, and (3) in what order they should be made [FREE83].

Not all methodologies will specifically include all of these aspects, and thus we should suspect that these methodologies are not sufficiently defined for repeatable use across different programming groups. Our own experiences show how readily different groups will modify a methodology to satisfy what they perceive as their unique environments. In some instances, the modifications are introduced for good and ample reasons, but in far too many cases they are introduced because the programming group either did not adequately learn the methodology, the methodology was not complete, or indeed the programmers simply believed they had a better way, right or wrong. Much of this is due to human nature, and we do not propose to try to change it, nor do we believe it will be changed, but a methodology that is not properly and completely defined will be the first to fall to

CURRENT STATE	INPUT	NEW STATE	OUTPUT
1	3	3	1
3	4	4	2
4	4	4	8
4	3	3	6
3	6	6	3

Figure 96. FSM Processing in Tabular Form

change. Maybe that is the way it should be, if we believe that evolution weeds out the weak through selection and change.

7.6.1 Functional Decomposition

Functional decomposition methodologies show how the flow from element to element in the structure is determined or directed by defining and relating functional subparts of the solution. Thus in our previous discussion of hierarchy we saw that the flow of the design solution could be either from top to bottom or from bottom to top depending on perspective.

When we later look at what has been labeled top-down design, we know immediately how the methodology wants us to perceive and direct the flow of design development. Alternately, the more loosely defined method of bottom-up design asks that first we define the bottom layer of our product, and then progressively work our way to the top. The former employs the activity of decomposition while the latter requires the activity of abstracting to higher level relationships.

Another methodology that is included in functional decomposition is structured programming.

We explore both top-down design and structured programming methodologies in Chapter 9 and Chapter 10.

7.6.2 Data Structure

Data structure methodologies do not focus so much on the flow and transformations that the data follows, as they do with clearly identifying the basic structure of both the input and output to a program and then defining the program structure based on both of these data structures. There are additional procedures that vary between the different methodology approaches.

Two of the most written about methodologies in this group are named after their originators: Jackson method and Warnier method. We discuss the Jackson method in Chapter 9 and Chapter 10.

7.6.3 Data Flow

With data flow design methodologies, we primarily focus on how the overall product's data flows through the program. Included in these methodologies are procedures to address and account for the transformations the data takes as it flows from input to the program and then becomes output. The network model rather than the hierarchical model is an underlying concept to show how the data goes through transformations: joining, diverging, or being stored with other data [PETE81].

Chief among these methodologies is the Structured Design or more specifically, Composite Design, developed by Stevens [STEV74], Myers [MYER78], Yourdon and Constantine [YOUR79]. We will spend a fair amount of time in discussing this methodology in Chapter 10.

Another approach that follows a data flow orientation is Structured Analysis and Design Techniques (SADT) of SofTech Corporation [CONN80].

7.6.4 Prescriptive

Prescriptive methods actually employ parts of other design methodologies, representations, and practices that seem to either make sense from an intuitive view or are based on the prescriber's experiences. These methods typically prescribe or dictate step by step procedures which the designer must follow to complete the design. It is hard to argue with methods based on successful experience, but many of these methods read either like a straight jacket or they approach motherhood statements which are hard to sell without a taxonomy of application. While we may class certain design methodologies as prescriptive, they have very little in common conceptually except that they have shown evidence of being successful in at least one environment, and they do exhibit a prescriptive nature [PETE81].

7.6.5 Object Oriented

This last area is more recent than the previous four approaches to design methodologies and has begun to demonstrate more popularity with the advent of Ada and its capability to define packages or data abstractions. It is these very packages or data abstractions that are referred to as objects and wherein "the approach recognizes the importance of discernible software objects, each with its own set of applicable operations" [BOOC83].

Among others who have also been advocating this methodology for design are Liskov and Zilles [LISK75], and Shankar [SHAN80].

We discuss this approach in more detail in Chapter 9 and Chapter 10, and especially describe how it can integrate itself into some of the other methodologies.

7.7 Design Representations

Design representations are the carriers or communication vehicles which are used to both capture the results of the design thought process and to move the design to other programming groups for their use. The argument of whether to hide design detail or show all design detail has existed long before software. In fact, there are alternative levels of design representation in fields like building architecture. Indeed, as we will see later, there are appropriate ways to reflect the needed detail at the appropriate time in a number of design representations.

The book, *Diagramming Techniques for Analysts and Programmers* [MART85B], gives an extensive breakdown of a large number of representation schemes. While this breakdown may not be complete, it will leave the reader understanding that there is a vast number of alternatives existent for software design representation.

The problem of large numbers of design representations is compounded if one tries to address all of the alternatives within one of the generic techniques. For example, at one time we were able to identify over 200 approaches to pseudocode. Most of them had large areas of similarity, but you have to pause to wonder how so many different dialects came to occur so quickly and for what purpose.

7.8 What Is Good Design?

It has been stated by some that good design can be defined as design that maps to the requirements clearly and conveys the solution to the coder. This is not only simple, it is an abdication of responsibility. For example, let us suppose the requirements have no mention of usability and that the user in fact concurs with the requirements. The designer completes the solution and the product is not usable. Who is at fault, the designer or the user? We would argue that it is the designer who was at fault for the Tacoma Narrows bridge and not the government agency that commissioned the design and building of the bridge. Surely, the user in most instances assumed the design would lead to a safe product and in fact had no way to ensure this except to assume the contracted design would make it so. Thus, design in our thinking carries with it the responsibility to make it good, based on some criteria that must be addressed, if not satisfied, by the designer.

The user, although he or she believes he knows what he wants and although he may be involved in reviews to evaluate the requirements, may not really have a good feeling for making explicit what is needed. Equally, the designer certainly cannot know what the user may or may not really want, but the good designer does know, especially after training and experience, that all products must address a set of attributes that help to define them as good products.

Included in this list of attributes are capability or functionality, usability, performance, reliability, installability, and maintainability. Although these are physical product attributes, the designer will know before anyone whether these attributes will exist in the product. If they are not existent or addressed in the specifications, and he does nothing to make them visible, then the product may be defective and the designer is culpable.

Enos and Van Tilburg suggest that there are indeed attributes for a good design that are achievable in all designs [ENOS79]. These are outlined in Figure 97 on page 230.

Aside from all these, we would argue that if the design is not cost effective, it is not good. Additionally, it should be understandable to enable its maintenance and enhancement.

- Necessity: putting into the design only those performance requirements and design functions necessary to meet the requirements of usability.

- Completeness: all modules in the structure are identified, all interfaces are specified, and all environments are specified.

- Consistency: design philosophy incompatibilities have been identified and resolved.

- Traceability: all design elements must be traceable to requirements.

- Visibility: trade-off decisions must be traceable.

- Feasibility: critical elements in the design must have been demonstrated to be attainable in the current state of the art.

Figure 97. Attributes of Good Design (from Enos and Van Tilburg)

7.8.1 Design Validation

Design validation is a way to check for the goodness of design against some pre-defined criteria. Design validation takes many of the same forms as other work product validation approaches. For example, at each discrete level of design completion, PLD, CLD, and MLD, a formal Inspection should be held. These inspections will establish that the refinement from the accepted requirements is in fact proceeding as desired through each transformation stage.

Additionally, users can be involved in a less formal review of either the PLD or a prototype of the product. These both will serve to give early warning of usability and capabilities issues.

On a more rigorous level, proof of correctness during design refinement offers some help. However, we must state that in complex or large systems programming formal proofs have rarely been successfully implemented. This appears to be due mostly to the high degree of effort involved in correctness proofs. Nonetheless, we will discuss this approach in some detail in Chapter 10.

7.9 Design Directions

Where will design methodologies, tools, and production practices need to change in order to evolve to a higher plane of repeatability, consistency, and quality of design? There are many areas and even more opinions from which to debate this question. We would like to focus briefly on four directions we believe will have a major effect on the design of software in the future.

1. Requirements to Design Bridge: There is no one completely satisfactory solution for this problem. Approaches such as PSL, SADT, SREM, and any of the structured analysis proposals, while usable at some levels of design and for some software problems, have not been widely applied or accepted. In some instances acceptance may be limited because of biases or entrenched prior approaches, but it also appears that these proposals sometimes have proven difficult to use and insufficient sometimes when working through the detail levels of design. As with a better mousetrap, a better requirements-to-design solution will have the world beating a path to its door.

2. Prototyping: Any language can be used to develop a prototype in software. Some are easier to use than others; some such as Basic Assembler Language are awkward to use at best and questionable as a choice. We are assuming here that prototyping occurs as early as possible in the design of a system, and that it is not eventually shipped as the product. Therefore, we are assuming that the prototype will be written in as high a level of language as is available, and that it will be executable or interpretable. There are many languages that satisfy this requirement. What we are suggesting is that a language or language environment is needed that makes prototypes easy to choose and use, is extendable into lower levels of details to complete the design, and allows maintenance of the prototype and design at different levels of the problem solution.

3. Design Automation: This need includes a design subsystem environment as part of the software development system environment. More can be, is being, and will be done to enrich design methodologies and tools within development environment solutions. This is necessary for business reasons, for as more software is required and the increase in numbers of programmers remains insufficient to solve the problem of demand, then automation must be brought into being to increase productivity. Embedded as a limitation to automation especially with respect to design is the fact that no automation can replace the need for creativity in developing solutions. Automation can only make the design tasks easier, more productive, and reliable, it cannot replace creativity.

4. Automatic Code Generation: On the other hand, automation may eliminate the need to transform design into code and thereby eliminate one of the major places of defect insertion during the development cycle. Perhaps we are only requiring a higher level language rather than a design-to-code generation solution. In either event, if we can raise the level of solution statement in design such that it can be executed, then we will have improved the software development process.

7.9.1 Summary

In this chapter we discussed design for software, and what we do when we design. As was seen from the works by Peters and Freeman, there are a number of activities that need to be performed which require time and resources if the design solution is to meet the needs of the users. We introduced the idea that there are three discrete levels for software design: Product Level Design, Component Level Design, and Module Level Design. We will explore each of these in more detail in Chapter 9 and Chapter 10. There are a number of concepts necessary for a software engineer to design, such as structure, hierarchy, networking, function, and finite state machines. We introduced the five prevalent design methodologies: (1) functional decomposition, (2) data structure, (3) data flow, (4) prescriptive, and (5) object oriented. Each will be discussed in detail in succeeding chapters. We briefly discussed the need for design representations as carriers of the solution and explored the idea of a "good design." We concluded the chapter with a discussion on design validation and possible future directions for design in software.

7.10 References

[BOEH75] B. W. Boehm, R. L. McClean, and D. B. Urfig, "Some Experience with Automated Aids to the Design of Large–Scale Reliable Software," *IEEE Transactions on Software Engineering*, Vol. SE-1, No. 1 (March 1975), pp. 125 – 33.

[BOOC83] G. Booch, "Object–Oriented Design," adapted from *Software Engineering with Ada*, Benjamin/Cummings Publishing Co. (1983).

[CONN80] M. F. Conner, "SADT: Structured Analysis and Design Techniques Introduction," *IEEE Management Conference Record*.

[ENOS79] J. C. Enos and R. L. Van Tilburg, "Chapter 3: Software Design," in *Software Engineering*, Randall W. Jensen and Charles C. Tonies, eds., Prentice-Hall (1979).

[FAIR85] R. E. Fairley, *Software Engineering Concepts*, McGraw-Hill Book Company (1985).

[FLOY79] R. W. Floyd, "The Paradigm of Programming," *Communications of the ACM*, Vol. 22, No. 8 (August 1979), pp. 455 – 60.

[FREE83] P. Freemen, "Fundamentals of Design," *Tutorial on Software Design Techniques*, IEEE Computer Society Press (1983).

[LING79] R. C. Linger, H. D. Mills, and B. J. Witt, *Structured Programming: Theory and Practice*, Addison-Wesley Publishing Company (1979).

[LISK75] B. Liskov and S. Zilles, "Specification Techniques for Data Abstractions," *IEEE Transactions on Software Engineering*, Vol. SE-1, No. 1 (March 1975), pp. 7 – 19.

[MART85B] J. Martin and C. McClure, *Diagramming Techniques for Analysts and Programmers*, Prentice-Hall (1985).

[MYER78] G. J. Myers, *Composite/Structured Design*, Van Nostrand Reinhold Company (1978).

[PETE78] L. J. Peters and L. L. Tripp, "A Model of Software Engineering," *Proceedings of the Third International Conference on Software Engineering*, New York, IEEE Computer Society (1978), pp. 63 – 70.

[PETE81] L. J. Peters, *Software Design: Methods and Techniques*, Yourdon Press (1981).

[SALT76] K. Salter, "A Methodology for Decomposing System Requirements into Data Processing Requirements," *Proceedings 2nd International Conference on Software Engineering* (October 1976).

[SHAN80] K. S. Shankar, "Data Structures, Types and Abstractions," *Computer* (April 1980).

[STEV74] W. P. Stevens, G. J. Myers, and L. L. Constantine, "Structured Design," *IBM Systems Journal*, Vol. 13, No. 2 (February 1974), pp. 115 – 39.

[YOUR79] E. Yourdon and L. L. Constantine, *Structured Design*, Prentice-Hall (1979).

Chapter 8. Validation and Verification

8.1 Introduction

Within the ETVX paradigm introduced in Chapter 2, we noted that for every task there must be a corresponding validation of that task. No activity within the development of a software product is completed without this validation. No work item should proceed into a new activity of product development without a validation step. To do otherwise is to open up the product to the potential of increased defect propagation. The best time to remove a defect is immediately after the work item has been completed. Thus, we should perform the validation immediately after a work item task has been completed. If we cannot do so immediately, we can certainly perform the validation prior to beginning a new level of development or refinement on the work item. For example, we would not begin Code until the results of the Module Level Design had been validated. To this point in the book we have been using the term validation in a generic sense within the ETVX model. Actually there are two views of correctness which are contained in our use of the term validation. Barry Boehm, in *Software Engineering Economics* draws out these views succinctly in his definitions.

Validation: "Are we building the right product?"

Verification: "Are we building the product right?" [BOEH81]

Here validation is concerned with the value or worth of the software product, while verification is concerned with the correct and consistent refinement of a product with respect to some higher level that has already been proven to be correct or of worth. Thus, we would assume that validation is of concern early in the development cycle; that is, are we developing a product that is worth developing? We might ask this question during Product Planning and Requirements Engineering. After we have determined that we are developing the product that is wanted by a user community, then we would begin to refine the requirements into a design and then into code. It is during these refinements that we should ask ourselves: "Are we building the product right?"; that is, are we refining the solution correctly?

We explore in this chapter why validation and verification are required in order to deliver high quality software products. We will address a number of alternative approaches that have been used, and we will focus on two primary recommended approaches: *Inspections* and *Proof of Correctness*. Additionally, we will give enough of the mechanics to enable the reader to begin using Inspections on their software products. Proof of Correctness will be discussed in more detail in Chapter 10 when we introduce a design language that enables proofs of design correctness.

8.2 Good Programmers Make Errors

How many times have you been convinced, absolutely convinced, that you had either created a defect-free program or had "tested out" all of the defects only to sadly discover that yet another bug was found? One wonders how we as programmers have been able to repeatedly survive this cruel onslaught to our egos.

We are not talking about the slovenly programmer who seems to develop as many defects as lines of code in the program. Neither are we referring to the programmer who is in a schedule crunch without enough time to develop the best work. Rather, we are talking about that very qualified programmer, who does have an ample schedule to produce a defect-free piece of work. Yet after the program is delivered to the user, fixes have to be provided to enable the product to work as advertised. We are not going to try to come to terms in this volume with why this may happen, for there truly are many reasons, and at least some, we dare say, we as an industry do not yet understand. Let it remain for now that good programmers do indeed make mistakes, and if this is true for the better programmers, then it must follow all the more so for the rest of the programming population.

If mistakes are made while producing a software product, a defect can be injected into the product. If these errors are not removed, then defects will be shipped with the product. Some of these defects may never become visible to the product user, but those that do will require service to upgrade the product. Fixing defects through product maintenance activities is more costly than fixing the defects prior to delivery to the user. This cost relationship has been shown numerous times in the literature: IBM [FAGA76], GTE [DALY77], TRW [BOEH81], and AT&T [STEP76]. In addition to the higher costs, user satisfaction can be affected by defects. In turn a lower user satisfaction can have an impact on continued sales for the product in the commercial market. For other products a defect might result in a catastrophic or critical, life or death situation. Clearly, software development has ample reasons for wanting to create zero-defect products.

8.3 Alternatives for Delivering Defect-Free Product

Is it possible to deliver a defect-free product? We believe it is. Has it been done? Not often. The real issue in our view is not how we can create defect-free products, but why it is not done more often. Another way to view the concern is to ask, why are software products as defective as they are? Why are they not better? What we are suggesting is that all software products can be made less defective. It becomes a question of choice.

First, the choice is in deciding whether it should be done; that is, should we spend more to improve quality. We would vote that is should always be done, but there is the cost. However, there is also a savings. Unfortunately, the cost is seen early and the savings are seen later in the development life cycle. Eventually the savings more than account for the costs, but the decision to spend more resources to produce a product than was historically spent on other products is always a difficult decision. A hypothetical example is shown in Figure 98 on page 237. In this example we see the costs required to remove defects with early detection compared with early detection and improved inspections [RADI82]. The one assumption we make is that the cost to find and fix a defect in any stage remains roughly equal in both scenarios. We see that test costs decrease as there are fewer errors to find in test. We see that maintenance costs also decrease as the shipped quality is better.

Thus, in this hypothetical example we see that by spending $1,000,000 earlier to improve the effectiveness of Inspections, that we save $4,020,000 in test and maintenance. This is not only a good return on investment, but it represents about a 30 percent improvement in overall productivity.

Second, the choice is in deciding among the different defect-removal alternatives to deliver products with better quality. Most of these alternatives are of the defect detection nature; that is, they occur after a work item has been completed. More significant is to prevent the defects from occurring in the first place. This is a newer focus in software and we will speak to it later in this chapter. For now

COSTS WITH EARLY DETECTION:

Stage	Error Detection Rate (errors/KLOC)	Cost to find and Fix an Error $/error	Cost of Errors K$	Programming Development Costs K$	Inspection Costs K$	Total Costs K$
PLD/CLD	8	50	40	300	---	340
MLD	12	100	120	300	---	420
Code	18	200	360	400	---	760
All Tests	22	1000	2200	2200	---	4400
Field Use	2	5000	10000	---	---	10000

TOTAL: 15,920

COSTS WITH EARLY DETECTION WITH IMPROVED INSPECTIONS EFFECTIVENESS:

Stage	Error Detection Rate	Cost to find and Fix an Error	Cost of Errors	Programming Development Costs	Inspection Costs	Total Costs
PLD/CLD	10	50	50	300	300	650
MLD	15	100	150	300	300	750
Code	20	200	400	400	400	1200
All Tests	16	1000	1600		---	3600
Field Use	1	5000	5000	---	---	5000

TOTAL: 11,200

Figure 98. Example of Cost Effectiveness of Early Defect Detection

let us discuss the prevalent defect-removal methods used to validate and verify a completed work item.

8.3.1 Peer Reviews

This is perhaps the easiest and simplest alternative. It requires only one other person who has the time to review, for example, another programmer's code. Any errors, questions, or concerns are noted and passed on to the author for consideration and correction. It is, however, only as effective as the person doing the review. More specifically it is dependent on the availability, frame of mind, experience, and thoroughness of the reviewer, among other factors that can militate against the success of the review. Success is defined here as finding all the defects. Anything less is less of a success. When this approach is successful, it is the least costly to perform. Our experience shows that the success factor is unfortunately low with this approach. This becomes a particular problem when the execution of a peer review leads one to higher expectations of quality which are not seen in program execution, because the reviews were ineffective.

8.3.2 Reviews and Walk-Throughs

Peer reviews certainly help; they are better than not doing any reviews. What they suggest, however, is that the vulnerability to success can be reduced by making the review less dependent on one individual reviewer. Thus, *reviews* and *walk-throughs* that tried to eliminate some of the vulnerabilities that existed in peer reviews evolved as the next level of defect-removal methodology. In these approaches a group of people get together to review a work item such as a module design. Typically the review/walk-through is scheduled in advance with some degree of preparation assumed to have been done prior to the group review meeting. At the review meeting the participants will "walk-through" the design, using a higher level product design or requirement statement as a base of comparison along with the design programmer. After the review the design programmer is responsible for making any necessary corrections.

This approach is an improvement over peer review, but due to its informal nature, it too leaves some doubts about its overall effectiveness and repeatability.

8.3.3 Inspections

The *Inspection* methodology initiated by Mike Fagan in IBM in 1972 tried to address the problems that were inherent in the review/walk-through approach. While it is in our view a superior approach which is widely practiced, it is by no means universally accepted. The chief obstacles seem to be commitment to maintain a rigorous approach and that it requires more of an upfront cost to do it well. When there is a commitment to use Inspections, they have worked extremely well and have earned back all their costs and then some [FAGA86].

An Inspection is a formal team review and evaluation of a programming product work item. The Inspection is led by an independent moderator with the intended purpose of effectively and efficiently finding defects early in the development process cycle, recording them as a basis for analysis and history, and initiating rework to correct the defects. The Inspection team sometimes uses a checklist to validate the work product against historical defect types. The Inspection results will indicate whether to allow the work item to continue into the next product stage by either passing or failing the work item based on predefined exit criteria. The Inspection is a validation of the completed work item under review.

A programming product that is composed of many work items must not be viewed as simply the coded program, although the program is certainly one of the set of work items that is part of the product. The programming product includes requirements statements, high level design specifications, module level design specifications, user manuals, test plans, and individual test cases among other work items. The complete set of work items for a product is defined by the specific process used to develop a final product for the users. All work items are candidates for Inspections.

Inspections themselves follow a process that includes the following activities:

1. Planning

2. Overview

3. Preparation

4. Inspection

5. Report

6. Rework

7. Follow-up

We discuss Inspections as one of our recommended choices for validation and verification in detail later in this chapter.

8.3.4 Prototyping

Prototypes are a key part of the development process, and we want to mention them here because of the significant feedback mechanism they can provide in the early product life cycle. Prototypes have long been a part of other engineering disciplines, and it makes sense that the idea be applied to software production also. Basically the reason for a prototype, or an early version of the final product, is to help determine if the final product is feasible and achievable; that is, is it usable and does it satisfy the requirements? A prototype is not and was never intended to be the final product. Never, that is, except in software. The industry is replete with examples of prototypes that have been redeveloped or shipped as final products. This might be acceptable if shipping the prototype had desirable attributes other than helping to contain a poorly planned schedule or a badly overrun project. This is not to suggest that there is anything wrong with developing a prototype for a software product. In fact, prototyping is encouraged. However, the prototype should be part of the process used to develop a superior product and not part of the product. There are rare exceptions to this, and shipping the prototype as the product should only be considered when quality and maintenance goals are not jeopardized.

A prototype offers most value when it is developed as early on in the life cycle as possible. Ideally this would be right after the Requirements stage exit. When the prototype is ready, it can then be used to validate the requirements statement. The prototype validation will work better if users can be involved in the validation of the requirements through the prototype.

Once the prototype exists, it can be maintained as an adjunct to the product to provide early validation of new requirements of design changes against the baseline prototype previously validated.

8.3.5 User Involvement

We spoke earlier in Chapter 5, Human Factors and Usability about user involvement. Where this can be accomplished, it offers an excellent approach to validating requirements and human factors aspects of the product. Additionally, it serves as the ultimate validation of requirements interpretation done during Requirements Engineering.

8.3.6 Proof of Correctness

It is arguable that proof of correctness techniques should be viewed as an alternative approach for defect removal [DUNN84]. There is no doubt in our minds that proof of correctness is a primary verification method. Basically it is a mathematical method of verifying the logic or function of a program or program part. There are a number of approaches to proof of correctness. We will explore in more detail in Chapter 10 the method taught at the Software Engineering Institute at IBM which is based on the work of Harlan Mills [LING79]. While this method currently is the most labor-intensive of the verification methods, it offers a consistent and repeatable approach. Once the refined specification or design has been proven to be correct against the higher level specification or design, it is correct and probably defect-free with respect to that base. The refinement has been done right. The argument which still exists is whether the higher level specification was the right statement of what is to be done. The assumption is that it is, and that it has been validated to show that it is.

8.3.7 Testing

The ultimate validation and verification prior to delivery of the product to the user lies in testing. If nothing has been validated or verified prior to testing, this is where validation and/or verification will first occur. Postponing validation until test is borrowing for trouble, so let us assume some validation and verification has previously occurred. Indeed, in a well-designed process it can be expected that each product work item, including those related to test, will have been validated or verified *prior* to the first test entry. Where this is done, the test can focus on testing, that is, validating the product rather than focusing on defect removal which is the traditional use of testing in software development. We will discuss test in detail in Volume 2 of this series.

8.3.8 Other Approaches

There are other approaches to verification, that typically involve tools. For example there are *pseudolanguage* processors that can analyze for such things as inconsistencies in the use of the pseudolanguage, for improper sequences of processing steps, and for interface inconsistencies [DUNN84]. Other tools include static analysis and dynamic analysis packages that can process the design or source code looking for various types or errors. While these tools are more focused on defect removal, they do offer a level of verification and are recommended for use within the environment where they exist.

8.4 Recommended Approaches

Figure 99 on page 242 shows where the different validation and verification methods could be used to best advantage within the stages defined in the Programming Process Architecture, PPA (Chapter 2). We recommend Inspections, in preference to Reviews, Walk-throughs, or Peer Reviews, which do not appear in the figure. We show the validation and verification methods from the viewpoint of Product Development only. Note that for all the other viewpoints defined in the PPA, the work items completed in the respective activities would also have a validation or verification step.

STAGE	PRODUCT DEVELOPMENT
Requirements and Planning	1. User Involvement 2. Inspection
Product Level Design	1. User Involvement 2. Prototype 3. Inspection
Component Level Design	1. Prototype 2. Inspections 3. Proof of Correctness
Module Level Design	1. Inspections 2. Proof of Correctness
Code	1. Inspections

Figure 99. Validation and Verification Within Stages

8.4.1 Inspections

As already mentioned, Inspections are preferred and recommended as a defect-removal method rather than Reviews, Walk-throughs, or Peer Reviews. This is because Inspections have resolved the deficiencies in the other approaches mentioned. Experience has shown Inspections to be very successful in systematically and consistently discovering defects.

Mike Fagan, in his article in the 1976 IBM Systems Journal, showed a chart that compared walk-throughs with Inspections [FAGA76]. The comparisons are shown in Figure 100 on page 243 and Figure 101 on page 244.

Inspections are systematic. In Figure 100 on page 243 there are seven steps or process operations for Inspections, while for Walk-throughs there are only two process operations. Note also that the objective of the Inspection step is solely to find defects, while that of Walk-throughs is additionally to provide group education and to discuss design alternatives. We will address this distinction shortly. We have taken the liberty to modify the original table from Fagan for Figure 100 on page 243 to include the planning and reporting operations, which have been added since 1976.

Figure 101 on page 244 makes evident the more formal and rigorous approach of Inspections versus Walk-throughs. The notion of a moderator, or formal leader is introduced. The notion of defining roles for each participant is intro-

INSPECTION		WALK-THROUGH	
PROCESS OPERATIONS	OBJECTIVES	PROCESS OPERATIONS	OBJECTIVES
1. Planning	Secure resources	---	---
2. Overview	Education (group)	---	---
3. Preparation	Education (individual)	1. Preparation	Education (individual)
4. Inspection	Find defects (group)	2. Walk-through	Education (group)
5. Report	Document problems		Discuss design alternatives
6. Rework	Fix problems	---	Find errors
7. Follow-up	Ensure all fixes correctly installed	---	---

Figure 100. Inspection and Walk-Through Processes and Objectives (from Fagan)

duced. The technique of using checklists and error distribution types to aid the finding of defects in introduced. Steps for follow-up to ensure that all defects are fixed are shown. The important aspects of feedback and analysis of data to improve the process are introduced.

We may conclude from this evaluation that Inspections are more disciplined than walk-throughs, leading to a more effective process for defect removal. The same conclusion also applies to reviews as defined in Yourdon [YOUR79A] and in Freedman and Weinberg [FREE82].

In all of these other methods for defect removal: walk-throughs, reviews, and peer reviews, we see that the process is less repeatable than Inspections, because of factors like inadequate formal training for the participants, lack of consistent checklists by which the process and product can be evaluated, inadequate data capture or data analysis, lack of cause analysis, and lack of feedback and re-evaluation of the process itself to determine if it can be made more effective.

PROPERTIES	INSPECTION	WALK-THROUGH
1. Formal moderator training	Yes	No
2. Definite participant roles	Yes	No
3. Who drives the inspection or walk-through	Moderator	Owner of mater. Designer or Coder
4. Use "How to Find Errors" checklists	Yes	No
5. Use distribution of error types to look for	Yes	No
6. Follow-up to reduce bad fixes	Yes	No
7. Less future errors because of detailed error feedback to individual programmer	Yes	Incidental
8. Improve inspection efficiency from analysis of results	Yes	No
9. Analysis of data --> process problems --> improvements	Yes	No

Figure 101. Comparison of Key Properties of Inspections and Walk-Throughs (from Fagan)

In the original studies in 1972 when Inspections were compared to walk-throughs one of the authors worked with Fagan and found that, aside from the differences in methods of performing Inspections and walk-throughs, Inspections were indeed more effective in finding defects.

It is important to note that in no cases are the data from the inspections to be used as input for appraising the programmer responsible for the material to be inspected. To do otherwise would defeat the primary intent of Inspections which is to find defects efficiently and effectively. If people are concerned that the data will reflect an appraisal of their work, human nature may prevail and the process may be sub-optimized to reflect that the work is nothing less than outstanding; no defects are found ... at least at the inspection.

8.4.2 Proof of Correctness

We also prefer and recommend that proof of correctness be used as a verification method. While it will be difficult to easily apply proofs to all programs, we believe it is important to try nonetheless, as proofs will provide the programmer with insights into the mathematical properties of the programs they are designing and implementing. When proofs are combined with Inspections we believe that a powerful verification methodology exists to provide higher levels of quality for software. This is to say that the design or code and the corresponding proofs can be read together during the Inspection to provide a more effective Inspection. Mills, among others, suggest that the proofs be developed while the design or code is being developed. We agree that this is the preferred approach, but suggest that the proof can be made more useful when incorporated into the Inspection process also.

If proofs are to be applied to design as well as code, then a design language which permits the expression for proofs would be advantageous. Indeed such languages already exist, for example, PDL-Ada used by the Federal Systems Development (FSD) group in IBM for some of its work. Grady Booch states that Ada itself is usable as a design language and demonstrates this in his book *Software Engineering with Ada* [BOOC83]. We introduce A Design Language, ADL, in Chapter 9 and Chapter 10, which we use to refine design and which allows the expression of formal proofs.

8.5 What Is an Inspection in Software Development?

In this section we will discuss in more detail what Inspections are, how they are performed, who is involved in the different process operations, when Inspections are performed, and when they can begin in a project which has not used them before.

In 1976 Fagan stated that "Inspections are a *formal, efficient,* and *economical* method of finding errors in design and code. All instructions are addressed at least once in the conduct of inspection" [FAGA76]. Only four years earlier the first design Inspection had been moderated by one of the authors of this book. At that time in 1972 we were only concerned with inspecting the work items resulting from Module Level Design and of Code. Since that time Inspections have evolved such that any work item which is either an initial statement of a product part or a refinement of a product part can be verified using Inspections.

Thus, today we inspect from the Program Development viewpoint the results of Product Planning, Requirements Engineering, PLD, CLD, MLD, and Code.

For the Publications viewpoint we inspect all plans, all drafts, and versions of a publication. For the testing viewpoint we inspect all test plans, test scenario designs, and test scenario implementations much as we do for Program Development. These latter inspections (for testing) are sometimes argued to be unnecessary, and indeed they do not have the same impact on the product that the user sees. Nonetheless, they are important as they verify that the testing is proceeding as desired in its own planning, design, and implementation stages. Test Inspections also remove defects in the test scenarios themselves, which if found during the actual test stages can cause delay in test, confusion as to which is in error (the test or the products), or further defect injection. In section 8.7 on "Cost and Benefits" we will discuss how Inspections can be tuned to achieve higher efficiencies without increasing risk in the quality of the product.

Sometimes it is suggested that inspections and testing are trying to accomplish the same thing for the product whether it is software or hardware. We would argue that testing attempts, or should attempt, to quantitatively measure properties such as performance, function, quality, or usability. Generically Inspections are not intended to measure properties of a product, rather Inspections are attempting to measure the process of developing a product. While we primarily focus on removing defects through Inspections today, we are in essence measuring how well the product has been made. The level of defects give us an indication of what we need to do to change the process. It also allows us to reject the product part for rework to correct the defects.

It is important for us to understand this distinction because we have a similar situation in software. In software testing we do indeed try to determine quantitative measures of certain properties, such as, response time, storage utilization, quality, recovery procedures, and presence of function. However, in many software operations today the testing is being used to ensure the presence of quality by finding the defects or "testing the quality into" a product.

Today Inspections for software focus on both ensuring the quality and in observing the process by which we put the product together. Other aspects such as usability and maintainability can also be addressed in Inspections, by adding specific focus on usability and maintainability error types in the Inspection checklists which are input to the Preparation step for the Inspection.

Inspections are a method to control quality by the application of certain preestablished criteria. They also involve, as Davis et al. say in their book, *The Testing and Inspection of Engineering Materials*, the rejection of substandard material.

> Material produced by a given manufacturing process is always, to some degree, of variable quality. A material that is satisfactory for a given type of service usually has requirements as to minimum level of quality, some-

times as to range of quality. In order to assume the presence of desired quality, a product is examined with the object of passing material that conforms to stated requirements and rejecting material that fails to conform. This is the essence of the inspection process. [DAVl64]

In the case of software, however, it is not so much the rejection of substandard material as it is causing the rework of substandard elements without allowing them to continue on through successive development stages where costs for rework increase. While rework exists to varying extents in hardware, it almost always exists in software. There are many similarities between software and hardware/manufacturing inspections, but there are some differences. For software the value of inspections in still sometimes debated, although this debate has diminished with the increasing interest in improving software quality. While inspections in software are relatively new, inspections in hardware or manufacturing have been in existence for a much longer time, because they have repeatedly shown their value to hardware/manufacturing quality.

Another of the differences is when the inspections occur. Software and hardware both have product development stages. Additionally, both software and hardware have manufacturing stages, where the product is physically made. The difference, however, is that for software the development and manufacturing stages are one and the same. Software does not require a manufacturing line to make repeated copies of the product. Thus, a primary distinction is that hardware is inspected during its manufacturing stage after its development stage is completed, and software is inspected during its development stage which is also its manufacturing stage.

Testing should be concerned with the determination of quality, not with trying to control quality. The control of quality should occur at the time of development. During test we want to determine the quality level regardless of the implication of the results. In some cases these results will tell us not to deliver the product as it exists, but to rework it and then to test it again. Another distinction today is that in hardware sampling inspections is an accepted method, while in software, sampling is barely beginning. Rather for software it is suggested that "all instructions are addressed at least once in the conduct of Inspection."

In addition to finding defects, which is the primary purpose today, there are three ancillary purposes for Inspections. They are education, early product assessment, and process assessment. It is important to realize that Inspections do not have education as a primary purpose for the participants. However, as a by-product, the participants will be educated in how the product work item that is under inspection functions as a part by itself and in relation to the parts with which it interfaces. The education is accomplished primarily through two steps of the overall Inspection process: the Overview step, in which the author of the material presents his perspective on the work item to the Inspection participants and the Preparation step, in which each Inspector reads the material to be inspected. The Overview can be held immediately before an actual Inspection, such as in a code Inspection where a module of small size is being inspected; or it can be held a few days prior to a scheduled Inspection, in cases when Requirements are being inspected or when a large section of the Product Level Design is being inspected. An Overview can last from a few minutes to a few days, depending on the complexity of the work item under Inspection.

The Inspection step itself should not be used directly as an education vehicle for the participants. It is recommended that the Inspection step not be extended to provide education through the surgical arena approach where groups of programmers "observe" an Inspection with the intent of trying to receive some knowledge by viewing the product under Inspection. There are far better ways to get new programmers educated. In both of these approaches to education, the process leads to more questions than can be answered productively at the Inspection. We must remember that Inspections are primarily intended to find errors and to find them economically. Therefore, if we include education as one of our primary purposes, we will be changing the economics and effectiveness of the Inspection process. This is not a problem so long as the cost of education is discernible from the cost for inspection or verification.

A second ancillary purpose for Inspections is early product assessment. This occurs because the quality level of the product is determined early in the product life cycle and signals management that actions are required to bring the product in line with pre-established quality goals.

Another ancillary purpose is process assessment. This means that data must be gathered about the process of doing the Inspection itself. This data covers all of the steps in the Inspection process from Planning through Follow-up. The types of data that need to be collected include time spent in preparation, time spent in the Inspection step, and numbers of defects found by specific classification. This data can then be analyzed with other process and product data to determine the effectiveness of the Inspection process against the project goals and targets. For example, if the goal is economics only, that is, to find the defects as early as possible and as cheaply as possible, then education has less significance. However, if we are willing to accept the cost for education, then we can factor this into the cost of Inspections. We should not, however, then try to argue against the higher cost of Inspections where we choose to include the cost of education.

In addition, during assessment of the process data, we can determine what we may wish to modify in the Inspection process. For example is there something about the preparation that can be handled differently? We can present this data to the people who are most knowledgeable about the Inspection process, that is, the programmers or the Inspection moderators, and ask them how the process can be improved.

Thus, we can assess the process dynamically and modify it dynamically to achieve our primary purpose for the project, that is, to find errors efficiently and effectively.

8.6 How Are Inspections Performed?

Observe Figure 102, in which it is shown that the Inspection process has Input; that is, entry criteria which must be satisfied prior to beginning the Inspection. There is Output in the form of exit criteria, which are specific, predetermined objectives that must be satisfied before the step can be considered complete. These outputs include the Inspection reports, the relevant data, and information resulting from the Inspection. The essential process steps shown in Figure 100 on page 243 go from planning through rework and follow-up. Each of these steps has a predefined list of entry and exit criteria. There is a methodology, which can be provided to the participants through training. This methodology shows how inspectors can best find defects, includes a checklist of common defect types for the subject Inspection, and includes a way of improving the process steps themselves. The checklists are developed for each type of work item developed during the product cycle. This checklist will vary based on the environment. For example, a checklist for code Inspections where FORTRAN is used would be different from one for Basic Assembler Language (BAL). There are also similarities in these two checklists because in both cases the work item results from the Code stage. A sample checklist is shown in Figure 103 on page 250 and in Figure 104 on page 251

8.6.1 Inspection Steps

The Inspection process, as noted earlier and as shown in Figure 100 on page 243, is composed of seven steps or operations.

Planning can occur at any point in time prior to the scheduled overview and inspection, but the lead time should not be compromised by making this a last-minute step. If it is done well, it makes all the remaining steps easier. Planning typically takes a global view and tries to account for all necessary Inspections for the product; therefore, it tends to be done in aggregate prior to the first inspection. However, it is rare to be able to account for all Inspections. Therefore, planning does continue throughout the project development. The primary concern is to ensure that enough time and resources are planned to be available in order to allow proper Inspections. Planning may be assigned to one group such as Process Control, but much of the detail scheduling of resources will probably be handled by the Inspection moderators.

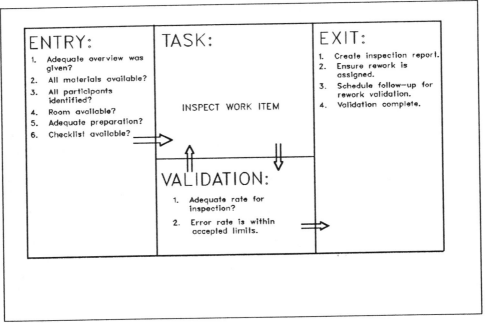

ENTRY:

1. Adequate overview was given?
2. All materials available?
3. All participants identified?
4. Room available?
5. Adequate preparation?
6. Checklist available?

TASK:

INSPECT WORK ITEM

EXIT:

1. Create inspection report.
2. Ensure rework is assigned.
3. Schedule follow-up for rework validation.
4. Validation complete.

VALIDATION:

1. Adequate rate for inspection?
2. Error rate is within accepted limits.

Figure 102. ETVX

Overview—The work item author first describes the overall area being addressed and then the specific area he has developed in detail-logic, paths, dependencies, and so forth. Documentation is distributed to all inspection participants on conclusion of the overview. For a code Inspection, no overview is necessary.

Preparation—Participants, using the documentation, literally do their homework to try to understand the work item, its intent and logic. To increase their error detection in the inspection, the inspection team should first study the ranked distributions of error types found by recent inspections. This study will prompt them to concentrate on the most fruitful areas for defect detection. Checklists of clues on finding these errors should also be studied.

Inspection—A "reader" chosen by the moderator describes the work items in his own words. He is expected to paraphrase the documentation as expressed by the author. Every piece of logic is covered at least once, and every branch is taken at least once. All higher level documentation, high level design specifications, logic specifications, and so on, and macro and control block listings at code Inspections must be available and present during the inspection.

Now that the design is understood, *the objective is to find errors*. An error is defined as any condition that causes malfunction or that precludes the attainment of expected or previously specified results. Thus, deviations from specifications

```
LOGIC

Missing

    1. Are all constants defined?
    2. Are all unique values explicitly tested on input parameters?
    3. Are values stored after they are calculated?
    4. Are all defaults checked explicitly tested on input parameters?
    5. If character strings are created, are they complete?  Are all
       delimiters shown?
    6. If a keyword has many unique values, are they all checked?
    7. If a queue is being manipulated, can the execution be interrupted?
    8. Are registers being restored on exits?
    9. In queuing/dequeuing should any value be decremented/incremented?
   10. Are all keywords tested in macro?
   11. Are all keyword related parameters tested in service routine?
   12. Are queues being held in isolation so that subsequent interrupting
       requestors are receiving spurious returns regarding the held queue?
   13. Should any registers be saved on entry?
   14. Are all increment counts properly initialized (0 or 1)?


Wrong

    1. Are absolutes shown where there should be symbolics?
    2. On comparison of two bytes, should all bits be compared?
    3. On build data strings, should they be character or hex?
    4. Are internal variables unique or confusing if concatenated?


Extra

    1. Are all blocks shown in design necessary or are they extraneous?
```

Figure 103. Sample Module Design Checklists (from Fagan)

are termed errors. The finding of errors is actually done during the reader's discourse. Questions raised are pursued only to the point at which an error is recognized. It is noted by the moderator; its type is classified, severity (major or minor) is identified, and the inspection is continued. Often the solution of a problem is obvious. If so, it is noted, but no specific solution hunting is to take place during inspection. The inspection is *not* intended to redesign, evaluate alternate design solutions, or to find solutions to errors; it is intended just to find errors!

SAMPLE COBOL PROGRAM CHECKLIST

During the I2 the unit being inspected should be examined for the following points:

1. **Identification Division**

   Remarks Paragraph

   Does the prose in the **REMARKS** paragraph function as a complete prologue for the program?

2. **Environment Division**

   Does each **SELECT** sentence explicitly define the external (system-dependent) specifications for the file?

3. **Data Division**

   File Section

   Are the File Definitions (**FD**s) in the same order as their respective **SELECT** sentences in the **ENVIRONMENT DIVISION**?

   Do the record and data item names conform to their usage?

   Does each **FD** contain comments regarding:

   Usage of the file (**RECORDING MODE,** Block Size, Record Length, Imbedded Keys, etc.)?

   Amount of activity (updated how often, used every time program is run, etc.)?

   Interaction with other data items. (Do its records contain objects of "Occurs...Depending On" clauses (**ODO**s); is the length of its records dependent on an ODO object elsewhere in the program, etc.?)

   Is the file **SORT**ed or **MERG**ed?

   Are statistics kept on file activity in a given run or series of runs?

Figure 104. Sample of a COBOL Checklist

Report—Within one day of conclusion of the inspection, the moderator should product a written report of the inspection and its findings to ensure that all issues raised in the inspection will be addressed in the rework and follow-up operations. Examples of these reports are given in three parts in Figure 105 on page 253.

Rework—All errors or problems noted in the inspection report are resolved by the author.

Follow-up—It is imperative that every issue, concern, and error be entirely resolved at this level, or errors that result can be 10 to 100 times more expensive to fix if found later in the process. It is the responsibility of the moderator to see that all issues, problems, and concerns discovered in the inspection operation have been resolved by the author. If more than 5 percent of the material has been reworked, the team should reconvene and carry out a 100 percent reinspection. Where less than 5 percent of the material has been reworked, the moderator at his discretion may verify the quality of the rework himself or reconvene the team to reinspect either the complete work or just the rework.

8.6.2 Who Participates in an Inspection?

There are three key participant types for Inspections:

1. Moderator
2. Author
3. Inspector

Inspectors can be further refined into different roles, such as:

1. Reader
2. Mapper
3. Receiver
4. Verifier

Moderator—the key person in a successful inspection. The moderator must be a competent programmer but need not be a technical expert on the program being inspected. To preserve objectivity and to increase the integrity of the Inspection, it is usually advantageous to use a moderator from an unrelated project. The moderator must manage the inspection team and offer leadership. Hence, the moderator must use personal sensitivity, tact, and drive in balanced measure. The moderator's use of the strengths of team members should produce a synergistic effect larger than their number. In other words, the moderator is the coach. The duties of moderator also include scheduling suitable meeting places, reporting inspection results within one day, and follow-up on rework. For best results the moderator should be specially trained. The moderator does not normally take on any of the other roles for Inspections as there will be more than

| I₂ Problem definition sheet | | | Page   of | | Date | |

Module	Component	System	
Inspection date	Duration	Man-hrs. prep.	
Moderator	Designer	Implementer	Tester
Is this a re-inspection?			

No.	Page	Line	Problem description	Definition		
				Type	Class (MWE)	Major minor

Total LOC inspected	Total errors found
Estimated LOC in rework	Estimated rework hours
Is re-inspection required?	Suggested date

Figure 105. Example Inspection Report

enough to do as moderator. However, in some cases the moderator may also function as an inspector.

Author—this is the programmer who was responsible for creating the work item to be inspected.

Inspectors—these are programmers who are not directly involved with the work item to be inspected, but who are capable of understanding it during their preparation and who are experienced enough to be able to discern work item defects. They are assumed to be at least technical peers of the author in order to efficiently and effectively find defects.

Reader—this is one of the inspectors and not the author. The author would have a tendency to read the work items materials as if they were correct and to read quickly due to his foreknowledge of the subject material. This works against the intent of the Inspection which is to find errors. The reader, when other than the author, will tend to read the material at a slower pace and in his own paraphrased terms. Other inspectors will follow the reading with their own annotated materials. If the reader's interpretation through the reading is other than what other inspectors assumed or what the author intended, this may indicate a defect in the material. For large work items the role of author can be rotated across the inspection team.

Mapper—this inspector ensures that the material under inspection and the higher level materials do indeed map. This will ensure that the inspection material and the materials from which it was refined are synchronized. Thus, MLD materials would be mapped back to the CLD baseline, Code would be mapped to MLD, and PLD would be mapped to requirements. If the materials do not map, one of them is in error.

Receiver—this inspector is the next person to receive the subject inspection materials for refinement. For example, if the inspection is for MLD, then the receiver is the programmer who will do the code implementation. This inspector should take the most demanding role as inspector, ensuring himself that he has received defect-free material. In some situations, the receiver and author will be the same individual, in which case the distinct role is not of importance.

Verifiers—these are all the other inspectors who may not have another assigned role. Their role is to find errors and to verify that the materials are defect-free after all the errors have been identified.

The inspection team will vary with the type of inspection. Thus, an inspection of the requirements may involve all the design team among other programmers on the project. This is an exception, as typically the material to be inspected is checked such that four to six people are the right team size boundaries. Typically, managers are not included in the inspection team, although, we are aware of one project where this worked successfully without any concern that the inspection would be used as an appraisal of the author. The team participants should be given ample time to plan and prepare for the inspection. Last-minute substitutes should only be accepted under rare situations.

The Inspection process was designed to be independent of any one individual participant in order to achieve consistently successful Inspections. This is to say that the team, because it works as a team with a predefined process, will counterbalance most, if not all, individual factors that could cause the Inspection to fail, or worse, to mislead by implying no errors exist because none were found.

Individual factors that might offset the effectiveness of Inspections would include failure to prepare adequately for the Inspection, the fear that recorded defects might be used against an individual, and strong-willed authors of the work item.

Essentially, with a predefined process and the necessary education of the participants, the Inspection process stands a high probability of working, regardless of individual variables. It also works especially well under difficulty, such as when an Inspection must be canceled and rescheduled. In this case the rescheduling permits the team to regroup at a later date under conditions that will enable the Inspections to be successful.

Inspections involve many people; Inspections are a team effort. It is for this reason that a necessary and sufficient education package must be defined for all the team members. This education will enable the team to learn the same set of ideas, values, standards, and practices of the complete and successful Inspection process. It is truly not enough to simply understand the intent of an Inspection; it is essential to share a culture of Inspections and this can only be achieved by engaging all participants in the same education and training.

8.6.3 When and Where Do Inspections Fit into the Programming Process?

There are basically twelve process development stages with various work items delivered from each of these stages, as we discussed in Chapter 2. The question of where Inspections fit into these stages is answered simply: Inspections can be applied to any work item that has reached a milestone of completion. Data can be gathered to ensure that the work item is at a satisfactory quality level. Defects can be removed that may have gotten into the product during work item construction and they can be prevented from being propagated into the subsequent process stages. For example, at the Requirements stage exit, the various requirements work items can be inspected before beginning to design against those requirements. The various design level documents can be inspected after they are completed and before we refine the design into code, and so on. The code can be inspected at the point of its completion. The test cases to be applied against the code can be inspected. The external publications for the product can be inspected. In essence, we can and should inspect any work item produced by a group or an individual for which we wish to establish a quality assessment before allowing it to proceed down the line to the next stage of production. What is basically being done is to determine the applicability of the work item for the next stage in the programming process. This will result in substantial savings in product development costs. See Figure 106 on page 257 as an example of the kinds of savings which can be realized.

During the series of inspections in the development process we will also be able to determine which parts of the product should be reworked before going into the next stage of development. Additionally, we will reinspect the subsequent reworked items to ensure their quality. These two steps combined allow us to literally pull a part off the development line, rework it at the most appropriate time in the process, and replace it in the development line, and thereby ensure that a higher level of quality is shipped to the testers and ultimately to the users of the product.

When should you start to do Inspections, if you are working on a project? The answer is simple: start now. There is no reason to wait for the "right time" to employ Inspections in a product. Begin immediately. Even if the project is half-way through the testing stage, the team can begin inspecting fixes to defects discovered during test. It is assumed that the necessary education and planning for Inspections have been completed. If the project is in the code stage, begin to inspect the code. There is no need to wait for the right time, because there never is a right time, except now. One will want to understand for a particular project what Inspections have to offer and what they will cost, and then put a plan in place to use Inspections starting now. Get the team trained, then go and do it.

The payoff is immediate. No sooner will Inspections be started than defects will begin to be removed which would only have been found later at a higher cost.

Training is easy once it is accepted as necessary to bring the team together. Training is also the key. Training is also the biggest pitfall that projects encounter when they begin to use Inspections. The usual argument given is that the programmers can learn all they need by reading a manual on Inspections rather than spending three days in a training session. The principles are simple, the ideas are easy. Why then train for three days? The answer is that if you do not train the team, you will not have good, repeatable Inspections. Worse you may not have people who are convinced that Inspections really work, so they may, without forethought, cause erosion in the Inspection effectiveness and efficiency.

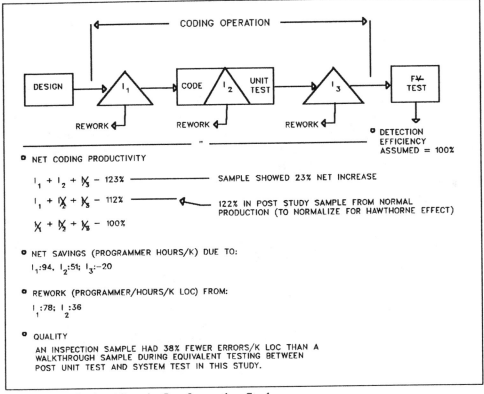

Figure 106. Savings Seen in One Inspection Study

8.7 Cost and Benefits

In this section we will look at numbers that will explain what it costs to do Inspections and what some of the benefits are from doing Inspections.

8.7.1 Cost

Inspections incur cost, just as any effort in developing a product incurs a cost. The cost will vary by the stage in which the Inspection is held. For example, during code, an Inspection will typically cost approximately 77 programmer hours per one thousand source lines of code to do a proper quality job. In the design stage, 70 hours is usually required. These are calculated by including the suggested rates from Fagan (Reference Figure 107 on page 259). These costs mean that we are choosing to spend resources earlier in the development process than we were prior to using Inspections. The payback comes later in improved testing and lower test and maintenance costs. This, in essence, is a form of capital investment, and as always with capital or up-front investments, it may not be available at the time it can be most advantageous.

STEP	RECOMMENDED RATE LOC/HR	COST HOURS/KLOC	RECOMMENDED RATE LOC/HR	COST HOURS/KLOC
Planning	NE	---	NE	---
Overview	500	2	NA	---
Preparation	100	10	125	8
Inspection	130	7.7	150	6.7
Report	NE	---	NE	---
Rework	20	50	16	62.7
Follow-up	NE	---	NE	---
TOTAL		69.7		77.2

Figure 107. Effect of Inspections on Defect-Removal Costs

What we need to do in these cases is re-evaluate our schedules to understand if there might be any impact to our delivery dates. This problem of deciding to make the up-front investment will occur when Inspections are used for the first time or when a product has already committed to a delivery date and is making quality a lower priority. The choice will ultimately have to be made between quality and schedule. For now, we should note that another trade-off exists between the cost of finding the defects early with Inspections and the cost of finding them later in test or when the product is in use, where costs to fix errors increase to roughly 20 times and 100 times, respectively. We should remember that the economics of the software business requires that we constantly tune the Inspection process as we gather data about its effect on the development process itself. These data and continued analysis will lead us to a continuing improvement in our costs.

8.7.2 Benefits

In the original study to test Inspections done in the early 1970s it was shown that productivity had increased by 23 percent and quality had apparently increased by 38 percent. The study was performed on a part of a new telecommunications access method. Three types of Inspections were held: I1, at the end of MLD; I2, at the end of the first clean compilation; and I3, after unit test was completed. Data was gathered and analyzed for each of these Inspections. The results are as summarized in Figure 106 on page 257 The I3 was dropped as it seemed to decrease productivity and did little to improve quality; test was a more productive method to remove defects in this case.

With this evidence Inspections became an accepted alternative for process management to improve quality. Since that time Inspections have gone on to be widely used in the industry.

In his most recent article, outlined in Figure 108, Fagan gives more evidence of benefits resulting from Inspections [FAGA86].

In terms of overall productivity, Inspections have had a positive effect. As Fagan says:

> Experience has shown that inspections have the effect of slightly front-end loading the commitment of people resources in development, adding to requirements and design, while greatly reducing the effort required during testing and for rework of design and code. The result is an overall *net* reduction in development resource, and usually in schedule too. [FAGA86]

Documented Case	Results
1. AETNA Life and Casualty 4439 LOC	- 0 defects in use - 25% reduction in development resource
2. IBM RESPOND, UK 6271 LOC	- 0 defects in use - 9% reduction in cost compared to walk-throughs
3. Standard Bank of South Africa 143,000 LOC	- 0.15 defects/KLOC in use - 9.5% reduction in corrective maintenance costs
4. American Express 13,000 LOC	- 0.3 defects in use
5. IBM S/370 software since 1974	- defects/KLOC reduced by two-thirds

Figure 108. Documented Benefit Examples (from Fagan)

Reference Figure 109 on page 261 for a representation of this statement.

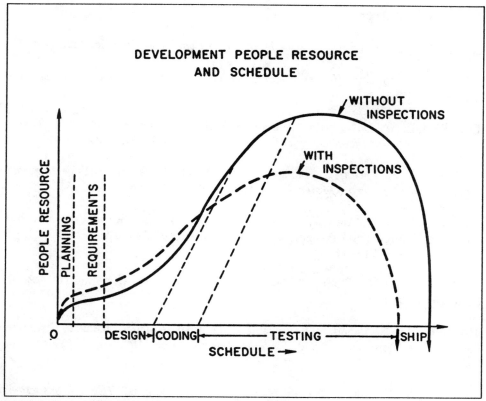

DEVELOPMENT PEOPLE RESOURCE
AND SCHEDULE

Figure 109. Development, People, Resource, and Schedule

8.8 Summary

We discussed in this chapter the fact that there are a number of alternatives for validating and verifying product work items. Among these are peer reviews, reviews and walk-throughs, inspections, prototyping, user involvement, proofs of correctness, and tests. All of these methods serve to checkpoint the correctness of the work item, some cost less to use and some lead to better quality than others. We recommend two primary approaches: Inspections and Proofs of Correctness. We believe these two approaches are especially powerful when used together. We recommend Inspections because the benefits have been proven numerous times. We recommend Proofs of Correctness because they enable the programmer to become involved and aware of the mathematical basis of programming. We discuss Proof of Correctness in Chapter 10.

8.9 References

[BOEH81] B. W. Boehm, *Software Engineering Economics*, Prentice-Hall (1981).

[BOOC83] G. Booch, *Software Engineering with Ada*, Benjamin/Cummings Publishing Co. (1983).

[DALY77] E. B. Daly, "Management of Software Engineering," *IEEE Transactions on Software Engineering* Vol. SE-3, No. 3 (May 1977), pp. 229 − 42.

[DAVI64] H. E. Davis, G. E. Troxell, and C. T. Wiskocil, *The Testing and Inspection of Engineering Materials*, McGraw-Hill Book Company (1964).

[DEMI79] R. A. DeMillo, F. J. Lipton, and A. J. Perlis, "Social Processes and Proofs of Theorems and Programs," *Communications of the ACM*, Vol. 22, No. 5 (May 1979), pp. 271 − 80.

[DUNN84] R. H. Dunn, *Software Defect Removal*, McGraw-Hill Book Company (1984).

[FAGA76] M. E. Fagan, "Design and Code Inspections to Reduce Errors in Program Development," *IBM Systems Journal*, Vol. 15, No. 3 (1976), pp. 182 − 211.

[FAGA86] M. E. Fagan, "Advances in Software Inspections," *IEEE Transactions on Software Engineering*, Vol. SE-12, No. 7 (July 1986), pp. 744 − 51.

[FREE82] D. Freedman and G. M. Weinberg, *Handbook of Walkthroughs, Inspections, and Technical Reviews: Evaluating Programs, Projects, and Products*, Little Brown (1982).

[LING79] R. C. Linger, H. D. Mills, and B. J. Witt, *Structured Programming: Theory and Practice*, Addison-Wesley Publishing Company (1979).

[RADI82] R. A. Radice, "Productivity Measures in Software," in *The Economics of Information Processing, Vol. 2*, Robert Goldberg and Harold Lorin, eds., John Wiley & Sons (1982).

[STEP76] W. E. Stephenson, "An Analysis of the Resources Used in the SAFE-GUARD System Software Developmen t," Bell Labs (August 1976).

[YOUR79A] E. Yourdon, *Structured Walk-Throughs*, Prentice-Hall Software Series (1979).

Additional Recommended Reading

IEEE Standard for Software Quality Assurance Plan, (1980).

Military Standard for Technical Reviews and Audits for Systems, Equipments, and Computer Software, (1985), MIL_STD_1521B.

Software Validation, Inspection-Testing-Verification-Alternatives: Proceedings of the Symposium on Software Validation, Darmstadt, Germany, (September 1983).

Quick, W. J., ed., *Verification and Validation of Real Time Software*, Springer-Verlag, (1985).

Part 4. Design and Coding Stages

Chapter 9. Product Level Design and Component Level Design

9.1 From Requirements to Product Level Design (PLD)

Following the sequence of the programming life cycle, we should have at the entry to PLD a completed level of objectives that were derived during the Requirements stage. Now we need to create a design solution for the problem as stated in the requirements specification, and match the design direction included in these requirements. Refer to Figure 110 on page 267 where we break out the user and developer views of the problem to be solved.

In Chapter 4, Requirements Engineering, we saw that, while the user has one view of the problem and tasks requiring a solution, the designer will typically have another view of the same problem and tasks. These views can be identical, but rarely are. Typically, the developer begins to bound or refine the problem with physical constraints or detailing solutions from his experiential base. We assume in this chapter that the the requirements problem statement and design direction have already been validated against the users' view during the Require-

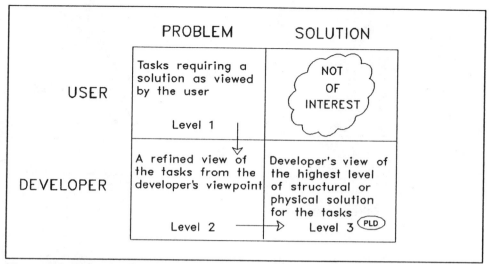

Figure 110. User and Developer Views of the Problem and Solution

ments Engineering process described in Chapter 4. This validation can take many forms but it must involve the user and it must result in a user agreed upon problem statement. If the user was not involved in the validation, the developer may very likely proceed to provide a solution for the wrong problem. It may be a good solution for the problem perceived by the developer, but it may be incorrect or incomplete from the user's viewpoint. Therefore, if given a project in which validation has not yet been done under the Requirements Engineering stage, it must be undertaken before the PLD stage begins.

When the developer has a refined and validated set of requirements or problem statement, he can proceed into the design or solution domain. This refinement is basically the divergence and transformation steps which we addressed in Chapter 8.

As we see in Figure 111 on page 268, the problem view is a task oriented view. The design or solution view, as we will shortly explain, is seen from a number of orientations different from the task oriented view. Among these design orientations are:

1. Function Flow Orientation

2. Data Flow Orientation

3. Data Structure Orientation

4. Object Orientation

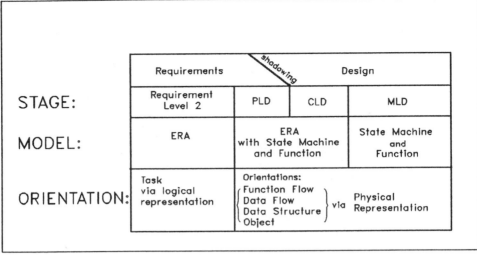

	Requirements	shadowing		Design
STAGE:	Requirement Level 2	PLD	CLD	MLD
MODEL:	ERA	ERA with State Machine and Function		State Machine and Function
ORIENTATION:	Task via logical representation	Orientations: Function Flow, Data Flow, Data Structure, Object } via		Physical Representation

Figure 111. Relationships of Problems and Solution Representations and Models

Although we identified five design methodologies in Chapter 8, we are not interested in the *prescriptive method* for this discussion, since it draws from the other four methodologies. What we need to resolve during this transformation from requirements to design, or problem to solution, is whether there is a mapping from a task orientation to any or all of the design orientations.

An additional problem we have to address during this transformation is that we have different conceptual models in requirements and design. The requirements statement may be based on an ER model. As we shall see, the design statement will be based on a function model or state machine model. Thus, we must be able to show that we have a mapping between these models.

This question of mapping becomes key when we understand that the points in time when we are most likely to create errors in developing software are when we go through transformation steps from one level of problem or solution representation to a refined problem or solution representation at another level. Thus, in Figure 110 on page 267, if the refinement from Level 1 into Level 2 is not complete and validated, then the problem as viewed by the user and developer will be different and the consequences are evident.

9.1.1 Requirements to Design Transformation Alternatives

There are five basic ways we can address the problem of transformation:

1. We can use a requirements language, such as PSL or SREM, through the Module Design Level stage. SREM, for example, has been successfully applied at the design level [SCHE85]. In general, however, ER languages find their most practical use at the more conceptual levels, while procedural languages seem better suited at the lower levels, where the need to express conditional logic and control flow are more prevalent.

2. We can employ an automated language transformer from requirements to design representations. There is some initial thinking that such an approach might be practical in an artificial intelligence environment with an expert system [SIMO86]. However, it remains to be demonstrated just how this would be done.

3. We can manually transform from a specification language representation to a design language. This has been and is still today the typical instance. In most cases, however, the approach appears unsatisfactory because parts are discovered to be incomplete or incorrect. Moreover, it has been almost impossible to keep the two representations up to date and synchronized. This latter problem would be less likely to arise if all requirements were made known at one time and never changed. Alas, the real world works otherwise, and, thus, we are constantly greeted with updates, changes, revisions, new ideas, and "absolutely necessary" requirements that were not understood when the project was initially commissioned.

4. We can "shadow" the requirements representation, which derives the solution, with an emerging design representation.

5. We can "shadow" the emerging design representation, which derives the solution, with a refined requirements representation.

The distinction between these last two choices is subtle and debatable. The issue is which representation is viewed as leading the design. We value these two choices equally, since they result in the same delivered work products. In both of these approaches we acknowledge the need for two representations which must be updated and synchronized. However, the "shadowing" requires a process criterion which consistently checks for level synchronization.

At this time, given the lack of a more rigorous requirements language, the lack of an automated solution, and the problems with manual transformation, we recommend the shadow approach as the best available alternative. It is perhaps unfortunate that two representations must be maintained in parallel, but the other alternatives are less desirable as quality of the product is a vital issue.

9.2 Concepts Relevant in PLD and CLD

There are six design principles that are particularly applicable to these two design stages. These principles are abstraction, problem decomposition, separation of concerns, encapsulation, design decision, and consistency. These principles are interrelated and they lead to satisfying two primary goals: (1) intellectual control over the design solution and (2) modularity within the design solution. They go back to many sources [DIJK72], [WIRT71], [LING79], [PARN72], and are presently the essential principles underlying the IBM Software Engineering Institute design workshops [CARP85].

9.2.1 Abstraction

Programmers have traditionally tried to get to the details of the solution as soon as possible, for in the details they believed they could see for themselves the viability of their solution. It is hard to argue with this approach when the methods, tools, and techniques available to the programmers may inhibit the ability to validate the proposed solution at higher levels of conception.

We are suggesting that abstraction is one part of the package which enables the programmer to successfully validate a staged design solution without having to resort to immediate detail.

Abstraction for our purposes in design must suppress undesirable details. It enables a higher level view of a design object or solution and at the same time maintains the precision, consistency, and completeness that will ultimately be existent in the detailed and final design statement. Abstractions require a carrier or representation that will permit the programmer to use them successfully to derive a solution. We will explore one such representation called "ADL" shortly.

Abstractions allow us, in programming and other disciplines, to speak in concepts or generics that will later be resolved into specifics. Thus, in the building trades an architect can talk about and represent a proposed building without having to show all or in some cases any details that will be contained in the final actual building. In software, we can talk about and relate concepts like telecommunication access methods or data base systems without having to know the details in our early discussions. At some point in time, the "suppressed details" of the actual hardware involved, of how the program executes, or of the representation of data base structures will become necessary for us to know in order to proceed with our solutions, but they are not necessary immediately and not for some time during the design stages.

Most importantly, it should be understood that while the details may be satisfying because they reflect something tangible, they are immediately restrictive in the necessary choices we need to make later. Premature attachment to details is likely to bind our thinking and our solutions. We must intellectually avoid or suppress the expression of details until we can no longer avoid expressing them. This is particularly a problem for designers when they "know" the details of the solution.

Thus, we want to avoid expressing the HOW versus the WHAT as long as necessary. We want to express a summary of the function to be performed versus the full expression of the function to be performed. At every level of refinement, we want to express as much of what we can in terms of already existing abstractions or to draw upon abstractions which we can defer for elaboration until later in the design stage.

In net, we want to simplify the task of understanding all the implications of what the design abstraction represents. Figure 112 on page 272 shows some relationships for abstracting in software and other fields.

9.2.2 Problem Decomposition

We discuss specifics of problem decomposition in section 9.5.1, "Stepwise Refinement" on page 279 when we explore stepwise refinement in detail. For now it is important to note that we want a repeatable method that allows us to move in orderly steps of specifications and consequent designs towards the final and detailed module design solution. Each step will elaborate on selected decisions that make the design actual, while other decisions may still be deferred in their design solution representations. Ultimately we will elaborate all our decisions into a target implementation language with equivalent function.

In essence, we will be dividing and conquering the solution space as we progress from the WHAT to the HOW in the final module level design solution. Decisions that are deferred at one step become the next decomposition step's WHAT specification. Thus, if we look at Figure 113 on page 273 and Figure 114 on page 274 we see a representation of this notion of problem decomposition.

In Figure 113 on page 273 we see at Level 1 one part of the design decision is deferred to be addressed later at Level 1.2, where again a design decision is deferred to be addressed still later at Level 1.2.2 where the final and remaining design decisions are made.

We proceed at each level to refine or defer design decisions as shown in Figure 113 on page 273. Figure 114 on page 274 shows the relationship between the (1) specification and design pieces and the (2) WHAT-HOW pair of problem decomposition.

| | | REQUIREMENTS | DESIGN |
		WHAT	HOW
Field of Interest:	Abstraction	Definition	Alternatives
Trigonometry:	SIN (angle a)	SIN (angle a)= opposite side/ hypotenuse	a. series expansion b. table look–up
Transportation:	car	A gasoline powered, four wheeled vehicle	a. sedan b. 4 X 4 c. van
Housing:	Single family house	A self–contained structure supporting family personal hygiene and social needs	a. split level b. ranch c. colonial
Software:	Stack	A data structure which allows elements to be added and deleted to the structure on a last in first out basis.	a. bounded b. unbounded c. protected d. concurrent e. sequential
Software:	Operating System	An operating system which enables personal computer application processing	a. CPDOS b. UNIX c. CPM d. MS/DOS

Figure 112. Abstractions in Different Fields of Interest

In Figure 114 on page 274 we see that the specification levels correspond to the levels of deferred design decisions in Figure 113 on page 273.

9.2.3 Separation of Concerns

There are two basic concerns we face in design: (1) the inherent problem complexities of the design problem itself, and (2) the complexities added due to the representation used. These complexities can be dealt with through separation of concerns, for example, at the highest level of separation at the user view and the developer view. As we progress through each level of design, this separation corresponds to the view of the WHAT versus the HOW for each level. The WHAT in each level is some remnant of the user view not yet defined until the final design.

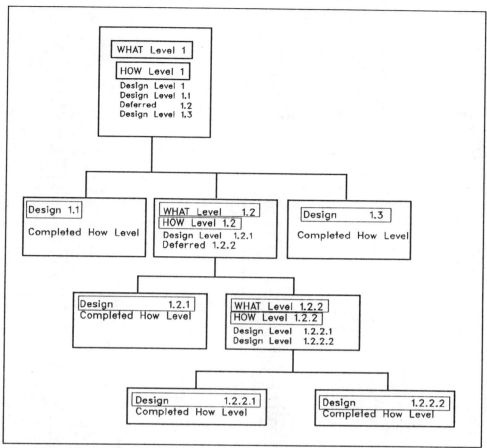

Figure 113. Specification Levels for Deferred Design Decision (Part 1)

We need to partition these concerns into two views at each level of design, that is, the specification view and the design view. At each level we will address the user's view separately from the developer's view. The specification or problem statement is always some part of the user's view and the design statement is the developer's view of the solution for the corresponding specifications.

Basically, we are separating the concerns of WHAT the user (or developer) wants to do from HOW the developer does it, or WHAT the user wants to access from HOW the developer represents the data that is accessed.

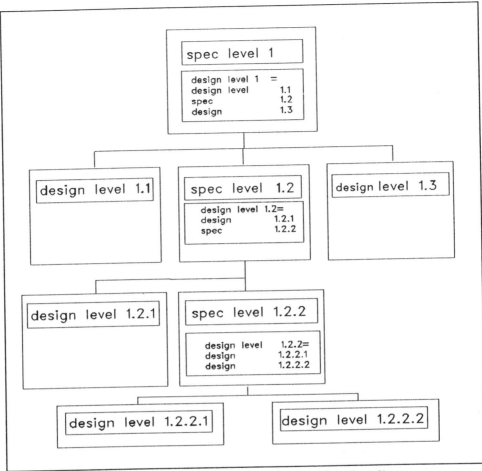

Figure 114. Specification Levels for Deferred Design Decision (Part 2)

9.2.4 Encapsulation

The specification or problem statement serves to encapsulate the design decisions that will be made in the next series of refinements. In the course of this encapsulation within the specification, the user or reader of the specification is insulated from the details of algorithms to solve functions, the data representation within the design solutions, and the design choices of how to carry out the specification. The purpose of encapsulation is to build a wall around the details of the solution.

9.2.5 Design Decisions

We addressed this subject somewhat in Chapter 7, but it bears repetition in this section as it is basic to our objective of achieving defect-free designs.

We already know that for each requirements statement or problem statement there are many possible design solutions. This choice among alternative solutions continues throughout each level of the design refinement process. It remains until all design decisions have been made at the lowest level needed to satisfy each necessary design module that will be a part of the design solution.

Thus, in Figure 112 on page 272 we see that there are a number of design alternatives that can be used to create a solution for the requirements whether they be for software or other fields. A decision must eventually be made selecting the one alternative that best fits the specification and constraints of the problem space. Ideally, this choice will have sufficiently addressed all the aspects of the problem, but this does not imply all of the aspects will be satisfied. Trade-offs sometimes must be made in order to reach a solution. Thus, for an embedded software system which may have memory constraints, the maintainability of the program may be compromised because it can be, whereas the memory is fixed and cannot be changed as a constraint.

9.2.6 Consistency

Bergland states there are a number of additional concepts that we must pursue in software design [BERG81]. Among them is consistency, or obtaining the "same" solution for any given problem with different designers. We are not quite at the desirable position in Software Engineering, with the methodologies available at this time, to achieve design consistency, though Jackson [JACK76B] would argue that consistency is achievable with his method.

9.3 Viewpoints in Product Level Design and Component Level Design

As in other process stages discussed in this book, we are primarily focusing on one viewpoint, that of program development. We must remember, however, that while program development is proceeding in full force, that various people on the project will be addressing the other viewpoints of testing, publications, usability, marketing and service, build and integration, and process management. Without these other viewpoints completing their part of the product solution, there is no product solution.

While it is not our purpose in this book to elaborate on the other viewpoints, we must continue to restate their importance to the product under development.

9.4 Entry Criteria

In accordance with the ETVX paradigm, explained in Chapter 2 on process, every stage has its entry criteria, and so do the PLD and CLD stages. The following list shows examples by viewpoint of entry criteria that must be satisfied prior to beginning the tasks of PLD or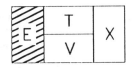
CLD, respectively. There are, of course, others, and the relevant set of criteria will be particular to the production environment, problems to be solved, and objectives of the solution.

The Entry Criteria for the PLD and CLD Stages is listed as follows:

PLD

- Requirements exit criteria have been satisfied.

- Program Development

    - Target objectives are defined and available from the Requirements stage.

    - Business case evaluation is completed, and demonstrates that the project should continue.

    - Procedures for requirements changes are defined and instituted for the Design stage.

- Process Management

    - A defined process exists, is documented, and is understood by the designers.

    - A defined disaster recovery plan exists to protect the product development assets.

- Publications

    - Defined objectives exist to complete necessary publications for the product.

- Usability

    - Definition of target users is updated based on user feedback from the Requirements stage.

    - Defined objectives are completed and available from the Requirements stage.

- Marketing and Service

  - Defined education training requirements are completed for marketing and service personnel for this product.

CLD

- PLD exit criteria have been satisfied

- Programming development

  - Refined objectives are resolved based on PLD experiences.

  - Product Level Design is completed and validated.

  - Product external design specifications are completed and available for review by other products.

  - Defined performance objectives are updated based on PLD input.

  - User validation is completed for PLD.

- Process Management

  - A tracking system for process management is updated with relevant data from the Requirements stage.

  - A project plan is updated with information learned during the Requirements stage and which may affect the existing project plan.

  - Quality and productivity plans are updated to reflect the goals for design based on data gathered during the Requirements stage.

  - A defined validation plan and procedures exist for PLD closure.

- Build and Integration

  - A build plan defining how the product is projected to proceed against an agreed-to schedule is completed.

- Testing

  - A defined test strategy is completed and approved.

- Publications

  - A defined publications delivery plan is completed and approved.

  - A defined publications validation plan and procedures are completed and integrated into the build plan.

- Usability

  - A defined usability test plan is completed and approved.

  - PLD is validated for usability.

- Marketing and Service

    - A defined distribution and product support plan is created.

    - A defined product service plan is created.

    - A defined service training plan is agreed to for service personnel.

    - Planning for user education is completed.

9.5 Functional Decomposition as a Methodology in PLD and CLD

Functional decomposition is related to stepwise refinement. These two methodologies are different, however, in that stepwise refinement implies an orderly view of successive elaboration from any given level of definition, while with functional decomposition the full view of the inherent or contained subparts may be immediate without a level of refinement.

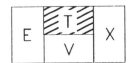

There is an implied hierarchy in functional decomposition with flow proceeding in a sequential order of top to bottom and left to right. There is a higher-level-to-lower-level progression with ever-increasing detail at the lower levels forming a tree. Typically the paths of execution are shown in a tree-like structure. Common function tends to be isolated, giving it high visibility in the tree and making it easily accessible to solve various similar needs of the problem.

The major problems to overcome are how to subdivide the tree and when to stop subdividing. Thus, the solution reached with functional decomposition will likely vary by programmer, as there is a high degree of choice amongst the alternatives of how to decompose the functions identified during the Requirements stage.

Martin and McClure suggest that there are three species of functional decomposition [MART85A]. These are:

1. A tree structure that relates to functions but not to the data used by those functions.

2. A form similar to the first, but the data types that are input and output to each function are shown.

3. A rigorous form, which forces the decomposition of solutions only in certain ways defined by mathematically precise axioms.

This latter form is exemplified by the Higher-Order Software (HOS) methodology [HOS82], which at this writing is not a widely used approach for functional decomposition. Functional decomposition typically exhibits a hierarchical structure rather than one of networks.

9.5.1 Stepwise Refinement

Stepwise refinement of function and data was publicly proposed by Niklaus Wirth in 1971 as a strategy to teach programming. Ever since then it has been rightfully adapted into the mainstream of most current programming design methodologies. The primary result of stepwise refinement is to give the designer intellectual control over the design act. It is a methodology that enables the designer to gradually and in an orderly way evolve the design from the highest level of abstraction and representation into a series of successively more detailed solution statements.

Wirth best describes the lessons it is necessary to follow in a stepwise refinement of design. They are:

1. "Program construction consists of a sequence of refinement steps. . . . Refinement of the description of program and data structure should proceed in parallel."

2. "The degree of modularity obtained in this way will determine the ease or difficulty with which a program can be adapted to change or extensions of the purpose or changes in the environment."

3. "During the process of stepwise refinement, a notation which is natural to the problem in hand should be used as long as possible. . . . This language should therefore allow us to express as naturally and clearly as possible the structures of program and data which emerge during the design process."

4. "Each refinement implies a number of design decisions based upon a set of design criteria. Among these criteria are efficiency, storage economy, clarity, and regularity of structure. Students must be taught to be conscious of the involved decisions and to critically examine and to reject solutions, sometimes even if they are correct as far as the result is concerned; they must learn to weigh the various aspects of design alternatives in the light of these criteria. In particular, they must be taught to revoke earlier decisions, and to back up, if necessary even to the top" [WIRT71].

This latter point is perhaps the most demanding part of stepwise refinement, and the most difficult to put into use. All too often programmers are tempted to believe that the solution they have derived is the correct solution. However, when weighed against a set of predetermined criteria that need to be satisfied, the "in hand correct solution" may not be the best correct solution.

Functional Refinement

Let us now look in more detail at stepwise refinement as it is used in industry [LING79] [CARP85] [SEW84].

In Chapter 10, where we address Structured Programming in detail, we will spend more time with the notion of a basis set of programming control structures. For now, let us assume as Dijkstra proposed [DIJK72] that we only need three control structures: sequence, if-then-else, and do-while. Reference Figure 115 on page 281. Using a design language (ADL), we begin in step 1 by stating that our program is some function F. In the next step we refine F into three functionally equivalent subparts, G, H, and I, and we copy F over as a comment which describes the program now refined and represented as G, H, and I. In step 3 we have refined H into a functionally equivalent if-then-else statement. In step 4 we have refined T into a functionally equivalent do-while.

In all refinements, a design decision is made and the solution emerges step by step. In each step we maintain a functional equivalence to the previous functional specification, which is shown as the functional commentary in,

```
<functional commentary>
```

before each refinement. Later when we explore program correctness we will address how this functional equivalence can be verified.

Data Refinement

Data as well as function can proceed along a refinement process. Data additionally has a basis set, which we will discuss in the section on data abstraction in 9.8, "Object Oriented" on page 302 of this chapter. In the example shown in Figure 116 on page 282, we see that at the highest level of thinking there is a variable named "channel" which is abstracted to be a "stream" without defining what is meant by stream. In step 2 of the design we want to visualize that "stream" is a "queue of blocks," but we may not want to reveal how those "blocks" look. In step 3, we decide that a "block" should have an array data structure, where the array has two dimensions. We do not need to make a decision on the specific description of the array elements. Finally in step 4, we require a definition of the array elements, which are defined as records with four fields.

```
Step 1        Step 2        Step 3        Step 4

  F           DO [F]        DO [F]        DO [F]
               G;            G;            G;
               H;           [H]           [H]
               I;            IF            IF
              ENDDO;          Q;            Q;
                            THEN          THEN
                              R;            R;
                            ELSE          ELSE [T]
                              T;           WHILE
                            ENDIF;          V;
                              I;           DO
                            ENDDO;           Z;
                                          ENDDO;
                                          ENDIF;
                                            I;
                                          ENDDO;
```

Figure 115. Functional Stepwise Refinement Example

Stepwise Refinement Process

There are five parts we will follow in each step of refinement, whether it be function or data [SEW84].

1. Plan several levels of expansion while working on the present step. This requires trying to look ahead, but without making a commitment to the detail in the next step.

2. Select the structures in the present level that will be used to represent the refined design function or data.

3. Invent expressions which carry your thoughts about the design, even if the expression does not validly exist as a type in the final design language. During the refinement process, you will be near your end refinement when it is necessary to designate your expressions from the basis set in the design language. You should delay the final level as long as you need to do this.

4. Record your thoughts and decisions in the control, function, and data commentary in order to communicate.

5. Verify each refinement. (We address this in detail in the next chapter.)

This refinement process is interactive, one step leading to another until the final design is reached and we quit designing. Each refined expression becomes the functional commentary or specification for the next step.

```
Step 1

    VAR channel : stream;

Step 2

    VAR channel : stream;

    TYPE stream = QUEUE OF block;

Step 3

    VAR channel : stream;

    TYPE stream = QUEUE OF block;

    TYPE block = ARRAY (index1, index2) OF matrix_item;

Step 4

    VAR channel : stream;

    TYPE stream = QUEUE OF block;

    TYPE block = ARRAY (index1, index2) OF matrix_item;

    TYPE matrix_item = REC
                          flda : INTEGER;
                          fldb : BOOLEAN;
                          fldc : BOOLEAN;
                          fldd : BOOLEAN;
                       ENDREC;
```

Figure 116. Data Stepwise Refinement Example

While we are iterating through our refinement steps, we must remember, as Wirth suggested, that we must critically examine each refined solution so we can back up and modify previous design decisions when we discover unexpected complexities or when we find that there is a better choice. This may not be easy, but it leads to better design and more elegant solutions. In fact, it is an excellent technique to learn to use, as we have seen, from our own design experiences. See Floyd's paper on Paradigms for his experiences [FLOY79].

When Do We Stop Refining?

A simple answer, but not entirely acceptable, is, when the next refinement step would be equivalent to code. A better answer is, when the goals of the design have been achieved, when all significant design decisions have been recorded, or when the design has "quiesced." These latter are more representative of what we do, but they are not explicitly definitive as completion criteria. A designer should be afforded the decision-making capability to say, "I am done," and he or she should base the decision on environmental constraints. In one situation, it may be necessary to design to a very low level of detail which is almost code equivalent. While in another situation, a higher abstraction might be sufficient detail. The key in both instances is that the final detail should be predefined in the criteria for design completeness, and these criteria need to be validated for completeness before the design solution is accepted as being final.

9.5.2 Top-Down Recording of Design

Top-down recording of design is another method within the functional decomposition approach. The term was coined by Harlan Mills who was its chief proponent [MILL70]. It is similar to stepwise refinement in its iterative refinement of detail.

There are six basic steps to top-down recording of design, which are undertaken only after the critical details of algorithms and data representation have been decided, based on the designer's experience and education, or on experimenting for feasibility. The steps are:

1. Break the task or problem to be solved into a design with a number of independent constituent functions or modules.

2. Break each module further into independent submodules.

3. Repeat until each module is small enough to be under intellectual span of control.

4. Hide the details of design between levels as much as possible.

5. Delay recording the details of data structures until they are necessary to continue the design.

6. Use "stubs" or null modules as place holders in the design tree. This allows the designer to focus on the critical or mainline paths in the design solution, while being sure that the stubbed parts will fit into the design. In this way, integration occurs from the beginning, and unexpected interface problems will surface in time to be resolved with minimum rework.

9.5.3 Bottom-Up Design

The early approaches to software design gravitated toward a bottom-up approach. Perhaps this is because it is inherently more immediately satisfying to "feel" the design at a detail level.

If there is an orderly approach to the bottom-up method it is that it tends to focus on the most difficult or limiting subfunction first. Then the remainder of the design is tailored to fit around these crucial parts. The major problems with this approach are that (1) it lacks data structure, and (2) it forces and constrains functional choices upon which the full design is dependent. When the crucial modules have a problem, the full solution can come down like a house of cards. Nonetheless, where there are particularly difficult subfunctions in a product, some bottom-up designs may be appropriate. In these instances a rigorous process helps to control the problems noted with this approach.

9.5.4 Iterative Design

This approach is a variant of the top-down method, and is probably the one most widely used under functional decomposition. Indeed, it is the most natural approach. The designer starts with a top-down approach, then as critical subfunctions are determined, they are isolated and decomposed to their final level of detail. The designer then goes back to the top and pick the next most crucial subfunction to decompose. This iteration continues until the full design solution is completed. In fact, iterative design is actually encompassed in the top-down approach when it is practiced correctly.

9.6 Data Flow

Functional decomposition methods focus more on the flow of the functions in the design solution than they do on the flow of the data. The approaches we address under data flow all state that the design will be best solved by considering and following the flow of the data 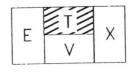 from its initial state as input to its final state as output. Approaches to a data flow design are known under a number of different names such as Myers' composite design [MYER78], structured analysis, structured design [YOUR79], structured analysis [DEMA78], but they are all basically the same in their purpose and result. We will treat them as one methodology in this book.

9.6.1 Data Flow Diagrams

Data Flow Diagrams, or DFDs, which are a representation of data flow, allow the designer to express a design solution at the product level. It can be used in any analysis of systems not just systems of software. The representation typically shows a network of relationships between component functions of the system and the interfaces among them. Figure 117 on page 286 shows an example of a DFD from DeMarco.

Figure 118 on page 287 explains the elements in the DFD representation. DFDs may have been an output from the latter part of the requirements analysis stage, if the project team were using a requirements methodology such as Structured Analysis [DEMA78] [MCME84]. If they were not created during the requirements stage, then the designer must create them before attempting structured designs.

The elements of a DFD as shown in Figure 117 on page 286 are few, and indeed this is one of the strengths of DFDs, as this allows almost immediate use of the diagrams by a designer who is not familiar with them.

Supporting the DFD in order to complete the design solution are (1) the data dictionary, which is a record for each file or data flow, and (2) a set of process specifications or mini-specs, which are step by step descriptions of the processing within the process element usually written in pseudocode. Figure 119 on page 288 shows the relationship between these design solution parts.

DFDs can be layered when all of the flow detail cannot be shown on a single diagram, which is the typical situation for a design solution. This layering introduces an aspect of hierarchy within the DFD as shown in Figure 120 on page 289.

The structure of individual DFDs typically exhibit a network relationship between the transform elements.

9.6.2 Structured and Composite Design

There are six primary aspects to Structured Design: (1) Data Flow Diagrams, which have just been discussed; (2) Transform Analysis; (3) Transaction Analysis; (4) Coupling and (5) Cohesion, both of which we discuss in the next chapter; and (6) Structure Charts.

DFDs are either input to the Design stage from the Requirement stage, or, as mentioned, they will need to be created by the designer. Transform and transactional analysis are addressed during the PLD/CLD stages. Coupling and

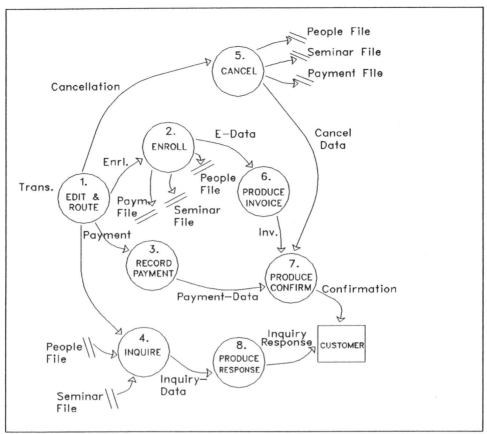

Figure 117. Example Data Flow Diagram (from DeMarco)

cohesion are most appropriately addressed during the MLD stage. Structure Charts are a representation which are best applied during the PLD/CLD stages.

Structured Design has been defined as the art of designing and selecting system components and their relationships in the way that will best solve a well-specified problem.

Myers gives the following five-step process for performing composite/structured analysis which will lead to a structured design [MYER78].

1. **Outline the structure of the problem.** This is unfortunately rather vague in that there is no guidance on how the designer should approach this outlining. Basically it boils down to common sense derived from experience and education, and is really nothing more than a first cut at function flow for the eventual solution. Figure 121 on page 290, Diagram A, shows an example for an outline of the structure for a simple problem.

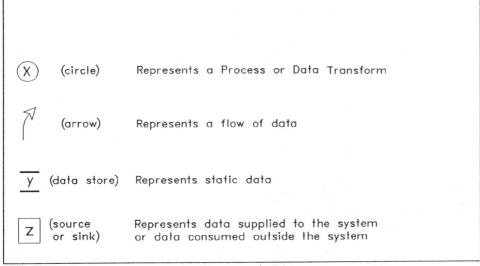

Figure 118. Data Flow Diagram Elements (from DeMarco)

2. **Identify major conceptual external streams of data**. This step asks that the input, output and flow from input to output be identified and imposed on the outline structure, which may be modified as a result. Thus Figure 121, Diagram B, shows the result of this step against the original problem structure outlined in Diagram A.

3. **Identify points of highest abstraction for both the input and output data**. These are points at which the data first exists as a logical view in the system rather than as the physical view which came into the system. This is a designer's decision and may vary from designer to designer, as "abstract" here is not well defined. Figure 121, Diagram C, shows the choice made for the problem under discussion.

4. **Define module functions in three basic groups: (a) sink, (b) source, and (c) transform**. Sink is composed of all the DFD bubbles up to that point which the designer identified as the highest abstraction for the input. Source is composed of all the DFD bubbles starting from the highest output abstraction point to the end in the diagram. Transform is what remains of the DFD bubbles. The figure continues with our example and shows these groupings in Diagram D.

5. **REPEAT THE PROCESS IN STEPS 1 TO 4 ON EACH SUBPROBLEM UNDER DESIGN IN THE SYSTEM UNTIL ALL MODULES HAVE BEEN DEFINED.**

Based on the nature of the problem, Myers states that one of three choices exists for design solution decomposition: (1) Transformational, (2) Transactional, and

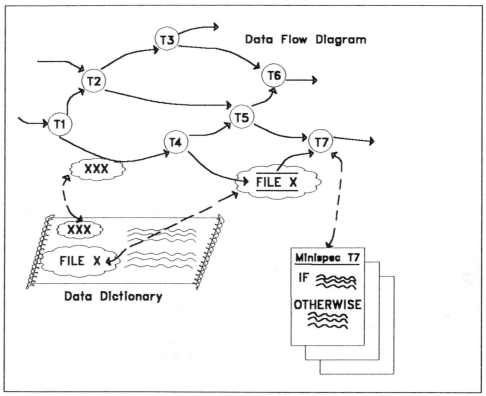

Figure 119. Data Flow Diagram Solution Parts (from DeMarco)

(3) Functional, which we have already addressed in section 9.5, "Functional Decomposition as a Methodology in PLD and CLD" on page 278. The admission of this latter choice is an indication of the many similarities seen between a functional flow approach and a data flow approach. The key difference is in identifying the data transforms or transaction centers.

So far we have only been addressing the part of structured design that is evident through the DFDs. Before we leave DFDs, we should understand how they relate to the Structure Charts which are the end product of structured design.

There are two processes we can follow: (1) complete the DFDs and then complete the structure charts, or (2) proceed to complete both in parallel. Both processes have been used, and both can lead to successful designs. The latter process does require that as changes are dynamically made to the DFDs which may affect completed structured design charts, that they be updated to maintain consistency. This change management control is essential and if not rigorously maintained will lead to unnecessary defects in the product. It is for this reason that we favor the process of completing DFDs before moving on to structured design charts.

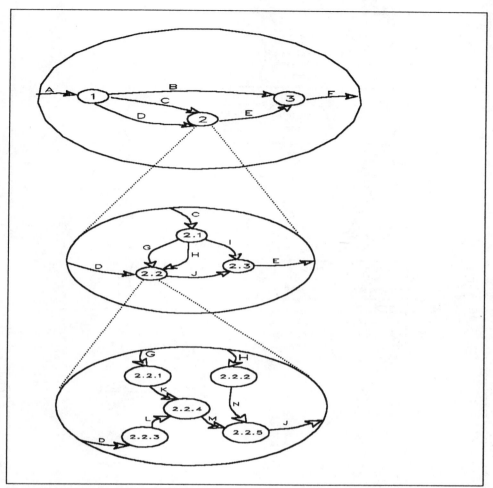

Figure 120. Hierarchy of DFD Charts

Unfortunately in later stages as design changes or problems become evident we cannot avoid having to change and keep synchronized both the DFDs and Structure Charts.

Regardless of which process is used, the DFDs must be converted, so we should understand how that is performed.

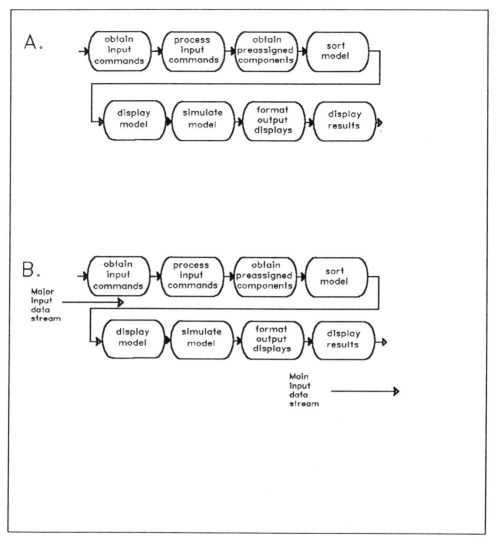

Figure 121 (Part 1 of 2). A Structured Analysis Example

Conversion Process

Myers has defined a five step process to convert DFDs to structured design charts:

1. Isolate the afferent part. This is equivalent to all elements up to the chosen point on the DFDs which reflects the most abstract data input point originating from the physical source. This is sometimes referred to as the source group.

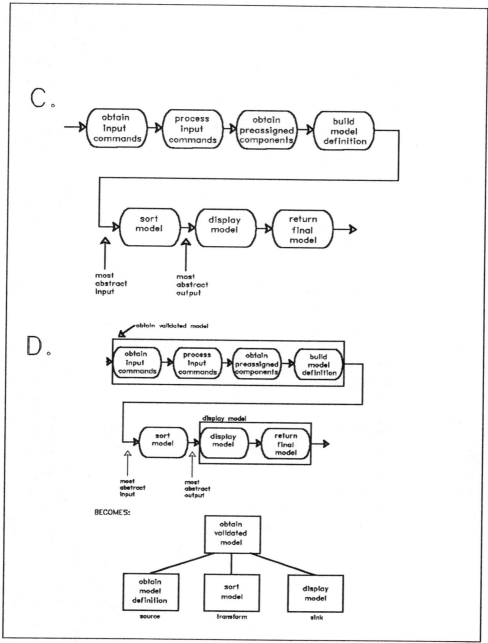

Figure 121 (Part 2 of 2). A Structured Analysis Example

2. Isolate the efferent part. This is respectively all the elements after the point which represents the most abstract data output culminating in the physical sink. This is sometimes referred to as the sink group.

3. Identify the Central Transform, which is every element between the afferent and efferent points.

4. Decide on Transformational or Transactional Design.

5. Construct the appropriate structure chart.

Transformational Design

Myers states that if there is a meaningful afferent and/or efferent part and a central transform, then the choice is transformational design. Otherwise, it is transactional design. Thus, we would view a transformational design as one in which the afferent, efferent, and central transform components are separately identified as module sets and are linked to a control module as shown in Figure 122 on page 293. The flow of processing control is indicated by the dashed lines through these system module clusters.

The control module may be the topmost module in the system or any module in the system which can be decomposed into its own afferent-transform-efferent set of modules.

Transactional Design

Given that we decide that the DFDs cannot be partitioned into identifiable afferent-transform-efferent parts, then we should use a transactional design approach. This is binary enough, but hardly satisfying as a method to choose a design approach.

Additionally we can determine that our design should follow a transactional approach if a selection process exists in the DFDs, or if a process node receives distinct types of input and each input implies that some different processing should occur. It is important to note that both transformational and transactional designs can exist within one complete DFD solution statement.

The flow of control in a transactional design is represented in Figure 123 on page 294. It flows from the transactional control module to one of the sub-process modules, and not to all of the subprocess modules, as is done through a transformational control module.

As there are no clearly identifiable afferent or efferent parts in a transactional design, the input and output processing is included in the transaction control module.

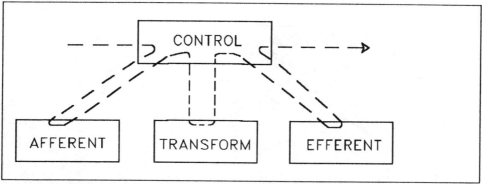

Figure 122. Transformational Design Processing Flow of Control

Structure Charts

Once we have partitioned the DFD into sets of modules representing functional clusters, we can proceed to complete the design structure charts. Basically, we already have the chart structure, but we do not have the data units which will flow, the data flow itself, or the control flow. We now need to show the design decisions for these aspects on the Structure Chart skeleton. Figure 124 on page 295 shows an example of a design Structure Chart with a list of related inputs and outputs for each block in the structure.

It is important to note that the design structure charts never show internal logic or internal data within any module. The notation used to express design in structure charts is shown and explained in Figure 125 on page 296, Figure 126 on page 297, and Figure 127 on page 298.

9.6.3 Critique of Data Flow

As mentioned previously, data flow is similar to functional decomposition in its approach. This is not a flaw in and of itself, especially when we understand that data flow offered solutions in the early 1970s that functional decomposition could not satisfy. Data flow is just one more tool in a richer bag of design tricks.

A more telling criticism is that the rules as specified by many of the data flow proponents, while lengthy, are often vague in that they do not offer a precise way to repeatably make the same design decisions. Most critical is that while data is key in this approach, the design of data is almost completely ignored.

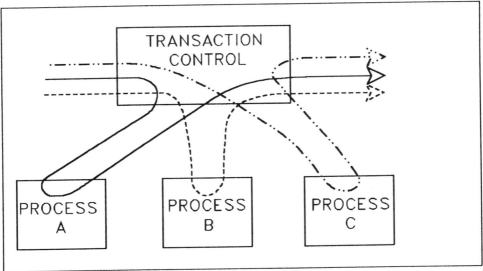

Figure 123. Transactional Design Processing Flow of Control

9.7 Data Structure

As the title of this group of methodologies implies, the
structure of the data plays an essential role in the design
solution. The two chief proponents of this approach
are Michael Jackson and Jean-Dominique Warnier.
Both have earned recognition through methodologies
which carry their names. We will look at the Jackson method in detail.

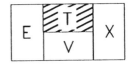

9.7.1 The Jackson Method

Jackson's method is fairly straightforward and has only four steps in its definition
[CAME83]:

1. **Data step**: the designer is required to draw a tree-structure diagram for each
   input data stream and each output data stream processable by the program.
   This is done as a prerequisite to trying to define the program structure. In
   fact, Jackson argues that once the data structures are defined, the program
   structure follows one for one. Under this premise, the variability between
   designers seemingly disappears, or at least is reduced.

2. **Program step**: the designer takes all the data structures previously defined in
   the data step and forms them into a single program structure. This works
   very nicely when the input and output structures have the same essence.
   When they do not, Jackson offers ways to resolve the conflicts or structure

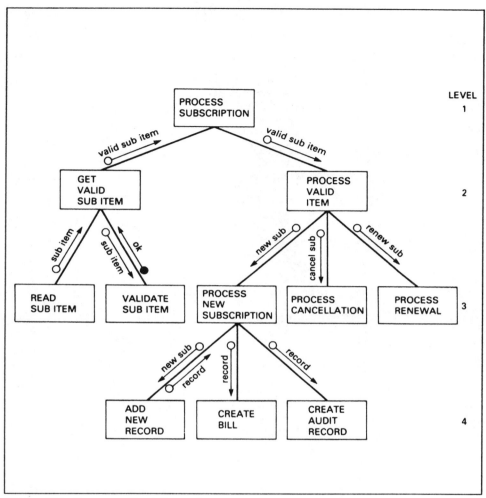

Figure 124. Structure Chart Example

clashes as he calls them. It can be a problem in completing the design if these structure clashes are too many and not easily solved.

3. **Operations step**: the designer must list all the elementary operations required to process the data. Then these operations must be allocated to the components in the program structure which will perform the operations. While this step may be obvious for a number of problems, it can be near impossible for others of large size. This suggests that Jackson's method works best with programs of a limited size, and indeed we are not aware of evidence to the contrary even after the many years of its existence as a methodology.

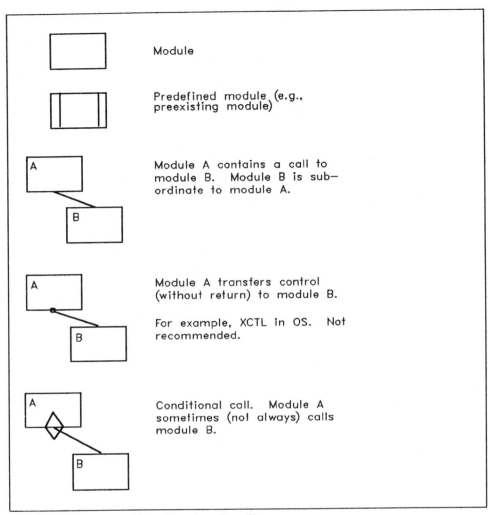

Figure 125. Structure Chart Notation (Part 1)

4. **Test step**: finally the designer must transcribe the program structure into a structured text of pseudocode adding the conditional logic for the designated operations to perform the execution of loops and selection structures.

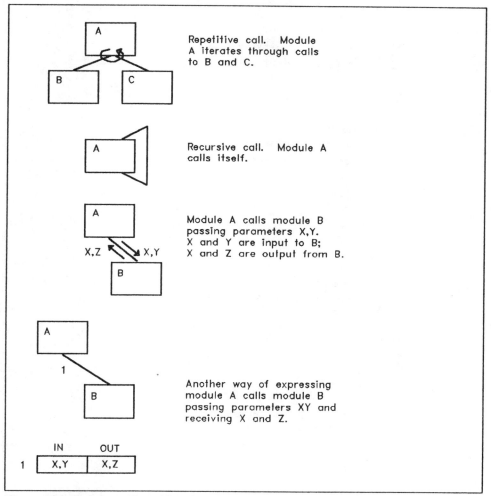

Figure 126. Structure Chart Notation (Part 2)

9.7.2 Jackson Representation

Jackson representation is directly tied to the need to be able to explicitly portray each of the data structures for each of the data streams involved in the problem. Each data structure is portrayed through a Structure Diagram which is a tree structure built from the three basic constructs of structured programming. See Figure 128 on page 299.

The root component of the data structure is given the name for the complete data stream. The elementary components then would be records of the data stream. Using these notations, all data structures can be portrayed. Since the

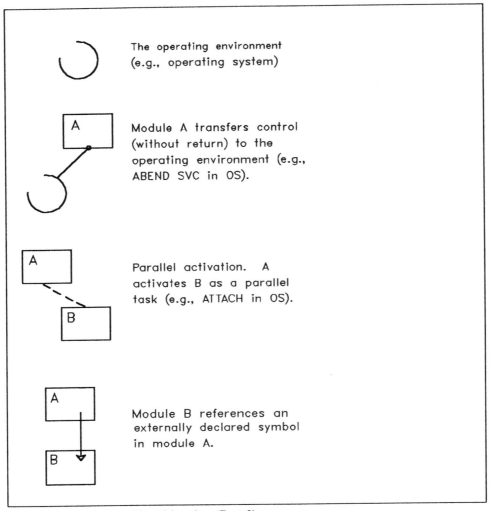

Figure 127. Structure Chart Notation (Part 3)

program structure is derived from the data structure, it is important that all relationships between data components must be noted.

9.7.3 Example

This example is taken directly from Jackson [JACK76A].

Example Specification:

A card file of punched cards is sorted into ascending sequence of values of a key

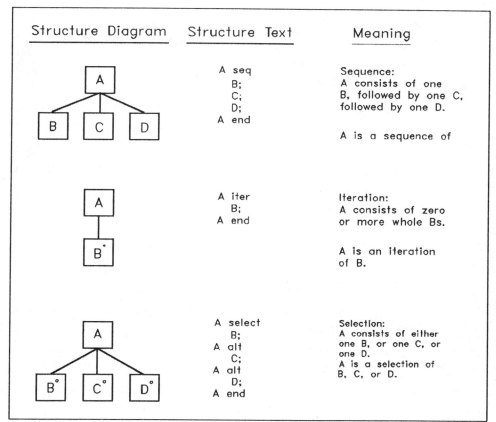

Structure Diagram	Structure Text	Meaning

	A seq
	  B;
	  C;
	  D;
	A end
		Sequence:
		A consists of one
		B, followed by one C,
		followed by one D.
		
		A is a sequence of

	A iter B; A end	Iteration: A consists of zero or more whole Bs. A is an iteration of B.

	A select
	  B;
	A alt
	  C;
	A alt
	  D;
	A end
		Selection:
		A consists of either
		one B, or one C, or
		one D.
		A is a selection of
		B, C, or D.

Figure 128. Jackson's Data Structure

which appears in each card. Within this sequence, the first card for each group of cards with a common key value is a header card, while the others are detail cards. Each detail card carries an integer amount. It is required to produce a report showing the totals of amount for all keys.

1. The first step in applying the method is to describe the structure of the data. A graphic notation is used to represent the structures as trees. See Figure 129 on page 300.

2. The second step is to compose these data structures into a program structure as shown in Figure 130 on page 301.

The structure has the following properties:

- It is related quite formally to each of the data structures. Any one data structure may be recovered from the program structure.

- The correspondences (**cardfile** : **report**) and (**group** : **totalline**) are determined by the problem statement. One report is derivable from one

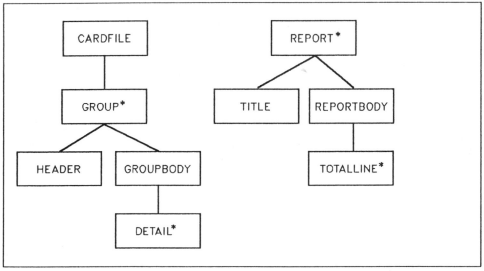

Figure 129. Structure of Data for Example (from Jackson)

      cardfile; one totalline is derivable from one group, and the totallines are in the same order as the groups.

- The structure is vacuous, in the sense that it contains no executable statements: it is a program that does nothing; it is a tree without real leaves.

3. The third step in applying the method is to list the executable operations required and to allocate each to its right place in the program structure. The operations are elementary executable statements of the programming language. They are enumerated, essentially, by working back from output to input along the data-flow paths. They are as follows for this example:

  a. write title

  b. write totalline (groupkey, total)

  c. total: = total + detail.amount

  d. total: = 0

  e. groupkey: = header.key

  f. open cardfile

  g. read cardfile

  h. close cardfile

Note almost every operation must have operands which are data objects. Allocation to a program structure is therefore a easy task if the program structure is correctly based on the data structures. This is a vital criterion of the success of

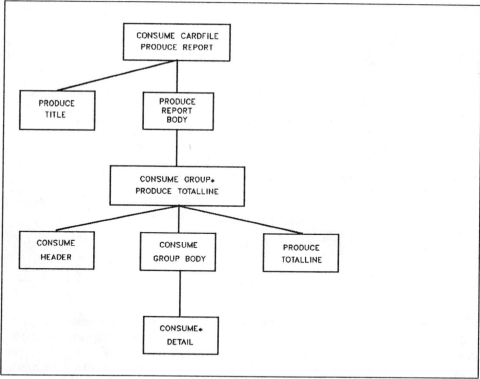

Figure 130. Program Structure for Jackson Example (from Jackson)

the first two steps. The resulting program, in a pseudocode notation (from Jackson), is shown in Figure 131 on page 302.

This program may now be transcribed into any other procedural programming language for implementation.

9.7.4 Critique

The Jackson method assumes that a complete and correct specification exists from which the designer can then glean out the data structures. This simply is not true for most complex or new problems. Additionally, as the specifications change, so too might the data structures, and with them the program structure. While change causes impact in all design methodologies, in the Jackson method it is practically unavoidable. Additionally, the required reworking of structure clashes can lead to other problems during design. The reader is referred to Jackson to understand how structure clashes are to be resolved.

```
CARD-REPORT sequence
  open cardfile;
  read cardfile;
  write title;
  REPORT-BODY iteration until cardfile.eof
    total:=0;
    groupkey:=header.key;
    read cardfile;
    GROUP-BODY iteration until cardfile.eof
             or detail.key=groupkey
      total:=total + detail.amount;
      read cardfile;
    GROUP-BODY end
    write totalline (groupkey, total);
  REPORT-BODY end
  close cardfile;
CARDFILE-REPORT end
```

Figure 131. Resulting Program for Jackson Example (from Jackson)

As mentioned, Jackson's method does seem to work well for a certain class of problems, but seems to be limited to simple systems or applications programs. Indeed, where it does work, it appears to work very well. Martin and McClure suggest [MART85A] that Jackson's method, when chosen for systems programming, should be limited to batch-processing systems, not on-line or data-base systems.

9.8 Object Oriented

Proponents of object oriented methodologies argue that a defined software object with its set of applicable operations will offset the inherent problems with other design methodologies. Rather than treating data and the procedures that act on them as if they are independent entities, an object oriented approach requires 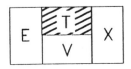 the designer to view the data and applicable operations on that data as one entity or object.

Other design methodologies have potential problems such as the wrong data being operated upon by a procedure, or the data being in the wrong form for the operating procedures. Data typing in a programming language helps to avoid some of these conflicts but not enough. In an object oriented approach it is suggested that these problems simply cannot happen.

The object oriented methodology is composed of three steps: (1) define the problem, (2) develop an informal strategy, (3) formalize the strategy [BOOC83]. This approach, writes Booch, is first attributed to R. J. Abbott of California State University, Northridge.

Define the Problem: This is an approach to gain an understanding of the problem and its structure. The methodology described in the chapter on requirements addresses in detail what needs to be done to complete this step.

Develop an Informal Strategy: This approach is used to create an informal strategy that will make use of the designer's experiences, the problem space, and constraints. The intent is to evolve as gracefully as possible to a formal strategy. This step is contained in the divergence and transformation phases of design which we addressed in Chapter 7.

Formalize the Strategy: This approach employs five steps [ABBO83].

1. **Identify objects and then attributes**. This is done by extracting from the specifications the nouns which represent objects and any qualifying adjectives which represent attributes of each object. This is basically a mechanical process.

2. **Identify operations on the objects**. Continuing the mechanical process, the verb phrases are identified in the specifications and represent the operations on the defined objects. Each operation must be associated with a specific object. To identify attributes of the operations we would class the adverb phrases with their respective verb phrases.

3. **Establish the interfaces**. This is equivalent to identifying the relationships among the objects. Thus, the visible interfaces to each object are formally described in the design language. Booch, in his book *Software Engineering with Ada* shows how this description can be carried out with Ada as the design language. In addition, the scope and visibility of each object needs to be determined, since any one object will not necessarily interact with all other objects.

4. **Implement the object with defined operations on them in the chosen programming language**. For Booch this is Ada, but it can be another language that supports the packaging notation. We suggest that ADL be used and elaborate on ADL in Chapter 10 and Appendix C.

5. **Repeat the process at all necessary levels** This is done until all necessary objects have been defined and implemented to achieve a complete solution.

Most of the advances to date in object oriented approaches have been at the implementation level. We are concerned here with design and therefore are reflecting the object orientation onto design. The language ADL which we discuss in 9.10.2, "Design Languages for Object Oriented Designs" on page 310 also allows us a representation of objects at design.

9.8.1 Information Hiding

We are concerned with concealing complex data structures such as pointers and arrays, complex design decisions, and highly vulnerable design decisions inside the modules that carry the structure or design. This is a key benefit in using an object oriented approach. Only selected service modules are allowed to know about the concealed data structure or logic. Modules that know the concealed data will probably be packaged together.

Each module in the solution hides the internal details of its processing. Modules communicate only through well-defined interfaces [PARN72]. Parnas states that design should focus first on (a) difficult design decisions and (b) design decisions that are likely to change. Then the module is designed to hide the details and information relevant to those decisions.

Fairley suggests that there are other candidates for information hiding [FAIR85]. These include:

1. A data structure, its internal linkage, and the implementation details of the procedure that manipulates it

2. The format of control blocks such as those for queries in an operating system

3. Character codes, ordering of character sets, and other implementation details

4. Shifting, marking, and other machine-dependent details

There is not an inherent or defined methodology that will make employing information hiding easier or more procedural. It, however, plays a vital role in object oriented design and in data abstractions which we discuss later. While information hiding is typically discussed when referring to design of a module, it is also used at each level of design refinement.

9.8.2 Abstractions

As was mentioned earlier, there are two types of stepwise refinements we can follow in design: functional and data. Likewise, there are two flows of abstraction: top down and bottom up. For the purposes of the book, we will be viewing abstractions in a top-down fashion, that is to say, each level of refinement is less abstract. If we were to address reverse engineering, however, a bottom to top view of abstraction would be the conceptual route, where each new level of reverse engineering is more abstract.

Each form of abstraction shows a separation of concerns. The two levels of concern are the two immediately related levels of the abstraction and its refinement. Thus, when we proceed from requirements to design, we separate the abstract WHAT from its refined HOW.

In a functional decomposition, one level separates WHAT a caller wants a specific function to do from HOW it is done or implemented by the lower-level called parts. A functional abstraction is recognized at various levels and in various languages by different terms. In Fortran it is called a subroutine, in hardware it is machine language, in ALGOL, Pascal or PL/1 it is a procedure, in BAL it would be called a MACRO, DSECT, or CSECT [SHAN80]. The level of abstraction is relative to the language of solution implementation.

When we speak of data abstraction, at any level of definition, the WHAT and HOW are separated until we reach the final level which would then have equivalence to the object types available in the implementation language. However, even with available language types we can have additional refinements of data representations in design. Thus in Pascal we might speak of records and then at another level show the record to be composed of integers and Boolean values. With *data abstractions* we will always note that in addition to the data, that we describe the abstraction in terms of the operations permitted on that data.

Shankar shows an excellent relationship between hardware data structures and programming language structures [SHAN80]. In Figure 132 on page 307 we see how each structure is understandable only as it is based on some lower level structure. Thus, at the hardware level, words are based on bytes, which in turn are based on bits, the final entity on which the more abstract structures are based. At the first level of programming language structure we see the traditional set of structures made available by languages in the early days of software compilers. All of these structures have a relationship which is defined by the hardware with which the compiler interfaces. At the second level of programming language structures, we see an enhanced mathematical set of data structures, which are in turn decomposable into lower levels of programming language structures. Indeed, in languages where these latter do not exist, we may think in terms of these structures as steps in our design solution refinement, but may have no way to directly represent them.

The criteria we follow in defining data abstractions are: (1) define the data, (2) hide the representation of the data inside of the data object, (3) define operations on the data, and (4) use them to manipulate the data only by the operation call and never directly on the defined data. These data abstractions essentially become new data types with this procedure, and as such we can then use them as any language defined data type in our design solutions.

Let us take a look at an example of a data type called "stack," which does not exist in most programming languages. We can define that this type *stack* has four operations which are permitted on it: Push, Pop, Top, and Depth. Conceptually, we know the data is a last-in, first-out series of elements, where we can put another element on the series through a PUSH, we can remove an element through a POP, we can determine what the TOP element is, and we can determine the length of the *series* through DEPTH. What we do not know, nor do we need to know it to complete our design, is whether the data is organized, for example, as a linked list or as an array. We do not need to know if the data is in main memory or on a disk. This information of HOW is kept hidden from us because it is not important to the nature of what we want to do in our design at this level of understanding.

Although the data types supplied with a programming language do define the data and permissible operations on that data, they often do not hide the representation of the data structure. As shown in Figure 132 on page 307 there is a mapping between data types and data abstractions. Thus, we can use the existing types to build more abstract types for our design thinking.

However, as Shankar notes, "this is unnatural as it forces programmers to think in terms of untyped data during design, and in terms of typed data during implementation." The solution would be to design in a language that permits thinking in terms of Abstract Data Types (ADTs) which draw on both the implementation language defined types and user defined types. The user defined types are eventually refined into the implementation language defined data types.

This flexibility allows designers to define and view ADTs from their perspective at the highest levels of abstraction and to successively refine these abstractions as the design decisions are made which eventually lead to a solution at the lowest level. The lowest level design refinements are in turn directly mappable to data types in the implementation language.

With a design language that enables abstractions, the designer has as an additional tool in his repertoire to create good designs of software problems.

9.9 Prototyping

A *prototype* is an early view of the final product to be produced. It permits a demonstration of an implementation of the problem specification. This by no means implies that a prototype has all of the function or characteristics of the final product. Rather, it typically embodies and manifests some selected parts of the product which the designers believe to be the most critical or most debatable as to the preferred solution.

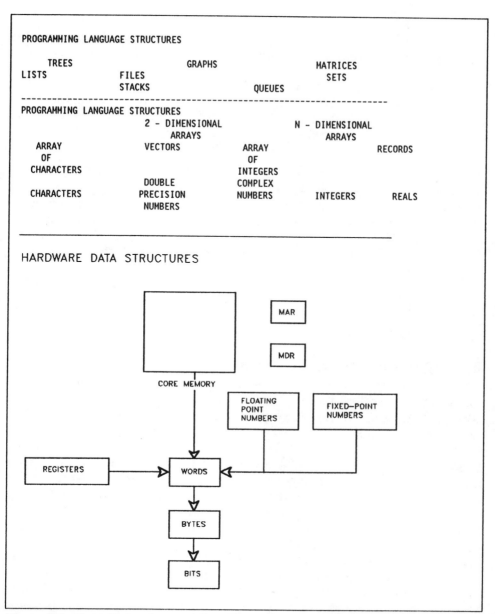

PROGRAMMING LANGUAGE STRUCTURES

TREES   GRAPHS   MATRICES
LISTS   FILES   SETS
                   STACKS   QUEUES

PROGRAMMING LANGUAGE STRUCTURES
                        2 - DIMENSIONAL   N - DIMENSIONAL
                            ARRAYS   ARRAYS
        ARRAY   VECTORS   ARRAY   RECORDS
         OF   OF
      CHARACTERS   INTEGERS
                        DOUBLE   COMPLEX
      CHARACTERS   PRECISION   NUMBERS   INTEGERS   REALS
                        NUMBERS

HARDWARE DATA STRUCTURES

                                    MAR

                                    MDR

                    CORE MEMORY

                              FLOATING   FIXED-POINT
                              POINT   NUMBERS
                              NUMBERS

        REGISTERS   WORDS

                              BYTES

                               BITS

Figure 132. Data Abstractions and Data Types (from Shankar)

Typically, the prototype has been written in the same language as the target language of the final product. This is a remnant of earlier days in software where the only language available was the eventual target language. Today, we have many other choices available, and indeed the designer who elects to develop a prototype should consider doing so in a language more powerful than the target language for the product. This will not only inhibit the development team from trying to ship the prototype as the product, but will allow the designer to work out a higher level of functional abstraction and complete the prototype earlier.

Basically then, a prototype is most useful when it can be done as early in the project life cycle as possible. However, when the prototype is completed early and if it is completed in the target implementation language, it carries with it the ever crying siren to be shipped as a product rather than to be thrown away. Fred Brooks states it perfectly:

> The management question, therefore, is not whether to build a pilot system and throw it away. You will do that. The only question is whether to plan in advance to build a throwaway, or to deliver a throwaway to the customers. Seen this way the answer is much clearer. Delivering the throwaway to the customer buys time, but it does so only at the cost of agony for the user, distraction for the builders while they do the redesign, and a bad reputation for the product that the best redesign will find hard to live down. Hence plan to throw one away; you will anyhow. [BROO82]

9.10 Design Representations

Just as there is an assortment of design methodologies, there is an even wider assortment of representations or languages which can be used to carry the intent and meaning of the design solution. Each methodology typically defines a recommended representation which should be used, but just as with any language, dialects all too soon seem to develop with their own subtleties. This is not necessarily a problem for any one common programming cultural group, but it can cause problems when programmers move between these cultures. We have already discussed two design representations with DFDs and with the Jackson method.

Since design representations are carriers of information just as natural languages are carriers of information, we should not be surprised that the problems inherent in natural languages are also to be found in design representations. These problems include (1) inhibitors to ease of use, (2) ease of misuse, (3) lack of precision as a carrier, and (4) ease of misinterpretation. Basically, we want a design representation to give us as much flexibility as we need, but no more, to aid us in clearly thinking through the problem. We want the representation to be easy to use. We want it to precisely and consistently represent our thoughts, and we want it to completely and sufficiently communicate those thoughts to someone who reads our design such that there is no misinterpretation of our thoughts.

Natural languages cannot fully satisfy these requirements, so we should hesitate to believe that invented languages are any better. They may be, but we should certainly determine that they are; otherwise we may suffer the consequences. Design representations based on mathematics have a better chance of improving the precision of communication, but they have proved difficult to use. Thus, trade-offs may have to be made. It is not clear that mathematics based languages are the best approach in large programming population groups today. This does not imply that these languages should not be taught or tried in large groups, but it does imply that the ease-of-use problem may stand in the way of quick, wide, and successful adoption of mathematics-based languages or representations unless tools are supplied to make the mathematics easier to use.

The reader is referred to Martin and McClure's, *Diagramming Techniques for Analysts and Programmers* for a comprehensive though not complete listing of the prevalent design representations in use today [MART85B].

We will explore two design representations in the next two subsections. The first, pseudocode, is more like a natural English language than other design represent-ations we have discussed. It has its flaws, but it is a good teaching aid and is among the easiest to use. The second, A Design Language (ADL), is a more rigorous approach, founded on a mathematical basis, and our preferred pedagog-ical solution for the design levels. ADL can be combined with ERA diagrams at the requirements level to provide a complete set of languages for the requirements to design "shadow" approach mentioned in Chapter 7.

Chapin, in his book, *Flowcharts* [CHAP71], gives seven criteria that should be met before a design representation should be considered for wide and universal programming environments. Although those criteria were derived in 1971, they are still applicable today. They are:

1. Is it easy to use?

2. Is the technique quick to use?

3. Is the technique simple?

4. Is the technique scannable, that is, can the reader quickly derive the meaning without having to read all the detail?

5. Is the level of detail controllable?

6. Is the technique free of ambiguity?

7. Is the technique independent of the computer and computer language?

We would add: (1) Is the technique processable via a tool? (2) Does it enforce the chosen method of design? and (3) Does it facilitate maintenance?

9.10.1 Pseudocode

Pseudocode is sometimes called structured English, but the two are different in that pseudocode looks more like code, yet is easier to read and tends to use a set of keywords familiar to the programmers. Pseudocode came into being shortly after or about the time of the introduction of structured programming. At that time flowcharts were the prevalent form of design representation, but they did not lend themselves well to encouraging structured design. Pseudocode, on the other hand, made it easy to eliminate labels, basically removing the need for GO TOs which are the critical cause of unstructured design and code.

Its popularity resulted, however, at one count, in over 200 varieties of pseudocode. Although there was much in common among these 200 varieties, nonetheless there were differences which sometimes caused confusion or irritation.

Figure 133 on page 311 shows an example in a *Design Programming Language* (DPL) written in 1974 [RADI75] and used on a number of large systems program designs. Figure 134 on page 312 shows the complete set of DPL statement types. Appendix B includes a definition of each of these statement types.

9.10.2 Design Languages for Object Oriented Designs

We have chosen object oriented design as our preferred design approach because this approach supports abstraction, problem decomposition, encapsulation, stepwise reference, and precise expression. We believe it will lead to improved quality in the design and product. We, therefore, will need a carrier or design representation which allows for ease of use during the design process. None are commercially available. Booch suggests using Ada. Software manufacturers are in the process of getting their proprietary choice used for their product designs. We found that we needed a language that would help us teach and therefore derived our own.

This representation we call *A Design Language* (ADL). It is not our intent to either provide a full solution or offer a candidate for wider acceptance. We use ADL solely for example. Appendix C contains the definition of the ADL syntax, which is derived from a number of sources including DPL [RADI75], CDL [SEW84], Ada [BOOC83], and PDL [LING79]. Examples using ADL are shown in Chapter 10, Module Level Design.

The intent is that ADL offer enough of a solution to enable it to support the Software Engineering principles of abstraction, problem decomposition, sepa-

```
EXAMPLE OF DPL:

     FORMAT:BGNSEGMENT(MAIN,MODULE,STANDALONE).
          FUNCTION IS TO PERFORM INDENTATIONS OF DPL STATEMENTS TO
          DO SYNTAX CHECKING, TO INSERT SUPPORT DEPENDENCY CODES,
          AND TO OPTIONALLY PLACE TITLES ON EACH PAGE, BUILD
          PORTIONS OF THE PROLOGUE, AND LIMIT LINE LENGTH.
     INPUT=FILES(DPLSCRC,DPLINPT),USER PARAMETERS(SC_CODE, TITLE,
          PROLOG,LINELNTH).
     CALL INIT TO CHECK OPTIONS AND ESTABLISH ENVIRONMENTAL VARIABLES
     DO WHILE THERE ARE RECORDS TO READ FROM DPLSRCE.
       IF LINE-IN-BUFFER-1 SWITCH IS OFF (A RECORD HAS NOT ALREADY
             READ INTO LINE BUFFER 1)
          THEN
             CALL READIN TO READ A RECORD INTO LINE BUFFER 1.
          ELSE (A RECORD HAS BEEN PREVIOUSLY READ INTO LINE BUFFER 2)
             SWAP LINE BUFFER 2 INTO LINE BUFFER 1.
             TURN LINE-IN-BUFFER 1 SWITCH OFF.
       ENDIF.
       INCREMENT DPL LINE COUNTER.
       CALL SCANBUF TO DETERMINE LINE MODE AND KEY ATTRIBUTE
             POSITIONS IN THE LINE BEING PROCESSED.
       IF CONTINUED LINE SWITCH IS GREATER THAN ZERO (A DPL STATEMENT)
             IS COMPOSED OF MORE THAN ONE INPUT LINE)
          THEN
             CALL SHIFT TO INDENT THIS LINE.
             CALL CONTINUE TO PROCESS THIS CONTINUED PORTION.
          ELSE
             CALL LINETYPE TO DETERMINE WHICH TYPE OF LINE IS TO
                  BE PROCESSED.
             CALL PUTLINE TO UPDATE THE DPL SOURCE WITH THE FORMATTED
                  LINE.
       ENDIF.
     ENDDO (RECORDS IN DPLSRCE).
     OUTPUT=FILES(DPLUPDT,DPLPRNT).
     ENDSEGMENT(FORMAT).
```

Figure 133. Example of DPL (Note: See Appendix B for definitions)

ration of concerns, encapsulation, structured programming in design, stepwise refinement, and precise expression of design.

The reader may be using an implementation language which does not support object orientation; therefore, it is important that a mapping of intersections and differences be made between ADL and the language implementation. These dif-

1. BGNSEGMENT AND ENDSEGMENT

2. FUNCTION

3. Interface Statements:

    a. INCLUDE

    b. ISSUE

    c. CALL

    d. INSET

4. IF THEN ELSE

5. DO UNTIL

6. DO WHILE

7. CASE

8. NOTE

9. INPUT and OUTPUT

10. Action Sequence Statements

    a. General Function

    b. EXPAND

    c. MESSAGE

11. Extended Structured Programming Figures

    a. DO INFINITE

    b. LEAVE

    c. SEARCH

Figure 134. DPL Statement Types

ferences should be accounted for in the functional commentary statements in ADL.

9.11 PLD and CLD Validation

Validation of PLD and CLD must be ensured before continuing on into MLD. This validation takes two forms: prototyping and inspections. Although prototyping really takes more of the form of validating the requirement, that is, "is it the right product?," it is an 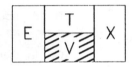 excellent choice where it can be made during the different Design stages.

Inspections are concerned with verifying that the solution is being done right. Inspections refer backward to previously verified and validated work items that initially started with the requirements statement. Refer to Chapter 8, Validation and Verification, to understand how to plan and hold an Inspection at the PLD and CLD levels.

9.12 Exit Criteria

The following are examples of the kinds of work items which should have a predefined criteria or definition that must be satisfied in order to be considered completed in PLD and CLD. There are, of course, others 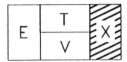 dependent on the product and its production environment.

- The product level and component level designs are complete and have been recorded in the appropriate documents and data bases.

- The usability walk-through has been held, problems identified, and a plan exists to address them.

- The following are complete and have been validated or verified:
  - PLD
    - External specification for other product areas
    - Usability objectives
    - Performance objectives
  - CLD
    - Final external specification is updated and refined
    - Usability plan

- In addition, the following have been created:
  - PLD

- Product workbook which houses the history of the product development

- Build plan which describes how the product is projected to proceed against an agreed schedule

- Comprehensive test plan describing the approach to all scheduled test stages

- Publication plan for all books to be made available with the product

- Publication objectives describing the purpose of each book

- Publication measurement plan describing how the product books will be measured and against which criteria

- Distribution and support plan for the marketing and service organizations

- Service plan describing how the product will be maintained

- Service training plan for the service personnel

- CLD

  - Functional verification test plan describing how the FVT will be performed

  - Performance test plan describing how performance will be measured

9.13 Summary

In this chapter we discussed the concepts of abstraction, problem decomposition, separation of concerns, encapsulation, design decision, and consistency. We view these concepts as necessary to completing good PLDs and CLDs. We applied the ETVX paradigm for PLD and CLD with defined entry criteria, validation techniques, and exit criteria. The task part itself was addressed in discussion of the four major design methodology groups: functional decomposition, data flow, data structure, and object oriented. The latter is our recommended approach for design.

During PLD the design solution is decomposed into component parts which become the basis of the individual CLD design refinement. The resultant parts identified from the CLD decomposition are modules that will be refined during MLD. Any one of the four design methodology types may be used to complete PLD and CLD. In industry, all are used today, and there does not seem to be any one overwhelmingly dominant choice. We discussed a number of design representations including DFDs, Jackson, pseudocode, and ADL. The latter is our recommended choice.

9.14 References

[ABBO83] R. J. Abbott, "Program Design by Informal English Descriptions," *Communications of the ACM*, Vol. 26, No. 11 (November 1983), pp. 882−94.

[BERG81] G. D. Bergland, "A Guided Tour of Program Design Methodologies," *Computer* (October 1981).

[BOOC83] G. Booch, *Software Engineering with Ada*, Benjamin/Cummings Publishing Co. (1983).

[BROO82] F. P. Brooks, Jr., *The Mythical Man-Month*, Addison-Wesley Publishing Company (1982).

[CAME83] J. R. Cameron, *Tutorial: JSP & JSD: The Jackson Approach to Software Development*, IEEE Computer Society (1983).

[CARP85] M. B. Carpenter and H. K. Hallman, "Quality Emphasis at IBM's Software Engineering Institute," *IBM Systems Journal*, Vol. 24, No. 2 (1985).

[CHAP71] N. Chapin, *Flowcharts*, Auerbach, (1971).

[DEMA78] T. DeMarco, *Structured Analysis and System Specification*, Yourdon Press (1978).

[DIJK72] E. W. Dijkstra, "Notes on Structured Programming," in *Structured Programming*, O. J. Dahl, ed., Academic Press (1972), pp. 1−82.

[FAIR85] R. E. Fairley, *Software Engineering Concepts*, McGraw-Hill Book Company (1985).

[FLOY79] R. W. Floyd, "The Paradigm of Programming," *Communications of the ACM*, Vol. 22, No. 8 (August 1979), pp. 455−60.

[HOS82] USE.IT Reference Manual, Higher Order Software, Cambridge, MA (1982).

[INSP] *Inspections in Application Development—Introduction and Implementation Guidelines*, GC20-2000, IBM.

[JACK76A] M. A. Jackson, *Lecture Notes in Computer Science*, Springer-Verlag, Vol. 44 (1976), pp. 236−62.

[JACK76B] M. A. Jackson, *JSP Handbook*, Michael Jackson Limited, London, (1981).

[LING79] R. C. Linger, H. D. Mills, and B. J. Witt, *Structured Programming: Theory and Practice*, Addison-Wesley Publishing Company (1979).

[MART85A] J. Martin and C. McClure, *Structured Techniques for Computing*, Prentice-Hall (1985).

[MART85B] J. Martin and C. McClure, *Diagramming Techniques for Analysts and Programmers*, Prentice-Hall (1985).

[MCME84] S. M. McMenamin and J. F. Palmer, *Essential Systems Analysis*, Yourdon Press (1984).

[MILL70] H. D. Mills, "Top Down Programming in Large Systems," *Courant Computer Science Symposium Debugging Techniques in Large System*, New York (1970).

[MYER78] G. J. Myers, *Composite/Structured Design*, Van Nostrand Reinhold Company (1978).

[PARN72] D. L. Parnas, "On the Criteria to Be Used in Decomposing Systems into Modules," *Communications of the ACM*, Vol. 15, No. 12 (December 1972), pp. 1053 − 58.

[RADI75] R. A. Radice, *Design Programming Language*, IBM TR 21.604 (August 4, 1975).

[SCHE85] P. A. Scheffer, A. H. Stone, W. E. Rzepka, "A Case Study of SREM," *IEEE Computer Magazine*, Vol. 18, No. 4 (April 1985), pp. 47 − 54.

[SEW84] *Software Engineering Workshop (SEW) Student Notebook*, Vol. 1 − 4, Software Engineering Institute, G325-0010, IBM Corporation.

[SHAN80] K. S. Shankar, "Data Structures, Types, and Abstractions," *Computer* (April 1980).

[SIMO86] H. A. Simon, "Whether Software Engineering Needs to Be Artificially Intellengent," *IEEE Transactions on Software Engineering*, Vol. SE-12, No. 7 (July 1986), pp. 726–32.

[WIRT71] N. Wirth, "Program Development by Stepwise Refinement," *Communications of the ACM*, Vol. 14, No. 4 (April 1971), pp. 221–27.

[YOUR79] E. Yourdon and L. L. Constantine, *Structured Design: Fundamentals of a Discipline of Computer Program and Systems Design*, Prentice-Hall (1979).

Chapter 10. Module Level Design (MLD)

10.1 Introduction

If the product has successfully completed the exit criteria for PLD and CLD, the development can now continue into Module Level Design (MLD). In this chapter we will discuss methodologies relevant to MLD including structured programming, cohesion and coupling, object oriented design, module verification through proof of correctness, and concurrent processing.

10.2 What Is a Module?

Primary to the definition of a *module* is the idea that it is a unit that represents a logical and self-contained task to be performed as part of a system or component in a system. The notion of modularity is not unique to software. In the housing industry, modular units are widely accepted to solve large economically driven developments. As economics and the need to better manage large software projects becomes more necessary, then the concept of *modularity* becomes more important in software. Aside from being a compiler issue where a solution was needed to enable program development across large groups, modularity came about through management's need to divide and conquer the software engineering problem and to control project complexity. This became known as *programming in the large*. These needs, however, could only be satisfied if language and operating system capabilities were provided that would allow the development of separate units which could later be combined to communicate with other units to present a cohesive system view. The program user does not really care how many modules may exist in a system or problem solution. The need for modules comes from the builder, not the user.

Parnas, in 1972, saw the need to add some intellectual order to the decision of module choice in his paper "On the Criteria to be Used in Decomposing Systems into Modules" [PARN72]. He argued that we should not define modules by decomposing a system into modules, rather that we should develop a list for the product under development of difficult designs and design decisions that will probably change during the design process. Then each module should be constructed to hide decisions from the other modules in the system. This became the now widely accepted concept of information hiding which eventually was absorbed into object oriented and data abstraction design approaches.

Martin and McClure give the following useful list of properties of a module [MART85A]:

- Each module represents one logical, self-contained task.

- Modules are simple.

- Modules are closed.

- Modules are discrete and visible.

- Modules are separately testable.

- Each module is implemented as a single, independent program function.

- Each module has a single entry point and a single exit point.

- Each module exits to a standard return point in the module from which it was executed.

- Modules may be combined into larger modules without the knowledge of the internal construction of the modules.

- Modules have well-defined interfaces. Modules have control connections via their entry points and exit points; modules have data connections via the services they perform for each other.

Most modules do not exhibit all these desirable attributes, and yet exist as parts of successful products. Thus, one can create modules that lack these attributes.

Since there is no free lunch, however, the price may be paid in longer schedules, lower productivity, poorer quality, or greater maintenance costs.

10.3 Module Level Design Concepts

Let us take a look at two concepts that are important at the module level:

- Cohesion
- Coupling

10.3.1 Cohesion

Cohesion, sometimes called *module strength*, is a measurement of the relationships among the elements within a single module. Myers defines several levels of module strength, where the higher the cohesion the better [MYER78]. They are:

1. A *coincidental strength* module (1) cannot be defined except by its logic, and/or (2) it performs multiple, completely unrelated functions. The module elements are only loosely connected or related to each other, while at the same time they may be closely related to elements within other modules. These modules lack an integrated identity.

2. A *logical strength* module is composed of elements that are logically related and perform a class of functions. The required imbedded function can be invoked by calling the module with a parameter or function argument. For example, three different print routines exist in one module and the specific required print routine is invoked via a defined parameter.

3. A *classical strength* module performs multiple sequential functions, and there is a weak relationship among the functions. For example, the relationship may be one of time, as in initialization or termination modules, or it may be in "trivial" tasks such as housekeeping or cleanup functions which are not specific to one function, but scattered across the product.

4. A *procedural strength* module has a set of elements that are related according to the procedure of the problem being solved. Thus, the procedural sequence of tasks to be performed binds this type of module.

5. *Communicational strength* modules are similar to procedural strength modules, but the elements are also related because the element either uses the same data or the output of one element is the input to another element in the module.

6. *Informational strength* modules look like function-strength modules, but all functions are related by a concept, data structure, or resource which is hidden within the overall module.

7. The highest form of strength is *functional strength* and is represented by a module that performs a single specific function where all elements contribute to an integral overall function. The Abstract Data Types (ADTs) discussed in Chapter 9 are examples of modules at a functional strength level.

10.3.2 Coupling

Coupling is a measure of the relationships between modules. There are seven categories of module coupling where the higher level or tightest coupling is the least desired, as it is the most dependent on changes in other modules [MYER78].

1. Modules with *no direct coupling* are just that. They exist in and of themselves as programs. They are self-contained. They are preferred as a module type.

2. *Data coupled* modules communicate in the form of passed data elements only via input and output arguments, and have no other form of coupling with other modules higher than this level.

3. *Stamp coupled* modules communicate by referencing data in the same non-global data structure, and have no higher levels of coupling.

4. *Control coupled* modules have one module that explicitly controls the logic of the other modules by passing explicit elements of control as arguments through function codes, switches, or flags as examples; they have no higher level of coupling.

5. *External coupled* modules reference a homogeneous global data item or have one module that makes reference to an externally declared symbol in another module; they have no higher level of coupling.

6. *Common coupled* modules occur among modules that reference a global data structure. It should be noted that global data areas used as communication between modules are the source of endless errors and inhibit reuse of function.

7. *Content coupled* modules are the worst level of coupling. This attribute exists in modules that make direct reference to contents of another module.

10.4 Viewpoints in the MLD Stage

The overriding viewpoint during the MLD stage, of course, is that of program development. However, coincidental activities will be occurring in the following product areas for each of the other product viewpoints:

- Program Development
- Testing

- Publications

- Marketing and Service

- Build and Integration

10.5 Entry Criteria for Module Level Design

The following list shows some examples by viewpoint of entry criteria which must be satisfied prior to beginning the tasks for MLD:

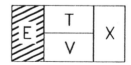

- All exit criteria from CLD have been satisfied.

- Program Development

  - Final external specifications are complete and available to the MLD designers.

  - All new and changed requirements have been documented and accounted for.

  - Performance and usability objectives are completely defined and agreed to.

  - CLD documentation is current and available for the MLD designer.

- Build and Integration

  - Build plan is kept current for the agreed to schedule and resources required.

- Testing

  - Final external specifications are available to the test group.

  - CLD documentation is available to the test group.

  - Performance objectives are available to the test group.

- Publications

  - Final external specifications are available for the publication writers.

  - CLD documentation is available for the publication writers.

10.6 Structured Programming

Structured programs as defined by Dijkstra are composed of three basis control structures: sequence, if then else, and do while [DIJK72]. These three structures are shown graphically in Figure 135 on page 323 using the basic nodes shown in Figure 136 on page 324 to construct a flow chart. We will define *flow chart* as a directed graph that depicts the flow of execution control of a program and the instructions to be executed [SEW84].

A *proper program* is defined as a program with a control structure characterized by [LING79]

- a single entry.
- a single exit.
- each node existing on a path from entry to exit.

Thus, Figure 137 on page 325 shows examples of proper programs, while Figure 138 on page 326 shows improper program parts.

A *proper subprogram* is a proper program consisting of some, but not all, of the nodes of a full proper program. Thus in Figure 10-3a if we exclude function node C the remainder is a proper subprogram of the given full proper program.

A *prime program* is a proper program that has no proper subprograms of more than one node. Thus, all the basis control structures are prime programs by default, but, for example, so is the program represented in Figure 10-3b. It is not reducible without restructure.

A *composite program* is a proper program that has at least one proper subprogram of more than one node. Thus, the program expressed in Figure 10-3a is a composite program and a proper program.

We may view *stepwise refinement* at the module level as the process of repeatedly replacing function nodes within a program by programs from the control structures in the basis set. Abstraction at the module level would proceed in a reverse order and would replace basis set control structures with function nodes. One test for a structured program is that it can be derived from a single function node using stepwise refinement, or it is a program that can be abstracted to a single function node at its last level of functional abstraction.

The *basis set* that we will use for structured programming is composed of the six figures which include the three in Figure 135 and the additional three shown in Figure 139 on page 327. Thus, when we are doing stepwise refinement or func-

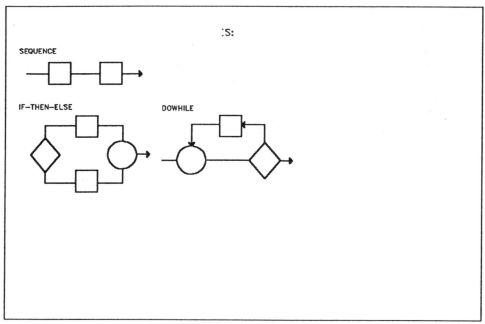

Figure 135. Basic Control Structures

tional abstraction we are limited to using structures from the basis set of these six figures to refine or elaborate our solution.

For more details on this extension of the basis set and structure theorem, the reader is referred to *Structured Programming: Theory and Practice* [LING79].

10.6.1 Structuring Unstructured Programs

Unfortunately not all programs are structured because (1) they may have been created prior to 1972, when structured programs began to affect the programming culture; (2) there is a lack of good design documentation which reflects the structure; (3) because structured programming, while known, was not practiced; or (4) the modules deteriorated from an initial structured form into unstructured programs through maintenance and enhancement. The debate about structured programming's value is still continuing, even at the writing of this book [RUBI87]. However, if we accept the value that structuring gives us, we may choose to try to bring structure to some existing unstructured modules.

There are five basic operations we need to understand in order to try to achieve structure in these cases:

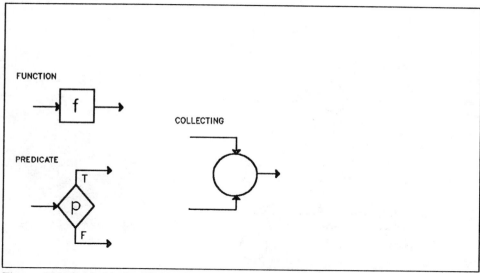

Figure 136. Basic Nodes Within Flow Charts

Interchange allows us to exchange at will the input and output lines of two or more adjacent collection nodes, as doing so will not affect function flow. Thus, Figure 10-6a is equivalent to Figure 10-6b, and Figure 10-7a is equivalent to Figure 10-7b.

Transposition allows us to transpose a function node with a predicate or collector node provided the logic of the program is not changed. Thus Figure 10-8a is equivalent to Figure 10-8b, and Figure 10-9a is equivalent to Figure 10-9b.

Combination allows us to combine two or more consecutive function nodes into one composite function node. Reference Figure 144 on page 332.

Resolution allows us to duplicate program flow prior to a given point by adding collector nodes as needed to complete the duplicate flow. Thus Figure 10-11a is equivalent to Figure 10-11b.

Substitution allows us to substitute a function node for any proper program or subprogram.

The reader is referred to Linger, Mills, and Witt's *Structured Programming: Theory and Practice* for a deeper analysis of these techniques [LING79]. Additionally, the reader should refer to Robert C. Tausworthe's *Standardized Development of Computer Software*, for an assessment and expansion on Mills' mathematical foundations [TAUS76].

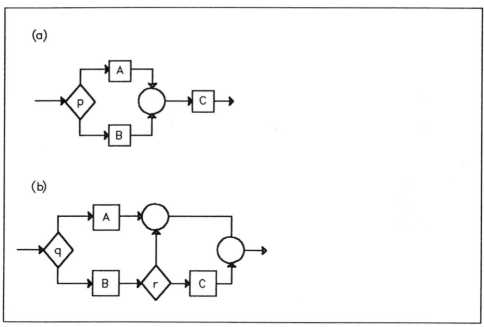

Figure 137. Examples of Structured Proper Programs

10.7 Composite/Structured Design

As mentioned in Chapter 9, the six primary aspects to Structured Design are: (1) Data Flow Diagrams; (2) Transform Analysis and (3) Transaction Analysis, which were covered under the PLD and CLD discussions; (4) Coupling and (5) Cohesion, which were covered in the concepts section of this chapter. The sixth aspect is Structure Charts, some of which was discussed in Chapter 9. The basic elements needed to complete Structure Charts are shown in Figure 146 on page 334 [YOUR79]. An example of a Structure Chart using these is shown in Figure 147 on page 335.

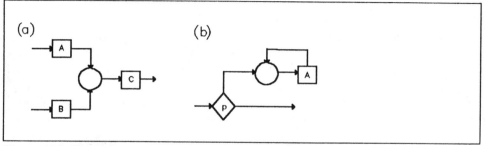

Figure 138. Examples of Improper and Unstructured Programs

10.8 Module Refinement

Module refinement is an extension to stepwise refinement [SEW84].

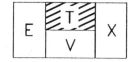

The need for module refinement lies in the real work situation where: (1) not all input to the design process is in evidence at the beginning, and (2) there are alternative design decisions which could define the final solution. Both stepwise refinement and module refinement are directed towards an orderly top-down design approach. Both struggle to reach design quiescence in an orderly and complete manner, and both can be used to define checkpoints to hold design inspections for work item completion at different design levels.

The keys points to remember are that in module design using, for example, ADL notation we progress from a SPEC or user viewable package to a DESIGN or package body with implementation details. We do this refinement in successive steps until the design is complete. We progress from more abstract data to more concrete data statements until the design is complete. Design refinement is shown graphically in Figure 148 on page 336.

We progress from mapping the defined operations on the abstract data to restated operations on the concrete data.

The key difference between stepwise refinement and module refinement is the difference of focusing on refining functions alone and including data type refinement. The latter contain both the function and the necessary data, both of which are refined until the design has quiesced. More specific differences are noted in Figure 149 on page 337.

What is design quiescence? SEW at IBM defines it as "a checkpoint in a design hierarchy where the designer has strong confidence that all the intended functions/state machines directly below the design quiescent point may be

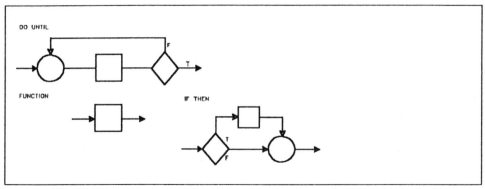

Figure 139. Additional Basic Set Figures

designed in a straightforward manner within all system constraints and with little or no input on the design above it" [SEW84]. When the design quiescent points are reached, this is the most appropriate point to hold a design inspection and acknowledge the MLD level as completed.

Figure 147 on page 335 from Martin [MART85A] is an example of a "simplified structure chart." Simplified, indeed. The basic elements of a Structure Chart are shown in Figure 146 on page 334.

10.9 Jackson at the Module Level

At the module level, Jackson employs a form of pseudocode which he calls structured text. The intent is to provide more rigor to some of the ambiguous pseudocodes by requiring the specific use of keyword pairs for sequence, selection, and iteration control structures.

The rules are shown in Figure 150 on page 338 where keywords are shown in bold face.

10.10 Object Oriented

Object oriented design methodologies begin with the assumption that a desirable entity includes function with related data and is to be viewed as one object type. This object includes the function and related operations to invoke the function. An object type is a language type much as *integer* is a type that permits operations such as add, subtract, multiply, and divide. At a higher level of abstraction, a symbol table may be viewed as a type that permits operations such as "add_symbol" and "delete_symbol."

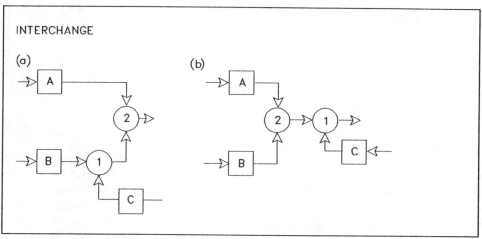

INTERCHANGE

(a)

(b)

Figure 140. Example of Interchange

Object orientation can be used at all levels of design, and even while in MLD the designer may find the need to create additional lower-level object types. We will now explore an approach to get us to use data and functional abstraction at the module level. The following subsections have their origin in the SEW design methodologies [SEW84]. A number of extensions and changes have been added, such that these sections now stand on their own.

10.10.1 Function Statements

By definition, a function is a set of ordered pairs such that each first element of the pair is unique. Thus: $[(1,1),(2,4),(3,9),(4,16)]$ is a function, but $[(1,1),(2,4),(2,6),(3,9)]$ is not.

For our purposes at this time, we do not care how the function is performed, thus we can view a function as a black box. We do care, however, that for each unique first element of an ordered pair we can predict the second element that will be returned through the black box mechanism.

Any program can be viewed as a function if the end result is such that the program satisfies the definition of a function. Thus,

```
SEGMENT increment_A PROGRAM (INOUT A:INTEGER ≥ 0);
    A=A+1;
ENDSEGMENT increment_A;
```

is a program and can be viewed as the mathematical function:

```
{(x,y)]x ≥ 0 and y = x+1}
```

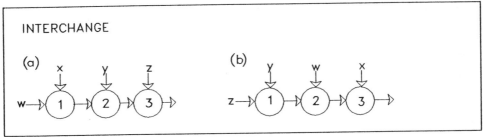

Figure 141. Additional Interchange Examples

If our program were more complex than the example *increment_A*, we should be able to summarize the overall program behavior to achieve a functional equivalence. We would include this function statement in the program preceding the code to which it applies. The function statement would look as follows:

$$<(x,y)x \geq) \text{ and } y=x+1>$$

In this form it represents the mapping of initial inputs to final outputs, and it hides the order of events which show how the input to output is transformed. This would be an example of abstracting the function statement from the code. If we began with the function statement we could refine it in a stepwise manner to achieve the function statement objectives.

We shall not deal in this book with deriving function statement from programs, be they sequence, conditional, or looping. The reader is referred to Linger, Mills, and Witt's *Structured Programming: Theory and Practice* for an excellent exposition on these techniques.

10.10.2 Data Abstraction

A data abstraction is an object in that it presents a view of data which describes a set of legal values and a set of valid operations on that data. While we may want to be able to create new data abstractions for our use during the design stage, we also want to be able to draw from an existing set of data abstractions. This existing set includes all data types that exist in the design language and those data abstractions previously made available for reuse through a library. New data abstractions are refined until resolved to the basis set of data types defined in the design language. The basis set may be different for each design language. These in turn will have to be mapped to the data types in the implementation language. Some data types in the design language are directly translatable into data types in the implementation language. Others will require refinement when the design to implementation transition is made. Even in the implementation language further refinement can occur. Thus, a RECORD type in Pascal may be refined into ARRAY and INTEGER types.

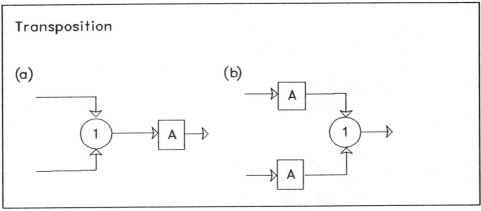

Figure 142. Examples of Transposition

Thus, during MLD we can use data abstractions types in these four forms:

1. A direct data type from the design language basis set, for example, VAR a:INTEGER. The basis set for ADL is defined in Appendix C.

2. An indirect type that will eventually be refined into a type in the design language basis set, for example:

```
Point 1 in design time = VAR input-data:stream;
Point 2 in design time = TYPE stream = QUEUE OF item;
Point 3 in design time = TYPE item = REC
                                    x: ....;
                                    y: ....;
                                 ENDREC;
```

3. A newly created data abstraction/type that defines the set of legal values and valid operations using a module as the carrier, for example:

```
VAR x:MOD to_be_defined (parms);
```

The designated module (to_be_defined) via the MOD keyword in ADL requires a SPEC to elaborate the legal values and valid operations. Thus, MOD requires a SPEC to complete the design specification of the new data abstraction.

4. A previously defined data abstraction available for reuse through local or global libraries.

This latter form offers the greatest potential for increases in productivity and quality during design and program development.

The basis set for the ADL structured types must later be refined into the implementation language data types during Code. In some environments, the term *concrete data type* is used to describe the data types in the implementation lan-

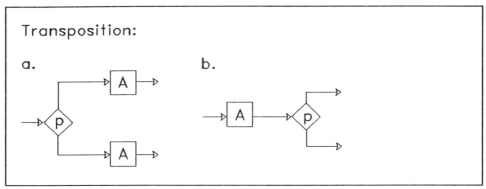

Transposition:

a.

b.

Figure 143. Additional Examples of Transposition

guage. The difference between abstract and concrete data types is that abstract data types are not directly executable on a target machine.

How then does one go about abstracting a design solution? First, identify the important features of the solution as it presently exists that need to be highlighted. Address the WHAT not the HOW. Summarize the function to be performed. Avoid detail. Second, identify the details that need to be suppressed at the design level of the work in progress. All function and data that explain HOW the function is performed or HOW the data is represented should be visibly suppressed. Finally, describe the object that embodies the function and data in terms of existing abstractions or basis types. Alternately, describe the functions and data in terms of deferred or indirect types or abstractions that will be refined at a later design point. Use the descriptive operations of the abstractions used. Use models of the data from the ADL basis set of data types.

Each data abstraction has an external and internal part. The external part makes evident

1. the type name

2. the definition of legal values

3. the definition of valid operations on the data model.

The internal part is not visible to the user of the abstraction. It contains (1) the refinement of the abstract model at the implementation level, and (2) procedures that will implement the defined operation.

A symbol table can be used as an example of a data abstraction. Here the data span is selected to be defined in terms of a set of records as the abstract data model, for example:

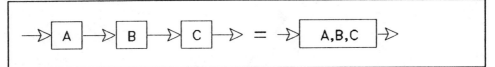

Figure 144. Example of Combination

```
SET of REC
        symbol_name: STRING;
        location: INTEGER;
    ENDREC;
```

The operations we may wish to define (there may be others) could be as follows:

```
CLEAR --------- set the symbol table to EMPTY.
ADDSYMBOL ----- a) if not in SET, add to set and
                    return status of OK.
                b) if already in SET, return status of IN_SET.
GETLOCATION --- a) if in SET, return location for symbol
                    and return status of OK.
                b) if not in SET, return status of undefined_symbol
```

The packaging of data abstractions using ADL has the following relationships:

1. If a procedure type of SEGMENT makes a reference to a deferred type via the keyword MOD which is not already defined, then a SPEC will need to be created. In the case where it is already defined, then the SPEC exists in some library for reuse.

2. A SPEC will satisfy the required deferred definition and provide the abstract view, or WHAT view, of the data type.

3. For each FUNCTION defined in the SPEC, there will be a SEGMENT(PROCEDURE) that will satisfy the required function of the operation.

4. A DESIGN will eventually be created for the SPEC and will satisfy the design view of the data type. The FUNCTIONS in the DESIGN will be implemented by the same PROCEDURE in the SPEC view.

This PROCEDURE to SPEC to DESIGN to PROCEDURE evolutionary process will continue as necessary until the full design solution for the problem is defined. See an example of this in Figure 148 on page 336.

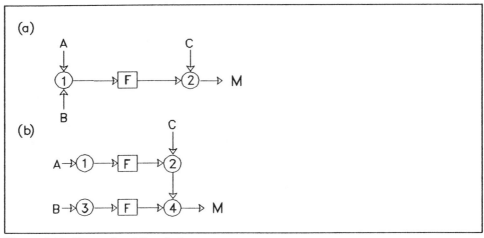

Figure 145. Example of Resolution

10.10.3 State Machine as a Model

We shall use the *state machine* as the model for creating data abstractions [LING79] [SEW84]. In 7.5.5, "Finite State Machine (FSM)" on page 223 we defined the state machine model, where it was explained that there are five main components to a state machine: input, transition rules (operations), output, state data which is returned, and an initial state that is assumed to be true when the machine is first entered.

We can view a data abstraction with these same five components:

1. INPUT, where the required variables for the defined abstraction (type) are provided in order to execute specified operations.

2. TRANSITION RULES, where the operations or functions are defined for this abstraction.

3. OUTPUT, where variables that are changed or produced and that are bounded by the abstraction (type) are delivered.

4. STATE DATA, where the abstract model for the abstraction is chosen. It is assumed that a new state is created from the combination of the input and current operation specified for the abstraction, that the new state is retained, and that the new state becomes the current state for any next invocation of the operation on this variable provided as input.

5. INITIAL STATE, which becomes the first current state on the variable. This initial state is manifested when variable of this type is declared.

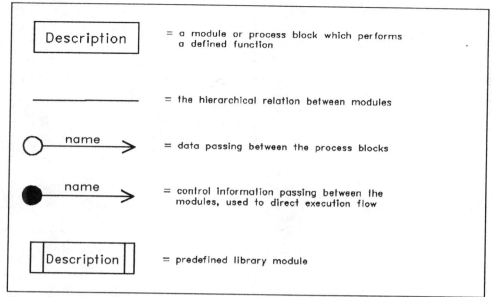

| Description | = a module or process block which performs a defined function |

| ——————————— | = the hierarchical relation between modules |

| ○——name——→ | = data passing between the process blocks |

| ●——name——→ | = control information passing between the modules, used to direct execution flow |

| ‖Description‖ | = predefined library module |

Figure 146. Basic Elements of Structure Charts

Both the SPEC and DESIGN package structures of ADL require that all these five components be defined in order to complete the definition of the SPEC or DESIGN packages. SPEC and DESIGN are fully defined in Appendix C.

10.10.4 Designs in ADL

Let us now take a look at a specific example of an abstract data type. If we were designing a compiler, we would find that we needed a symbol table. We might then view this symbol table as an abstract data type; that is, it has a defined data space and it has permissible operation on that data space.

Continuing with our designated example and using the ADL syntax, we could construct our example of the ADT named *symbol table* as shown Figure 151 on page 339.

Thus, we have chosen to view our symbol table as a set of records with an invariant condition which inhibits two items in the symbol table from having the same name. Initially we view the set as being empty.

We have chosen three legal operations which will be allowed on this data space; that is, we may CLEAR the symbol table, we may ADD_SYMBOL to the table, or we may GET_LOCATION of a symbol. Each operation shows its equivalent function commentary.

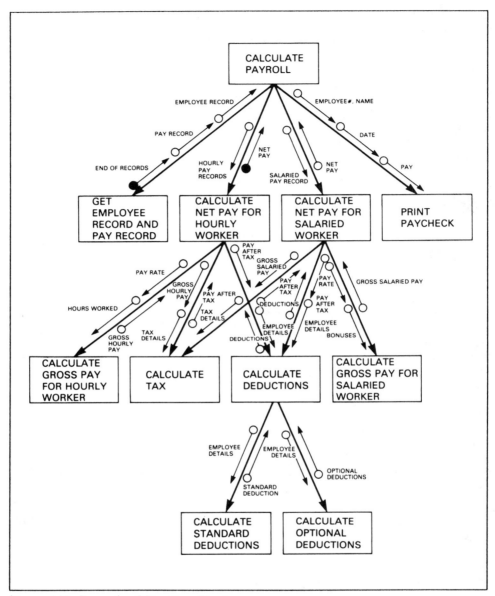

Figure 147. Example of Structure Chart

We have defined our data space and legal values on the date space, and we have specified our view of this abstract data type named *symbol_table* using the FSM as a model.

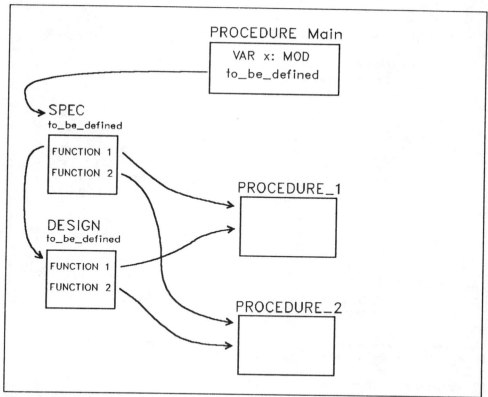

Figure 148. Design Refinement Shown Graphically

10.10.5 Module Invariants

Data space invariants designated through the keyword INVARIANT in the SPEC-ENDSPEC package are included because we may wish to restrict the data space such that values that evaluate true for the INVARIANT condition are disallowed. These values would cause an error in the processing of the implementation if they were not guarded or screened out. We do not always require an INVARIANT, but it is rare to not find a restriction on the data space.

A simple form of INVARIANT would be for the data type INTEGER, where we designate the INTEGER must be ≥ 0 to disallow negative values. We may have more than one INVARIANT if we choose or require that our data space be more precise.

INVARIANTS can be written in three basic forms:

1. Simple English narrative

	Stepwise Refinement	Module Refinement
Begins with	A specification of intended function	A module specification, SPEC or the package in Ada frequently with abstract state data
Refines into	A design composed of a structure from the basis set containing program functions	A design or package body in Ada with more concrete state data and contain intended functions to be refined, and potentially, additional abstract variables MOD requiring further levels of module refinement
Verifies	That intended function and program function correspond	SPEC and DESIGN correspond

Figure 149. Module Refinement Compared with Stepwise Refinement

2. Procedural English narrative

3. Mathematical

Examples of these for the abstract data type *symbol_table* used in the previous section, 10.10.4, "Designs in ADL" on page 336, would look as follows:

1. INVARIANT: No duplicate symbols can exits in the STACK;

2. INVARIANT: There does not exist an i and j, between 1 and max, such that symbol(i) equals symbol(j) and i does not equal j;

3. INVARIANT: $(\neg EXIST(i,j), 1 \leq (i,j) \leq max \ \& \ i \neq j)$ AND
$\qquad\qquad\qquad symbol(i) = symbol(j);$

```
    Sequence:
        Name seq
                part_1;
                part_2;
                part_3;
        Name end;

    Selection:
        Name select (condition_1)
            part_1;
        Name (condition_2)
            part_2;
        .
        .
        .

        Name (condition_n)
            part_n;
        Name end;

    Iteration:
        Name iter while (condition)
            part;
        Name end;
```

Figure 150. Jackson Pseudocode Example

10.10.6 Generic Types

Once we have begun to get comfortable with creating SPECs as part of our
designs, we may begin to sense that many of our SPECs have similarities. If we
can identify where these similarities exist, we may be able to define a TYPE that
is generic to all of those that have an essential similarity. However, since there
are undoubtedly some differences between each of the previous types, we will
have to allow for those differences.

This notion of creating a "super" type which can be modified to reflect differences is called a *generic type*. It allows us to create families of data types which
have some essential similarity in common. More importantly it allows us to
promote reuse through the generic "super" type. It allows inheritance of the
generic type's attributes to be passed on to the specific instantiated type. The
instantiation also permits modification of the generic type attributes through
parameters which override the generic defaults.

```
SPEC symbol_table;
   STATE
     TYPE symbol_table=SET of REC
                                symbol_name:STRING;
                                location:INTEGER;
                             END;
     INVARIANT (¬EXIST (i,j),1≤(i,j)≤max & i≠j)
        AND (symbol_name(i) = symbol_name(j))
     INITIAL SET symbol_table: = EMPTY;
   OPERATIONS
     FUNCTION CLEAR (INOUT s:symbol_table) <S:=EMPTY>;
     FUNCTION ADD_SYMBOL (INOUT s:symbol_table,
        IN new_symbol:STRING,new_location:INTEGER,
        OUT status:(OK, MULTI-DEFINED))
           <EXISTS (i,s) (symbol_name(i)=new symbol)--->
           status:=MULTI-DEFINED | TRUE --->s,status:=
           s+(new_symbol,new_location,OK)>;
     FUNCTION GET_LOCATION (IN s:symbol_table,new_symbol:STRING,
        OUT loc:INTEGER,
        status:(OK,UNDEFINED);
        <EXIST (i,s) (symbol_name(i)=new_symbol)---->loc,
        status:=
        location(i), OK | TRUE ---> status:=UNDEFINED>;
   ENDSPEC symbol_table;
```

Figure 151. ADL Example of Symbol_Table ADT

The differences required for each member of the data type family are reflected through personalization or parameterization of each declared variable in the SPEC package structure in conjunction with a VAR statement that triggers the specific instance of some type family "member." The invocation of a specific instance of a generic type is called *instantiation*.

Thus, we might have a SPEC defined as a generic type as shown in Figure 152 on page 341.

In this example, the generic savearea has been instantiated for two purposes, and we now have two types that have been defined with less effort than if we had to start from scratch on each. Clearly this is in the best interests of productivity and quality in software. Thus, we see that generic types allow us reusability and ease of completion for different instances.

This example did not show any parameter override in the generic type, as there was only one variable of interest, that is, max. However, we could have defined the generic type as shown in Figure 153 on page 342.

```
        SPEC savearea(saverec:TYPE,max:INTEGER ≥ 1);
where saverec and max are parameters which must be included in all
instantiations of savearea.
For example;
        VAR savearea_1:MOD savearea(format_1,1000);
is one instance of completing the SPEC.  In this case saverec
is defined as format_1 through the instantiation, and max
is set to 1000.
        VAR savearea_2:MOD savearea(format_2,2048);
is a different instantiation of the same generic type named
savearea.
Alternately, we could have defined two SPECs as follows:
        SPEC savearea_1:(saverec:format_1,1000);
and
        SPEC savearea_2:(saverec:format_2,2048);
```

Figure 152. Generic SPEC

Module Verification

As was mentioned with stepwise refinement and module refinement, we as designers are declaring our specification or intended function at one level in the solution and then refining it into a design at the next level of solution completeness. As we derive our design we want to ensure that it corresponds to the intended function of the specification. We discussed Inspections in Chapter 8 as one approach to this verification. In this section we wish to explore a more formal approach, that of *proof of correctness*. This section is based on the work of Linger, Mills, Witt [LING79] and IBM's Software Engineering Institute [SEW84].

Although we believe that proofs of correctness are the more rigorous form of verification at the MLD, we must advise the reader that they are not easy to do, and are somewhat prone to error themselves. The strength of proofs lies in their mathematical basis, and this is indeed a basis of significance. However, mathemathical proofs themselves contain errors. Evidence to this point is cited by Davis [DAVI72] in Shooman [SHOO83]:

1. Over 130 errors have been committed since antiquity by mathematicians of the first and second rank.

2. A previous editor of *Mathematical Reviews* estimates that about half of all published mathematical papers contain errors.

3. Several errors were found in the *Handbook of Mathematical Functions*.

```
      SPEC savearea
         (saverec:TYPE,max:INTEGER≥1,range:STRING='UNBOUNDED');

In this case, if we instantiated savearea as:
      VAR savearea_1:MOD savearea(format_1,1000);

we would have a savearea of 1000 elements and the default has been
been accepted as UNBOUNDED, that is the savearea is dynamic in its
size.

On the other hand had we instantiated savearea as:
      VAR savearea_1:MOD savearea(format_1,1000,'BOUNDED');

we would have a savearea which is BOUNDED, that is the
savearea has a fixed upper bound on size.
```

Figure 153. Generic Type with Parameter Override

Nonetheless, we believe that as the programming community comes closer to the
mathematical basis of software solutions, the reliability of software products will
improve substantially. Whether software solutions will ever consistently be error
free is doubtful.

10.10.7 Method of Proofs

Correctness can be complete or sufficient. Figure 154
on page 343 shows these two levels of correctness. For
our purposes the sufficiently correct solution is acceptable in our proofs.

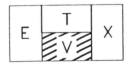

We follow a consistent method in our proofs. The steps are:

1. Record the specification.

2. Record the design.

3. Record the proof argument.

4. Indicate PASS or FAIL as our proof decision.

We will show the proof paradigms for the control figure in our basis set. With
these paradigms, any program can be shown to be correct or incorrect given a
specification and a design.

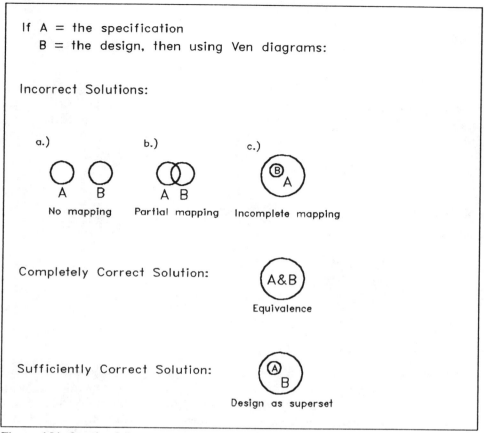

If A = the specification
   B = the design, then using Ven diagrams:

Incorrect Solutions:

a.)   b.)   c.)

A   B   A   B   Incomplete mapping

No mapping   Partial mapping

Completely Correct Solution: A&B

                                   Equivalence

Sufficiently Correct Solution: A
                                      B

                                 Design as superset

Figure 154. Levels of Correctness

Sequence Proof

Some sequences of design statements can be verified directly using a mental verification because the derivation is obvious, in such as:

```
<y:=x*x>;
BEGIN
    y:=x;
    y:=y*y;
END;
```

In other instances the series of sequence statements must be derived. For example, if the specification indicates: x,y: = y,x, that is, the function required is to swap values for the given variables, and the design which has been written takes the form

```
<x,y: = y,x>;
  BEGIN
    x:=x+y;
    y:=x-y;
    x:=x-y;
  END;
```

then we must use the verification method to determine if these specifications and design are equivalent, that is, that the design is correct with respect to the intended function in the specification. Thus for this problem:

1. Record the specification

   • As given

2. Record the design

   • As given

3. Record the proof argument:

time step	x	y
1. x:=x+y;	x1=x0+y0	y1=y0
2. y:=x-y;	x2=x1	y2=x1-y1
3. x:=x-y;	x3=x2-y2	y3=y2

This is to say that for the first time sequence statement x becomes $x+y$ and y remains unchanged. At the second time sequence statement x remains unchanged from the previous statement but y now becomes the difference of the x and y values at time 1 in the sequence execution, and at time 3 y remains unchanged from the previous sequence statement while x becomes the difference of x and y at their time 2 value.

Now through algebraic substitution for x3 and y3 we derive the following:

```
x3=x2-y2            y3=y2
  =x1-(x1-y1)=y       =x1-y1
                      =x0+y0-y0
  =y0                 =x0
```

4. Thus x,y: = y,x, and we can indicate that this design PASSes as a proof or is equivalent to the intended function in the given specification.

IF THEN ELSE Proof

With the IF THEN ELSE control structure we split the domain of the intended function into two parts, the THEN (true) part and the ELSE (false) part. Thus, if the IF predicate is evaluated as true we will execute the THEN part, and if the IF predicate evaluates as false we execute the ELSE part.

Our proof, therefore, must account for both parts, and both parts must PASS in order for the design to be equivalent to the intended function of the specification. Thus, we might have the following example for an absolute value function:

1. Record the specification:

   ```
   x≤y--->x,y:=x,abs(x-y)|
   x>y--->x,y:=abs(x-y),y
   ```

2. Record the design:

   ```
   IF x>y
   THEN
     x:=x-y;
   ELSE
     y:=y-x;
   ENDIF;
   ```

3. Record the proof argument:

   a. IF predicate evaluated TRUE; that is, x>y;
      <x,y:=abs(x-y),y> is the intended function of the THEN part,
      x:=x-y;   is the derived THEN part for x.
      y:=y;   is implied for y.
   Thus, the specification and THEN part design are equivalent, or
   PASSes as the one statement design x:=x-y, is equivalent to

      x: = abs (x-y) when x > y.

   b. <x,y:=x,abs(x-y> is the intended function of the ELSE part, and
      x:=x;   is implied.
      y:=x-y;   is the derived ELSE part; but as y is always greater
                or equal to x, then indeed y:=y-x.
   Thus, the specification and the ELSE part design are equivalent,
   or PASSes as the design state y:=y-x.

4. Since both the THEN part and ELSE part PASS, the design for the
   complete structure and the specification are equivalent or PASS.

CASE Proof

With the IF THEN ELSE structure we partitioned the functional domain into two parts. With the CASE control structure, we would partition the functional domain into as many parts as there are WHEN conditions.

Once we have partitioned the domain we may proceed to complete the proof as we did with the IF THEN ELSE control structure which had only two parts. For this control structure, all partitions or WHENs must PASS in order for the CASE to PASS.

DO WHILE and DO UNTIL Proofs

For looping programs we must ensure two aspects in order to complete a proof:

1. We must assure the loop terminates

2. We must, using the proof rules of a function-equivalent IF THEN, prove equivalence.

Let us look at the second step first. If the loop terminates and we are given the following:

```
<f>
DO WHILE p
  q;
ENDDO;
```

we construct a function equivalent IF THEN as follows:

```
<f>
IF p;
THEN
  g;
  f;
ENDIF;
```

This is the paradigm we will always follow for looping programs. From the constructed function equivalent IF THEN we would then proceed to try to prove that the IF THEN program is equivalent to the intended function <f>. If so, then the proof holds. How do we ensure the first step, that is, that the loop terminates? In some cases it is obvious that the loop terminates, but those are the trivial cases. In others we will have to assure ourselves that some variable in the loop must eventually cause an exit from the loop to occur. Alternately we may be able to observe that a predicate which was initially true on the loop entry will become false during execution and thus allow a loop exit to occur. Unfortunately in some cases we will not be able to observe a loop exit, which shall then cause us to think about simplifying the looping conditions such that an exit is observable. For DO UNTIL programs we would first convert to a DO WHILE structure and then to the corresponding IF THEN.

For a more complete assessment and expository of proofs of correctness including their mathematical basis the reader is referred to Linger, Mills, and Witt's *Structured Programming: Theory and Practice* [LING79].

10.11 Concurrent Processing

To this point we have only been concerned with design solutions that proceeded as if only one process sequence were occurring at any given time. We must now acknowledge that this is the simple world of processing, and that it sometimes is necessary to have two or more processes logically occurring in parallel. This is the idea of *concurrent processing*. We should be able to specify our design such that it is independent of physically knowing whether two or more processors are acting on the concurrent processes or whether we are constrained to one processor with interleaved execution. In fact, the problem at a logical design level is the same; that is, two or more processes need to act on the same shared data or critical sections of a defined data space for the problem being processed. Concurrency was typically a concern for operating system or subsystem, or real-time programs in the past. Today as software applications get more complex, concurrency becomes of concern in this programming domain, also.

A number of approaches exist to address the problems inherent in concurrent processing. Among these are:

1. Dekker's algorithm

2. Semaphores

3. LOCK and UNLOCK

4. Message passing

5. MONITORS

For an in-depth explanation and examples of each approach, the reader is referred to Hoare's paper "Monitors: an Operating System Structuring Concept" [HOAR74], Papadimitriou's *The Theory of Database Concurrency Control* [PAPA86], and *Structured Concurrent Programming with Operating System Applications* by Holt, Graham, Lazowska, and Scott [HOLT78]. Additionally, the reader should read the chapter on Tasks in Grady Booch's book *Software Engineering with Ada.* [BOOC83]

10.11.1 Monitors

A *monitor* is a construct that permits concurrency. It contains the data and the procedures needed to allocate a shared resource. Our recommended choice for concurrent processing is monitors, where we can guarantee the following necessary aspects of concurrency:

1. Mutual exclusion, ensuring that the shared data is protected from being manipulated by more than one process at a time. Without this guarantee any one of a number of undesirable errors can occur as two or more processes could concurrently change the shared data.

2. Blocking, whereby a process that needs to manipulate some shared data is permitted to wait in a queue for its turn to process that data. It is assumed that while a process is enqueued on some shared data that its processing is blocked from continuing until the resource is made available.

3. Waking up, whereby an enqueued process is notified that it may use the requested shared data and then continue.

Section 8 in Appendix C contains the ADL that permits designing concurrent programs. Using an example problem from Booch, that of bank customer and a teller, we might see the following in ADL (reference Figure 155 on page 349): (Note: For our purposes here we will assume that the MONITOR specification has been previously defined and we will complete the design using MONITOR_DESIGN.)

Any one of these three entries (MAKE_DEPOSIT, MAKE_DRIVE_UP_DEPOSIT, or DO_FILING) can be called from a PRO-CEDURE or FUNCTION. If any one of the three is called and IN_USE is TRUE, then the calling process must enqueue on the teller resource through the WAIT statement. When the teller is completed with whichever entry it is processing, then it will signal that it is available for additional processing by using a POST. Then the next queued caller will be given control in the requested ENTRY.

An example from Holt, Graham, Lazowska, and Scott written in the ADL syntax is shown in Figure 156 on page 350.

Note: Again we will assume the MONITOR specification had been defined, and we will complete the MONITOR_DESIGN.

Here we are assuming that some resource is protected by a monitor. Exclusive access to the resource is desired by processing units, such that "a process wishing to gain access to the resources calls the monitor entry ACQUIRE and a process returning control of the resource calls the monitor entry RELEASE. This situ-

```
MONITOR_DESIGN TELLER;
    DATA
        VAR IN_USE: BOOLEAN;
        COND AVAILABLE;
        INITIAL IN_USE = FALSE;
    OPERATIONS
        ENTRY MAKE_DEPOSIT (IN ID:INTEGER, AMOUNT:REAL,
            BALANCE:RECORD, OUT BALANCE:RECORD);
            IF IN_USE
              THEN
                 WAIT (AVAILABLE);
            ENDIF;
            IN_USE:=TRUE;
            .
            .
            .
            BALANCE(ID):=BALANCE(ID) + AMOUNT;
            IN_USE:=FALSE;
            POST (AVAILABLE);
        ENDENTRY MAKE_DEPOSIT;

        ENTRY MAKE_DRIVE_UP_DEPOSIT (IN ID:INTEGER, AMOUNT:REAL,
            BALANCE:RECORD, OUT BALANCE:RECORD);
            IF IN_USE
              THEN
                 WAIT (AVAILABLE);
            ENDIF;
            IN_USE:=TRUE;
            .
            .
            .
            BALANCE(ID):=BALANCE(ID) + AMOUNT;
            IN_USE:=FALSE;
            POST (CONDITIONAL);
        ENDENTRY MAKE_DRIVE_UP_DEPOSIT;

        ENTRY DO_FILING;
            IF IN_USE
              THEN
                 WAIT (AVAILABLE);
            ENDIF;
            IN_USE:=TRUE;
            DELAY 30 MINUTES;
              DO UNTIL delay is complete
                 Filing;
              ENDDO;
            IN_USE:=FALSE;
            POST (AVAILABLE);
        ENDENTRY DO_FILING;
END_MONITOR_DESIGN TELLER;
```

Figure 155. Concurrency Example

ation occurs often in operating systems. For example, the resource may be a file on a peripheral device and the processes may be waiting to update it" [HOLT78].

The state indicator of the resource is always under the control of the monitor. The resource in this example could be some global shared data which is directly

```
MONITOR_DESIGN RESOURCE;
  DATA
        VAR IN_USE:BOOLEAN;
        COND AVAILABLE;
        INITIAL IN_USE=FALSE;
  OPERATIONS
        ENTRY ACQUIRE;
          IF IN_USE
            THEN
                WAIT (AVAILABLE);
          ENDIF;
          IN_USE:=TRUE;
        ENDENTRY ACQUIRE;
        ENTRY RELEASE;
          IN_USE:=FALSE;
          POST (AVAILABLE);
        ENDENTRY RELEASE;
 END_MONITOR_DESIGN RESOURCE;
```

Figure 156. Monitor Example

accessed by the processing units. The assumption is that the processing units for this example will only access the resource by invoking the ACQUIRE entry.

If the resource has been previously acquired and another process calls ACQUIRE it will be enqueued via the WAIT. Later when the resource is posted as AVAIL-ABLE this enqueued process will be resumed.

Deadlock *Deadlock* is undesirable during processing and can occur, for example, when one task (TASK1) is waiting for a resource owned by another task (TASK2), which is itself waiting for a resource owned by TASK1. Since neither task can process until it gets the required resource and since both are in a wait state, the system is in a hung or deadlock situation. Sometimes, deadlock occurs because locked shared data is inadvertently not unlocked.

Deadlock can be avoided by requiring that resources be defined in a hierarchy and requiring locks to follow the order of the hierarchy. Each resource is defined to be in an ordered series of classes from 1 to n. Once the order is set a task must only request a resource in the defined order. Thus, for example, a task holding a resource at level 3 can lock any resource at a lower level. If, however, locks are already being held, then only resources at level 4 can be locked by a level 3 task.

10.12 MLD Validation

As with all work items and particularly the PLD and
CLD stages which preceded the MLD, an inspection is
required to validate the solution. Again, the inspections
refer back to the previously validated PLD and CLD
statements, which represent the basis for transformation

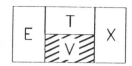

into a MLD. We also may use proof of correctness as discussed in section 10.9
to verify the design. While this is a more rigorous method, it seems to require
more determination to complete, and may not be appropriate for all programs at
this time. Where it is used it should be combined with Inspections as a more
powerful verification of the MLD.

In some instances, prototyping may proceed as far down as MLD solutions, as
when performance is a critical issue.

10.13 Exit Criteria

As with each stage in the product life cycle, MLD has a
predefined set of exit criteria. The following are some
examples:

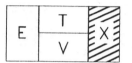

- The module level design is complete and has been recorded in the appropriate documents and data bases.

- The serviceability walk-through has been successfully completed.

- The installability walk-through has been successfully completed for products
with new or complex installation scenarios.

- The following have been completed:

  - Unit test plan

  - Functional verification test plan

  - Product verification test plan

  - Performance test plan

  - Publication plan

  - Publication measurement plan

  - Initial plan to support early program users

10.14 Summary

In this chapter on Module Level Design we discussed why it is more desirable to have modules with strong internal relationships (cohesion) and weak external relationships (coupling). We examined Structured Programming in terms of a basis set of control structures which give us intellectual control over the design act. We reviewed an approach for structuring unstructured programs. We then reviewed the design methodolgy for Composite/Structured Design, Jackson's method, and Object Oriented Design as they apply to MLD. Since we prefer an object oriented approach, we discussed in more detail function statements as they relate to the intent of the design, data abstractions, and the use of state diagrams as a model for design. We then introduced examples and details of ADL, particularly as ADL applies to creating generic types during design. For verification of MLD we explored detail proofs of correctness for each of the structured programming basis set control structures. We gave examples of how ADL could be used to design for concurrent processing, and completed the chapter with MLD validation and exit criteria.

10.15 References

[BOOC83] G. Booch, *Software Engineering with Ada*, Benjamin/Cummings Publishing Co. (1983).

[DAVI72] P. J. Davis, "Fidelity in Mathematical Discourse: Is One and One Really Two?," *American Mathematical Monthly* (March 1972), pp. 252−263.

[DIJK72] E. W. Dijkstra, "Notes on Structured Programming," in *Structured Programming*, O. J. Dahl, ed., Academic Press (1972), pp. 1−82.

[HOAR74] C. A. R. Hoare, "Monitors: an Operating System Structuring Concept," *Communications of the ACM*, Vol. 17, No. 10 (October 1974).

[HOLT78] R. C. Holt, G. S. Graham, E. D. Lazowska, and M. A. Scott, *Structured Concurrent Programming with Operating System Applications*, Addison-Wesley Publishing Company (1978).

[LING79] R. C. Linger, H. D. Mills, and B. J. Witt, *Structured Programming: Theory and Practice*, Addison-Wesley Publishing Company (1979), pp. 549−557.

[MART85A] J. Martin and C. McClure, *Structured Techniques for Computing*, Prentice-Hall (1985).

[MYER78] G. J. Myers, *Composite/Structured Design*, Van Nostrand Reinhold Company (1978).

[PAPA86] C. Papadimitriou, *The Theory of Database Concurrency Control*, Computer Science Press (1986).

[PARN72] D. L. Parnas, "On the Criteria to Be Used in Decomposing Systems into Modules," *Communications of the ACM*, (December 1972), pp. 1053 – 1058.

[RUBI87] F. Rubin, "GOTO Considered Harmful," *Communications of the ACM*, (March 1987), pp. 195 – 196.

[SEW84] *(SEW) Software Engineering Workshop Student Notebooks*, Vol. 1 – 4 , Software Engineering Institute, G325-0010, IBM Corporation.

[SHOO83] Martin L. Shooman, *Software Engineering*, McGraw-Hill Book Company (1983).

[STEV74] W. P. Stevens, G. J. Myers, L. L. Constantine, "Structured Design," *IBM Systems Journal*, Vol. 13, No. 2 (1974), pp. 115 – 139.

[TAUS76] Robert C. Tausworthe, *Standardized Development of Computer Software*, Jet Propulsion Laboratory under Contract No. NAS 7-100 (July 1976), for sale by the Superintendent of Documents, U.S. Government Printing Office, Washington, DC 20402.

[YOUR79] E. Yourdan and L. L. Constantine, *Structured Design*, Prentice-Hall (1979).

Chapter 11. Code

11.1 Introduction

To this point in the book, we have completed the design stages through Module Level Design. The Code stage begins here and results in code that is inspected, ready for the Unit Test stage and subsequent entry to the formal test stages.

In this chapter, we look at some of the current code issues and problems, discuss various viewpoints of individual roles during the code stage, and discuss typical implementation methods and tools for coding and validating the code. Finally, we look at some of the implications that "automatic programming" might have on coding activities of the future.

11.2 Key Concepts of This Chapter

The purpose of the Code stage is to create source code from the Module Level Design material, to verify that the code meets the required standards, and to validate it against the design through inspections, making it ready for unit testing.

This text focuses on the *process* aspects of the Code stage and thus will not describe specific coding standards, coding techniques, and coding styles. We will discuss coding styles and conventions, and how they can affect the development and maintenance of the product, in Volume 2 of this text series.

11.3 Viewpoints

Program Development In many large-scale projects, individual programmers are designated as *module owners* of a functional group of the modules being created or updated. The module owner is responsible for implementing a specific function in a set of affected modules, and for fixing defects that are discovered during the formal test stages. The module owner is usually the one who also performed the module level design for the module(s) being coded.

Build and Integration Build and Integration refers to a central function in all large-scale system development projects that consolidates code at preplanned levels of development into test versions called *drivers*. The drivers, in turn, are used by all developers as the most current level of all the functions under development in the system. These drivers form the testing environment for unit testing and for subsequent formal testing stages. Depending upon the characteristics of the project, drivers may be built monthly, or even more often.

Testing During the Implementation stage, test organizations are completing the test plans for the formal test stages, and are implementing test cases. These people interact with the module owner to get input and do reviews of their detailed test plans.

Product Publications During the Code stage, product publications such as user guides and service manuals are being brought to final draft state. The refinement and completion of these manuals depend upon input and reviews from the module owner.

Marketing and Service Service plans are being brought to their final state, service personnel are being trained in the new product, and service data bases are being initialized with service information about the product.

Performance On many large projects, a performance plan and a set of tests will be written by programmers who specialize in performance. During the coding stage, these plans and test cases will be undergoing their final reviews and Inspections. Reviews of the Module Level Design and of the code itself may also be taking place to identify potential performance bottlenecks.

11.4 Code Stage Problem Areas

Coding on a large project can be very event-driven and fraught with crises. From the module owner's view, at the very time when coding and unit testing is most intense, the entire world seems to converge and make further demands for time. Publication writers need input for the final draft of the product publication, test plans for upcoming test stages need participation of the module owner for reviews and inspections, and the number of code inspections, in addition to one's own, that the module owner must participate in is sometimes overwhelming. Module owners also provide input to product training programs for service, testing, and product publications personnel.

In addition to being an event-driven activity, the Code stage finds related problem areas in the build and integration process and in change control.

Build and Integration Process

It is the module owner's responsibility to have the code developed and unit-tested in support of previously negotiated functions and driver integration dates. In a well run, large-system project, build and integration people work closely with module owners to develop a schedule on which each incremental set of functions will be made available for integration into individual test systems (drivers). This is called the *driver build plan*. It is critical that, once committed, the module owner stick to the delivery dates for each functional level of his component. Each is highly dependent upon the other: If a driver is late, or will not work properly, development testing is inhibited, and planned new function is in turn made late for integration in subsequent drivers. When the driver build process gets out of control in this fashion, the domino effect can soon devastate an entire project during the Code stage.

Change Control

On a typical project, at least three versions, or *change levels*, of a module are under the jurisdiction of the module owner at any given time. They are:

1. The *base level(s)*: the one or more versions in current field use

2. The *integrated level*: the version currently undergoing formal testing

3. The *development level*: the version currently being enhanced with new and changed code, that is, the version currently in the Code stage

Module level control is a subpart of a broader topic called configuration management. Configuration management includes program library systems that create the environment for the implementation and testing stages, and assist in module level control, rework change control, and control of the build and integration process. Such systems fall under a broader category called *configuration management*, which will be discussed in detail in Volume 2 of this text series.

If the library system or other controls in the coding process are not rigorous, the amount of rework due to confusion over levels of code can consume vital resources and time needed to complete the project.

11.5 Entry Criteria

Coding should not be started until some key "coding strategy" decisions have been made, based upon the completed Module Level Design. Examples are:

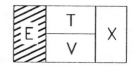

- The base code ("old code") on which the new code will be built should be thoroughly understood.
- The modules, and areas within them, that need modification (sometimes called "module hits") should be identified, along with a rough estimate of the amount and nature of the change needed for each area.

- Modules that will need to be restructured or divided into two modules due to size increases or performance considerations should be thoroughly identified and planned.

Examples of work items that should be completed before coding starts are:

- Final Programming Specifications
- Final draft of Program Logic Specifications
- Unit test plan
- Updated program size estimates
- Project workbook and related materials updated and kept current

11.6 Tasks of the Code Stage

The coding task consists basically of writing code and compiling it. This set of tasks can be further divided into (1) transforming MLD information to source code and (2) transforming the resultant source code to efficient source code. There is of course, much more to

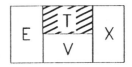

coding than the foregoing oversimplification would indicate. This volume will focus on the *process* of the Code stage, leaving for a subsequent volume detailed coverage of coding methods and techniques, code standards and practices, the effect of coding style on maintainability, and techniques for writing efficient code.

For more detail on these aspects of coding, we refer the reader to two books, both written by J. L. Bentley, entitled "Programming Pearls" [BENT86] and "Writing Efficient Programs" [BENT82].

11.6.1 Preparation

A significant amount of preparation for coding is actually accomplished during the Module Level Design stage, as described in 11.5, "Entry Criteria" on page 357. Upon entering the Code stage, there is some additional planning activity that must be undertaken. These preparation tasks include:

- Review base design and old code.

- Review applicable standards, for example, register usage.

- Review applicable practices, for example, requirements for structured programming, and guidelines for comments.

- Review code flagging for traceability to new function, design changes, fixes made for defects discovered during testing, and fixes made for defects discovered throughout field use of the baselined code.

11.6.2 Training Assistance

During the Code stage, training programs are being established and conducted for individuals in testing organizations who will execute the test cases, service training is being prepared for those who will service the new product, and briefings are taking place for product publications personnel. The module owner is often consulted for technical input for all these activities.

11.6.3 Processing Defects in Integration-level Code

When the code for the new release is integrated in the test drivers, formal testing begins, and an iterative rework process starts around the following tasks:

- Discovering defects

- Creating fixes

- Inspecting the fixes

- Unit-testing the fixes

- Integrating the updated modules containing the fixes

This is the basic code change process, and the control of this process is called *code change control*. It is important to note that the code change process should follow the normal development process in all respects. That is, no special shortcuts should be in place just because the changes seem relatively small compared to the initial development changes.

In the code change process, the module owner must always be alert to the possibility of affecting the design as well as the code, and the product publications as well as the code. All to often, in the press of processing coding changes rapidly, both these important viewpoints are overlooked, thereby shortcutting an essential part of the process. Furthermore, once the design change request has been initiated, it is imperative that it proceed through the normal development process as well, and not be shortcut in any way.

The module owner must also ensure that all fixes go through the normal inspection and unit testing processes for validation before integration in the official test drivers. Consideration must also be given to potential additions or changes to the test plan for properly validating the fix when it arrives in the formal test environment.

11.6.4 Processing Defects in Shipped-Level Code

The Unit Test, Functional Verification Test, Product Verification Test, and System Verification Test stages preceding the shipment of each new release result in the discovery and fixing of defects in the new and changed code for that release. Simultaneous with this activity, field use of prior releases is causing defects to be discovered in the baseline code of the product under development. Since the defects also exist in the baseline code of the new release under development, they must be integrated in the new release before shipment so as not to regress future users of the new release. This activity is sometimes called *retrofitting* of the field fixes to the baseline code.

In large projects, such defects are diagnosed and fixed by service teams, separate from development. In well run projects, the fixes produced by the service groups are reviewed by the module owner and jointly certified by the person creating the fix and the module owner as OK to integrate in the next driver build cycle for the new release. Figure 157 illustrates the relationship between discoveries of defects in the baseline code and discoveries of defects in the new code during testing. The curves in the figure are called *defect depletion curves*, and represent the number of defects remaining to be discovered at any given time during the product life cycle. The initial value of each curve depicts the number of new defects in the new and changed code for each new each release, at the start of formal testing for that release.

11.6.5 Analyzing for Cause and Prevention of Defect

Most defects discovered during testing indicate simply a bug in the implementation. However, many defect discoveries indicate a flaw in the Module Level or Component Level Design. In some cases, defects can even be traced to flaws in the Product Level Design and initial requirements definition. Such defects indicate something else too; there was a deficiency in the design process and perhaps in the Requirements Engineering process as well. A process must be in place to ensure that the discovery of such defects are fed back to the design process for evaluation and implemented as permanent process improvements such that the same type of defect will not happen again [JONE85]. This process is called the design change process, and is triggered by some sort of formal request document, which we are calling a Design Change Request (DCR) in this text.

11.7 Validation

Validation activities are prominent during the Code stage. First and foremost are the Code Inspections that validate the code against its design specifications and ascertain its readiness for Unit Test [FAGA86]. The code Inspection process is described in Chapter 8.

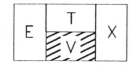

In addition to Code Inspections, the product in a broader sense is being validated by usability reviews, serviceability reviews, quality reviews, publication Inspections and reviews.

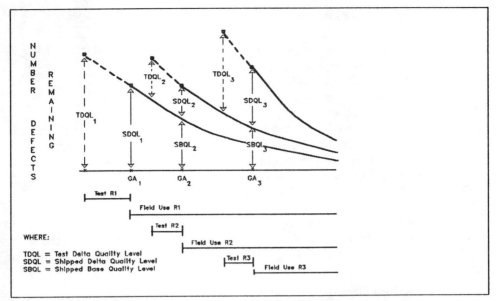

Figure 157. Defects Remaining in New and Baselined Code

The types of validation activities mentioned so far all validate various forms of the product directly. The module owner also participates in a series of second-order validation activities during the Code stage: those that create or validate the validation "tools" to be used in subsequent stages. Examples are:

- Plan unit tests

- Review the unit test plan

- Implement unit test cases

- Inspect Function, Component, System and Performance test plans

All the above direct and second-order validation activities are highly labor-intensive, requiring large quantities of human analysis, evaluation, and technical decision-making to achieve a result that will effectively ensure the product. Ironically, all too often it is these very activities that are the first to be compromised or eliminated when a project develops schedule problems. Refer to Chapter 8 for further discussion. Process management aspects of phenomenon will be discussed in Volume 2 of this text book series.

11.8 Exit Criteria

Exit from the Code stage for a particular function marks readiness for its Unit Test stage, and hence into the formal test stages. Although testing will be discussed in a subsequent volume, it is appropriate to mention here that successful completion of unit test certifies that the 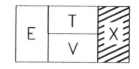 module(s) may be integrated in the driver and ready for formal testing. For the module owner it signifies, "my code is complete, tested to the best of my ability, and ready to ship to my customers." Note this depicts the programmer as viewing the formal test process as a means of validating the truth of the product, and not as simply another series of stages for debugging his buggy code.

As mentioned in the previous section, new function is coded, unit tested, and integrated in test drivers in preplanned, incremental levels, according to the driver build plan. The exit criteria for each of these incremental "packages" of function are:

1. All inspections are completed, and the code is verified for

   a. Completeness

   b. Consistency

   c. Conformance to standards and good coding practices

   d. Correctness, validated against the Module Level Design

2. All rework from the code inspections is completed and verified/validated as above.

3. All necessary updates to the Module Level Design documentation are completed.

4. Any changes to the Component or Product Level Design suggested as a result of the coding activity are properly recorded through Design Change Requests (DCRs), evaluated by the design function, approved, implemented, and validated according to the normal process.

5. Publication drafts are inspected and in process for external review.

In addition to the exit criteria for incremental versions of the product work items described above, exit from the entire Code stage requires that

1. All appropriate updates to the project workbook are completed.

2. FVT test cases are completed.

3. CVT/SVT/Performance test implementation is in progress.

4. Serviceability walkthroughs are completed.

11.9 Summary

The purpose of the Code stage is to create source code that has been validated through Inspections and ready for Unit Testing.

Coding for a particular function may begin when the Module Level Design for that function is complete and validated by means of Inspection. Coding and Module Level Design for a particular function is usually done by one individual module owner.

The Code stage is usually filled with intense activity for the module owner, due to the convergence of several work items and tasks at once in the process, such as product publication drafts, final drafts of test plans for upcoming test stages, and the code being developed by his peers. All these work items require the module owner's participation in reviews and Inspections. In addition, the module owner must fix defects discovered during the testing of new function previously integrated in drivers, as well as review and certify fixes made to the baseline code by service organizations.

11.10 Future Directions

In the order of evolution of Software Engineering, the Code stages are probably the next target for complete automation. As discussed in Chapter 2 of this text, and by Balzer, Hoffnagle, and others [BALZ85] [HOFF85] an automated coding environment will include functions for

- library control and automatic level control
- automated driver builds and test environments
- process management
- automatic code generation

Will this automated environment eliminate the need for module owners as described in this chapter? Not likely. The current-day activities of adding or modifying program logic, implementing design changes, fixing bugs discovered during testing and during field use will simply be refocused from the coding level of today, to the Component and Module Level Design. This will have a significant effect on the responsibilities and skills of the module owner because each individual will exercise control and influence over much larger portions of the product being developed than is possible today. Along with the increased sphere of influence afforded each individual in such a future environment, comes increased responsibilities and challenges.

In addition to the automated environment mentioned above, other factors are also converging on the Code and Module Level Design stages of our life cycle model, such as Ada, and the added effect of using Fourth Generation Languages (4GL), placing this stage on the threshold of some very exciting changes and offering many interesting challenges to the software engineers of today and tomorrow.

11.11 References

[BALZ85] R. Balzer, "A 15 Year Perspective on Automatic Programming," *IEEE Transactions on Software Engineering*, Vol. SE-11, No. 11 (November 1985), pp. 1257 – 68.

[BENT82] J. L. Bentley, *Writing Efficient Programs*, Prentice-Hall (1982).

[BENT86] J. L. Bentley, *Programming Pearls*, Addison-Wesley Publishing Company (1986).

[FAGA86] M. E. Fagan, "Advances in Software Inspections," *IEEE Transactions on Software Engineering*, Vol. SE-12, No. 7 (July 1986), pp. 744 – 51.

[HOFF85] F. G. Hoffnagle and W. E. Beregi, "Automating the Software Development Process," *IBM Systems Journal*, Vol. 24, No. 2 (1985), pp. 102 – 20.

[JONE85] C. L. Jones, "A Process-Integrated Approach to Defect Prevention," *IBM Systems Journal*, Vol. 24, No. 2 (1985), pp. 150 – 67.

Part 5. Appendixes

Appendix A. A Specification Language (ASL) Reference

A.1 Introduction

A Specification Language (ASL) is an Entity-Relation (E-R) language for specifying programming Requirements and Product-Level Design specifications. ASL object types are represented as templates which may be instantiated to real object definitions to form a specification.

ASL object types are derived from a smaller set of generic object types, called *meta types*, shown in Figure 158 on page 367. The ASL object types as shown in the figure are grouped according to the RPLD Model perspectives, as defined in 4.5.4, "RPLD Model" on page 90.

A.2 Universal ASL Object Heading

ASL syntactic forms may be constructed by filling in the templates shown in the following sections. Each form thus constructed should include all or part of the universal heading information shown in Figure 159 on page 368, as appropriate to the object being defined.

```
        ASL TYPE                    META-TYPE

┌─ Environment ──────────────────────────────────────────────┐
│                                                             │
│        USER ENTERPRISE           ENVIRONMENT                │
│        USER                      ENVIRONMENT                │
│        SYSTEM ENVIRONMENT        ENVIRONMENT                │
│        INPUT                     INPUT                      │
│        OUTPUT                    OUTPUT                     │
│                                                             │
└─────────────────────────────────────────────────────────────┘

┌─ Current and Target Process ───────────────────────────────┐
│                                                             │
│        CURRENT ACTIVITY          TASK                       │
│        TARGET ACTIVITY           TASK                       │
│        WORK ITEM                 DATA OBJECT                │
│        DECISION                  DECISION                   │
│        CONDITION                 CONDITION                  │
│        EVENT                     EVENT                      │
│                                                             │
└─────────────────────────────────────────────────────────────┘

┌─ Problem/Solution Statements ──────────────────────────────┐
│                                                             │
│        PROBLEM                   PROBLEM                    │
│        SOLUTION                  SOLUTION                   │
│                                                             │
└─────────────────────────────────────────────────────────────┘

┌─ Current and Target Product ───────────────────────────────┐
│                                                             │
│        FSM                       FSM                        │
│        TOOL                      AGENT                      │
│        PERSON                    AGENT                      │
│        WORK ITEM                 DATA OBJECT                │
│        STATE DATA                DATA OBJECT                │
│        REPOSITORY                REPOSITORY                 │
│        SKELETON                  DATA OBJECT                │
│        USER PROFILE              DATA OBJECT                │
│        CONDITION                 CONDITION                  │
│        EVENT                     EVENT                      │
│                                                             │
└─────────────────────────────────────────────────────────────┘

┌─ Universal Objects ────────────────────────────────────────┐
│                                                             │
│        ATTRIBUTE                 ATTRIBUTE                  │
│        REFERENCE                 REFERENCE                  │
│                                                             │
└─────────────────────────────────────────────────────────────┘
```

Figure 158. ASL Object Types and Source Meta-types

```
TYPE: <USER DEFINED TYPE NAME>                    <Object_Name>  ;
META TYPE: <META TYPE NAME>

    DESCRIPTION;
        <Narrative input to a reviewer or designer > ;
  ┌─ Classification ──────────────────────────────────────────────┐
  │                                                                │
  │     VIEW-KEY IS            '<string(s)> ;                      │
  │     SYNONYMS ARE            <Name(s)> ;                        │
  │     PERSPECTIVE            '<string(s)>'  ;                    │
  │     DEFINER IS             '<name>' ;                          │
  │     OBJECT OWNER IS        '<name>' ;                          │
  │     ATTRIBUTES ARE         Attribute_Name  '<string>',         │
  │                               [,Attribute_Name '<string>']... ; │
  │     REFER TO               <Reference_Name(s)> ;               │
  │                                                                │
  └────────────────────────────────────────────────────────────────┘
```

Figure 159. Universal Information for all ASL Templates

A.2.1 Prose Descriptions

Objects in a RPLD Specification may have a prose description, or commentary, assigned to it by means of the word "DESCRIPTION." Such descriptions can add clarity for the reader of the ASL reports. Given an appropriate tool, narrative descriptions could also be retrieved and printed separately in a structured order, without the accompanying ASL statements, to create a more or less conventional-looking description for the reviewer not familiar with the ASL syntax.

A.2.2 References

Documents external to the RPLD Specification are of the type "REFERENCE," and are pointed to from any other ASL object type by the expression "REFER TO." For example, the statement

```
        REFER TO   'ANSI-Standards'
```

points to a document containing further information related to the object being described. The referenced document may reside either within or outside of the RPLD Specification data base.

Attributes

Attributes for objects within the RPLD may be assigned by the "ATTRIBUTES ARE" expression.

For example, when describing a compiler, the expression,

```
ATTRIBUTES ARE  Object_Code_Performance
                  'Primary importance',
                Compiler_Performance
                  'Secondary importance',
                Current_Status
                  'Completed' ;
```

implies that object code performance is to be given priority over compiler performance during the design process.

A.2.3 Keywords

Keywords may be assigned any object in the RPLD Specification to assist in machine analysis.

For example, the expression

```
        VIEW-KEY IS    'Overview Level' ;
```

could facilitate a machine search for all objects that are of interest to a high-level manager.

A.2.4 Synonyms

Synonyms may be used as name qualifiers. For example

```
SYNONYMS ARE    The_Compiler,
                FORTRAN,
                The_Target_System  ;
```

could all be synonyms for "The_FORTRAN_Compiler."

A.3 Templates for Universal Objects

A.3.1 Attribute

```
TYPE: ATTRIBUTE                           <Attribute_Name>  ;
META TYPE: ATTRIBUTE
  ┌─ Structure ──────────────────────────────────────────────┐
  │                                                            │
  │    HAS PARTS        <Attribute_Name(s)>  ;                 │
  │    PART OF          <Attribute_Name>  ;                    │
  │                                                            │
  └────────────────────────────────────────────────────────────┘

  ┌─ Values ─────────────────────────────────────────────────┐
  │                                                            │
  │    VALUES ARE    '<string>' FOR     <non-Attribute_Name>   │
  │                [,'<string>' FOR     <non_Attribute_Name>,....] ; │
  │                                                            │
  └────────────────────────────────────────────────────────────┘
```

Figure 160. The Attribute Template

A.3.2 Reference

```
TYPE: REFERENCE                        <Reference_Name> ;
META TYPE: REFERENCE
  ┌─ Structure ─────────────────────────────────────────────────┐
  │                                                              │
  │    HAS PARTS          <Reference_Name(s)> ;                  │
  │    PART OF            <Reference_Name>   ;                   │
  │                                                              │
  └──────────────────────────────────────────────────────────────┘

  ┌─ Use ───────────────────────────────────────────────────────┐
  │                                                              │
  │    APPLIES TO     {Agent_Name(s)        } ,                  │
  │                   {Attribute_Name(s)    },                   │
  │                   {Environment_Name(s)} ,                    │
  │                   {FSM_Name(s)          } ,                  │
  │                   {Output_Name(s)       } ,                  │
  │                   {Problem_Name(s)      } ,                  │
  │                   {Solution_Name(s)     } ,                  │
  │                   {State_Data_Name(s)   } ,                  │
  │                   {Activity_Name(s)     } ,                  │
  │                   {Work_Item_Name(s)    } ;                  │
  │                                                              │
  └──────────────────────────────────────────────────────────────┘
```

Figure 161. The Reference Template

A.4 Templates for Product Environment Perspective

A.4.1 User Enterprise

```
TYPE: USER ENTERPRISE            <Enterprise_Object_Name> ;
META TYPE: ENVIRONMENT

   ┌─ Structure ─────────────────────────────────────────────┐
   │                                                          │
   │    HAS PARTS              <Enterprise_Object_Name(s)>  ; │
   │    PART OF                <Enterprise_Object_Name>     ; │
   │                                                          │
   └──────────────────────────────────────────────────────────┘

   ┌─ Input/Output ──────────────────────────────────────────┐
   │                                                          │
   │    GENERATES              <Input_Name(s)>   ;            │
   │    RECEIVES               <Output_Name(s)>  ;            │
   │                                                          │
   └──────────────────────────────────────────────────────────┘
```

Figure 162. User Enterprise Template

A.4.2 User

```
TYPE: USER                       <User_Type_Name> ;
META TYPE: ENVIRONMENT

   ┌─ Structure ─────────────────────────────────────────────┐
   │                                                          │
   │    HAS PARTS              <User_Type_Name(s)>  ;         │
   │    PART OF                <User_Type_Name>     ;         │
   │                                                          │
   └──────────────────────────────────────────────────────────┘

   ┌─ Input/Output ──────────────────────────────────────────┐
   │                                                          │
   │    GENERATES              <Input_Name(s)>   ;            │
   │    RECEIVES               <Output_Name(s)>  ;            │
   │                                                          │
   └──────────────────────────────────────────────────────────┘
```

Figure 163. The User Template

```
TYPE: SYSTEM ENVIRONMENT          <System_Envmt_Name> ;
META TYPE: ENVIRONMENT

 ┌─ Input/Output ──────────────────────────────────────────────┐
 │                                                              │
 │    HAS PARTS              <System_Envmt_Name(s)> ;           │
 │    PART OF                <System_Envmt_Name>   ;            │
 │                                                              │
 └──────────────────────────────────────────────────────────────┘

 ┌─ Input/Output ──────────────────────────────────────────────┐
 │                                                              │
 │    GENERATES             <Input_Name(s)>  ;                  │
 │    RECEIVES              <Output_Name(s)>  ;                 │
 │                                                              │
 └──────────────────────────────────────────────────────────────┘
```

Figure 164. The System Environment Template

A.4.3 Input

```
TYPE: INPUT                     <Input_Name> ;
META TYPE: INPUT

 ┌─ Structure ─────────────────────────────────────────────────┐
 │                                                              │
 │    HAS SUBSETS           <Input_Name(s)> ;                   │
 │    SUBSET OF             <Input_Name>  ;                     │
 │                                                              │
 └──────────────────────────────────────────────────────────────┘

 ┌─ Input/Output ──────────────────────────────────────────────┐
 │                                                              │
 │    GENERATED BY          <Environment_Name(s)>  ;            │
 │    RECEIVED BY           <FSM_Name(s)> ;                     │
 │                                                              │
 └──────────────────────────────────────────────────────────────┘

 ┌─ Use ───────────────────────────────────────────────────────┐
 │                                                              │
 │    USED    [ BY   {Activity_Name(s)}, ]                      │
 │            [      {FSM_Name(s)      } ]                      │
 │       TO  {CREATE}                                           │
 │           {CHANGE}  <Work_Item_Name(s)  [TO STATE <State_Name>] ;  │
 │                                                              │
 └──────────────────────────────────────────────────────────────┘
```

Figure 165. The Input Template

A.4.4 Output

```
 ┌─────────────────────────────────────────────────────────────────┐
 │                                                                   │
 │  TYPE: OUTPUT                      <Output_Name> ;                │
 │  META TYPE: OUTPUT                                                │
 │  ┌─ Structure ──────────────────────────────────────────────┐    │
 │  │                                                           │    │
 │  │   HAS SUBSETS          <Output_Name(s)> ;                 │    │
 │  │   SUBSET OF            <Output_Name>   ;                  │    │
 │  │                                                           │    │
 │  └───────────────────────────────────────────────────────────┘    │
 │                                                                   │
 │  ┌─ Input/Output ───────────────────────────────────────────┐    │
 │  │                                                           │    │
 │  │   GENERATED BY         <FSM_Name(s)> ;                    │    │
 │  │       [ USING <Work_Item_Name(s)>  [IN STATE <State_Name> ],...] ; │
 │  │   RECEIVED  BY          <Environment_Name(s)>  ;          │    │
 │  │                                                           │    │
 │  └───────────────────────────────────────────────────────────┘    │
 │                                                                   │
 └─────────────────────────────────────────────────────────────────┘
```

Figure 166. The Output Template

A.5 Templates for Current and Target Process Perspectives

A.5.1 Current Activity

```
TYPE: CURRENT ACTIVITY              <(Activity)_Name>  ;
META TYPE: TASK
   ┌─ Structure ──────────────────────────────────────────────┐
   │                                                            │
   │   HAS PARTS           <Activity_Name(s)>  ;                │
   │   PART OF             <Activity_Name>   ;                  │
   │   UTILIZES            <FSM_Name(s)> ;                      │
   │                         [ TO GENERATE <Output_Name(s)> ]   │
   │                         [ TO {CREATE  } <Work_Item_Name(s)> ] ; │
   │                              {CHANGE  }                    │
   │                              {VALIDATE}                    │
   └────────────────────────────────────────────────────────────┘

   ┌─ Operations ─────────────────────────────────────────────┐
   │                                                           │
   │   {CREATES  }                                             │
   │   {UPDATES  }   <Work_Item_Name(s)> [TO STATE <State_Name>] │
   │   {VALIDATES}                                             │
   │       [USING  <Work_Item_Name(s)> [IN STATE <State_Name>]],..] ; │
   │   MAKES   PROBLEM  <Problem_Name(s)>     TRUE  ;          │
   └───────────────────────────────────────────────────────────┘

   ┌─ Entry/Exit Criteria ────────────────────────────────────┐
   │                                                           │
   │   {ENTRY ENABLED}                                         │
   │   {SUSPENDED    }                                         │
   │   {EXIT ENABLED }                                         │
   │       WHEN     {Work_Item_Name(s) IN STATE <State_Name>}  │
   │                {Condition_Name(s)                     }   │
   │                {Event_Name(s)                         }   │
   │                            BECOMES  {TRUE }    [AND]      │
   │                                     {FALSE}    [OR ] ;    │
   │   CAUSES        <Event_Name(s)>  ;                        │
   └───────────────────────────────────────────────────────────┘
```

Figure 167. The Current Activity Template

A.5.2 Target Activity

```
TYPE: TARGET ACTIVITY                  <(Activity)_Name>  ;
META TYPE: TASK
```

┌─ **Structure** ───┐
```
    HAS PARTS          <Activity_Name(s)>  ;
    PART OF            <Activity_Name>   ;
    UTILIZES           <FSM_Name(s)> ;
                       [ TO GENERATE <Output_Name(s)> ]
                       [ TO {CREATE  } <Work_Item_Name(s)> ] ;
                            {CHANGE  }
                            {VALIDATE}
```
└───┘

┌─ **Operations** ──┐
```
    {CREATES  }
    {UPDATES  }   <Work_Item_Name(s)> [TO STATE <State_Name>]
    {VALIDATES}
        [USING  <Work_Item_Name(s)> [IN STATE <State_Name>]],..] ;
    MAKES   PROBLEM  <Problem_Name(s)>    FALSE  ;
    MAKES   SOLUTION <Solution_Name(s)>   TRUE   ;
```
└───┘

┌─ **Entry/Exit Criteria** ───────────────────────────────────────┐
```
    {ENTRY ENABLED}
    {SUSPENDED    }
    {EXIT ENABLED }
           WHEN     {Work_Item_Name(s) IN STATE <State_Name>}
                    {Condition_Name(s)                      }
                    {Event_Name(s)                          }
                                  BECOMES  {TRUE }   [AND]
                                           {FALSE}   [OR ] ;
    CAUSES          <Event_Name(s)>  ;
```
└───┘

Figure 168. The Target Activity Template

A.5.3 Work Item

```
TYPE: WORK ITEM                          <(Work_Item)_Name> ;
META TYPE: DATA OBJECT

┌─ Structure ────────────────────────────────────────────────────────┐
│                                                                      │
│   HAS SUBSETS          <Work_Item_Name(s)> ;                         │
│   SUBSET OF            <Work_Item_Name>  ;                           │
│                                                                      │
└──────────────────────────────────────────────────────────────────────┘

┌─ Derivation ────────────────────────────────────────────────────────┐
│                                                                      │
│   {CREATED  }                                                        │
│   {CHANGED  }  [TO STATE <State_Name>] }                             │
│   {VALIDATED}                                                        │
│     [BY  {Activity_Name(s)},                              ]          │
│     [     {FSM_Name(s) }                                  ]          │
│     [                                                     ]          │
│     [  [ USING  {Work_Item_Name(s) [IN STATE <State_Name>]}]]        │
│     [  [          {Skeleton_Name(s)                  }]]             │
│     [  [          {User_Profile_Name(s)              }]]             │
│     [  [          {Input_Name(s)                     }]],...] ;      │
│                                                                      │
└──────────────────────────────────────────────────────────────────────┘
```

Figure 169 (Part 1 of 2). The Work Item Template

```
┌─────────────────────────────────────────────────────────────────────┐
│  ┌─ Use ───────────────────────────────────────────────────────────┐ │
│  │                                                                   │ │
│     USED    [IN STATE <State_Name>]  [ BY   {Activity_Name(s)}, ]      │
│                                      [      {FSM_Name(s)     } ]       │
│        TO    {CREATE  }                                               │
│              {CHANGE  }  <Work_Item_Name(s)> [TO STATE <State_Name> ] ;│
│              {VALIDATE}                                                │
│                                                                       │
│     BECOMING   {TRUE }    IN STATE <State_Name>                        │
│                {FALSE}                                                 │
│                            {ENABLES ENTRY TO }                         │
│                            {SUSPENDS         }    <Activity_Name(s)> ; │
│                            {ENABLES EXIT FROM}                         │
│                                                                       │
│     BECOMING   {TRUE }    IN STATE <State_Name>                        │
│                {FALSE}                                                 │
│                                ENABLES ENTRY TO    <Decision_Name(s)> ;│
│     BECOMING   {TRUE }                                                 │
│                {FALSE}    IN STATE <State_Name>                        │
│                                {TRIGGERS   }                           │
│                                {INTERRUPTS }        <FSM_Name(s)> ;     │
│                                {TERMINATES }                           │
│                                                                       │
│     BECOMING   {TRUE }    IN STATE <State_Name>                        │
│                {FALSE}                                                 │
│                                MAKES <Condition_Name(s)>  {TRUE }       │
│                                                          {FALSE}  ;     │
│     {PUT   TO     }   <Repository_Name(s)>  BY  <FSM_Name(s)> ;         │
│     {GOTTEN FROM}                                                       │
│                                                                       │
│  └───────────────────────────────────────────────────────────────────┘
└─────────────────────────────────────────────────────────────────────┘
```

Figure 169 (Part 2 of 2). The Work Item Template

A.5.4 Decision

```
TYPE: DECISION                         <(Decision)_Name>  ;
META TYPE: DECISION

  ┌─ Entry Criteria ─────────────────────────────────────────────┐
  │                                                               │
  │   ENTRY ENABLED  WHEN                                         │
  │        {<Work_Item_Name(s)>  IN STATE  <State_Name>} ,       │
  │        {<Condition_Name(s)>                         } ,      │
  │        {<Event_Name(s)>                             }        │
  │                                                               │
  │                           BECOMES  {TRUE }    [AND]          │
  │                                    {FALSE}    [OR ]  ;       │
  │                                                               │
  └───────────────────────────────────────────────────────────────┘

  ┌─ Decision Criteria ──────────────────────────────────────────┐
  │                                                               │
  │   MAKES    <Condition_Name(s)>    {TRUE }                    │
  │                                   {FALSE}                    │
  │     [ WHEN  {<Work_Item_Name(s)>  IN STATE  <State_Name>},]  │
  │     [       {<Condition_Name(s)> } ,                      ]  │
  │     [       {<Event_Name(s)> }                           ]  │
  │     [                         BECOMES  {TRUE }   [AND] ]     │
  │     [                                  {FALSE}   [OR ] ] ;   │
  │   CAUSES    <Event_Name(s)>   ;                             │
  │                                                               │
  └───────────────────────────────────────────────────────────────┘
```

Figure 170. The Decision Template

A.5.5 Condition

```
TYPE: CONDITION                        <(Condition)_Name>  ;
META TYPE: CONDITION
┌─ Cause ──────────────────────────────────────────────────────────┐
│                                                                    │
│   MADE       {TRUE }    [ BY  <Decision_Name(s)> ]                 │
│              {FALSE}                                               │
│      WHEN  {<Work_Item_Name(s)>  IN STATE  <State_Name>} ,         │
│            {<Condition_Name(s)>                        } ,         │
│            {<Event_Name(s)>                            }           │
│                                     BECOMES   {TRUE }   [AND]      │
│                                               {FALSE}   [OR ]  ;   │
│                                                                    │
└────────────────────────────────────────────────────────────────────┘

┌─ Effect ──────────────────────────────────────────────────────────┐
│                                                                    │
│   BECOMING    {TRUE }    {ENABLES ENTRY TO    {Activity_Name(s) },  │
│               {FALSE}                         {Decision_Name(s) } ; │
│   BECOMING    {TRUE }    {SUSPENDS         }  <Activity_Name(s)> ;  │
│               {FALSE}    {ENABLES EXIT FROM}                        │
│   BECOMING    {TRUE }    {TRIGGERS   }                             │
│               {FALSE}    {INTERRUPTS}         <FSM_Name(s)> ;       │
│                          {TERMINATES}                              │
│                                                                    │
└────────────────────────────────────────────────────────────────────┘
```

Figure 171. The Condition Template

A.5.6 Event

```
TYPE: EVENT                           <(Event)_Name>  ;
META TYPE: EVENT

┌─ Cause ──────────────────────────────────────────────────┐
│                                                           │
│   CAUSED BY                {Event_Name(s)    },           │
│                            {Decision_Name(s)},            │
│                            {Activity_Name(s)},            │
│                            {FSM_Name(s)      }  ;          │
│                                                           │
└───────────────────────────────────────────────────────────┘

┌─ Effect ─────────────────────────────────────────────────┐
│                                                           │
│   CAUSES                   <Event_Name(s)>  ;             │
│   ENABLES ENTRY TO         <Decision_Name(s)> ;          │
│   {ENABLES ENTRY TO }                                     │
│   {SUSPENDS          }     <Activity_Name(s)> ;          │
│   {ENABLES EXIT FROM }                                    │
│                                                           │
│   {TRIGGERS    }                                          │
│   {INTERRUPTS }            <FSM_Name(s)> ;               │
│   {TERMINATES }                                           │
│                                                           │
└───────────────────────────────────────────────────────────┘
```

Figure 172. The Event Template

A.6 Templates for Problem/Solution Perspectives

A.6.1 Problem

```
TYPE: PROBLEM                     <(Problem)_Name>  ;
META TYPE: PROBLEM

  ┌─ Structure ──────────────────────────────────────────┐
  │                                                       │
  │   HAS PARTS          <Problem_Name(s)>  ;             │
  │   PART OF            <Problem_Name>  ;                │
  │                                                       │
  └───────────────────────────────────────────────────────┘

  ┌─ Resolution ─────────────────────────────────────────┐
  │                                                       │
  │   MADE  TRUE    BY   <Activity_Name(s)> ;            │
  │   MADE  FALSE   BY   <Activity_Name(s)>  ;           │
  │   RESOLVED BY        <Solution_Name(s)> ;            │
  │                                                       │
  └───────────────────────────────────────────────────────┘
```

Figure 173. The Problem Analysis Template

A.6.2 Solution

```
TYPE: SOLUTION                    <(Solution)_Name>  ;
META TYPE: SOLUTION

  ┌─ Structure ──────────────────────────────────────────┐
  │                                                       │
  │   HAS PARTS          <Solution_Name(s)>  ;           │
  │   PART OF            <Solution_Name>  ;              │
  │                                                       │
  └───────────────────────────────────────────────────────┘

  ┌─ Resolution ─────────────────────────────────────────┐
  │                                                       │
  │   MADE  TRUE    BY   <Activity_Name(s)> ;            │
  │   RESOLVES           <Problem_Name(s)> ;             │
  │                                                       │
  └───────────────────────────────────────────────────────┘
```

Figure 174. The Solution Definition Template

A.7 Templates for Current and Target Product Perspectives

A.7.1 Finite State Machine

```
TYPE: FSM                              <FSM_Name>  ;
META TYPE: FSM

┌─ Structure ──────────────────────────────────────────────────┐
│                                                                │
│    HAS PARTS          <FSM_Name(s)>  ;                         │
│    PART OF            <FSM_Name>   ;                           │
│                                                                │
└────────────────────────────────────────────────────────────────┘

┌─ Usage ──────────────────────────────────────────────────────┐
│                                                                │
│    UTILIZES           <FSM_Name(s)> ;                          │
│                         [ TO GENERATE <Output_Name(s)> ]       │
│                         [ TO {CREATE  } <Work_Item_Name(s)> ] ;│
│                              {CHANGE  }                        │
│                              {VALIDATE}                        │
│    UTILIZED BY        {Activity_Name(s)},                      │
│                       {FSM_Name(s)      }  ;                   │
│                         [ TO GENERATE <Output_Name(s)> ]       │
│                         [ TO {CREATE  } <Work_Item_Name(s)> ] ;│
│                              {CHANGE  }                        │
│                              {VALIDATE}                        │
│    PERFORMED BY       <Agent_Name(s)>    ;                     │
│                                                                │
└────────────────────────────────────────────────────────────────┘
```

Figure 175 (Part 1 of 2). Finite State Machine Template

```
┌─────────────────────────────────────────────────────────────────┐
│                                                                   │
│  ┌─ Trigger/Terminate Criteria ───────────────────────────────┐  │
│  │                                                             │  │
│  │    {TRIGGERED  }                                            │  │
│  │    {INTERRUPTED}                                            │  │
│  │    {TERMINATED }                                            │  │
│  │        WHEN   {Work_Item_Name(s) IN STATE <State_Name>},    │  │
│  │               {Condition_Name(s)                      },    │  │
│  │               {Event_Name(s)                          }     │  │
│  │                              BECOMES  {TRUE }    [AND]       │  │
│  │                                       {FALSE}    [OR ] ;     │  │
│  │        CAUSES        <Event_Name(s)>   ;                    │  │
│  │                                                             │  │
│  └─────────────────────────────────────────────────────────────┘  │
│                                                                   │
│  ┌─ Operations ────────────────────────────────────────────────┐  │
│  │                                                              │  │
│  │    {CREATES  }                                               │  │
│  │    {UPDATES  }    <Work_Item_Name(s)> [TO STATE <State_Name>]│  │
│  │    {VALIDATES}                                               │  │
│  │        [USING  <Work_Item_Name(s)> [IN STATE <State_Name>]],..] ; │
│  │    GENERATES       <Output_Name(s)>                          │  │
│  │        [ USING  <Work_Item_Name(s)> [IN STATE <State_Name>]],..] ; │
│  │    RECEIVES       <Input_Name(s)>   ;                        │  │
│  │    PUTS       <Work_Item_Name(s)>    TO    <Repository_Name(s)> ; │
│  │    GETS       <Work_Item_Name(s)>    FROM  <Repository_Name(s)> ; │
│  │                                                              │  │
│  └─────────────────────────────────────────────────────────────┘  │
│                                                                   │
└─────────────────────────────────────────────────────────────────┘
```

Figure 175 (Part 2 of 2). Finite State Machine Template

A.7.2 State Data

```
TYPE: STATE DATA                    <(State_Data)_Name> ;
META TYPE: DATA OBJECT
```

┌─ **Structure** ──┐
│   │
│   HAS SUBSETS   <State_Data_Name(s)> ;   │
│   SUBSET OF   <State_Data_Name> ;   │
│   │
└───┘

┌─ **Derivation** ───┐
│   {CREATED }   │
│   {CHANGED } [TO STATE <State_Name>] }   │
│   {VALIDATED}   │
│   [BY FSM_Name(s)   ]   │
│   [   ]   │
│   [[USING {Work_Item_Name(s) [IN STATE <State_Name>]}]] │
│   [[{Skeleton_Name(s)   }]]   │
│   [[{User_Profile_Name(s)   }]]   │
│   [[{Input_Name(s)   }]],...] ; │
└───┘

┌─ **Use** ──┐
│   USED   [IN STATE <State_Name>] [BY   FSM_Name(s)]   │
│   TO   {CREATE }   │
│   {CHANGE } <State_Data_Name(s)> [TO STATE <State_Name>] ; │
│   {VALIDATE}   │
│   BECOMING   {TRUE }   │
│   {FALSE}   IN STATE <State_Name>   │
│   {TRIGGERS   }   │
│   {INTERRUPTS }   <FSM_Name(s)> ; │
│   {TERMINATES }   │
│   BECOMING   {TRUE }   IN STATE <State_Name>   │
│   {FALSE}   │
│   MAKES <Condition_Name(s)> {TRUE } │
│   {FALSE} ; │
│   {PUT TO   }   <Repository_Name(s)> BY <FSM_Name(s)> ;   │
│   {GOTTEN FROM}   │
└───┘

Figure 176. The State Data Template

A.7.3 Repository

```
TYPE: REPOSITORY                    <(Repository)_Name> ;
META TYPE: REPOSITORY
┌─ Structure ────────────────────────────────────────────────┐
│                                                             │
│    PARTITIONS ARE        <Repository_Name(s)> ;             │
│    PARTITION OF          <Repository_Name>  ;               │
│                                                             │
└─────────────────────────────────────────────────────────────┘

┌─ Use ──────────────────────────────────────────────────────┐
│                                                             │
│    HAS   {Work_Item_Name(s)   },                            │
│          {Input_Name(s)        }    PUT BY      <FSM_Name(s)> ; │
│    HAS   {Work_Item_Name(s)   },                            │
│          {Output_Name(s)       }    GOTTEN BY   <FSM_Name(s)> ; │
│                                                             │
└─────────────────────────────────────────────────────────────┘
```

Figure 177. The Repository Template

A.7.4 Skeleton

```
TYPE: SKELETON                    <Skeleton_Name> ;
META TYPE: DATA OBJECT
┌─ Structure ────────────────────────────────────────────────┐
│                                                             │
│    HAS SUBSETS          <Skeleton_Name(s)> ;                │
│    SUBSET OF            <Skeleton_Name>  ;                   │
│                                                             │
└─────────────────────────────────────────────────────────────┘

┌─ Use ──────────────────────────────────────────────────────┐
│                                                             │
│    USED  [ BY  {FSM_Name(s)       },]                       │
│          [     {Activity_Name(s)} ] TO CREATE <Work_Item_Name(s)> ; │
│                                                             │
└─────────────────────────────────────────────────────────────┘
```

Figure 178. The Skeleton

A.7.5 User Profile

```
TYPE: USER PROFILE                    <(Profile_Element)_Name> ;
META TYPE: DATA OBJECT
```

┌─ **Structure** ───┐
```
    HAS SUBSETS           <Profile_Element_Name(s)> ;
    SUBSET OF             <Profile_Element_Name>  ;
```
└───┘

┌─ **Use** ───┐
```
    USED   [IN STATE <State_Name>]  [ BY   {Activity_Name(s)}, ]
                                    [      {FSM_Name(s) } ]
      TO    {CREATE  }
            {CHANGE  } <Work_Item_Name(s)> [TO STATE <State_Name> ] ;
            {VALIDATE}
    BECOMING  {TRUE }   IN STATE <State_Name>
              {FALSE}

                          {ENABLES ENTRY TO }
                          {SUSPENDS         }      <Activity_Name(s)> ;
                          {ENABLES EXIT FROM}
    BECOMING  {TRUE }   IN STATE <State_Name>
              {FALSE}

                          ENABLES ENTRY TO     <Decision_Name(s)> ;

    BECOMING  {TRUE }
              {FALSE}    IN STATE <State_Name>


                          {TRIGGERS   }
                          {INTERRUPTS }            <FSM_Name(s)> ;
                          {TERMINATES }
    BECOMING  {TRUE }   IN STATE <State_Name>
              {FALSE}

                          MAKES <Condition_Name(s)>  {TRUE }
                                                     {FALSE} ;
    {PUT  TO    }  <Repository_Name(s)>  BY  <FSM_Name(s)> ;
    {GOTTEN FROM}
```
└───┘

Figure 179. The User Profile Template

A.7.6 Tool

```
TYPE: TOOL                          <(Tool)_Name>  ;
META TYPE: AGENT
```

┌─ **Structure** ──────────────────────────────────────┐
```
   HAS PARTS            <Tool_Name(s)> ;
   PART OF              <Tool_Name> ;
```
└──┘

┌─ **Operations** ─────────────────────────────────────┐
```
   PERFORMS             <FSM_Name(s)> ;
```
└──┘

Figure 180. The Tool Template

A.7.7 Person Role

```
TYPE: PERSON                        <(Person_Role)_Name>  ;
META TYPE: AGENT
```

┌─ **Structure** ──────────────────────────────────────┐
```
   HAS PARTS            <Person_Role_Name(s)> ;
   PART OF              <Person_Role_Name> ;
```
└──┘

┌─ **Operations** ─────────────────────────────────────┐
```
   PERFORMS             <FSM_Name(s)> ;
```
└──┘

Figure 181. The Person Role Template

A.8 ASL Syntax Conventions

1. ASL names must be 30, nonblank characters, or less.

2. The Underscore character should be used to connect words in a name.

3. For ease of reading, all names should be in mixed case - that is, the first letter of each word should be capitalized.

4. For ease of comprehension

   a. All names of objects of Meta-Type ACTIVITY, should be *verb* names. (example: "Generate_The_Code").

   b. All names of objects of Meta_Type FSM should be *noun* names (example: "Code_Generator").

5. All ASL keywords must be in upper case.

6. Conventions for the ASL skeletons:

   a. All keywords are optional.

   b. All names bounded by carets (" < This_Name > ") are to be substituted with real names, dropping the carets.

   c. When two or more names appear within braces ("{This_Name}"), one must be chosen.

   d. Statements within brackets ("[KEYWORD   < This_Name >]") are optional.

7. Reserved words and synonyms cannot be used in a name.

8. An ASL string is a sequence of 30 characters or less, enclosed by primes (') at both ends. The string may include any character, including blanks.

9. All ASL statements must be terminated with a semicolon.

10. Comments may be included in the ASL source code by preceding them with /* and ending them with */.

Appendix B. Design Programming Language (DPL) Reference

B.1 BGNSEGMENT and ENDSEGMENT

Definition:

A *segment* is a logical functional entity which can be composed of logic, data, or prologue information. All segments must be delimited by the BGNSEGMENT and ENDSEGMENT statements.

Syntax Format:

```
name:BGNSEGMENT.

MAIN|BLOCK|SUBROUTINE|DATA|PROLOGUE.

 Other DPL Statements

ENDSEGMENT(name).
```

name=The segment name.
MAIN=The top segment in a procedure.
BLOCK=Any segment internal to the procedure that can
     be INCLUDEd in its entirety into another logic
     segment or which can be written in-line (INSETed).
SUBROUTINE=Any segment (internal or external) that can
     be CALLed from another logic segment.
DATA=Any internal segment containing data that is to be
     INCLUDEd into a logic segment (BLOCK, MAIN, or
     SUBROUTINE) or another data segment.
PROLOGUE=The segment containing all Prologue data for
     the module.

Syntax Rules:

1. For each BGNSEGMENT there must be an ENDSEGMENT.
2. Name and ENDSEGMENT start in the same column.
3. FUNCTION is the only valid DPL statement that
   may immediately succeed the BGNSEGMENT statement.
4. Other DPL statements:
   a. Separate lines for each statement
   b. Indented from beginning column of the
      name according to the indentation rules

B.2 FUNCTION

Definition:

A concise description of the logical function of each segment.

Syntax Format:

```
FUNCTION is to describe.
describe=see section B.1.12 for details.
```

Syntax Rules:

1. FUNCTION starts in same column as **name** on BGNSEGMENT.

2. Other DPL statements

    a. are indented from FUNCTION according to the indentation rules.

    b. have a separate line for each statement.

Example:

```
XYZ:BGNSEGMENT(BLOCK).

FUNCTION is to convert responses to the proper format
for analysis by the normal FID1 inbound processes.
```

B.3 NOTE

Definition:

Any statement used to clarify or expand the design specification. Used to aid the interpretation of another statement or to explain the rationale behind the logic description. Can be used to bring level of detail to a finer specification, when needed.

Syntax Format:

```
NOTE-expansion.
```

expansion=statements clarifying or detailing design logic or intent.

Example:

```
NOTE-This program will only read initial amount, which may
not be sufficient, in which case the attention handler will
cause the remainder to be read.
```

B.4 INTERFACES

Definition:

An interface is established when a relationship exists
between two distinct pieces of design such that control
of logic flow is passed from one piece to another.

INCLUDE

Definition:

Used to incorporate a BLOCK segment into the segment
of a procedure.

Syntax Format:

INCLUDE name TO describe.

name = is the name of the BLOCK segment.
Names should be meaningfully descriptive.

describe = see section B.1.12 for details.

ISSUE

Definition:

Used to invoke a service through a macro statement.

Syntax Format:

ISSUE macro-name TO parameter_describe.

macro-name = the name of the macro as it will exist in the implementation maclib.

parameter_describe = a brief description of each macro parameter that is critical to how the macro is invoked. Defaults should be shown when they are key.

CALL

Definition:

Used to invoke a SUBROUTINE segment or another module.

Syntax Format:

CALL name EXTERNAL|INTERNAL TO describe.

name = the procedure name that is invoked.

describe = see section B.1.12 for details.

EXTERNAL = any procedure outside the code of this procedure.

INTERNAL = any segment of code inside this procedure.

INSET

Definition:

Used to show where a BLOCK will be coded in-line in another logic segment.

Syntax Format:

INSET name TO describe.

name = the name of the BLOCK segment that will be coded in-line.

describe = see section B.1.12 for details.

NOTE: A CALLed segment implies branching to get to the call segment. INCLUDEd or INSETed segments do not require a branch to get to it; rather it is implanted at the position of INCLUDE or INSET.

Examples:

INCLUDE XYZ TO BUILD FSB.

CALL A123 TO GET STORAGE AND FORMAT IT.

ISSUE GETMAIN TO GET STORAGE FROM SUBPOOL 0 FOR THE ABC.

INSET PIPPOP TO TEST FOR INVALID CODES.

B.5 IF THEN ELSE

Definition:

A decision to determine if one or more conditions exist which will determine one of two paths to execute. If all conditions are satisfied as true the THEN logic will be executed; otherwise the ELSE logic will be executed.

Syntax Format:

IF condition [describe], [AND|OR condition [describe]]

THEN [describe]

 DPL Statements

[ELSE [describe]]

 [DPL Statements]

ENDIF [describe].

condition = Any valid test of resources

describe = see section B.1.12 for details

Syntax Rules:

1. For every IF there must be an ENDIF.

2. IF and ENDIF begin in the same column.

3. THEN and ELSE begin in the same column.

4. THEN and ELSE are indented two columns.

5. ELSE is optional.

6. Other DPL statements:

   - indented from THEN of ELSE according to the indentation rules

   - separate lines for each statement

Example:

    IF all input is valid

    THEN (keep processing)
        DPL statements
        .
        .
        .

    ELSE (quit and exit)
        DPL statements
        .
        .
        .

    ENDIF.

B.6 DO UNTIL

Definition:

A trailing decision to determine if one or more conditions
exist, which will cause a repetitive process to stop. When
all conditions are satisfied, an exit will be made from the
loop; otherwise the logic within the DO domain is executed
and the loop processing continues.

Syntax Format:

    DO UNTIL condition [describe] [,AND|OR condition
        [describe]...]
        DPL Statements

    ENDDO [describe].

    condition = any valid test of resources

    describe = see section B.1.12 for details

Syntax Rules:

1. For every DO there must be an ENDDO.

2. DO and ENDDO begin in the same column.

3. Other DPL statements:

   a. separate lines for each statement

   b. indented from DO according to the indentation rules

Example:

    DO UNTIL the last block is attached.
      Move pointers into attached block.
      Establish base counters.
        .
        .

    ENDDO.

B.7 DO WHILE

Definition:

A leading decision to determine if one or more conditions exist that will initiate or repeat a flow of logic. If all conditions are satisfied, the logic in the DO domain will be executed and loop processing continues; otherwise an exit will be made from the loop.

Syntax Format:

    DO WHILE condition [describe] [, AND|OR] condition
        [describe]...].
      DPL Statements

    ENDDO [describe].

condition = any valid test or resource

describe = see section B.1.12 for details

Syntax Rules:

1. For ever DO there must be an ENDDO.

2. DO and ENDDO begin in the same column.

3. Other DPL statements:

   a. separate lines for each statement

   b. indented from DO according to the indentation rules

Example:

    DO WHILE there is still storage to zero out.
        ISSUE XYX TO FIND ABC.
        Zero out next block of storage.
        .
        .
        .

    ENDDO.

B.8 CASE

Definition:

    A branch table mechanism for executing different blocks
    of logic that are determined by an input indexing factor.

Syntax Format:

CASENTRY [describe].

  CASE   [NULL|name|FOLLOWS]   IF condition

  [DPL Statements, if FOLLOWS is selected]

     .

     .

     .

     .

ENDCASE [describe].

condition = any condition which is or can be translated into an indexing factor in a branch table series.

name = any internal logic segment to be given control.

NULL = a position in the indexing factor will that not occur for transfer of control.

FOLLOWS the logic to be executed follows this CASE statement.

describe = see Section B.1.12 for details.

Syntax Rules:

1. For every CASENTRY there must be an ENDCASE.

2. CASENTRY ENDCASE begin in the same column.

3. CASE is indented two columns from CASENTRY

   a. separate lines for each DPL statement

   b. indented from CASE according to indentation rules

Example:
CASENTRY (after returning from error processor).
   CASE A IF return code is 0
   CASE NULL IF return code is 4
   CASE B IF return code is 8
   CASE C IF return code is 12
   CASE FOLLOWS IF return code is 16
      ISSUE TPEXIT TO TERMINATE processing this request
ENDCASE.

Design Notes:

1. At least three CASE statements are suggested before use is made of this figure, although it will work with one CASE statement. For less that three cases, the IF THEN ELSE should apply.

2. There must be a CASE statement for each possible increment even if it has no assigned logic, where the NULL applies on the CASE statement.

3. Logic may precede the CASENTRY statement to translate randomly ordered conditions to an indexing factor.

B.9 INPUT and OUTPUT

Description:

- INPUT - The statement used to list all data that is referenced or set by the segment.

- OUTPUT - The statement used to list all data that is changed by the segment.

Syntax Format
        INPUT   (data,data,...).
        OUTPUT (data,data,...).

Syntax Rules:

1. INPUT can only appear after the FUNCTION statement.

2. OUTPUT can only precede the ENDSEGMENT statement.

3. INPUT and OUTPUT are optional, but when one is used so must the other.

4. INPUT and OUTPUT begin in the same column as FUNCTION.

Example:
        INPUT (TCB,FMCB).
            .
            .
            .
        OUTPUT (TCBCOUNT,FMCBXX).

B.10 Sequence Statements

B.10.1 General Function

Any statement that defines a process or logical act, but excludes any branching technique. See section B.1.12 on *describe* for more detail.

B.10.2 EXPAND

Description:

Used to indicate logic which is to be generated for macro caller, versus logic internal to the macro which generates the EXPANDED logic.

Syntax Format:

EXPAND TO describe.

Describe = see section on describe for details.

Example:

EXPAND TO LOAD Reg1 with address of parameter list.

B.10.3 MESSAGE

Description:

Used to indicate that the stated message is to be written.

Syntax Format:

MESSAGE id-message.

id = the message ID

message = the message text

Example:

MESSAGE IHA999-INVALID MACRO PARAMETER.

B.11 Extended Structured Programming Figure

B.11.1 DO INFINITE

Definition:

A closed loop without any implied exit for termination of execution.

Note: It is not the intent to discuss the advantages or requirements for this statement type in this specification.

Syntax Format:

DO INFINITE [describe]

DPL Statements

ENDDO.

describe = see section B.1.12 for details.

Syntax Rules:

1. An ENDDO for each DO.

2. DO and ENDDO begin in same column.

3. DPL statements are indented two columns from DO.

Example:

DO INFINITE

Function A.

LEAVE on p ANDDO

Function B.

ENDLEAVE.

Function C.

ENDDO.

B.11.2 LEAVE

Definition:

A controlled exit from a DO loop, a segment, or a program.
The exit may be conditional or unconditional.

Syntax Format:

LEAVE   [DO|SEGMENT|PROGRAM|SEARCH]
         [ON condition [ANDDO]]

         [DPL Statements]

         [ENDLEAVE.]

DO = exit from the innermost or single DO containing the LEAVE
    DO is the default.
SEGMENT = exit from the segment containing the LEAVE
PROGRAM = exit from the program module containing the LEAVE
condition = any valid test of resources
SEARCH = exit from the SEARCH control structure.

Syntax Rules:

1. If prior to taking the exit some function is to be performed,
   then the ANDDO must be written.

2. If ANDDO is written, the ENDLEAVE statement is expected as the
   terminator for the function to be executed prior to exit.

3. LEAVE and ENDLEAVE are written in the same column.

4. The optional statements to be executed prior to exit are
   indented two columns from LEAVE.

Example:
```
DO WHILE p
 LEAVE ON q ANDDO
   Clean up all data areas.
 ENDLEAVE.
   .

   .

   .
 ENDDO.
```

NOTE: LEAVEs cannot be nested

B.11.3 SEARCH

Definition:

A table search flow where an exit is taken and a process is to be performed if the searched-for element is found. Otherwise, if the list is exhausted before finding the searched-for entry, another process is to be performed before leaving the search loop.

Syntax Format:
```
SEARCH condition [describe].
   DPL Statements
   LEAVE SEARCH ON condition    [ANDDO]
   [DPL Statements]
    OTHERWISE
      DPL Statements
   ENDLEAVE.
   DPL Statements
ENDSEARCH.
```

condition = any valid test of resources.
describe = See Section B.1.12.

Syntax Rules:

1. SEARCH and ENDSEARCH begin in same column.

2. SEARCHs cannot be nested.

3. LEAVE rules apply as defined in B.2.11.

4. OTHERWISE must be specified.

5. Each place where "DPL Statements" is shown in the Syntax Format, there must be some design process except after the LEAVE.

```
Example:
        SEARCH the TCB chain.
        DPL Statements
        LEAVE SEARCH ON finding the highest priority task.
        OTHERWISE
          DPL Statements
        ENDLEAVE
          DPL Statements
        ENDSEARCH.
```

B.12 Describe

1. Length of statement

   - limit of 120 characters

2. Content

   a. FUNCTION: a synopsis of what the segment or procedure does

   b. NOTE: as much as is necessary, without consistently talking bit-level Design

   c. Interfaces

      1) one-line synopsis for INCLUDE, CALL, INSET

      2) parameters needed to ISSUE a macro call

   d. IF, DO, CASE

      - An interpretation of the condition to make the design more understandable

   e. EXPAND: the actual macro generated instruction

3. Format

   [action|information|explanation]   [(CB Fields)]

   action = what is to be done   (sequence,EXPAND,ISSUE)
   information = a help to get it done   (NOTE,FUNCTION,interface)
   explanation = why it is being done   (IF,DO,CASE)

   CB Fields = the name of the fields written to or read from

4. Style

   - Some programmers have a tendency to write their designs as if they were coding at the same time; others are too esoteric or vague in their use of values, actions, and so forth. DPL cannot change these peculiarities. It is not the intent to inhibit style; in fact it is one of the advantages of DPL that it does not demand too rigorous a discipline, but rather it takes into account that programmers are also people.

It is suggested, however, that the writers of DPL or any design language read their results and designs as if they were the next programmer to inherit the design. If the designer does his best to communicate his ideas, he will find that DPL will help rather than retard his efforts.

B.13 Data Segments

Can contain any description of data needed for the logic statements.

It is common usage to put control block format or definitions in the data segment when they are integral to the design. It is also common usage to indicate the contents of built or modified control blocks in the data segment when most of the control block is involved.

- Types of Data
  - Options—data supplied by the user when calling the MAIN segment
  - Switches—also known as bits or flags
  - Counters—values initialized and incremented or decremented by the segments
  - Buffers—data areas used to hold data for immediate or later use; also called "save" areas
  - Values—data set dynamically during logic flow; different from counters in that they are not incremented or decremented, but may be entirely reset
  - Constants—self-defined and preset, unchanging data
  - Messages—preset character data to be dynamically outputted under specific conditions
  - Files—Input and output data sets

```
┌─ EXAMPLE ─────────────────────────────────────────────────────────┐

DATA: BGNSEGMENT (DATA)
FUNCTION IS TO DESCRIBE ALL DATA FOR FORMAT PROGRAM.

  OPTIONS=
    TITLE-DEFAULT IS NO, USER OPTIONALLY SUPPLIES
    PROLOG-DEFAULT IS NO, USER OPTIONALLY SUPPLIES
    LINELGTH-DEFAULT IS 120 CHARACTERS, USER CAN OPTIONALLY CHANGE

  SWITCHES=
    CONTINUED 'IF' STATEMENT=AN 'IF' LINE IS BEING CONTINUED
    FINAL CONTINUE SWITCH=THE LAST SECTION OF A CONTINUED 'IF' HAS BEEN FOUND
    LINE-IN-BUFFER=DATA LINE IS ALREADY IN BUFFER
    LINE-IN-TEMPORARY-AREA SWITCH=DATA IS TEMPORARILY SAVED

  COUNTERS=
    ENDIF=THE NUMBER OF REQUIRED ENDIF'S TO MATCH IF'S
    DPL LINE=THE NUMBER OF INPUT LINES PROCESSED
    PRINTED LINE=THE NUMBER OF LINES WRITTEN TO PRESENT PAGE

  BUFFERS=
    TITLE LINE BUFFER=THE AREA FOR THE TITLE CARD DATA
    LINE BUFFER 1=THE INPUT READ IN AREA
    LINE BUFFER 2=THE INPUT LOOK AHEAD AREA

  SAVE AREAS=
    SEQUENCE NUMBER=THE SEQUENCE NUMBER FOR THE LINE IN PROCESS

  CONSTANTS=
    FIXED MODE CHARACTER='|'

  MESSAGES=
    DPLMSG1-NON DPL LINE ENCOUNTERED IN OPEN SEGMENT.  THE LINE IS IGNORED
    DPLMSG2-INVALID TITLE CARD KEYWORK XXXXXXX-IGNORED
    DPLMSG3-NO DATA IN SPECIFIED DPL DATA SET-PROCESSING TERMINATED
    DPLMSG11-WARNING-FIXED MODE LINE CHARACTER FOUND BUT NOT IN
         EXPECTED COLUMN-LINE TREATED AS FIXED MODE
    DPLMSG13-SEVERE-MISSING ENDDO STATEMENT(S) IN THIS SEGMENT
    DPLMSG14-SEVERE-MISSING ENDIF STATEMENT(S) IN THIS SEGMENT
    DPLMSG15-SEVERE-MISSING ENDCASE STATEMENT(S) IN THIS SEGMENT

  FILES=
    DPLSRCE=THE DPL SOURCE INPUT FILE
    DPLINPT=THE TITLE LINE CARD FILE
    DPLPRINT=THE FORMATTED TEXT PRINT FILE

ENDSEGMENT (DATA).

└───────────────────────────────────────────────────────────────────┘
```

B.14 Syntax Rules

1. Use only the allowed DPL statements.

2. A period (.) must end every DPL statement, except the IF, THEN, and ELSE statements. The period, when followed by more than two blank characters, will indicate a termination of statement.

   If a line has as its last character a period in the last allowable column and the next line has less than three blanks before first printable character, this will be taken as an indicator of termination for the statement.

3. When the number of characters between an open parenthesis and close parenthesis is eight or less, the content in the parenthesis will be assumed to be a control block field name.

4. Keywords:

   When used in their prescribed contexts, they take on specific meanings. Otherwise, they are free form.

BLOCK	ELSE	PROLOGUE
MAIN	ENDIF	BGNSEGMENT
SUBROUTING	DO	CALL
DATA	ENDDO	FUNCTION
ENDSEGMENT	CASENTRY	NOTE
INCLUDE	CASE	MESSAGE
ISSUE	ENDCASE	INPUT
IF	EXPAND	OUTPUT
THEN	INSET	LEAVE
		ENDLEAVE
		SEARCH

B.15 Indentation Rules

The following rules apply:

1. FUNCTION statement begins in the same column as BGNSEGMENT.

2. All THEN and ELSE lines will be indented two columns from the previous IF statement start position.

3. All DPL statements immediately following THEN, ELSE, DO, LEAVE, or CASE will be indented two columns.

4. All CONTINUATION LINES OF A STATEMENT will be indented five columns from the statement start position.

5. All ENDDO, ENDIF, ENDCASE, ENDLEAVE, and ENDSEGMENT statements will line up with the respective DO, IF, CASENTRY, LEAVE or BGNSEGMENT associated with it.

6. A new statement begins when a period is found on any DPL statement except the IF, THEN, ELSE or OTHERWISE statement.

7. The user may fix the format of indentation length on any line by having a vertical slash (|) as the first character on that line.

8. Each segment will begin a new physical page.

Appendix C. A Design Language (ADL) Reference

ADL is derived from DPL, CDL (an internal IBM design language), Ada, and the PDL syntax denoted in Linger, Mills, and Witt's, *Structured Programming: Theory and Practice*. ADL is used here for pedagogical purposes only. It does not pretend to be a complete design language. However, it is sufficient to teach the principles of design discussed in this book, and is a usable design representation.

C.1 Packaging Structures

1. **SEGMENT - ENDSEGMENT** are used to define a self-contained package or part of a design solution.

```
┌─────────────────────────────────────────────────────────────┐
│  ┌─ FORMAT ────────────────────────────────────────────────  │
│                                                               │
│    SEGMENT name PROGRAM│PROCEDURE│BLOCK                        │
│       (parmlist) <function commentary>;                       │
│       Statement_1;                                            │
│          .                                                    │
│          .                                                    │
│          .                                                    │
│                                                               │
│       Statement_n;                                            │
│    ENDSEGMENT name;                                           │
│                                                               │
└─────────────────────────────────────────────────────────────┘


┌─────────────────────────────────────────────────────────────┐
│  ┌─ DEFINITION ───────────────────────────────────────────   │
│                                                               │
│      name for PROGRAM is a unique identifier for the          │
│         main segment of a program or a FUNCTION refinement.   │
│      name for PROCEDURE is a unique identifier for a          │
│         self-contained subunit of a program or a FUNCTION refinement. │
│      name for BLOCK is a logical grouping of data,            │
│         function commentary, or logic statements.             │
│      parmlist takes the form (IN inparms, OUT outparms,       │
│         INOUT inoutparms)                                     │
│         inparms are input data which are not changed during   │
│            execution.                                         │
│         outparms are output data derived during execution.    │
│         inoutparms are input data which are changed to some   │
│            output value during execution.  Note:  not valid when │
│            a SEGMENT is a refinement of a FUNCTION.           │
│      inparms, outparms, and inoutparms take the form of:      │
│            parms_1:type,...,parms_n:type                      │
│               where                                           │
│               parms_1,...,parms_n may be one or more          │
│               variable names.                                 │
│         type is any of the acceptable type definitions in section │
│            C.6, "Data Types"                                  │
│      function commentary is the intended function of the      │
│         segment; refer to "Function Commentary," section C.5. │
│                                                               │
└─────────────────────────────────────────────────────────────┘
```

```
┌─────────────────────────────────────────────────────────────────┐
│  ┌─ EXAMPLE ──────────────────────────────────────────────────┐  │
│  │                                                             │  │
│  │   SEGMENT example PROGRAM (parm_1,parm_2) <this is an example>; │
│  │              .                                              │  │
│  │              .                                              │  │
│  │              .                                              │  │
│  │              .                                              │  │
│  │                                                             │  │
│  │   ENDSEGMENT example;                                       │  │
│  │                                                             │  │
│  └─────────────────────────────────────────────────────────────┘  │
└─────────────────────────────────────────────────────────────────┘
```

2. **SPEC-ENDSPEC** are used to define an abstract view of a module.

```
┌─────────────────────────────────────────────────────────────────┐
│  ┌─ FORMAT ───────────────────────────────────────────────────┐  │
│  │                                                             │  │
│  │   SPEC modulename (generic parameters);                     │  │
│  │      STATE modulename                                       │  │
│  │         TYPE modulename = type;                             │  │
│  │         INVARIANT module invariant;                         │  │
│  │         INITIAL module initialization;                      │  │
│  │      OPERATIONS:                                            │  │
│  │         FUNCTION name_1 (parmlist) <function commentary>;   │  │
│  │                  .                                          │  │
│  │                  .                                          │  │
│  │                  .                                          │  │
│  │         FUNCTION name_n (parmlist) <function commentary>;   │  │
│  │      ENDSPEC modulename;                                    │  │
│  │                                                             │  │
│  └─────────────────────────────────────────────────────────────┘  │
└─────────────────────────────────────────────────────────────────┘
```

modulename is the identifier of the module.

generic parameters define parameters that are to be supplied by the user when variables for the type modulename are defined through a VAR statement. If the user does not supply a defined generic parameter, then a default will be inherited for that specific parameter.

type is any of the data type definitions in section C.6, "Data Types," including any deferred types.

module invariant defines restrictions on the data space defined in this specification.

module initialization defines the initial state of the declared variables of type modulename.

name_1,...,name_n are the unique identifiers for the permitted operations on type modulename.

parmlist takes the form (**IN inparms, OUT outparms, INOUT inoutparms**)

    inparms are input data which are not changed during execution;

    outparms are output data derived during execution;

    inoutparms are input which may be changed during execution.

    inparms, outparms, and inouparms take the form of:

        parms_1:type,...,parms_n:type

            where

            parms_1,...,parms_n may be one or more variable names.

function commentary defines the intended function for the operation.

See the symbol_table example in Figure 151 on page 339

3. **DESIGN-ENDDESIGN** are used to define the concrete design view of a module and is *not* seen by the module user. For each SPEC-ENDSPEC there is a corresponding DESIGN-ENDDESIGN.

```
FORMAT

    DESIGN modulename;
        STATE
            TYPE modulename = type;
            INVARIANT module invariant;
            INITIAL module intialization;
        OPERATIONS
            FUNCTION name_1 (parmlist) <function commentary>;
                .
                .
                .
            FUNCTION name_n (parmlist) <function commentary>;
    ENDDESIGN modulename;
```

modulename is the identifier of the module.

type is any of the data type definitions in section C.6,
"Data Types" including a deferred type.

module invariant defines restrictions on the data space
defined using either TYPE or VAR in this design refinement.

module initialization defines the initial state of the declared
variables of type modulename.

name_1,...,name_n are the unique identifiers for the permitted
operations on type modulename.

parmlist takes the form (**IN inparms, OUT outparms**)

  inparms are input data which are not changed
    during execution

  outparms are output data derived during
    execution

inparms take the form of:

  parms_1:type ,...,parms_n:type
    where
      parms_1...parms_n may be zero or
      more variable names.

outparms take the form of:

  parms_1:type ,...,parms_n:type
    where
      parms_1...parms_n may be one or more
      variable names.

function commentary defines the intended functions for the
operation.

See the symbol_table example inFigure 151 on page 339

C.2 Control Structures

1. **IF THEN ELSE - ENDIF** A control element in which one of two patterns is satisfied depending on the resolution of the condition statement. If TRUE, the THEN path is executed, otherwise the ELSE path is taken if present. If not present, the THEN path is bypassed.

```
FORMAT

    <if structure function commentary>
    IF condition
       THEN <then_part function commentary>
          statement_1;

                .
                .
                .

          statement_n;
       [ELSE <else_part function commentary>
          statement_1;

                .
                .
                .

          statement_n;]
    ENDIF;
```

```
DEFINITION

      if structure function commentary defines the intended
         function for the entire IF THEN ELSE-ENDIF control structure.
      condition is a predicate or expression which evaluates
         to TRUE or FALSE.
      then_part function commentary defines the intended
         function if the condition evaluates TRUE.
      else_part function commentary defines the intended
         function if the condition evaluates FALSE.
```

2. **DO UNTIL-ENDDO** A loop control structure in which the function executed is continued until the condition for loop termination is satisfied. Function is always executed at least once.

```
FORMAT
        <do until structure function commentary>
        DO UNTIL condition <do_part function commentary>;
           statement_1;
              .
              .
              .
           statement_n;
        ENDDO;
```

```
DEFINITION
        do until function commentary defines the intended
           function for the entire DO UNTIL-ENDDO control structure.
        condition is a predicate or expression which evaluates
           to TRUE or FALSE.
        do_part function commentary defines the intended function
           of one execution of statement_1 through statement_n.
```

3. **DO WHILE-ENDDO** Another looping control structure in which the function execution is not permitted if the condition is satisfied.

```
┌─ FORMAT ──────────────────────────────────────────────────┐
│                                                            │
│    <do while function commentary>                          │
│    DO WHILE condition <do_while function commentary>;      │
│       statement_1;                                         │
│            .                                               │
│            .                                               │
│            .                                               │
│       statement_n;                                         │
│    ENDDO;                                                  │
│                                                            │
└────────────────────────────────────────────────────────────┘
```

```
┌─ DEFINITION ──────────────────────────────────────────────┐
│                                                            │
│    do_while function commentary defines the intended       │
│       function for the entire DO WHILE-ENDDO control       │
│       structure.                                           │
│    condition is a predicate or expression which            │
│       evaluates to TRUE or FALSE.                          │
│    do_part function commentary defines the intended        │
│       function of one execution of statement_1 through     │
│       statement_n.                                         │
│                                                            │
└────────────────────────────────────────────────────────────┘
```

4. **CASE**: A branch table control structure where one of many paths will be executed based on the condition resolution.

```
  FORMAT

      <case structure function commentary>
      CASE (condition test)
         WHEN (case_condition 1)
            <case_part 1 function commentary>;
               case_part 1;
                  .
                  .
                  .

         WHEN (case_condition n)
            <case_part n function commentary>;
               case_part n;
                  .
                  .
                  .

         OTHERWISE <otherwise part function commentary>;
               otherwise_part;
      ENDCASE;
```

5. **BEGIN-END** is a logical internal grouping of ADL statements.

```
┌─ FORMAT ──────────────────────────────────────────────────────┐
│                                                                │
│     <begin structure function commentary>                      │
│     BEGIN                                                       │
│        statement_1;                                            │
│                  .                                             │
│                  .                                             │
│                  .                                             │
│        statement_n;                                            │
│     END;                                                       │
│                                                                │
└────────────────────────────────────────────────────────────────┘
```

```
┌─────────────────────────────────────────────────────────────────┐
│  ┌─ EXAMPLE ────────────────────────────────────────────────────┐│
│  │                                                               ││
│  │    <x,y:=y,x>                                                  ││
│  │    BEGIN                                                       ││
│  │       x:=x+y;                                                  ││
│  │       y:=x-y;                                                  ││
│  │       x:=x-y;                                                  ││
│  │    END;                                                        ││
│  │                                                               ││
│  └───────────────────────────────────────────────────────────────┘│
└─────────────────────────────────────────────────────────────────┘
```

C.3 Interfaces

1. **INCLUDE** is used to cause substitution of the included **BLOCK** statements in place of the INCLUDE statement.

```
┌─────────────────────────────────────────────────────────────────┐
│  ┌─ FORMAT ─────────────────────────────────────────────────────┐│
│  │                                                               ││
│  │    <include function commentary>                              ││
│  │    INCLUDE blockname (parmlist);                              ││
│  │                                                               ││
│  └───────────────────────────────────────────────────────────────┘│
└─────────────────────────────────────────────────────────────────┘
```

2. **CALL** is used to invoke a **PROCEDURE|PROGRAM**.

```
┌─────────────────────────────────────────────────────────────┐
│  ┌─ DEFINITION ────────────────────────────────────────────┐ │
│  │                                                          │ │
│  │     call function commentary defines the intended function│ │
│  │        of the PROCEDURE│PROGRAM being CALLed.            │ │
│  │                                                          │ │
│  │     parmlist takes the form (IN inparms, OUT outparms, INOUT│ │
│  │        inoutparms)                                       │ │
│  │                                                          │ │
│  │       inparms are input data which are not changed       │ │
│  │          during execution;                               │ │
│  │                                                          │ │
│  │       outparms are output data derived during execution; │ │
│  │                                                          │ │
│  │       inoutparms are input data which are changed to     │ │
│  │          some value during execution.                    │ │
│  │                                                          │ │
│  │     inparms, outparms, and inoutparms take the form of:  │ │
│  │                                                          │ │
│  │     parms_1:type,...,parms_n:type                        │ │
│  │        where parms_1...parms_n may be one or more        │ │
│  │        variable names.                                   │ │
│  │                                                          │ │
│  └──────────────────────────────────────────────────────────┘ │
└─────────────────────────────────────────────────────────────┘
```

3. **EXECUTE** is used to cause an execution of the FUNCTION named.

```
┌─────────────────────────────────────────────────────────────┐
│  ┌─ FORMAT ─────────────────────────────────────────────────┐ │
│  │                                                          │ │
│  │     <execute function commentary>                        │ │
│  │     EXECUTE name (parmlist);                             │ │
│  │                                                          │ │
│  └──────────────────────────────────────────────────────────┘ │
└─────────────────────────────────────────────────────────────┘
```

```
┌──────────────────────────────────────────────────────────────┐
│  ┌─ DEFINITION ──────────────────────────────────────────┐    │
│  │                                                        │    │
│  │    execute function commentary defines the FUNCTION    │    │
│  │       to be executed.                                  │    │
│  │                                                        │    │
│  │    name is the unique identifier for the functional    │    │
│  │       operation invoked.                               │    │
│  │                                                        │    │
│  │    parmlist takes the form (IN inparms, OUT outparms)  │    │
│  │                                                        │    │
│  │      inparms are input data which are not changed      │    │
│  │         during execution.  There may be zero or more   │    │
│  │         inparms.                                       │    │
│  │                                                        │    │
│  │      outparms is output derived during the function    │    │
│  │         execution.                                     │    │
│  │                                                        │    │
│  │      inparms take the form of:                         │    │
│  │         parms_1:type,...,parms_n:type                  │    │
│  │            where parms_1,...,parm_n may be zero or more │    │
│  │            variable names                              │    │
│  │                                                        │    │
│  │      outparms takes the form of:                       │    │
│  │         parms_1:type,...,parms_n:type                  │    │
│  │            where parms_1,...,parms_n may be one or more │    │
│  │            variable names.                             │    │
│  │                                                        │    │
│  └────────────────────────────────────────────────────────┘    │
└──────────────────────────────────────────────────────────────┘


┌──────────────────────────────────────────────────────────────┐
│  ┌─ EXAMPLE ─────────────────────────────────────────────┐    │
│  │                                                        │    │
│  │    <an example of the EXECUTE statement>               │    │
│  │    EXECUTE ADD (IN subtotal:REAL,new_value:REAL,OUT    │    │
│  │                 total:REAL)                            │    │
│  │                                                        │    │
│  └────────────────────────────────────────────────────────┘    │
└──────────────────────────────────────────────────────────────┘
```

C.4 Assignment and Data

1. An Assignment statement is used to fix values to variables.

```
┌─ FORMAT ─────────────────────────────────────────────

    1.  simple:
        variable:=expression;

    2.  concurrent simple:
        varname_list:=expression_list;

    3.  conditional:
        condition_1-->assignment_1, ...,
        condition_n-->assignment_n;

    4.  factored conditional:
        varname_list:=
        ((condition_1-->expression_list_1),...,
          (condition_n-->expression_list_n));
```

┌─ EXAMPLES ──┐

1. x:=a+b;

2. x,y:=y,x;

3. x<0-->y:=0;

4. x,y:=((x<0-->y,x),(x<y-->0,0));

└──┘

2. **CONST** is used to define constant values.

3. **TYPE** is used to define a new typename to be used in **VARs**, other **TYPE** statements, or paramenter definitions.

```
┌─────────────────────────────────────────────────────────────┐
│  ┌─ FORMAT ──────────────────────────────────────────────┐   │
│  │                                                        │   │
│  │      TYPE typename = type;                             │   │
│  │                                                        │   │
│  └────────────────────────────────────────────────────────   │
└─────────────────────────────────────────────────────────────┘
```

```
┌─────────────────────────────────────────────────────────────┐
│  ┌─ DEFINITION ──────────────────────────────────────────┐   │
│  │                                                        │   │
│  │      typename is a unique identifier.                  │   │
│  │                                                        │   │
│  │      type can be any of the type definitions in section C.6, │
│  │         "Data Types" including any deferred type.      │   │
│  │                                                        │   │
│  └────────────────────────────────────────────────────────   │
└─────────────────────────────────────────────────────────────┘
```

4. **VAR** is used to define one or more variables and the type of the allowable content in the variable. Additionaly VAR may be used to instantiate or refine the definition of a predefined generic type.

```
┌─────────────────────────────────────────────────────────────┐
│  ┌─ FORMAT ──────────────────────────────────────────────┐   │
│  │                                                        │   │
│  │      VAR varname_list:type MOD modulename (passed_parms); │
│  │                                                        │   │
│  └────────────────────────────────────────────────────────   │
└─────────────────────────────────────────────────────────────┘
```

```
┌─────────────────────────────────────────────────────────────────┐
│  ┌─ DEFINITION ──────────────────────────────────────────────┐   │
│  │                                                            │   │
│  │     varname_list is one or more variable identifiers       │   │
│  │        separated by commas.                                │   │
│  │                                                            │   │
│  │     type can be any of the type definitions in section     │   │
│  │        C.6, "Data Types," including any deferred type.      │   │
│  │                                                            │   │
│  │     modulename is the identifier of the user defined       │   │
│  │        data type via the SPEC that defines the data type.   │   │
│  │        It may be generic.                                   │   │
│  │                                                            │   │
│  │     passed_parms are the parameters to refine or override   │   │
│  │        a default in the generic specification. Defaults     │   │
│  │        not overridden are inherited.                        │   │
│  │                                                            │   │
│  └────────────────────────────────────────────────────────────┘   │
└─────────────────────────────────────────────────────────────────┘


┌─────────────────────────────────────────────────────────────────┐
│  ┌─ EXAMPLES ────────────────────────────────────────────────┐   │
│  │                                                            │   │
│  │     VAR abc:CHAR;                                           │   │
│  │                                                            │   │
│  │     VAR abc:MOD tester(parm);                               │   │
│  │                                                            │   │
│  │     VAR abc:MOD modname;                                    │   │
│  │                                                            │   │
│  └────────────────────────────────────────────────────────────┘   │
└─────────────────────────────────────────────────────────────────┘
```

C.5 Function Commentary

FUNCTION COMMENTARY is used to describe the intended function of a logical group of statements.

```
┌─ FORMAT ──────────────────────────────────────────────┐

    <function commentary>

└───────────────────────────────────────────────────────┘
```

```
┌─ DEFINITION ──────────────────────────────────────────┐

    function commentary can take one of three forms:
    a.  Simple English language statements
    b.  Procedural English narrative
    c.  Mathematical expression using variables,
        constants, or operations that produce a
        functional value

└───────────────────────────────────────────────────────┘
```

```
┌─ EXAMPLE ─────────────────────────────────────────────┐

    See section 10.9.5 for examples of each of these three forms.

└───────────────────────────────────────────────────────┘
```

C.5.1 Input and Output

INPUT and OUTPUT define data passed between Programs, Procedures, Blocks, and Functions.

┌─ DEFINITION ───┐

   inparms are input data which are not changed during
      execution.
   outparms are output data derived during execution.
   inoutparms are input data which are changed to some
      value during execution.
   inparms, outparms, and inoutparms take the form of:
      parms_1:typeuse,...,parms_n:type
         where parms_1...parms_n may be one or more
            variable names.
└──┘

┌─ EXAMPLES ───┐

   (IN a:INTEGER, OUT b:CHAR, INOUT c:STRING)
└──┘

C.6 Data Types

There are three type classes which are permitted with ADL:

- Scalar
- Structured
- Deferred

1. SCALAR: a data form without a structure.

TYPE	OPERATIONS	EXAMPLES
INTEGER	+,-,*,**,/,REM,=,<,≤,>,≥	1, 19, 1923
REAL	+,-,*,**,/,=,<,≤,>,≥	3.14
BOOLEAN	AND,NOT,OR,XOR,=	TRUE,FALSE
CHAR	||,<,≤,>,≥	'A','B'
STRING	||,=,<,≤,>,≥	'abcde'
Enumerated	PRED, SUCC,<,≤,>≥	(A,B,C) (2,4,6)
Subrange	<,≤,>,≥	(1...3)

2. STRUCTURED:

a. ARRAY

A data structure defining a vector or matrix of numbers all having the same data type.

```
┌─ FORMAT ──────────────────────────────
    ARRAY (indextype) of type;
```

OPERATIONS	DEFINITION	EXAMPLES
Construction	Builds the array	VAR a:ARRAY(1..4) OF CHAR;
Definition	Initializes the array	a:=('b','c','d','e');
Access	Obtains a value from the array	a(3) gets d
Update	Defines a value in the array	a(3):=h

b. RECORD

A data structure containing a collection of named data structures.

OPERATIONS	DEFINITION	EXAMPLES
Construction	Builds the record	VAR A:REC SIZE:INTEGER; AMOUNT:REAL; ITEM:STRING; ENDREC;
Definition	Initialize the record	A:=(38,10.99,'SHIRT');
Access	Obtains value in record	A.ITEM gets 'SHIRT'
Update	Defines a value in record	A.ITEM:='BLOUSE'

c. **LIST**

A sequence of data values all having the same type.

OPERATIONS	DEFINITION	EXAMPLES
Construction	Build the list	VAR L: LIST of INTEGER;
Definition	Initialize the list	L:=(1,2,3,4,5,6);

FIRST	Returns first element
	    of list
		FIRST(L)
		    returns 1

LAST	Returns last element
	    of list
		LAST(L)
		    returns 6

TAIL	Returns list without
	    the first element
		TAIL(L)
		    returns 3,4,5

FRONT	Returns list without
	    the last element
		FRONT(L)
		    returns 3,4

EMPTY?	Test for a NULL
	    list
		EMPTY?(L)
		    gets FALSE

CLEAR	Clears the contents
	    of the designated
	    list
		CLEAR(L)
		    returns a
		    NULL list L;
		    EMPTY?(L)
		    returns TRUE

d. QUEUE

```
┌─────────────────────────────────────────────────────────────┐
│  ┌─ FORMAT ──────────────────────────────────────────────┐   │
│  │                                                        │   │
│  │    QUEUE OF type                                       │   │
│  │                                                        │   │
│  │        A sequence of data elements where the elements  │   │
│  │        are accessed on a first-in, first-out manner.   │   │
│  │                                                        │   │
│  └────────────────────────────────────────────────────────┘   │
└─────────────────────────────────────────────────────────────┘
```

```
┌─────────────────────────────────────────────────────────────┐
│  ┌─ DEFINITION ──────────────────────────────────────────┐   │
│  │                                                        │   │
│  │      type is any data type name or data type           │   │
│  │      definition in section C.6, "Data Types," or any   │   │
│  │      deferred type.                                    │   │
│  │                                                        │   │
│  └────────────────────────────────────────────────────────┘   │
└─────────────────────────────────────────────────────────────┘
```

OPERATIONS	DEFINITION	EXAMPLES
Construction	Builds the queue	VAR Q:QUEUE of INTEGER;
Definition	Initializes the queue	Q:=(1,2,3,4);

ENQUE	Adds an element to
	the end of the
	of the queue
		ENQUE(Q,5)
		   returns
		   Q=(1,2,3,4,5)

DEQUE	Returns the first
	value of the queue and
	deletes the value from
	the queue
		DEQUE(q,a)
		   returns
		   Q=(2,3,4,5)
		   where A=1

EMPTY?	Tests queue for NULL state	EMPTY? q returns FALSE

CLEAR	Clears the queue to
	NULL
		CLEAR Q
		   returns NULL;
		   EMPTY? now
		   returns TRUE

FRONT	Returns value of
	first element of
	queue without
	dequeing it
		FRONT (Q,X)
		   returns
		   X=2 and
		   Q=(2,3,4,5)

LENGTH	Returns the number
	of elements in the
	queue
		LENGTH
		   (q,x)returns
		   x=4

e. **STACK**

A sequence of data elements where the elements are accessed on a last in, first out manner.

```
┌─────────────────────────────────────────────────────────────┐
│  ┌─ FORMAT ─────────────────────────────────────────────────┐│
│  │                                                           ││
│  │    STACK OF type                                          ││
│  └───────────────────────────────────────────────────────────┘│
│                                                                │
└────────────────────────────────────────────────────────────────┘
```

```
┌─────────────────────────────────────────────────────────────┐
│  ┌─ DEFINITION ─────────────────────────────────────────────┐│
│  │                                                           ││
│  │    type is any data type definition in section C.6, "Data ││
│  │       Types," including any deferred type.                ││
│  └───────────────────────────────────────────────────────────┘│
│                                                                │
└────────────────────────────────────────────────────────────────┘
```

OPERATIONS	DEFINITION	EXAMPLES
Construction	Builds the stack	VAR S:STACK of INTEGER;
Definition	Initializes the stack	S:=(1,2,3,4);
PUSH	Adds an element to the top of the stack	WHERE D:=5, PUSH(S,D) returns S=(5,1,2,3,4)
POP	Deletes an element from the top of the stack and places it in the designated item	POP(S,X) returns X=5 and S=(1,2,3,4)
EMPTY	Tests the stack for a NULL state	EMPTY?(S) returns FALSE
CLEAR	Sets the stack to NULL state	CLEAR(S)
TOP	Returns value of top element without POPing	TOP (S,X) returns X=1 and does not change the stack
DEPTH	Returns the number of elements in the stack	DEPTH(S) returns 4

f. **SET** is a collection of data elements all of the same type.

FORMAT

    SET (number) OF type

DEFINITION

    number is the upperbound set size. If no value is designated,
    the set is unbounded.

    type is any data type definition in section C.6, "Data
    Types," including any deferred type.

OPERATIONS	DEFINITION	EXAMPLES
Construction	Build the set	VAR S:SET of CHAR;
Definition	Initialize the set	S:=('A','B','C','D');
EXISTIN?	An item is tested for membership in a set	'B'EXISTIN(S) returns TRUE
CARD	Returns the number of elements in the set	CARD(S) returns 4

Union	An item or set of items is added to the original set; assumes items are of the same type as original set	S:=S+A, adds the
		   item for variable
		   A to the set

Difference	An item or set of items is deleted from the set	S:=S-A, deletes the
		   item for variable
		   A from set S

Intersection	Returns the set intersection of sets S and T	I=SxT, returns
		   all items which
		   are in both sets

EMPTY?	The set is tested for NULL condition	EMPTY? S
		   returns FALSE
		   for set S

CLEAR	The set is cleared to NULL	CLEAR S
		   returns set S
		   NULL

3. DEFERRED

Any declared or referenced data type that is not part of the basis basis set of ADL data types. During the design refinement it will be refined into a basis set data type.

C.7 Concurrent Processing

1. **MONITOR - END_MONITOR** packaging statement set is used to define the specifications for a structure that controls access to shared data.

```
┌─ FORMAT ──────────────────────────────────────────────┐

      MONITOR monitor_name <commentary>;
         DATA
            TYPE typenamelist:type;
               or
            VAR varnamelist: type;
            COND condition_name list;
         INITIAL varname initialization;
      OPERATIONS
         ENTRY entry_name_1 (parmlist) <commentary>;
         ENTRY entry_name_n (parmlist) <commentary>;
      ENDMONITOR monitor_name;
```

┌─ DEFINITION ───┐

   monitor_name is the identifier of the shared data monitor.

   typenamelist is one or more NAMES for TYPES.

   varnamelist is one or more names for variables.

   type is any of the acceptable type definitions in section C.6,
      "Data Types," or a deferred type.

   condition_name_list is one or more conditions which are
      resources that serve as signals to the **ENTRY** caller.

   entry_name is the identifier of an **ENTRY** in the
      MONITOR.

   parmlist takes the form (**IN inparms,OUT outparms,INOUT
      inoutparms**).
      inparms are input data which are not changed
         during execution;
      outparms are output data derived during execution;
      inoutparms are input data which are changed to some
         value during execution.

NOTE:
   ENTRYs are optional. A **MONITOR** without an
   ENTRY may be used to initialize global variables.

└──┘

2. **MONITOR_DESIGN - END_MONITOR_DESIGN** packaging statement set is used to make explicit the design for the specification noted in its related MONITOR-ENDMONITOR structure.

```
┌─ FORMAT ────────────────────────────────────────────

      MONITOR_DESIGN name <commentary>;
        DATA
          TYPE typenamelist:type;
               or
          VAR varnamelist:type;
          COND condition_name list;
          INITIAL varname initialization;
        OPERATIONS
          ENTRY entry_name1 (parmlist) <commentary>;

              .
              .

              action processing;

              .
              .

          END_ENTRY entry_name1;

            .
            .
            .

          ENTRY entry_name_n (parmlist) <commentary>;

              .
              .

              action processing;

              .
              .

          END_ENTRY entry_name_n;
      END_MONITOR_DESIGN name;
```

```
┌──────────────────────────────────────────────────────────────┐
│  ┌─ DEFINITION ────────────────────────────────────────────┐  │
│  │                                                          │  │
│  │      monitor_name is the identifier of the shared data   │  │
│  │          monitor.                                        │  │
│  │                                                          │  │
│  │      typenamelist is one or more names for types.        │  │
│  │                                                          │  │
│  │      varnamelist is one or more names for variables.     │  │
│  │                                                          │  │
│  │      type is any of the acceptable type definitions in   │  │
│  │          section C.6, "Data Types," or a deferred type.  │  │
│  │                                                          │  │
│  │      condition_name_list is one or more conditions which │  │
│  │          are resources that serve as signals to the      │  │
│  │          ENTRY caller.                                   │  │
│  │                                                          │  │
│  │      entry_name is the identifier of an ENTRY in the     │  │
│  │          MONITOR.                                        │  │
│  │                                                          │  │
│  │      parmlist takes the form (IN inparms OUT outparms,   │  │
│  │          INOUT inoutparms).                              │  │
│  │                                                          │  │
│  │          inparms are input data which are not changed    │  │
│  │          during execution;                               │  │
│  │          outparms are output data derived during         │  │
│  │          execution;                                      │  │
│  │          inoutparms are input data which are changed to  │  │
│  │          some value during execution.                    │  │
│  │                                                          │  │
│  └──────────────────────────────────────────────────────────┘
└──────────────────────────────────────────────────────────────┘
```

3. **ENTER** is used to invoke a call to a **MONITOR ENTRY**.

```
┌──────────────────────────────────────────────────────────────┐
│  ┌─ FORMAT ────────────────────────────────────────────────┐  │
│  │                                                          │  │
│  │      <enter function commentary>                         │  │
│  │      ENTER name (parmlist);                              │  │
│  │                                                          │  │
│  └──────────────────────────────────────────────────────────┘
└──────────────────────────────────────────────────────────────┘
```

```
┌─ DEFINITION ──────────────────────────────────────────────────┐
│                                                                │
│     enter function commentary defines the intended function    │
│        of the invoked ENTRY.                                   │
│                                                                │
│     parmlist takes the form                                    │
│                                                                │
│        (IN inparms, OUT outparms, INOUT inoutparms)            │
│        of the MONITOR ENTRY being called.                      │
│                                                                │
│     inparms are input data which are not changed during        │
│        execution;                                              │
│                                                                │
│     outparms are output data derived during execution;         │
│                                                                │
│     NOTE:  name is the name of the MONITOR ENTRY, and takes    │
│        the form of monitor_name.entry_name.                    │
│                                                                │
└────────────────────────────────────────────────────────────────┘
```

4. **WAIT** is used to queue up processing through an **ENTRY**.

```
┌─ FORMAT ──────────────────────────────────────────────────────┐
│                                                                │
│     WAIT (condition);                                          │
│                                                                │
└────────────────────────────────────────────────────────────────┘
```

```
┌─ DEFINITION ──────────────────────────────────────────────────┐
│                                                                │
│     condition is an identifier which indicates state transitions│
│        in process on the shared data.  Conditions are Boolean types by │
│        default.                                                │
│                                                                │
└────────────────────────────────────────────────────────────────┘
```

5. **POST** is used to signal that an **ENTRY** has been released for additional processing.

condition is an identifier which indicates state transition has been completed on the shared data.

NOTE: **POST** signals not only that the shared data is available for further processing, but it causes the next queued up process to take immediate control of the shared data through the **ENTRY.**

6. **DELAY** is used to suspend processing for the designated time period.

period designates some time period in which processing is suspended.

Index

PDM
  example input document   86
  example problem analysis
    document   86
  example solution definition
    document   87
  work items   90
peer reviews   238
performance   46, 63
personal computers   6
Peters, L. J.   206, 210
PF keys   162
phases to design   210
Phillips, R. W.   84, 133
planning   242
Planning and Design Methodology
  See PDM
planning problems   174
planning tasks and methods   180
PLD   266
postmortem   38, 52
PPA   33
practices   47
preliminary sales estimate   62
prescriptive   227, 268
Pressman, R. S.   57, 174
problem decomposition   271
Problem Statement Analyzer
  See PSA
Problem Statement Language
  See PSL
process
  activities   36
  automation   22
  definition   47
  evolution   29
  iteration   38, 39
  management   9, 38, 49
  management principles   36
  parallelism   37
  principles   10
  stages   41
  standardization   52
  viewpoints   48
product announce   46
product attributes   63
Product Level Design   212, 215, 266

product planning   56, 66
product publications viewpoint
  Requirements and Planning stage   57
profit and loss   65
program development   48, 49
Program Logic Specification   357
programmerless programming   21
programming in the large   319
Programming Process Architecture   33,
  185
project inception proposal   57
project management system   193
project planning viewpoint
  Requirements and Planning stage   57
project process definition   185, 186
  attributes   187
  change management system   190
  process management system   186
  project management system   193
  relationships   188
  states   188
Project Workbook   357
proof of correctness   230, 245, 341
  case   346
  do until   346
  do while   346
  if then else   345
  sequence   343
proofs of correctness   5
prototype   306
prototyping   39, 231, 239
PSA   97
pseudocode   228, 309, 310, 328
pseudolanguage   241
PSL   97, 231, 269
  complementary form of expression   98
  object types   97
  tutorial   97
publications   10, 49
Putnam Estimation Model   181
Putnam, L.   181

Q

quality focus   47
quality plan   38
Quality-Productivity Plan   193

454

R

R-NETS 105
Radice, Roth, O'Hara, Ciarfella 185
Radice, R. A. 33
Rayleigh-Norden curve 182
readability indices 157
  Flesch, R. 158
  Fog 158
  forecast reading level 158
  Fry, E. 158
reliability 12, 63
report 242
representations
  definition 208
Requirements Engineering 11
  activities 83
  aspects 83
  domain 70
  future goals and trends 134
  ideal process defined 133
  perspectives 83
  problem areas 72
Requirements Engineering Validation
  System *See* REVS
requirements inputs, typical 76
requirements sources 72
Requirements Specification Language
  See RSL
requirements to design bridge 231
requirements to design transformation
  alternatives 269
resource estimation 181
resource estimation models 181
  dynamic multi-variable models 181
  static multiple variable models 181
  static single variable model 181
response time 165
retrofitting fixes 359, 360
reuse 15
  types of 17
reverse engineering 15
reviews 238
REVS 104
risk factors 65
Roman, G. 63, 72, 106
Ross, D. T. 106

Roth, N. K. 38
Royce, W. W. 31
RPLD Model 90, 110
  environment to process
    bridges 92
  perspectives 90
  process to product bridges 93
RPLD Specification 70, 108
RPLD Specifications 82
RSL 104
rugby team approach 31

S

SADT 106, 227, 231
  activity model 107
  data model 107
Scheffer, P. A. 104, 132
Schneiderman, B. 140
Schneier, C. A. 142, 147
screen formats 164
SEE 34
semaphores 347
separation of concerns 272
service 10, 49
SEW 327, 341
shadow approach 309
Shankar, K. S. 228, 305
Simon, H. A. 72, 135
sink group 292
sink module 287
skunk works 31
software
  management of 8
  types of 18
software engineering 3
  challenges 24
  goals 5
software engineering environments 34
Software Engineering Institute 240
Software Engineering Requirements
  Methodology *See* SREM
Software Engineering with Ada 303
software psychology 140
source module 287
SREM 104, 231, 269